Kevin L. Spawn
"As It Is Written" and Other Citation
Formulae in the Old Testament

Beihefte zur Zeitschrift für die
alttestamentliche Wissenschaft

Herausgegeben von
Otto Kaiser

Band 311

Walter de Gruyter · Berlin · New York
2002

Kevin L. Spawn

"As It Is Written" and Other Citation Formulae in the Old Testament

Their Use, Development, Syntax, and Significance

Walter de Gruyter · Berlin · New York

♾ Printed on acid-free paper which falls within the guidelines of the ANSI
to ensure permanence and durability.

Library of Congress Cataloging-in-Publication-Data

Spawn, Kevin L.:
"As it is written" and other citation formulae in the Old Testament :
their use, development, syntax, and significance / Kevin L. Spawn. –
Berlin ; New York : de Gruyter, 2001
   (Beihefte zur Zeitschrift für die alttestamentliche Wissenschaft ;
Bd. 311)
   Zugl.: Oxford, Univ., Diss., 1998
   ISBN 3-11-017161-9   1 0 0 2 6 6 9 4 3 3

Printed in Germany
Cover design: Christopher Schneider, Berlin
Printing and binding: Hubert & Co., Göttingen

Preface

This monograph is a slight revision of my doctoral thesis defended in the University of Oxford in December 1998. It is a delight to record my gratitude to my thesis supervisor, Prof. H. G. M. Williamson, whose incisiveness, command of scholarship, and gentlemanly bearing not only guided me during this research project, but also served as a model for scholarship. I must also record his support of my applications for lectureships in Biblical Hebrew at the Oriental Institute, University of Oxford (Hilary Terms 1997 & 1998), and at The Oxford Centre for Hebrew & Jewish Studies (1996-98). Aside from other obvious advantages, these opportunities were key to meeting my commitments during the writing of this thesis.

Other monies were awarded to me by various agencies. I am indebted to the Committee of Vice Chancellors and Principals of the Universities of the United Kingdom for the Overseas Research Award Scheme (1995-97). I also wish to thank the managers of the Pusey and Ellerton Fund at the Oriental Institute for their gracious support. In 1996, another body of trustees at the Institute granted me the Segal Award, which again greatly eased my burden. A grant awarded by the Tyndale House Committee enabled me to take advantage of the superb facilities in Cambridge during the spring of 1997. I also want to express my gratitude to Drs. R. Ivy and D. Cook for the opportunity to teach a course in Old Testament Theology for the Randolph-Macon Woman's College at the University of Reading (1996).

For their careful work, I am indebted to my examiners (Prof. J. Barton, Dr. P. Joyce, and Dr. G. Khan). I wish to thank Prof. O. Kaiser for the invitation to submit my manuscript to BZAW. My thanks to Klaus Otterburig (de Gruyter) for his guidance in seeing this manuscript into print.

My dear wife, Nyla, has been unflagging in her support of me and my work throughout the majority of my education. Her dedication takes many forms and has frequently included her personal sacrifice. Without her selflessness, belief in me, and wit, this monograph, as well as the research behind it, would never have been completed.

Table of Contents

Abbreviations

General

AB	The Anchor Bible
ABD	D. N. Freedman *et al.* (eds.), *The Anchor Bible Dictionary*, 6 Vols. (London: Doubleday & Co. Inc., 1987).
AL	*Afroasiatic Linguistics*
ATD	Das Alte Testament Deutsch
ATSAT	Arbeiten zu Text und Sprache im Alten Testament
AF	Authorization Formula
BA	Biblical Aramaic
BDB	F. Brown, S. R. Driver and C. A. Briggs, *Hebrew and English Lexicon of the Old Testament* (Oxford: Clarendon Press, 1907)
BEATAJ	Beiträge zur Erforschung des alten Testaments und des antiken Judentums
BH	Biblical Hebrew
BHS	*Biblia Hebraica Stuttgartensia*
BIOSCS	Bulletin of the International Organization for Septuagint and Cognate Studies
BJS	Brown Judaic Studies
BKAT	Biblische Kommentar Altes Testament
BSac	*Bibliotheca Sacra*
BZ	*Biblische Zeitschrift*
BZAW	Beihefte zur Z*A*W
CAT	Commentaire de l'ancien Testament
CB	Century Bible
CBQ	*Catholic Biblical Quarterly*
CBSC	The Cambridge Bible for Schools and Colleges
CD	Damascus Document
Chr	Chronicler
CTA	A. Herdner, *Corpus des tablettes en cunéiformes*

	alphabétiques découvertes à Ras Shamra — *Ugarit de 1929 à 1939,* MRS 10 (Paris: Imprimerie nationale, 1963)
DD	Direct Discourse
DDD	K. van der Toorn, B. Becking and P. W. van der Horst (eds.), *Dictionary of Deities and Demons in the Bible (DDD)* (Leiden: E. J. Brill, 1995)
DG	J. C. L. Gibson, *Davidson's Introductory Hebrew Grammar - Syntax,* 4th edn (Edinburgh: T. & T. Clark, 1994)
DSB	Daily Study Bible
DtrH	Deuteronomistic History
Ex	Extraposition
FOTL	Forms of the Old Testament Literature
FRLANT	Forschungen zur Religion und Literatur des Alten und Neuen Testaments
FTS	Freiburger Theologische Studien
𝔊	The Septuagint
𝔊A	The Septuagint, codex Alexandrinus
𝔊B	The Septuagint, codex Vaticanus
𝔊L	The Septuagint, textus Graecus ex recensione Luciani
Gen	Genesis
GK	*Gesenius' Hebrew Grammar as edited and enlarged by the late E. Kautzsch,* trans. by A. E. Cowley, 2nd edn (Oxford: Clarendon Press, 1909)
HAT	Handbuch zum Alten Testament
HSAT	Die heilige Schrift des Alten Testaments
HSM	Harvard Semitic Monographs
IB	*The Interpreter's Bible*
IBHS	B. K. Waltke and M. O'Connor, *An Introduction to Biblical Hebrew Syntax* (Winona Lake, Indiana: Eisenbrauns, 1990)
ICC	International Critical Commentary

ir	intermediate referent
JB	Jerusalem Bible
JBL	*Journal of Biblical Literature*
JBLMS	*JBL*, Monograph Series
JBS	Jerusalem Biblical Studies
JJS	*Journal of Jewish Studies*
JM	P. Joüon, *A Grammar of Biblical Hebrew*, 2 vols, trans. and rev. by T. Muraoka, reprint of 1st edn (1991) with corrections, SB 14/I & II (Roma: Editrice Pontificio Istituto Biblico, 1993)
JNSL	*Journal of North-West Semitic Languages*
JPS	The Jewish Publication Society Bible
JQR	*Jewish Quarterly Review*
JSOT	*Journal for the Study of the Old Testament*
JSOTS	*JSOT* Supplement Series
JTS	*Journal of Theological Studies*
K	Kethib
KAT	Kommentar zum Alten Testament
KHAT	Kurzer Hand-Kommentar zum Alten Testament
LBH	Late Biblical Hebrew
LOS	London Oriental Series
LXX	The Septuagint
MRS	Mission de Ras Shamra
MS	Manuscript
MSS	Manuscripts
MT	The Massoretic Text
NAS	New American Standard Bible
NCB	New Century Bible Commentary
NEB	New English Bible
N.F.	neue Folge
NICOT	New International Commentary on the Old Testament
NIV	New International Version
NRSV	New Revised Standard Version
NS	New Series
O	object
OT	Old Testament

OTL	Old Testament Library
OTS	*Oudtestamentische Studiën*
P	Priestly Source
PAR	Pronominal agreement constructions with resumptive pronouns
Q	Qere
RF	Regulation Formula
RSV	Revised Standard Version
S	subject
ܣ	The Syriac version of the Old Testament
ɯ	The Samaritan Hebrew Pentateuch
SB	subsidia biblica
SBH	Standard Biblical Hebrew
SBLDS	Society of Biblical Literature, Dissertation Series
SBLMS	Society of Biblical Literature, Monograph Series
SOTBT	Studies in Old Testament Biblical Theology
𝕮	The Targum(s)
𝕮ᴶ	*Targum Pseudo-Jonathan*
TBC	Torch Bible Commentaries
TDOT	G. Botterweck and H. Ringgren (eds.), *Theological Dictionary of the Old Testament,* trans. by J. T. Willis *et al.* (Grand Rapids, MI: Eerdmans, 1974-)
THAT	E. Jenni and C. Westermann (eds.), *Theologische Handwörterbuch zum Alten Testament,* 2 Vols (Zurich/Munich: Chr. Kaiser-Verlag, Theologischer Verlag, 1971-76)
TOTC	Tyndale Old Testament Commentaries
TWAT	G. Botterweck and H. Ringgren (eds.), *Theologisches Wörterbuch zum Alten Testament* (Stuttgart: Kohlhammer, 1970-)
UF	*Ugarit-Forschungen*
V	verb
ܠ	Vulgate
VT	*Vetus Testamentum*

VTS	Supplements to *Vetus Testamentum*
v(v)	verse(s)
WMANT	Wissenschaftliche Monographien zum Alten und Neuen Testament
WBC	Word Biblical Commentary
ZAH	*Zeitschrift für Althebraistik*
ZAW	*Zeitschrift für die alttestamentliche Wissenschaft*
1QS	*Rule of the Community, Manual of Discipline*
4QFlor	*Florilegium* from Qumran Cave 4

Old Testament

Gen	Genesis	Eccl	Ecclesiastes
Exod	Exodus	Cant	Song of Solomon
Lev	Leviticus	Isa	Isaiah
Num	Numbers	Jer	Jeremiah
Deut	Deuteronomy	Lam	Lamentations
Josh	Joshua	Ezek	Ezekiel
Judg	Judges	Dan	Daniel
Ruth	Ruth	Hos	Hosea
1 Sam	1 Samuel	Joel	Joel
2 Sam	2 Samuel	Amos	Amos
1 Kgs	1 Kings	Obad	Obadiah
2 Kgs	2 Kings	Jon	Jonah
1 Chr	1 Chronicles	Mic	Micah
2 Chr	2 Chronicles	Nah	Nahum
Ezra	Ezra	Hab	Habakkuk
Neh	Nehemiah	Zeph	Zephaniah
Esth	Esther	Hag	Haggai
Job	Job	Zech	Zechariah
Psa	Psalms	Mal	Malachi
Prov	Proverbs		

Chapter 1: The Present State of the Analysis of Citation Formulæ in the Old Testament and a Way Forward

I. Introduction

In recent scholarship, the use of the law in the post-exilic community of Judah has received various treatments. One aspect of this situation concerns the evaluation of citation formulæ ("as it is written in the law"; "according to the commandment of Moses"; etc.). A central issue with regard to the use of such formulæ involves the correct identification of the element in the prevailing context that is being ascribed to a source. In a short or simple sentence such an identification is usually not problematic due to the lack of rival referents[1]. In a complex sentence, however, the identification of the referent is compounded by the presence of several elements that could be identified as the topic or act being attributed to another source. There are even times when the relationship between a citation formula and its referent in simpler constructions is not self-evident.

The relationship between citation formulæ and their referents in the post-exilic historiography is technical in nature and is a central concern in the field of inner-biblical exegesis. As Thiselton observes, "the subject of inter-textual relations within the Old Testament...remains a delicate, complex and specialized one"[2]. In order to come to terms with the intricacies inherent to this subject, the demonstration of the present state of the problem regarding the relationship between citation formulæ and their referents will best proceed by a detailed survey of a

---

1   The term "referent" is preferred to "antecedent" since not every citation formula has a grammatical relation to the word, phrase, clause, etc. that it attributes to another source.

2   Anthony C. Thiselton, *New Horizons in Hermeneutics* (London: HarperCollins, 1992) 40.

representative passage. This approach will not only highlight the significance of this issue, but it will also be instrumental in the development of a method whereby progress might be made. Even though we will address only one passage immediately below the issues and problems that surface in this discussion are relevant to the study of citation formulae throughout the OT. The debates which are associated with these citation formulæ will be presented in subsequent chapters.

II. The Lack of Consensus and Method in Scholarship

The treatment of Neh 10:35 (34), for instance, in modern scholarship is representative of the lack of criteria used to identify the referents of citation formulæ in the OT.

וְהַגּוֹרָלוֹת הִפַּלְנוּ עַל־קָרְבַּן הָעֵצִים הַכֹּהֲנִים הַלְוִיִּם וְהָעָם לְהָבִיא
לְבֵית אֱלֹהֵינוּ לְבֵית־אֲבֹתֵינוּ לְעִתִּים מְזֻמָּנִים שָׁנָה בְשָׁנָה לְבַעֵר
עַל־מִזְבַּח יְהוָה אֱלֹהֵינוּ כַּכָּתוּב בַּתּוֹרָה (Neh 10:35 [34])

This passage contains twenty-four Hebrew lexemes of which the last two are the citation formula כַּכָּתוּב בַּתּוֹרָה ("as it is written in the law"). Recent examinations of this passage draw a number of conclusions regarding the relationship between this citation formula and the referent in the prevailing context that it is crediting to תּוֹרָה. The following survey of scholarship demonstrates the lack of consensus and method in the treatment of כַּכָּתוּב בַּתּוֹרָה in Neh 10:35 (34) throughout the modern era of biblical criticism.

Firstly, most scholars maintain that a discernible relationship exists between the citation formula כַּכָּתוּב בַּתּוֹרָה and its referent. Despite this common belief, there is no unanimity among scholars concerning which word, phrase, or clause constitutes the proper referent. Two referents have received the most support but they are by no means the only ones maintained. The two referents most frequently identified by scholars are: "the offering, or delivery, of wood" (הָעֵצִים קָרְבַּן)[3]; and "the continual burning of wood for a fire on the altar"[4]. Furthermore,

---

3 E.g., Judson R. Shaver, *Torah and the Chronicler's History Work: An Inquiry into the Chronicler's References to Laws, Festivals, and Cultic Institutions in Relationship to Pentateuchal Legislation*, BJS 196 (Atlanta, Georgia: Scholars Press, 1989) 84, 89, 127; Simon J. DeVries, "Moses and David as Cult Founders in Chronicles", *JBL* 107 (1988) 623, n. 10; Antonius H. J. Gunneweg, *Nehemia*, KAT (Gütersloh: Gütersloher Verlagshaus Gerd Mohn, 1987) 138; Michael Fishbane, *Biblical Interpretation in Ancient Israel* (Oxford: Clarendon Press, 1985) 213; Robert North, "The Chronicler: 1-2 Chronicles, Ezra, Nehemiah", in *The New Jerome Biblical Commentary*, ed. by R. E. Browne *et al.* 2nd edn (London: Geoffrey Chapman, 1990/1968) 437-38; Laurence E. Browne, *Early Judaism* (Cambridge: University Press, 1920) 192-93; G. Jahn, *Die Bücher Esra (A und B) und Nehemja, Text-Kritisch und Historisch-Kritisch untersucht mit Erklärung der Einschlägigen Prophetenstellen und einem Anhang über hebräische Eigennamen* (Leiden: E. J. Brill, 1909) 142, cf. xiv; T. Witton Davies, *Ezra, Nehemiah and Esther*, CB (London: Caxton, 1909) 250; A. Bertholet, *Die Bücher Esra und Nehemia*, KHAT (Tübingen: Mohr, 1902) 79; C. C. Torrey, *Ezra Studies* (Chicago: University Press, 1910) 277, n. g; H. E. Ryle, *The Books of Ezra and Nehemiah*, CBSC (Cambridge: Cambridge University Press, 1897) 276-77; Julius Wellhausen, "Die Rückkehr der Juden aus dem babylonischen Exil", in *Nachrichten von der königlichen Gesellschaft der Wissenschaften zu Göttingen: Philologisch-historische Klasse*, 1895, Heft 2, 174, n. 1; W. H. Kosters, *Het herstel van Israël in het Perzische tijdvak* (Leiden: E. J. Brill, 1894) 94, n. 1.

4 D. J. A. Clines, "Nehemiah 10 as an Example of Early Jewish Biblical Exegesis", *JSOT* 21 (1981) 112; *ibid., Ezra, Nehemiah, Esther,* NCB (London: Marshall, Morgan & Scott, 1984) 208. See also, H. G. M. Williamson, "History", in *It is Written: Scripture Citing Scripture*, ed. by D. A. Carson *et al.* (Cambridge: Cambridge University Press, 1988) 28; *ibid., Ezra, Nehemiah*, WBC (Waco, TX: Word, 1985) 336; J. M. Myers, *Ezra. Nehemiah*, AB (Garden City: Doubleday, 1965) 179; H. Schneider, *Die Bücher Esra und Nehemia*, HSAT (Bonn: Peter Hanstein, 1959) 226; Y. Kaufmann, *History of the Religion of Israel. Volume IV: From the Babylonian Captivity to the End of Prophecy*, trans. by C. W. Efroymson (New York: Ktav Publ., 1977) 425, n. 47, in Hebrew, תולדות האמונה הישראלית מימי קדם עד סוף בית שני (Jerusalem: Ktav Publ., 1956) 334, n. 47; Kurt Galling, *Die Bücher der Chronik, Esra, Nehemia*, ATD (Göttingen: Vandenhoeck & Ruprecht, 1954) 243; Johannes Geißler, *Die litterarischen Beziehungen der Esramemoiren, insbesondere zur Chronik und den hexateuchischen Quellschriften* (Chemnitz: J. C. F. Pickenhahn & Sohn, 1899) 39; Eduard Meyer, *Die Entstehung des Judenthums: eine historische Untersuchung* (Halle a. S.: Max Niemeyer, 1896) 211; Carl F. Keil, *The Books of Ezra, Nehemiah, and Esther,* trans. by Sophia

both of these alternatives have been advocated throughout the modern era of biblical criticism.

The present problem in scholarship, however, is considerably more involved than merely the two rival referents above. There are several other views that have been advocated by scholars regarding the relationship between כַּכָּתוּב בַּתּוֹרָה and its referent(s).

The analysis of some scholars regards the relationship between this citation formula and its referent to be ambiguous. Some maintain this view consciously while others simply do not treat the issue clearly. Houtman, for example, represents this latter category. After Houtman identifies the wood offering as the referent of this citation formula he immediately retreats from this position, admitting the burning of wood on the altar could be intended[5]. In another place, Houtman surmises still another possible meaning to be attached to this citation formula in v. 35 (34). This situation, according to Houtman, results from the two citation formulæ כַּכָּתוּב בַּתּוֹרָה in v. 35 (34) and v. 37 (36) being introduced with the heading in v. 30 (29) ("[the separated people] are taking on themselves a curse and an oath to walk in God's law, which was given through Moses, God's servant, and to keep and to observe all the commandments of God our LORD, and His ordinances and His statutes…"). Commenting on the community pledge in Neh 10:29-40 (28-39), he states,

> in view of the fact that two times in these verses it is stated explicitly that they will act *"as prescribed in the law"* (vv. 35, 37), it may be assumed that the enumeration of obligations or at least a part of it, is to be understood as an exact reflection of the rules of the law[6].

Here Houtman is suggesting that the citation formula in v. 35 (34) functions with both the citation formula כַּכָּתוּב בַּתּוֹרָה in v. 37 (36) and the heading in v. 30 (29) in order to indicate that the entirety of the pledge in Neh 10:29ff. (28ff.) has been accomplished "according to the law".

Taylor (Edinburgh: T. & T. Clark, 1873) 253-54, in German see, *ibid.*, *Chronik, Esra, Nehemia und Esther* (Leipzig: Dörffling und Franke, 1870) 569.

5   C. Houtman, "Ezra and the Law", *OTS* 21 (1981) 106.

6   *Ibid.*, 105.

The imprecision of his statement (i.e., "the enumeration of obligations or at least a part of it") in addition to his equivocation over the meaning of the formula in v. 35 (34), however, make his analysis muddled. In the end, Houtman gives us no less than three, and perhaps more, answers to the question: "What does the citation formula כָּתוּב בַּתּוֹרָה in v. 35 (34) ascribe to the law?" Remarkably, Houtman is unaware of the variability of his comments. However, among Houtman's proposals he does introduce to our survey the view that the entire pledge to observe the law in Neh 10:29-40 (28-39) could be identified as a possible referent. Additionally, he suggests that the citation formula in Neh 10:35 (34) functions in a synergistic manner with both the heading of the pericope and another citation formula in the immediate context.

Rudolph also considers the citation formula in v. 35 (34) to have more than one possible referent. However, his position is clearly distinguishable from Houtman since he consciously maintains that the relationship between the citation formula and its referent is ambiguous. According to Rudolph, "es ist nicht deutlich, ob sich das ‚wie im Gesetz geschrieben steht' nur auf die Verbrennung des Holzes auf dem Altar (38b [*sic*]) oder auf den ganzen Satz, also auf die durchs Los zu bestimmende Herbeischaffung des Holzes bezieht"[7].

Rudolph's second proposal introduces another potential referent to the debate in Neh 10:35 (34). In contrast to the frequently identified referents ("the continual burning of wood for a fire on the altar" and "the wood offering"), Rudolph's second suggestion includes all the accompanying details in "den ganzen Satz"[8]. If indeed the whole

---

7   Wilhelm Rudolph, *Esra und Nehemia,* HAT (Tübingen: J. C. B. Mohr, 1949) 180; for the manner in which Rudolph has been followed, see R. A. Bowman, "Introduction and Exegesis to the Book of Ezra and the Book of Nehemiah", in *IB,* Vol. III (New York: Abingdon, 1954) 765. He states, "*as it is written* is perplexing...[and]...is not clear whether the statement refers to Lev 6:12 alone or to the entire matter of the wood offering" (765).

8   Rudolph's succinct statement could be confusing if he had not clarified what he meant with the syntactic comment "den ganzen Satz". This phrase shows that he intends "die durch los zu bestimmende Herbeischaffung des Holzes" to be a summary of the entire sentence. This view also corresponds with the analysis of those who advocate "the wood offering" as the referent of the citation formula and normally label it "Holzlieferung". Rudolph clearly means something other

sentence was the referent, then the activity to which the citation formula was attributing a legal basis would consist of the following: "the casting of lots by the Levites, priests, and people for the delivery of wood as brought: 1) according to households of the fathers; and, 2) at set times annually"[9]. Even though Rudolph does not resolve which referent is to be identified, the review of his treatment adds yet another possible option to our list of rival referents for כַּכָּתוּב in Neh 10:35 (34).

Rudolph's indecision is unquestionably the most weighty conclusion of his analysis of this verse. The implication of Rudolph's statement is that the exegetical tools of the post-exilic community functioned, at least at times, in an incoherent manner. This is a striking conclusion insofar as it contradicts the presumed function of citation formulæ. The question that begs to be answered is: "Why was the citation formula used if it is unintelligible?" This is certainly a weighty conclusion to be attributed to such an exegetical device. Rudolph never addresses the obvious implication of his statement.

Rudolph's conclusion implies something more as well. Since the citation formula is a prepositional phrase that functions as an adverbial construction, then it follows from Rudolph's irresolution that such syntactic structures also function ambiguously. There is no doubt that the dynamism of language is such that grammar and syntax cannot always be easily classified. However, for Rudolph's point to carry weight he would clearly have to substantiate the view that prepositional phrases relate ambiguously to their contexts. Since he simply poses the dilemma it appears that he did not see the ramifications of his statement which implies far-reaching syntactic and hermeneutic conclusions to which we will return below.

Despite the problems we have noted with Rudolph's treatment, the review of his position has demonstrated that the identification of the referents of citation formulæ is inextricably linked to syntactic considerations. This will prove to be an important point in our development of a method below.

Not all scholars have ignored the fact that there are rival referents for the citation formula כַּכָּתוּב בַּתּוֹרָה in Neh 10:35 (34). In light of what

---

by "Herbeischaffung" which is no doubt clarified by his statement "den ganzen Satz".

9   The infinitive phrase would then mark the purpose of this activity.

we have seen so far, it is not surprising that some scholars have felt the need to appeal to objective criteria to decide between the rival referents in Neh 10:35 (34). Rather than resolving the debate, however, this general approach has resulted in an even greater breadth of opinion regarding the proper identification of the referent in Neh 10:35 (34).

Ryle debates between the rival referents of "the wood offering" and "the continual burning on the altar". Unlike Rudolph, however, he is able to resolve this debate by the consideration of one criterion. Ryle claims, "against [the continual burning on the altar] it may fairly be urged that 'the wood offering,' being the principal subject of the verse, is also the most probable subject for this quotation from Scripture"[10]. The problem with Ryle's reasoning is that a description of what constitutes the "principal subject" of the sentence is never addressed. Contrary to Ryle's assumption, this is not self-evident since even according to his own conclusion it is something other than the grammatical subject of the sentence.

In modern terms, an appeal to the "principal subject" of a sentence may refer to the binary information structure of a sentence. In an earlier part of the twentieth century, this binary structure was referred to as the Psychological Subject/Psychological Predicate of a sentence; the present nomenclature is Topic/Comment. This approach includes the "analysis of sentences according to communicative criteria into the topic (what is being talked about) and comment (what is being said about the topic)"[11]. However, this analytical approach is not a reliable guide for the identification of the referents of citation formulæ. As Crystal has recently indicated, "the topic/comment contrast is…sometimes difficult to establish…and in many types of sentence the analysis is…problematic"[12]. In fact, since Neh 10:35 (34) is part of a *list* of obligations that the community is placing upon itself, it simply is not amenable to the topic/comment analysis which applies chiefly to literary

---

10 Ryle, 276.
11 Hadumond Bussman, *Routledge Dictionary of Language and Linguistics,* trans. and ed. by Gregory Trauth *et al.* (London: Routledge, 1996) 487.
12 David Crystal, *A Dictionary of Linguistics and Phonetics,* 4th edn (Oxford: Blackwell Publishers, 1997) 392. Neither does the Theme/Rheme analysis of a sentence apply to Ryle's statement. For the specific development of Theme/Rheme from Topic/Comment, see M. A. K. Halliday, *An Introduction to Functional Grammar,* 2nd edn (London: Edward Arnold, 1994) 38-39.

works. The reference to the principal subject of the sentence does not in fact provide us with an objective standard for the identification of referents. While he did not have this method explicitly in mind, Ryle's analysis warns against such an approach. If Ryle's analysis is to be understood in a way other than our reference to the binary sentence structure above, this is not clear from his treatment.

Gunneweg considers the same two referents as Ryle and concludes that the wood offering for the altar is the proper referent of the citation formula. Gunneweg similarly argues against one referent in order to identify the other. However, Gunneweg's substantiation is vastly different:

> Allerdings kann man den Verweis auf das Gesetz grammatisch auch auf das Verbrennen des Holzes beziehen (Lev 6,5f.); aber diese Interpretation ist unwahrscheinlich, weil ja nicht die Verwendung, sondern die Lieferung von Holz geregelt werden soll[13].

Gunneweg's statement, however, reveals his inadequate understanding of the debate and this is particularly borne out by the following *non-sequitur* in his statement. It simply does not follow that what the citation formula attributes to the law must be identical with the act in Neh 10:35 (34) that is based on a legal tradition. It is the differentiation of these two aspects in this passage that constitutes the other main view among scholars. That is, those who advocate "the continual burning of wood on the altar" observe two hermeneutical horizons present in v. 35 (34). On one hand, a reference to the law is made by the statement "to burn [wood] on the altar of the LORD" (according to this view the referent is the continual burning of wood on the altar based on Lev 6:5-6). On the other hand, the second hermeneutical horizon concerns the exegetical adaptation that was necessary in the post-exilic community to fulfil the requirements of Lev 6:5-6, i.e., the wood offering[14]. Such an

---

13 Gunneweg, 138.
14 Scholars describe these two horizons differently but they nevertheless share a common view. Galling distinguished between *what was in the law* and *what was regulated from it* (243, my emphasis). Other descriptions of these two hermeneutical horizons include: "Pentateuchal laws" and the "creation of facilitating law" (Clines, "Nehemiah 10", 112; *ibid., Ezra, Nehemiah, Esther,* 208); "text and interpretation" (Williamson, "History", 29).

offering was enacted in the post-exilic community to fulfil the pentateuchal regulation that a fire should burn continually on the altar. The services of the Gibeonites (Josh 9:22-27) who formerly provided the wood were no longer available. Hence, facilitating measures had to be taken in the post-exilic community to fulfil Lev 6:5-6. Since Gunneweg does not take into consideration the possibility that there are two hermeneutical horizons (*what was in the law* and *what was regulated from it*) in Neh 10:35 (34) the cogency of his argument is undermined. Ironically, his concession that "the continual burning of wood on the altar" is grammatically possible as a referent in fact suggests the position that he rejects.

The treatments of Fensham and Brockington should be mentioned in connection with Gunneweg since all three of these scholars refer to "the use of wood" in connection with this citation formula. Fensham and Brockington both attribute the legislation of a wood offering developed in Neh 10:35 (34) to the mention of the use of wood in Lev 1:17 and the abundance of wood in Lev 6:5 [15]. Aside from this approach not clearly demonstrating why it should be preferred over other views, we would emphasise here the fact that "the use of wood" is yet another referent that scholars have credited to כַּכָּתוּב in Neh 10:35 (34). Interestingly, it is unclear precisely what word or phrase it is in the context of this formula that these scholars would regard as its referent. Such a use of a citation formula appears to have no definable function. We contend that the view advocated by Fensham and Brockingham is representative of a lack of method and a misunderstanding of the function of citation formulæ.

The categorisation of the views of certain other scholars is impossible since they do not clearly address the relation between the citation formula and the word, phrase, clause, etc. in the context to which it refers [16].

---

15 E.g., F. Charles Fensham, *The Books of Ezra and Nehemiah,* NICOT (Grand Rapids, MI: Eerdmans, 1982) 240; L. H. Brockington, *Ezra, Nehemiah and Esther,* NCB (London: Nelson, 1969) 184-85.

16 F. Michaeli, *Les livres des Chroniques, d'Esdras et de Néhémie,* CAT (Neuchâtel: Delachaux & Niestlé, 1967) 347; Joseph Blenkinsopp, *Ezra-Nehemiah: A Commentary,* OTL (London: SCM Press Ltd., 1988) 317; Derek Kidner, *Ezra and Nehemiah,* TOTC (Leicester: Inter-Varsity Press, 1979) 116.

Another problem among both of the main positions reviewed above is the identification of a referent by supposition. This was especially evident in the debate between Jahn, Geißler, Kosters, and Meyer a century ago. For example, Jahn merely asserted that, "das ככתוב bezieht man *am natürlichsten* mit Kosters auf den ganzen Vers, nicht mit Geißler bloß auf b"[17]. Conversely, Meyer just claimed, "dass die Flamme ständig auf dem Altar brennen soll, wird dagegen Lev. 6, 1-6 vorgeschrieben; diese Stelle wird also v. 35 *ausdrücklich citirt*"[18]. However, these scholars merely provide assertions and do not submit any evidence to support their position.

Even today, scholars on both sides of the main debate still typically champion one referent over another merely by supposition. For example, Clines has provided a study of the use of law in Neh 10 and is an advocate of the referent "the continual burning of wood for a fire on the altar", but he does not address the lack of consensus among scholars on this issue[19]. Unless the referent that he advocates can be shown to be correct, then the present disarray in scholarship casts doubt on his analysis of this verse. Conversely, the same can be observed with regard to two recent advocates of "the wood offering" referent. For example, Shaver states, "the obligation to contribute the wood offering...*is specifically identified* as a requirement of the written law..."[20]. But neither Shaver nor Fishbane support their identification of this referent over against the one that Clines advocates. According to Shaver, Neh 10:35 (34) is one of seven passages that support the view that "at least for the Chronicler, the canonization of the Torah had not yet occurred"[21]. Since he assigns such great significance to this passage, it is surprising and methodologically dubious that he does not address this debate.

---

17 Jahn, 142, my emphasis.
18 Meyer, 211, my emphasis.
19 Clines, "Nehemiah 10", 112; *Ibid., Ezra, Nehemiah, Esther*, 208.
20 Shaver, 89, my emphasis. Fishbane similarly claims, "...striking among...post-exilic shorthand allusions to Pentateuchal sources is the reference to the 'wood-sacrifice' in Neh. 10: 35, which the priests, Levites, and Israelites were to bring to the Temple yearly, on special occasions 'as written in the Torah'" (213).
21 Shaver, 128.

In light of the sustained debate that we have surveyed above the assertion of one's view is no longer acceptable. We contend that the assignment of referents to citation formulæ like Neh 10:35 (34) in modern scholarship has been accomplished by intuition and not sound method. Insofar as this passage is representative of many others in the OT, this constitutes a fundamental problem in the present evaluation of inner-biblical exegesis and the use of citation formulæ in the post-exilic community.

It is striking that the most recent analysis of כַּכָּתוּב in Neh 10:35 (34) leaves the identification of the referent unresolved. Donner states,

> Eine Bestimmung über Brennholzlieferungen für den Tempel findet sich allerdings im Pentateuch nirgendwo. Daß überhaupt Brennholz auf dem Altar Jahwes verwendet wurde, steht in Lev 6,5. Sollte sich die Formel „wie geschrieben steht" auf den ganzen V.35 beziehen, dann müßte man annehmen, daß die einschlägige pentateuchische Anordnung verlorengegangen ist. Es könnte aber auch sein, daß die Formel nur für V.35b gelten soll: dann bezöge sie sich auf alle Stellen im Pentateuch, die Feuer auf dem Altare beschreiben oder voraussetzen[22].

In general, our review of scholarship has demonstrated first of all a considerable lack of consensus concerning what is the proper referent of the citation formula כַּכָּתוּב in Neh 10:35 (34). Altogether there are six referents that have been identified by scholars: "the wood offering/the delivery of wood"; "the continual burning of wood for a fire on the altar"; "the use of wood"; the entire complex act in Neh 10:35 (34); the whole pledge to observe the law in Neh 10:29-40 (28-39); and the view that the referent is ambiguous. Another aspect of the survey has shown that even those scholars who have appealed to criteria to identify the correct referent have employed faulty reasoning to resolve the debate. In fact, no one has attempted an analysis of the relationship between citation formulæ and their referents according to a defined or explicit method. This survey has led us to conclude that it has normally been the intuition of scholars that has guided the identification of a referent.

---

22 Herbert Donner, "‚Wie geschrieben steht'. Herkunft und Sinn einer Formel", in his *Aufsätze zum Alten Testament aus vier Jahrzehnten* (Berlin: Walter de Gruyter, 1994) 231; also in *Sitzungsberichte der Wissenschaftlichen Gesellschaft an der Johann Wolfgang Goethe-Universität Frankfurt a. M.*, Bd XXIX, Nr 4 (Stuttgart: Franz Steiner Verlag, 1992) 154.

In light of the impasse that has resulted from this approach, there is need
for a sustained examination of citation formulæ in the OT.

We seek to address this lack of consensus and method that has
become evident in the survey of scholarship on כַּכָּתוּב in Neh 10:35
(34), a representative example. More can be learned from this survey in
constructing a method for our research but before we address this we
should be clear as to the magnitude of the issues at hand.

III. The Significance of the Proper Reading of Citation Formulæ

The significance of the correct identification of the referent of each
citation formula cannot be disputed. Part of the need for a study of this
issue rests on the fact that different and contradictory assessments of the
interpretation practiced by the post-exilic community are understood
depending on the referent that is identified.

A review of some of the conclusions scholars have reached based on
the identification of the six referents in Neh 10:35 (34) clearly
demonstrates the magnitude of this issue. Two recent views of the
exegetical processes reflected in Neh 10:35 (34) disagree precisely
because of the difference in the identification of the referent: "the
Chronicler attributed to the Torah book legislation not found in the
Pentateuch or...the Hebrew Bible"[23]; and, "creation of facilitating
law...enabl[ing] the law of Leviticus 6:1-6...to be carried out"[24].

Both of these main positions have been further developed. On one
hand, some have taken the former view further and concluded, based on
a late dating of P, that "...man [hat] auch hier einfach anzuerkennen,
dass der Pentateuch noch nach Esra mancherlei Veränderungen erfahren
hat"[25]. Brockington, on the other hand, is closer to Clines' position
and draws a further conclusion based on this evidence of new legislation

---

23   Shaver, 127. T. Witton Davies similarly asserts concerning Neh 10:35 (34),
     "we have here clear proof that Ezra's law was not our Pentateuch" (250). See
     also L. Browne, 193; F. Michaeli, 347; Bowman, 765.
24   Clines, "Nehemiah 10", 112.
25   Bertholet, 79; see also Wellhausen, 174, n. 1. Shaver concludes that for the Chr
     the canon of the Pentateuch was not closed.

in Neh 10:35 (34). He states, "we may perhaps see here the building up of detailed laws supplementing what was written in the Pentateuch; they were finally written down in the Mishnah"[26].

Torrey, in contrast to all of the views above, seeks another avenue to explain the wood offering referent. He maintains that Neh 10:35 (34) "is a very good example of the Chronicler's heedless and irresponsible mode of citation, giving merely what he happened to remember, or thought he remembered"[27].

Perhaps the best representation of the importance of deciding between the rival referents in Neh 10:35 (34) is seen in the ramifications of Rudolph's conclusion. Rudolph never resolved the debate between the two referents, "the continual burning of wood for a fire" and "all of the details of the sentence". Consequently, this indecision carries over into his description of the relation between Neh 10:35 (34) and the legal tradition. Commenting on these two referents he states,

> im ersten Fall ist an Lv 6 5 f. gedacht, und die Verlosung ist eine erst von Nehemia getroffene Regelung, im zweiten Fall haben wir wieder (vgl. 33) anzunehmen, daß eine entsprechende Vorschrift des Esragesetzes uns heute nicht mehr erhalten ist[28].

By entertaining the two conclusions that stem from each of his readings of כָּתוּב in Neh 10:35 (34), Rudolph demonstrates the importance of the correct identification of the referent of a citation formula. That is, each reading results in a different understanding of the relation of the pledge in Neh 10:35 (34) to Israel's legal tradition. Rudolph's indecision implies that the identification of a referent is impossible in Neh 10:35 (34) and that the meaning of this post-exilic exegetical device is equivocal. However, if these implications of Rudolph's view are correct, then these are significant conclusions that should be established by a comprehensive analysis of several citation formulæ.

The identification of the correct referent is a pivotal issue in assessing the interpretation reflected in passages that use citation formulæ. It will be recalled that the lack of consensus and method that we have seen in Neh 10:35 (34) represents a problem that exists in several passages with

---

26   Brockington, 185.
27   Torrey, 277, n. g; he draws a similar conclusion for Neh 8:14.
28   Rudolph, 180.

citation formulæ (see below). The importance of the correct identification of referents is no small problem in the field of inner-biblical exegesis. Consequently, there is a need for the study of the relation between citation formulæ and their referents in the OT. The method of such a study should seek to overcome the subjectivity of the intuitive readings that have characterised previous scholarly treatments of the identification of referents.

IV. The Development of a Method

What we have not indicated yet is the manner in which every identification of a referent assumes, wittingly or unwittingly, some understanding of the syntax of prepositional phrases. That is, the identification of the referent of כַּכָּתוּב בַּתּוֹרָה in Neh 10:35 (34) is inextricably linked to the syntax of such sentence constituents. Since the syntax of Classical Hebrew has received considerable analysis, this resource must be a central part of our method and should provide some direction to the state of the problem reviewed in the previous section. In short, the predicament represented by כַּכָּתוּב בַּתּוֹרָה in Neh 10:35 (34) can be translated into a single syntactic question: "How does a prepositional phrase introduced with כְּ that functions as an adverbial construction[29] relate to its environment?"[30] In light of the lack of unanimity regarding the correct identification of referents, a study of the syntax of the context of these citation formulæ may advance the present

---

29 The preposition כְּ does not form phrasal verbs like בְּ and עַל (see DG §§ 89e, 118c). Many prepositions, unlike כְּ, *may* form verbal phrases with certain stems (e.g., נִלְחַם בְּ "to fight with", נִלְחַם עַל "to fight for/against", etc.). In such a case, DG explains, "the prep. does not function adverbially within the clause, modifying the verb in terms of place, time, manner, etc., but rather adverbially within the verbal phrase itself, telling us something about the mode of the action" (DG § 118 c). Some linguists refer to this as the valence of the verb. For a brief overview of the valence of אָרַר, see W. Richter, *Untersuchungen*, §3.5.

30 This question deliberately does not limit relations to the sentence. Even though we disagree with Houtman's analysis above for the reasons listed there, this does not eliminate discourse relations altogether from our examination.

scholarly impasse regarding these exegetical devices. Hence, the syntax of adverbial constructions will be invaluable in identifying the referents of these citation formulæ.

However, we are met here with a serious challenge. The study of adverbial constructions constitutes a lacuna in the syntactic research of Ancient Hebrew. There is no place in the scholarship of Ancient Hebrew where one can find a study of the manner in which a prepositional phrase that functions as an adverbial construction relates to its syntactic environment, especially a complex sentence[31]. There can be little doubt that this lacuna is a chief reason for the multiplicity of scholarly views that we have surveyed above.

Jenni's recent treatment of the semantic range of the monoconsonantal prepositions will prove to be an important resource. While his examination concentrates on the categorisation of the semantics of these prepositions Jenni does provide an up-to-date summary of the syntactic research of כ[32]. However, Jenni admits that his section on the syntax of expressions introduced with כ is in need of further attention[33]. Hence, in our study of referents we will also be

---

31 For one study of Hebrew adverbs and adverbial constructions, see Joshua Blau, *An Adverbial Construction in Hebrew and Arabic: Sentence Adverbials in Frontal Position Separated from the Rest of the Sentence*, The Israel Academy of Sciences and Humanities Proceedings VI (Jerusalem: Central Press, 1977). Blau's work is a culminative study of his basic approach reflected in his "Adverbia als psychologische und grammatische Subjecte/Praedikate im Bibelhebräische", *VT* 9 (1959) 130-37; and, "תוארי־פועל כנושאים ונשואים דקדוקים והגיונים בעברית", *Leshonenu* 20 (1955/56) 30-40. Blau's study, however, is limited to adverbs and adverbial constructions that function as the "Topic" of the prevailing discourse. In other words, Blau's study addresses a limited aspect of these adverbs and adverbial constructions.

Despite these limitations, even the recent treatment of adverbs by *IBHS* remains dependent on Blau to a great degree.

For the first treatment of Hebrew adverbial constructions based on their analog of adverbs, see the recent revision of Davidson's syntax by J. C. L. Gibson (DG §§ 114-130). However, the necessary succinctness of a textbook prevents this work from assisting our enquiry. For example, the discussion of the modifying capacity of adverbial constructions (§116, *Rem 2*) addresses only the simplest sentence structures, unlike that found in Neh 10:35 (34).

32 Ernst Jenni, *Die hebräischen Präpositionen Band 2: Die Präposition Kaph* (Stuttgart: W. Kohlhammer, 1994) 26-34.

33 *Ibid.*, 26.

researching the syntax of adverbial constructions introduced by כְּ in Classical Hebrew. At the appropriate place below we will relate Jenni's syntactic summary to our examination.

Another important methodological consideration concerns the fact that there are related constructions and expressions that are relevant to an examination of comparative citation formulæ. As will be seen below, these structures share a similar function as the citation formula כַּכָּתוּב in that they attribute a word, phrase, clause, etc. to another source. While some recent studies have concentrated on one or more citation formulæ (Donner studies כַּכָּתוּב; DeVries analyses כַּכָּתוּב, כַּמִּצְוָה and כַּמִּשְׁפָּט), we hope to demonstrate the value in expanding the scope of research to include other terms. For example, other relevant prepositional phrases entail כַּתּוֹרָה, כַּחֻקָּה and כַּדָּת. After an exhaustive examination of these formulæ which consist of predominantly legal terms we will address a selected number of terms such as √אמר and √דבר as well as their nominal cognates[34].

Another set of constructions are related to some of the citation formulæ above. For instance, כַּמִּצְוָה and כַּדָּבָר are related to the comparative clauses כַּאֲשֶׁר צוה√ and כַּאֲשֶׁר דבר√ respectively. Jenni refers to such prepositional phrases introduced with כְּ as abbreviations (Verkürzungen) of the comparative clause introduced with כַּאֲשֶׁר[35]. For instance, the constructions in 2 Chr 35:16 and Num 26:4 below both ascribe a command to an authority figure.

...and to offer burnt offerings on the altar of the LORD *according to the command of King Josiah* [כְּמִצְוַת הַמֶּלֶךְ יֹאשִׁיָּהוּ]. (2 Chr 35:16)

Take a census of the people from twenty years old and upward *as the LORD has commanded* [כַּאֲשֶׁר צִוָּה יְהוָה]. (Num 26:4)

From our study, we hope to show various ways that the use of some citation formulæ in the post-exilic historiography reflects development.

---

34   For the need for these *verba dicendi* to be treated together, see S. Meier, *Speaking of Speaking: Marking Direct Discourse in the Hebrew Bible*, VTS 46 (Leiden: E. J. Brill, 1992).

35   Jenni, 30-31, 130-36.

It appears that the development of such expressions in the Hebrew Scriptures is part of a wider evolution of exegetical devices which continues into the post-biblical era. Among the Dead Sea Scrolls, for instance, the Damascus Document demonstrates how the prepositional phrase כַּכָּתוּב was further abbreviated to ככ/"as it is written" (CD 19:1). Even though the scope of our analysis cannot include these later developments, a necessary precursor for such a study is a comprehensive study of citation formulæ and their plenary constructions in the OT.

Such a study should not be limited just to comparative constructions. There are other constructions that also use the passive participle כָּתוּב to cite the law. For example, √מצא is sometimes used with כָּתוּב.

> *And they found it written in the law* [וַיִּמְצְאוּ כָּתוּב בַּתּוֹרָה]. (Neh 8:14[36])

Another related formulation concerns those structures that use כל with the above citations.

> …our fathers have not observed the word of the LORD, to do *according to all that is written* [כְּכָל־הַכָּתוּב] in this book. (2 Chr 34:21)

Various relative constructions fall within our study as well. Dan 9:11, for example, uses the same passive participle to attribute a referent to תּוֹרַת מֹשֶׁה.

> …the curse has been poured out on us, along with the oath *which is written in the law of Moses* [אֲשֶׁר כְּתוּבָה בְּתוֹרַת מֹשֶׁה] the servant of God. (Dan 9:11)

The other relative constructions that will be addressed include אֲשֶׁר √צוה, הַכָּתוּבוֹת, and relative constructions based on the other verb stems we have listed above.

The vast majority of the comparative and relative exegetical devices addressed so far ascribe a legal referent to another source. However, it will also be helpful to examine the citation of non-legal referents. For

---

36　Neh 13:1 נִמְצָא כָתוּב בּוֹ אֲשֶׁר. See also in the New Testament, for example, εὗρεν τὸν τόπον οὗ ἦν γεγραμμένον (Luke 4:17b, this passage introduces a citation of Isa 61:1-2).

example, we will examine the regnal source formulæ that also use the passive participle כָּתוּב.

> Now the rest of the acts of Zechariah, *they are written in the Book of the Chronicles of the Kings of Israel* [הִנָּם כְּתוּבִים עַל־סֵפֶר דִּבְרֵי הַיָּמִים לְמַלְכֵי יִשְׂרָאֵל]. (2 Kgs 15:11)

Even though these constructions consist of a different syntactic form they are still relevant for our study since this clause also ascribes a referent, here "the rest of the acts of the king", to another corpus. In fact, we will see that several different types of non-legal referents (e.g., lamentations, prophetic oracles, official correspondence, genealogies, etc.) are attributed to other sources (e.g., "the Book of the Just", "the annals of the kings of Media and Persia", etc.) by the same distinctive citation pattern used in the regnal source formulæ. These constructions with non-legal referents will also provide a useful point of comparison for assessing the use of formulæ with legal referents.

So far the description of our method has included syntactic considerations (comparative and relative constructions) and various terms (מִצְוָה, √צוה, כָּתוּב, etc.). Such a syntactic and semantic analysis, however, does not account for all of the relations that exist between citation devices and their respective referents. Other factors include certain linguistic and *Textlinguistik* concepts (i.e., pro-forms, discourse analysis, Topic/Comment, etc.). The work of linguists in Classical Hebrew has been particularly instructive in these and other matters[37]. We hope that our analysis will demonstrate some of the usefulness of these resources to OT studies.

This latter group of non-syntactic and non-semantic characteristics constitute a specialised discipline within linguistics called pragmatics or *Textpragmatik*. Hence, our survey of scholarship and our inductive analysis has led us to a three-part method centered on the syntactic,

---

37 Geoffrey Khan, *Studies in Semitic Syntax*, LOS, Vol. 38 (Oxford: Oxford University Press, 1988); Francis I. Andersen, *The Sentence in Biblical Hebrew*, Janua Linguarum, Series Practica, 231 (The Hague: Mouton, 1974); Wolfgang Richter, *Grundlagen einer althebräischen Grammatik*, ATSAT, Bd. 8: I. *Das Wort (Morphologie)*, Bd. 10: II. *Die Wortfügung (Morphosyntax)*, Bd. 13: III. *Der Satz (Satztheorie)* (Sankt Ottilien: EOS Verlag, 1978-80); Wolfgang Schneider, *Grammatik des biblischen Hebräisch* (Munich: Cladius, 1974).

semantic, and pragmatic considerations of the text. Interestingly, our survey and analysis has led us to a method that has also been articulated by Heinrich F. Plett, who has described the "drei semiotischen Dimensionen" of a text as "Textsyntax, Textsemantik, und Textpragmatik"[38]. While our approach remains largely grounded in syntax, it nevertheless touches on modern linguistics as applied to Classical Hebrew by a few recent Semitic scholars and *Textlinguistics* as reflected in Plett[39].

Another important outcome of the survey of scholarship above has been to demonstrate the need for a clear definition of terms in the analysis of citation formulæ in the OT. Citation formulæ assign a referent from their prevailing contexts to another source. This source can be another literary corpus or a person. The discussion of the use of citation formulæ must explicitly identify its referent(s); otherwise it is not a satisfactory treatment. The referent consists of a word, phrase, clause, etc. which the exegetical device attributes to another source.

Scholars sometimes refer to the terms we will be analysing as "citation formulæ". However, since these terms are not always formulaic, we will use the phrase "citation base" to refer to the constructions that ascribe a referent to another source.

Two other phrases which pertain to certain basic issues should be described at this stage. As we have already observed with כֹּל, a term can be used in conjunction with a citation base. The effect of this and certain other terms is that the citation base generally has a broader referent than without it. The passages that occur with such terms will be categorised separately as "citation bases with broadening terms". Another main category consists of two citation bases functioning

---

38   Heinrich F. Plett, *Textwissenschaft und Textanalyse* (Heidelberg: Quelle und Meyer, 1975) 55, cf. 52-92. In English, see Stephen C. Levinson, *Pragmatics*, Cambridge Textbooks in Linguistics (Cambridge: Cambridge University Press, 1983) 236-37; and Geoffrey Leech, *Principles of Pragmatics* (London: Longman, 1983). For some of these issues in Biblical Hebrew, see George W. Savran, *Telling and Retelling: Quotation in Biblical Narrative* (Bloomington & Indianapolis: Indiana University Press, 1988).

39   For an integration of the methods of Richter and Plett, see the series *Textwissenschaft · Theologie Hermeneutik Linguistik · Literaturanalyse Informatik*, ed. by Harald Schweizer, 1991- .

together as a "compound citation base". For example, the expression
(enlarged) in 2 Sam 24:19 is a compound citation base.

וַיַּעַל דָּוִד כִּדְבַר־גָּד כַּאֲשֶׁר צִוָּה יְהוָה (2 Sam 24:19)

Conversely, when a citation base consists of a single construction (e.g.,
כַּכָּתוּב בַּתּוֹרָה in Neh 10:35 [34]) it may be referred to as an
"independent citation base".

These are the most basic terms that will be employed throughout our
research and we will develop them as we proceed.

V. Conclusion

The above survey has used Neh 10:35 (34) to represent the lack of
consensus and method in scholarship concerning the treatment of the
relationship between citation formulæ and their referents in the OT. At
present, this situation results in confusion regarding the use of citation
formulæ and aspects of inner-biblical exegesis. In formulating a method
to address this situation, our survey of scholarship suggests that an
analysis of the syntax of these forms may prove helpful in advancing the
present state of the debate. The review of scholarship above has also
been formative in the development and definition of our terms as well as
alerting us to relevant constructions for a thorough examination. It
appears that a predominantly syntactic analysis of the constructions
covered in this chapter is merited and may advance the present state of
scholarship concerning the use of these exegetical devices in the OT as
well as the study of inner-biblical exegesis.

Chapter 2: Citation Bases with כָּתוּב

I. Introduction

The passive participle form of √כתב occurs 113 times in the OT.
There are a handful of relevant passages in BA and one citation formula
that, we will argue, should be reconstructed from the LXX[1]. In more
than ninety instances one of these forms functions as part of a citation
base providing a link between a referent and its source[2]. Among these
occurrences, both legal and non-legal referents are attributed to either a
corpus or a person. We will first address the manner in which non-legal
referents are linked to a source by the constructions that use כָּתוּב.
Even though these referents cover a vast range of topics, the way they
link a referent to a source consists of a remarkable degree of common
elements and relationships. In fact, the law is cited with כָּתוּב less
frequently than these non-legal topics.

---

1   Two Aramaic peil verbs כְּתִיב occur in Ezra 5:7; 6:2. There is only one
    occurrence of the noun כְּתָב in a citation base (Ezra 6:18). For the citation
    formula reconstructed from the LXX, see our treatment of 3 Reigns 8:53a
    below.

2   In the remaining instances, this form of √כתב does not link a referent to
    another source. In these passages, the participle functions either in: a
    descriptive way (Exod 31:18; 32:15b, c; Num 11:26; Deut 9:10; Josh 23:6; 2
    Kgs 22:13; Jer 51:60; Psa 149:9; Ezra 4:7; Neh 12:22; 1 Chr 4:41; 16:40 [see
    Jenni, *Die hebräischen Präpositionen. Band 3: Die Präposition Lamed*
    (Stuttgart: Kohlhammer, 2000) 299]); a figurative sense (Isa 65:6; Jer 17:1); a
    vision (Ezek 2:10a, b); or an eschatological passage (Dan 12:1; Isa 4:3). Psalm
    40:8 (7), Eccl 12:10, and Neh 6:6 use the passive participle as a finite verb and
    are to be distinguished from citation formulæ and expressions. "The ptcp.
    without subj. tends to be used occasionally for 3rd pers. like finite verb. . . .
    Neh 6. 6; . . . . and in Psalms" (DG § 113, *Rem 5*).

II. כָּתוּב Citation Bases with Non-Legal Referents

The topics and items that occur among the non-legal citation constructions can be classified as follows: the rest of the deeds of various kings; laments; poetic fragments attributed to "the Book of the Just"; genealogies; official correspondence; and excerpts from the books of prophecies or from court annals. The passages concerning "the rest of the deeds of kings" are cited more times than the law.

A. The Regnal Source Formulæ

1. A Categorisation of the Evidence

In the books of Kings and Chronicles the masculine plural passive participle of √כתב customarily refers to a body of literature which contains the deeds of a certain king. This type of reference occurs forty-nine times including Esth 10:2. An analysis of these passages demonstrates that there are typically four elements which exist in a reference to "the rest of the deeds of a king". The four elements that comprise this citation formula are: 1. "the rest of the deeds...", good or bad, of a given king; 2. a resumptive third person pronoun, separable or inseparable, with either the particle הִנֵּה or a negative interrogative הֲלֹא; 3. the passive participle כְּתוּבִים; and 4. the name of another corpus of literature.

Since we are concerned with the proper identification of the referent of citation bases, we will concentrate on the first three elements of this four-part citation pattern. The following detailed categorisation of these elements of the regnal source formulæ will facilitate our analysis of the relation between the citation base and the referent as well as its reformulations.

1. "The rest of the deeds of a king", good or bad, are referred to by two sets of distinguishable vocabulary.

   a. The vocabulary used in 1 and 2 Kings includes:

      i. ויתר דברי [a king] [3]

      ii. passages that add (וכל) אשר עשה to "i.":

        a) ויתר דברי [a king] וכל־אשר עשה [4]

        b) ויתר דברי [a king] אשר עשה [5]

      iii. passages that add גבורתו to "i." and "ii.":

        a) ויתר דברי [a king] וכל־גבורתו ואשר עשה [6]

        b) ויתר דברי [a king] וכל־אשר עשה וכל־גבורתו [7]

        c) ויתר דברי [a king] וכל־אשר עשה וגבורתו [8]

        d) ויתר דברי [a king] (ו) אשר עשה וגבורתו [9]

      iv. passages that add נלחם to "i." or "iii.":

        a) ויתר דברי [a king] וכל־אשר עשה וגבורתו• [10]

            אשר נלחם [a specific king or kingdom]

        b) ויתר דברי [a king] אשר נלחם ואשר מלך [11]

        c) ויתר דברי [a king] וגבורתו אשר־עשה ואשר נלחם [12]

      v. ויתר דברי [a king] וקשרו אשר קשר [13]

---

3   Passages which use this language exclusively are 2 Kgs 14:18; 15:11.

4   1 Kgs 14:29; 15:7, 31; 16:14; 22:39 (continues with details); 2 Kgs 8:23; 12:20 (19); 15:6, 21, 26, 31; 21:17 (adds וחטאתו אשר חטא); 23:28; 24:5; 1 Kgs 11:41 (adds וחכמתו).

5   2 Kgs 1:18; 15:36 (some Mss and versions add וכל like 1.a.ii.a); 16:19; 21:25.

6   1 Kgs 15:23 (read with 𝔊S; MT adds כל twice plus והערים אשר בנה); 2 Kgs 20:20 (continues with details).

7   2 Kgs 10:34.

8   2 Kgs 13:8.

9   1 Kgs 16:5, 27 (delete a second אשר עשה).

10 2 Kgs 13:12; 14:15 (some Mss and S𝔗f וכל), 28 (read with MT and most Mss 𝔊).

11 1 Kgs 14:19.

12 1 Kgs 22:46 (45).

13 1 Kgs 16:20; 2 Kgs 15:15.

vi. ‏ויתר דברי אחאב וכל־אשר עשה ובית השן אשר בנה‎ 14
‏וכל־הערים אשר בנה‎

b. The vocabulary used in 1 and 2 Chronicles includes:

  i. passages using ‏ויתר דברי‎ and ‏נים‏(ו)‏הראשנים והאחר‎:

    a) ‏נים‏(ו)‏ויתר דברי‎ [a king] ‏הראשנים והאחר‎ 15

    b) ‏ויתר דבריו וכל־דרכיו הראשנים והאחרונים‎ 16

  ii. deviations from "i."

    a) passages lacking ‏יתר‎

      1) ‏ודברי‎ [a king] ‏נים והאחר‏(ו)‏הראש‏(ו)‏נים‎ 17

      2) ‏ודבריו הראשנים והאחרנים‎ 18

    b) passages lacking ‏נים‏(ו)‏נים והאחר‏(ו)‏הראש‎

      1) ‏ויתר דברי‎ [a king] ‏וכל־מלחמתיו ודרכיו‎ 19

      2) ‏ויתר דברי‎ [a king] ‏וחסדיו‎ 20

    c) ‏ובניו ורב המשא עליו ויסוד בית האלהים‎ 21

    d) ‏ויתר דברי‎ [a king] ‏ותעבתיו אשר־עשה והנמצא עליו‎ 22

    e) 2 Chr 33:18-19 23

c. Esther 10:2 (see below)

---

14   1 Kgs 22:39.

15   2 Chr 20:34; 25:26. 2 Chr 9:29 uses the synonym ‏שאר‎ in place of ‏יתר‎.

16   2 Chr 28:26. The unique construction of this passage results from the mention of Ahaz's name, the antecedent of the pronominal suffixes, in v. 24. Otherwise, we would expect the same construction as in 1.b.i.a).

17   1 Chr 29:29 (the Chr adds the king's title only with David, ‏דָּוִיד הַמֶּלֶךְ‎); 2 Chr 12:15; 16:11 (introduces sentence with ‏והנה‎ instead of ‏ו‎).

18   2 Chr 35:27. This passage deviates from 1.b.ii.a) 1) which mentions the typical referent ‏ויתר דברי‎ and Josiah's name.

19   2 Chr 27:7 (read with MT; 𝔊 has one αὐτοῦ for both coordinated nouns).

20   2 Chr 32:32.

21   2 Chr 24:27 (read with MT).

22   2 Chr 36:8 which is not in *Vorlage*.

23   As is well-known, the Chr reworks Manasseh's account in 2 Chr 33:18-19. In fact, as we will see below, the formula and referent of his *Vorlage* are a focal point of the Chr's rewriting.

2. The second element is a resumptive third person pronoun with either
    the particle הִנֵּה or the negative interrogative הֲלֹא.

    a. instances of הִנֵּה with an inseparable third person masculine
        plural pronoun:

        הנם 24

    b. instances of a negative interrogative הֲלֹא with a separable third
        person masculine plural pronoun:

        i. הלא־הם 25
        ii. הלא־המה 26

    c. there is one passage where this second element does not exist
        resulting in a contiguous relation between the first and third
        elements (2 Chr 13:22)27.

3. The third element is the passive participle כְּתוּבִים 28.

4. The fourth element is the appellation of the body of literature29.

Below is a list of the standard variations among the first three elements
of these regnal source formulæ:

(1 Kgs 14:19) ...הִנָּם כְּתוּבִים [the rest of Jeroboam's deeds]

---

24 1 Kgs 14:19; 2 Kgs 15:11, 15, 26, 31; 1 Chr 29:29; 2 Chr 16:11; 20:34;
    24:27; 27:7; 28:26; 32:32; 33:19; 35:26-27; 36:8.
25 1 Kgs 11:41; 15:7, 31; 16:5, 14, 20, 27; 22:39, 46 (45); 2 Kgs 8:23; 10:34;
    12:20 (19); 13:8, 12; 14:15, 18, 28; 15:6, 21, 36; 16:19; 20:20; 21:17, 25;
    23:28; 24:5; 2 Chr 9:29; 12:15; Esth 10:2. The above passages include both
    the full (לוֹא) and defective (לֹא) spelling of the negative particle.
26 1 Kgs 14:29; 15:23; 2 Kgs 1:18.
27 2 Chr 13:22 will be addressed below.
28 כְּתֻבִים occurs in 1Kgs 11:41 and 2 Kgs 15:15.
29 For recent studies of these titles, see S. Japhet, *I & II Chronicles,* OTL
    (Louisville, Kentucky: Westminster/John Knox Press, 1993) 19-23; H. G. M.
    Williamson, *1 and 2 Chronicles,* NCB (London: Marshall, Morgan & Scott
    Publ. Ltd., 1982) 17-23.

(1 Kgs 14:29) ...הֲלֹא־הֵמָּה כְתוּבִים [the rest of Rehoboam's deeds]

(1 Kgs 15:7) ...הֲלוֹא־הֵם כְּתוּבִים [the rest of Abijam's deeds]

2. An Analysis of the Elements of the Regnal Source Formulæ

In order to analyse the relationship between the citation base כְּתוּבִים and the referent, we must initially address the first three elements of the four-part citation formula individually.

a. The First Element

i. The Terms Used in the First Element

Regarding the first element of these regnal source formulæ, the books of Kings and Chronicles customarily employ the phrase וְיֶתֶר דברי ("and the rest of the deeds of"). Despite this similarity, each of these books employ their own characteristic range of terms to elaborate on this phrase.

Kings typically elaborates on this phrase with expressions which include: (כל) אֲשֶׁר עָשָׂה ("[everything] that he did"), (כל) גבורתו ("[all of] his might"), and אֲשֶׁר נלחם ("the manner in which he fought"). Chronicles, on the other hand, details these deeds of the kings with terms that entail the merismus הראשׁנים והאחרנים ("the first and the last things"), but also the words דָּבָר and דֶּרֶךְ. From the first element of these formulæ the Chr always omits גְּבוּרָה, לחם√, קֶשֶׁר, קשׁר√, and other non-recurring forms[30].

---

30 As with most scholars, we are assuming that Chronicles is based on Kings,
   contra A. G. Auld (*Kings Without Privilege: David and Moses in the Story of
   the Bible's Kings* [Edinburgh: T. & T. Clark, 1994]) who suggests that Sam-
   Kgs have been rewritten from a source that was also used by the Chr in
   composing his history.

A brief analysis of the Chr's rewriting of the first element of this four-part citation pattern is instructive for the examination of the use of these regnal formulæ. The Chr's most common alteration of his *Vorlage* in the first elements of this four-part citation pattern concerns his use of the phrase "the first and the last things". This merismus is at times simply added to his *Vorlage* (1 Chr 29:29; 2 Chr 25:26) or it may replace one of the following deuteronomistic elaborations: the expression כל) אשר עשה) (1 Kgs 11:41/ 2 Chr 9:29; 1 Kgs 14:29/2 Chr 12:15; 1 Kgs 15:23/2 Chr 16:11; 2 Kgs 16:19/2 Chr 28:26; 2 Kgs 23:28/2 Chr 35:27)[31]; or וגבורתו אשר עשה ואשר נלחם (1 Kgs 22:46 [45][32]/2 Chr 20:34)[33]. Japhet has observed that the Chr's rephrasing with this merismus is restricted to nine Judean kings[34].

Even though the Chr may alter the regnal formulæ, the categorisation above shows that he does not typically alter their four-part structure.

Next we must consider the referent of Esther 10:2 in comparison to those just examined in Kings and Chronicles. We should first note the distinct provenance of the book of Esther which makes the regnal source formula in 10:2 of considerable importance[35]. In fact, several scholars maintain that Esther 9:20-10:3 has a separate provenance from the rest of the book. However, there is an even greater lack of consensus among scholars concerning the origin of this section of Esther which

---

31 This phrase accounts for only part of the Chr's rewriting in 2 Chr 9:29; 16:11; 28:26; 35:27.

32 Read with MT.

33 A similar rewriting occurs in 2 Chr 26:22 but this passage does not entail a regnal source formula.

34 Japhet, 644.

35 There is no unanimity among scholars concerning the date of the composition of Esther. Opinions vary from the fifth to first century B.C. (see Clines, 272-73). Most recently, J. D. Levenson states, "when the book of Esther was written is unknown" (*Esther: A Commentary*, OTL [London: SCM Press Ltd, 1997] 25). He suggests that it was probably in the fourth or third century B.C. (26). Dr. Stephanie Dalley has defended the view that the book was composed in the Achaemenid period ("The Mesopotamian Background to the Hebrew Book of Esther", Oxford Old Testament Seminar, 3 ii 1997). For a recent argument against the parallel of Marduk with Mordecai, see Clines "In Quest of the Historical Mordecai", *VT* 41 (1991) 126-39.

contains the regnal source formula we are examining. For example, Patton argued for a different provenance for Esther 9:20-10:3 from the rest of the book based on the view that it was added to legitimatise the Festival of Purim[36]. Recently, Clines tentatively stated, "it is tempting to suppose that the material that now occupies chs. 9 and 10 is of secondary origin and was composed by a narrator (or authors) of inferior artistry"[37]. However, other scholars maintain that 9:20-10:3 is an original part of the book since it is integral to the message and "full understanding" of the book[38]. There is a lack of consensus among scholars regarding the relation of 9:20-10:3 to the rest of the book.

Despite this disagreement concerning the origin of Esth 9:20-10:3, the distinctiveness of the extant book of Esther among the Hebrew Scriptures has been supported in a number of ways. Commenting on the citation formula in Esth 10:2, Gordis suggests that the book of Esther should be understood as a unique literary genre in the Hebrew Scriptures since it is written "in the form a chronicle of the Persian court, written by a Gentile scribe"[39]. Most scholars would consider Esther's uniqueness in the Old Testament to pertain to at least some of the following issues: its worldview (e.g., relations with a foreign king, vengeful slaughter, etc.); its subject matter (a diaspora community during the restoration period); and, of course, its lack of a reference to Israel's God. Furthermore, Esther is the only book in the Hebrew Scriptures not attested in the documents at Qumran. The force of these considerations has made the question of the canonicity of Esther a

---

36 L. B. Patton, *A Critical and Exegetical Commentary on the Book of Esther,* ICC (Edinburgh: T. & T. Clark, 1908) 57-60. M. V. Fox (*The Redaction of the Books of Esther: On Reading Composite Texts,* SBLMS 40 [Atlanta, GA: Scholars Press, 1991]) has argued that a redactor (R-MT) reworked "proto-Esther" which resulted in the MT. The bulk of this redaction, according to Fox, was the addition of chapters 8-10.

37 Clines, 320.

38 E. g., B. W. Jones, "The So-Called Appendix of the Book of Esther", *Semitics* 6 (1978) 36-43; *ibid.,* "Two Misconceptions about the Book of Esther", *CBQ* 39 (1977) 171-81; see also C. A. Moore, *Studies in the Book of Esther* (New York: Ktav Pub. House, 1982) 437-47.

39 R. Gordis, "Religion, Wisdom and History in the Book of Esther—A New Solution to an Ancient Crux", *JBL* 100 (1981) 375.

recurring issue in both Jewish (Council of Jamnia) and Christian communities (e.g., Luther).

Additionally, the citation base in Esther 10:2 does not refer to the same source as that of Kings or Chronicles. The literature cited above in Kings and Chronicles reflects a Jewish source while the formula in Esth 10:2 attributes the deeds of a Persian monarch to a document by the name of "the Annals of the Kings of Media and Persia". In fact, the author of Esther also appears to have no small knowledge of the Persian court[40].

In light of the exceptional nature of the book of Esther in the OT, it is not surprising that the referent of this regnal source formula employs vocabulary which is distinguishable from the language used in either Kings or Chronicles.

וְכָל־מַעֲשֵׂה תָקְפּוֹ וּגְבוּרָתוֹ וּפָרָשַׁת גְּדֻלַּת מָרְדֳּכַי אֲשֶׁר גִּדְּלוֹ הַמֶּלֶךְ הֲלוֹא־הֵם כְּתוּבִים עַל־סֵפֶר דִּבְרֵי הַיָּמִים לְמַלְכֵי מָדַי וּפָרָס (Esth 10:2)

Despite all of the distinctive characteristics of Esther and the possible separate provenance of 9:20-10:3, the same four-part citation pattern is used. Hence, like the Chr, the writer of Esther has used the first element of the four-part citation pattern for his own purposes but has retained the distinctive structure of this formula.

This expression in Esth 10:2 stands out among all regnal source formulæ. An explanation of the presence of this four-part formula in such an individualistic work suggests that its use here is best accounted for by attributing it to a shared literary convention for citing (court) records among the communities that produced Kings, Chronicles, and Esther. The alternative view that this formula in Esth 10:2 is due to the influence of Kings or Chronicles appears less likely. In light of the nature of the book of Esther as well as the section 9:20-10:3 reviewed above, it appears implausible to conclude that an influence between such distinguishable works would only be attested in such a tangential issue as the use of this distinctive four-part citation pattern (see below).

---

40 For the manner in which the author of Esther reflects knowledge of Persian court behaviour as it is attested in Herodotus, see E. Yamauchi, "The Archaeological Background of Esther", *BSac* 137 (1980) 104.

Hence the evidence, which is admittedly slim, nevertheless suggests that such a literary convention may have been shared by the communities responsible for Kings, Chronicles, and Esther (see further below)[41].

ii. The Syntax and Semantic Nature of the Nominal Phrases of the First Element

Syntactically, the referents of these regnal source formulæ include various nominal constructions that are in *casus pendens*. According to Muraoka, "casus pendens plays an active and important role in the whole structure of Biblical Hebrew *Satzlehre*"[42]. It is noteworthy that

---

41 Such a putative literary convention for the citation of court records may have survived anywhere from 60-ca.500 years in light of the range of dates scholars assign to these books. The *terminus a quo* for Kings is 561 B.C. (cf. 2 Kgs 25:27-30). It appears best to understand the *terminus ad quem* as 539 B.C. since the narrative of Kings ends at a point shortly before the overthrow of Babylon which is a watershed event that would probably have been included by the historiographer of the Israelite monarchy. Concerning the date of Chronicles, Japhet has recently summarised the consensus of scholarship (S. R. Driver, Eissfeldt, Curtis, Rudolph, Williamson, etc.). She states, "on the whole...the most common view is...placing the book's composition some time in the fourth century BCE or towards its end" (Japhet, 24). See also the post-exilic genealogies of Davidides in 1 Chr 3:24ff. For a dating of Chronicles contemporary with the DtrH which has not been generally followed, see A. C. Welch, *The Work of the Chronicler: Its Purpose and Its Date* (London: The British Academy, 1939) 149-60. For the dating of 1 Chr 10-2 Chr 34, Chr$_1$, to 520-515 B.C., see F. M. Cross, "A Reconstruction of the Judean Restoration", *JBL* 94 (1975) 4-18.

42 T. Muraoka, *Emphatic Words and Structures in Biblical Hebrew* (Jerusalem-Leiden: The Magnes Press/E. J. Brill, 1985) 94. In his chapter on *casus pendens,* Muraoka treats only verbal clauses (94, n. 6) while a limited number of nominal clauses are treated under pronominal copula (67-77). Since the pronouns in the sentence structure of the regnal formulæ are not copula but resumptive pronouns adjoined to different particles, Muraoka's study of *casus pendens* does not apply to our study of these formulæ. Muraoka's research on הִנֵּה, however, does apply to our study and we will address this below. For the classic treatment of *casus pendens,* see S. R. Driver, *A Treatise on The Use of the Tenses in Hebrew,* 3rd edn (Oxford: Clarendon Press, 1892) §§ 196ff.

the sentence structure chosen for this regnal source formula gives prominence and emphasis to the referent[43].

The significance of this sentence structure in Semitic languages has been recently illuminated by Khan's *Studies in Semitic Syntax*. Among the constructions that Semitists have traditionally called *casus pendens,* Khan has differentiated between extraposed nominal structures (Ex) and pronominal agreement constructions[44]. Khan's differentiation between Ex and "pronominal agreement constructions with resumptive pronouns" (PAR) illuminates the significance of extraposition in these regnal source formulæ. Structurally, "the crucial point of differentiation is that in pronominal agreement the nominal stands immediately inside the predication whereas in extraposition the nominal is structually isolated from the predication and is integrated within it vacariously [*sic*] by the co-referential pronoun"[45]. Hence, the extraposed referents of the regnal source formulæ receive greater prominence than if they had been placed in a PAR.

The difference between Ex and PAR concerns not only structure but also the type of nouns or nominal constructions that they include. According to Khan, "the slot at the front of PAR-clauses is restricted to highly individuated nominals whereas the equivalent slot in Ex-clauses

---

43 For the sentence structure used in these formulæ, the type of emphasis concerns both *casus pendens* and the specific manner by which the extraposed nominal phrase is reintegrated into the sentence. Since the resumptive pronoun in regnal formulæ is always affixed to a particle, either הנה or the negative interrogative הלא, the entire construction that expresses the subject "extraposed nominal phrase - particle - resumptive pronoun" must be addressed as a whole (see below) in order to define the specific type of emphasis marked by this structure. Hence, we content ourselves at this point with describing the *casus pendens* merely as emphasis which will be defined more specifically below.

44 Khan, xxv-xxviii, 65-97. According to Khan, an initial nominal word or phrase is extraposed when its role in the sentence (subject, object, etc.) is marked only by the placement of the co-referential pronoun. In this case, the syntactic role of the extraposed noun in the sentence is indicated by the placement of the resumptive pronoun which is fully integrated in the clause. On the other hand, pronominal agreement constructions differ from extraposition in that these mark the grammatical relation by adjoining to the noun or nominal phrase a "relational particle" (i.e., preposition, direct object marker אֶת־, inflection in languages with this feature, etc.).

45 *Ibid.,* xxviii.

admits nominals which are lower on the individuation scale"[46]. A nominal may be low on the individuation scale by being a familiar concept to the hearer/reader. Khan explains,

> a nominal may be assumed to be familiar by virtue of either (a) being closely related to a previously mentioned nominal, or (b) being in the permanent knowledge store of the hearer/reader. The most obvious kind of close relationship between two nominals is co-reference, i.e. the referent of the nominal has already been "evoked" or "given" in the prior discourse[47].

The semantic nature of the first element in most regnal source formulæ (e.g., "the rest of the deeds of David") rests in their close relation to the preceding narrative.

Khan's study has made the use of Ex in regnal source formulæ even more noteworthy than we initially thought since he has shown that the extraposed referent receives greater prominence by being placed outside of the predicate than *casus pendens* constructions in general. The full significance of this isolation of the referent, however, can only be appreciated after we have examined the other elements of the four-part citation pattern. This is especially true regarding the distinctive manner in which the referent is integrated into the predication, to which we turn next.

b. The Second Element

The two particles that may occur in the second element of these formulæ have a distinctive use and relation between each other. First, the particle הִנֵּה and the negative interrogative הֲלֹא are used synonymously in these regnal source formulæ. According to Gibson, "the particle הֲלֹא implying an affirmative answer is in effect equivalent to הִנֵּה"[48]. GK also equates these two particles and comments on their role as formulæ. "The formula of quotation...הֲלֹא־הֵם כְּתוּבִים [is]

---

46 *Ibid.*, 97.
47 *Ibid.*, xxxviii. For further elaboration of the hierarchies of semantic individuation, see *ibid.*, xxxvii-xxxix.
48 DG § 152.

equivalent to *surely it is, they are* written...synonymous with the simple formula of assertion הִנֵּה כְתוּבָה ..., and הִנָּם כְּתוּבִים"[49]. Kropat has observed "II [Chr] 20 34 u. öfter setzt der Chroniker הִנָּם כְּתוּבִים statt rhetorischer Frage der *Vorlage* הֲלֹא הֵם כְּתוּבִים"[50].

Secondly, scholars describe a role for these interchangeable particles in formulæ which corresponds to Khan's analysis of the type of nominals that are permitted by extraposition. According to GK, the role of these particles in these formulæ "serves merely to express the conviction that the contents of the statement are well known to the hearer, and are unconditionally admitted by him"[51]. Brongers follows GK insofar as he concludes that the use of these "mutually exchangeable" particles "is only to ask attention for something obvious"[52]. Regarding their use in citation formulæ, he suggests the rendering "as you know"[53].

Lastly, these particles are always construed with a resumptive pronoun that is in grammatical agreement with the extraposed nominal phrase[54].

---

49   GK § 150e.

50   Arno Kropat, *Die Syntax des Author der Chronik verglichen mit der seiner Quellen: Ein Beitrag zur historischen Syntax des Hebräischen*, BZAW 16 (Gießen: A. Töpelmann, 1909) 31. DG points out other places where the Chronicler changes between these two particles, "in Chr. הִנֵּה is sometimes used for הֲלֹא of earlier books, comp. 2 Chr. 16. 11 with 1 K. 15. 23" (§ 152, p. 184).

51   *Ibid.*; see also JM § 164d.

52   For the distinction of the emphatic use of the negative interrogative הֲלֹא from its use as a synonym of הִנֵּה, see H. A. Brongers, "Some Remarks on the Biblical Particle *hᵃlo*'", *OTS* 21 (1981) 180-185. Among his observations for the synonymity of these two particles Brongers notes that the LXX occasionally translates הֲלֹא with ἰδού (cf. Josh 1:9; Judg 6:14; Ruth 2:9). He continues, "one is struck by the fact that [הֲלֹא] and [הִנֵּה] are mutually exchangeable". Brongers cites the interchangeability of these particles in roles other than citation formulæ. For example, in 1 Sam 9:21 and Judg 6:15, these particles are used to draw attention "to a modest social status" (181). According to Brongers, Isa 37:11 could have used either particle.

53   *Ibid.*, 178.

54   On the unique example of הִנֵּה כְתוּבָה in 2 Sam 1:18, which is cited by GK, see our analysis below.

c. The Third Element

The passive participle of √כתב always agrees with the extraposed nominal construction and is placed in a contiguous relation to the resumptive pronoun. In regnal source formulæ, the participle is always inflected in the masculine plural.

Haag suggests that the relative infrequency of √כתב in the Old Testament compared to √אמר and √דבר "indicates that in Israel the spoken word played an incomparably more important role than the written word as a medium of both human communication and divine revelation"[55]. Undoubtedly there was an ancient oral tradition in Israel, but a mere statistical comparison of √כתב with these *verba dicendi* is misleading. Aside from the fact that he makes a comparison with only two *verba dicendi* Haag does not account for the uses of such forms in citing written texts (e.g., כמצוה, further below). In fact, the citations of "the Book of the Just" (e.g., Josh 10:13; 2 Sam 1:18) and "the Book of the Wars of the LORD" (Num 21:14) give far more weight to a tradition of writing in ancient Israel than Haag suggests. Several scholars consider such corpora early[56]. Hence, there is no need for Haag's argument to denigrate the importance of the written word in Israel.

3. The Relation Between the First Three Elements of the Four-Part Regnal Citation Formulæ

Having examined the individual elements of these regnal source formulæ, we will next address the manner in which these elements relate to each other.

There is a consistent use of the four-part regnal source formula despite the Chr's rephrasing of the referents, his interchanging of the

---

55 *TDOT,* Vol. VII, 374; in German, *TWAT,* Bd. IV, 388.

56 E.g., A. A. Anderson, *2 Samuel,* WBC (Dallas, Texas: Word Books, 1989) 14; T. C. Butler, *Joshua,* WBC (Waco, Texas: Word Books, 1983) 117; J. Gray, *Joshua, Judges, Ruth,* NCB (Basingstoke: Marshall, Morgan & Scott, 1986) 108-9; J. Mauchline, *1 and 2 Samuel,* NCB (London: Marshall, Morgan & Scott, 1971) 199.

two emphatic particles, and the distinct provenance of Esther. There are a handful of passages where the Chr's rewriting of these formulæ alters this four-part citation pattern. It will be shown below that the Chr's rewriting of these formulæ is related to certain pivotal pericopæ in his history. However, we will first examine the syntactic relation of the vast majority of these source formulæ together. The recurring pattern among these formulæ which is sustained for anywhere between 60-ca. 500 years and from distinguishable provenances consists of:

1. an extraposed nominal construction;
2. a particle with a resumptive pronoun;
3. כְּתוּבִים; and
4. a corpus of literature.

Our examination of the interrelation of these elements will demonstrate the marked degree of emphasis indicated by this formula and, based on Khan's analysis, a possible motivation for the selection of this construction.

First, Muraoka has analysed the different levels of emphasis among the various constructions that employ הִנֵּה. His procedure includes the examination of eleven different ways that a subject is expressed with הִנֵּה in verbal and nominal clauses. In order to assess the various degrees of emphasis among these structures he analyses all the possible combinations of pronouns (separable, inseparable, extraposed, resumptive) to express the subject of a clause with הִנֵּה. Among the five possible configurations of pronoun(s) with הִנֵּה in a verbless clause (e.g., הנני טוב, הנני אני טוב , הנה אני טוב , etc.), the type reflected in Gen 9:9 below, according to Muraoka, receives the greatest degree of emphasis (see also 6:17; Exod 14:17; Jer 40:10)[57]

And behold I myself will establish [וַאֲנִי הִנְנִי מֵקִים] my covenant with you and your seed after you (Gen 9:9).

---

57 Michael Rosenbaum (*Word-Order Variation in Isaiah 40-55: A Functional Perspective,* Studia Semitica Neerlandica 35 [The Netherlands: Van Gorcum Publ., 1997]) argues against the use of the word "emphasis" in verbal clauses due to word-order (216).

Muraoka intends his analysis of pronouns to be applicable to any noun or nominal phrase that assumes the place of the pronoun in his study[58]. Since the verbless clause in Gen 9:9 consists of the same sentence structure that we have analysed in the regnal source formulæ that use הִנֵּה, Muraoka's study demonstrates that these regnal formulæ give the highest degree of emphasis possible to a nominal phrase in a verbless clause with הִנֵּה.

The interchangeability of the particles הִנֵּה and הֲלֹא observed above in the section on the second element suggests that this insight applies to all of the source formulæ. Since the negative interrogative is not used in as many ways as הִנֵּה, Muraoka does not study the degrees of emphasis associated with the negative interrogative הֲלֹא. Dyk's analysis of the environment of the participle in the Old Testament enables us to relate the use of the negative interrogative הֲלֹא to Muraoka's analysis of הִנֵּה above. Although the occurrences of a participle with a preceding negative interrogative הֲלֹא are not exclusive to these regnal source formulæ, they are in fact extremely rare (0.03%)[59]. In light of the rare use of the negative interrogative הֲלֹא in this manner, it is best to understand its use in the regnal source formulæ in terms of the interchangeability of these two particles that we have already noted.

Hence, Muraoka's examination supports the view that the first three elements of the regnal formula constitute a complete emphatic structure which marks the greatest degree of stress possible for הִנֵּה in a verbless clause.

---

58   See Muraoka 139 n. 95, 140.

59   For Dyk's assessment of these constructions, see those passages that agree with the coding 1695--xx-- (J. W. Dyk, *Participles in Context: A Computer-Assisted Study of Old Testament Hebrew* [Amsterdam: VU University Press, 1994] 337). According to Dyk's analysis, there is only one occurrence of a negative interrogative הלוא before a pronominal subject preceding a participle in the 3,144 representative participles (0.03%) in her study. The texts that Dyk addresses as representative of the use of the participle in the Old Testament do not include the passages with regnal source formulæ.

The second issue in this section on the relation between the elements of the regnal formulæ concerns the meaning of the degree of emphasis reviewed above. Since the extraposed nominal phrase has a high degree of familiarity to the reader (see Khan above), the use of the emphatic structure does not appear to be best understood as drawing attention to a new concept as we might expect. Rather we suggest that the use of this emphatic structure is best accounted for in light of the usual placement of these regnal formulæ at the end of a monarch's history in Kings. In context, the distinctive structure and the nature of these formulæ suggest a function that is akin to the modern literary convention of a footnote. Such a role is best rendered in these cases, for example, as:

The rest of the deeds of David — they are written in the books of the kings of Judah.

While no scholar has addressed these formulæ in this manner heretofore, two linguists have identified such an off-line function for the syntactic construction used in the regnal source formulæ.

One of the novelties of Khan's study of Ex and PAR is to address their functions. In addition to the categorisation of syntactic structures, Khan also attempts to move into the "rich web of interpersonal and textual functions of syntax"[60]. According to Khan, the lack of interest that Semitic philologists have in this sort of enquiry "is a major deficiency in basic grammatical description since very often considerations of interpersonal or textual function are the primary criteria for the choice of one syntactic construction in contrast to another"[61]. Khan's analysis of the function of Ex/PAR can illuminate the author's motivations in the selection of the distinct syntactic construction that we have described above.

Khan has identified one function of Ex and PAR clauses that supports our translation of the regnal source formulæ above. He states,

An Ex/PAR clause may be used to signal a shift from foreground to background information. In other words the Ex/PAR clause together with clauses which are

---

60 Khan, xxv.
61 *Ibid.*

sequential to this clause (i.e. in the same "background" span) express an event or circumstance which is incidental to the main thrust of the discourse[62].

Hence, extraposition can be used for the marking of off-line information; this is the function that we have attributed to the regnal source formulæ above.

F. I. Andersen's study of adjunctive clauses has also analysed the sentence structure that we have encountered in the regnal source formulæ. Andersen's analysis grounds our conclusion from another vantage point since his examination of this function includes more features than extraposition. Andersen's class of adjunctive clause accounts for the extraposed nominal structure, the initial ו of these regnal source formulæ[63] and, more importantly, the resumptive pronoun. In fact, according to Andersen, these are the integral parts of an adjunctive clause. In his description of the structure of an adjunctive clause, Andersen states,

> There is always explicit coordination by means of we-, *and*, rarely gam or wegam. A marked break in the flow of discourse is achieved by fresh topicalization (*casus pendens*) whose opening sequence of we- +S[ubject] resembles a salient pattern in circumstantial clauses. ...but adjunctive clauses differ from circumstantial clauses [which are closest to them in form]...by the obligatory use of an explicit resumptive pronoun. ...the suspended topic is commonly resumed by the grammatic subject...[64].

According to Andersen, the sentence structure in the regnal source formulæ concerns a specific class of construction called an adjunctive clause.

It is not surprising that clauses that use the strongest emphatic structure (Ex - particle - resumptive pronoun in non-verbal clauses) would also have a discernible function. Andersen continues to describe the customary function of adjunctive clauses which further grounds the translation and function we assigned to these formulæ above. Explaining the contents of adjunctive clauses, Andersen states,

---

62 *Ibid.,* 83.
63 The scope of Andersen's enquiry concerns the twelve different types of coordination that are to be found in Hebrew clauses.
64 Andersen, 92.

> The information supplied in an adjunctive clause is generally less germane to the main discourse than the information typically supplied in a circumstantial clause. It resembles the kind of material which in English would be introduced by means of *By the way,....* It is tangential rather than marginal...[65].

Continuing the description of the function of such clauses, Andersen states, "an adjunctive clause deviates momentarily down a little side-track, to make a remark about somebody who does not figure anywhere else in the story, ...or to say something about a character that does not contribute to the plot..."[66]. Andersen emphasises that the conjunction ו, the extraposed nominal construction, and resumptive pronoun are necessary parts of these clauses.

The studies of Khan and Andersen corroborate the role and translation that we have ascribed to these regnal source formulæ. That is, the function of the highest degree of emphasis (Muraoka) of the subject in such cases serves to mark a break in the narrative and to provide background information to the on-going prosaic account. Viewing these regnal formulæ as a sort of ancient footnote appears to be well-grounded. Perhaps our rendering of this construction ("The rest of the deeds of David — they are written in the books of the kings of Judah") demonstrates how extraposition was used in these formulæ to mark a break in the narrative.

We conclude that the specific literary convention that we have seen so far in Kings, Chronicles, and Esther is best understood as an ancient footnote. Below we will see that this convention was used for other types of non-legal referents and in other books in the Old Testament. We will also address the way that the Chr rephrases a handful of these constructions.

Our translation above, then, ascribes no semantic value to the particle of the second element of these formulæ. Rather it appears to function as a "structural ballast", a term introduced by Khan, to place the topic of the footnote first[67]. By placing the nominal phrase first in

---

65 *Ibid.*
66 *Ibid.*, 93.
67 Another function that Khan attributes to this structure that appears to be relevant is that Ex makes the nominal construction "cognitively dominant" (230-31). Khan explains the cognitive psychology behind this construction in terms that its initial position facilitates the processing of information (by placing the Ex at the onset of a section) which also makes it more memorable (229-30).

this manner a break in the narrative is marked in order to provide background information. This treatment of the syntax of these passages appears to explain why the interchangeability between הִנֵּה and the negative interrogative הֲלֹא occurs between these formulæ without altering the function of the entire construction.

Hence, our analysis has shown that these regnal source formulæ are sophisticated constructions. As Khan has shown, certain syntactical structures were chosen by ancient writers for various textual functions. In the present case, the regnal source formulæ appear to have been deliberately constructed to function like a footnote. In the ancient world, such a role appears to have been signalled by a distinct syntactic construction "conjunction - extraposed nominal phrase - particle - resumptive pronoun" in a verbless clause. We conclude then that the four-part pattern of the regnal source formula, which includes this distinctive syntactic construction, is a sophisticated literary device. The structure employed marks a break with the foregoing narrative in order to introduce background information in the history of the monarchs. The evidence from the book of Esther might even suggest that this structure constituted an ancient literary convention for indicating background information in a narrative account.

4. The Chr's Alteration of Certain Regnal Source Formulæ

As we have seen, the Chr customarily follows the four-part formula pattern examined above. Sometimes, however, the Chr alters these formulæ so that they function in a way that includes something more than just supplying background information.

The Abijah narrative in the Chr's history includes a unique rephrasing of the four-part regnal source formula.

וְיֶתֶר דִּבְרֵי אֲבִיָם וְכָל־אֲשֶׁר עָשָׂה הֲלוֹא־הֵם כְּתוּבִים עַל־סֵפֶר
דִּבְרֵי הַיָּמִים לְמַלְכֵי יְהוּדָה (1 Kgs 15:7a)

וְיֶתֶר דִּבְרֵי אֲבִיָּה וּדְרָכָיו וּדְבָרָיו כְּתוּבִים בְּמִדְרַשׁ הַנָּבִיא
עִדּוֹ (2 Chr 13:22)

The regnal source formula in 2 Chr 13:22 is the only time he omits the second element (particle with a resumptive pronoun) of the four-part citation pattern[68]. The Chr's rewriting in 2 Chr 13:22 includes other rarities as well. First, this passage includes the unique expansion of the first element with the phrase וּדְרָכָיו וּדְבָרָיו ("and his ways and his words"). Secondly, the appellation given to the corpus contains two rare features. For instance, מִדְרָשׁ occurs elsewhere only in 2 Chr 24:27, and Iddo is mentioned in other regnal formulæ only in 2 Chr 9:29 and 12:15.

In fact, the Chr's unique alterations in the regnal source formula in v. 22 correspond with the nature of his representation of Abijah's reign which is vastly different from his *Vorlage*. Aside from being more than three times longer than the corresponding pericope in the DtrH[69], the Chr's account of Abijah has transformed the assessment of 1 Kgs 15:3 ("he committed all the sins that his father did before him; his heart was not true to the LORD his God, like the heart of his father David"). According to the Chr, Abijah was a champion of the Davidic dynasty whose valour, faithfulness, and exact obedience were exemplary. Abijah is not only a defender of Yahwism, but an exhorter as well.

Several scholars agree that the Chr's account of Abijah is central to his history. Commenting on the Chr's novel material, Japhet states,

> Even a superficial reading of vv. 3-21 reveals that they reflect not only the Chronicler's own language and style, but some of his most significant attitudes as well; about this there is practically no controversy.... The overall history of Abijah in Chronicles leaves us with the distinct impression that while the reign of Rehoboam was just an unsuccessful digression, it was Abijah who was the true successor of Solomon[70].

Commenting on the importance of chapter 13 in the Chr's history, Williamson has previously stated,

> it cannot be denied that for the development of the Chronicler's narrative this chapter is of crucial importance. The explanation it supplies of the situation

---

68 For a recent defense of the Chr's history not including Ezra-Neh, see Japhet, 23-28.
69 Japhet, 686.
70 *Ibid.*, 687.

within the divided monarchy prevails as far as ch. 28, and the principles on which that explanation is based were undoubtedly of abiding significance in the Chronicler's opinion[71].

The reason for the Chr's unique alteration of the four-part formula in 2 Chr 13:22 is related to his use of the unique phrase ודרכיו ודבריו. Commenting on this phrase, Japhet states, "here, sensitive to the context, the Chronicler uses the unique 'his ways and his sayings' (somewhat differently, II Chron. 28.26; but cf. JPS 'his conduct and his acts')"[72]. Hence, it appears that the Chr was intent on reemphasising the salient points of his new history of Abijah by using the phrase ודרכיו ודבריו at the end of this narrative in the regnal source formula. Rather than using the formula strictly to provide background information the Chr has deliberately rewritten the citation formula to bolster the message of this pivotal pericope. While the Chr does rephrase the formulæ to emphasise his point throughout his history, in the pivotal history of Abijah he has also alterred the basic four-pattern citation pattern by omitting הלוא־הם[73].

The Chr's account of Joash in 2 Chr 24 represents another considerable rewriting of his *Vorlage* that also affects the regnal source formula. As can be seen, the referent has been rephrased to stress his message in much greater detail than we have observed to be the Chr's customary practice (see 1b above).

וְיֶתֶר דִּבְרֵי יוֹאָשׁ וְכָל־אֲשֶׁר עָשָׂה הֲלוֹא־הֵם כְּתוּבִים
עַל־סֵפֶר דִּבְרֵי הַיָּמִים לְמַלְכֵי יְהוּדָה ([19]) (2 Kgs 12:20)

וּבָנָיו וְרֹב הַמַּשָּׂא עָלָיו וִיסוֹד בֵּית הָאֱלֹהִים הִנָּם כְּתוּבִים
עַל־מִדְרָשׁ סֵפֶר הַמְּלָכִים (2 Chr 24:27a)[74]

---

71 Williamson, 250.
72 Japhet, 699.
73 For scholars who view the Chr's account to be based on a reliable source, see Japhet, 688; Williamson, 250; R. B. Dillard, *2 Chronicles*, WBC (Waco, TX: Word Books, 1987) 105-6; D. G. Deboys, "The Chronicler's Portrait of Abijah", *Biblica* 71 (1990) 61-62.
74 Read with K.

The changes include a transformation of the standard referent of his *Vorlage* ("and the rest of the acts of Joash, and all that he did") to a much more specific referent ("as to his sons and the many oracles against him and the rebuilding of the house of God"). The Chr's rewriting reinforces both the faithfulness and apostasy of Joash. The Chr is in fact taking advantage of the formula, which is positioned at the end of the pericope, to summarise the purpose of his revised history of Joash. The Chr also has replaced the negative interrogative הלא of his *Vorlage* with the particle הנה. Furthermore, the only two occurrences of מדרש in the appellation occur in connection with the extensively reworked regnal source formulæ in the important narratives of Abijah and Joash.

As we observed in the Abijah narrative, the Chr alters a regnal formula to conclude an extensively rewritten narrative. The Chr offers another "radical" new history, but Joash's reign is depicted with greater nuance than that of Abijah's. The Chr presents both the positive and negative characteristics of Joash's reign and these have been summarised in the first element of the citation formula. The referent appears to reinforce the fact that the Chr's history departs substantially from his less nuanced *Vorlage*. Japhet has recently described the new history of Joash provided by the Chr. She states,

> The Chronicler...views the reign of Joash as composed of two completely distinct periods. In the first, Joash indeed does "what was right in the eyes of the Lord" and fares well (vv. 1-16); then comes a turning point, the death of Jehoiada. Joash now forsakes the way of the Lord, for which he is justly punished (vv. 17-27). The Chronicler's reworking bears fruit in a lucid, theologically coherent composition[75].

In this manner, the citation formula does not appear to function simply to provide background information.

The Chr has chosen to reflect the rewriting of his accounts of Abijah and Joash in the regnal formulæ that conclude each pericope. These marked changes include the use of more specific referents that summarise the Chr's message, the two uses of מדרש for the corpora cited, and the omission of the four-part pattern in 2 Chr 13:22. Insofar

---

75 Japhet, 840.

as scholars agree that these are important pericopæ in his history, it is
clear that the Chr took advantage of the final placement of these formulæ
at the end of each monarch's history as an opportune place to reinforce
his message.

No greater rewriting of the regnal source formulæ, however, is to
be found than in 2 Chr 33:18-19.

וְיֶתֶר דִּבְרֵי מְנַשֶּׁה וְכָל־אֲשֶׁר עָשָׂה וְחַטָּאתוֹ אֲשֶׁר חָטָא הֲלֹא־הֵם
כְּתוּבִים עַל־סֵפֶר דִּבְרֵי הַיָּמִים לְמַלְכֵי יְהוּדָה (2 Kgs 21:17)

וְיֶתֶר דִּבְרֵי מְנַשֶּׁה וּתְפִלָּתוֹ אֶל־אֱלֹהָיו וְדִבְרֵי הַחֹזִים
הַמְדַבְּרִים אֵלָיו בְּשֵׁם יְהוָה אֱלֹהֵי יִשְׂרָאֵל הִנָּם עַל־דִּבְרֵי
מַלְכֵי יִשְׂרָאֵל וּתְפִלָּתוֹ וְהֵעָתֶר־לוֹ וְכָל־חַטָּאתוֹ וּמַעְלוֹ
וְהַמְּקֹמוֹת אֲשֶׁר בָּנָה בָהֶם בָּמוֹת וְהֶעֱמִיד הָאֲשֵׁרִים וְהַפְּסִלִים
לִפְנֵי הִכָּנְעוֹ הִנָּם כְּתוּבִים עַל דִּבְרֵי חוֹזָי (2 Chr 33:18-19) [76]

The Chr's presentation of Manasseh is another thoroughly reworked
passage which is also reflected in the regnal source formula. The most
outstanding feature of the constructions in 2 Chr 33:18-19 is that the
Chr *repeats* some of the elements of the four-part pattern: two sets of
extraposed referents; two occurrences of הִנָּם; and two literary works
are cited. Note how the Chr's repetition of הִנָּם is based on the negative
interrogative הלא from his *Vorlage*[77]. In light of the repetition of these
elements of the four-part citation pattern it is surprising that the Chr
omits the citation base כתובים in v. 18. Further examination of 2 Chr
33, however, suggests a compelling reason for this lacuna in v. 18.

The uniqueness of these regnal source formulæ in 2 Chr 33:18-19
and the distinctiveness of the Manasseh narrative in Chronicles present a
key place to analyse the Chr's historiography. In his analysis of the
Chr's writing technique in 2 Chr 33:18-19, Schniedewind has focused
on these formulæ and gives special attention to the repetition of וּתְפִלָּתוֹ
in these verses. Schniedewind maintains,

---

76 Read with MT.

77 Note that the Chr always omits וכל אשר עשה from his *Vorlage* in these
    regnal source formulæ.

in Manasseh's source citation, the repetition of [וַתְפִלָּתוֹ] reflects the Chr's addition of an interpretation to an earlier source which is preserved in v. 18. In other words, in v. 18 the Chr is largely dependent on a source (not in Kings), while v. 19 is the Chr's free composition[78].

According to Schniedewind, v. 18b has no links with the Chr's account of Manasseh while v. 19 reflects the Chr's distinctive additions. Schniedewind basically thinks that there is a contrast between v. 18 and v. 19. The Chr's motivation for composing v. 19, according to Schniedewind, was that he "was not entirely comfortable [with v. 18b] and thus, by using a repetitive resumption of [וַתְפִלָּתוֹ], the Chr interpreted and 'clarified' the elements which troubled him"[79]. His argument, however, is not convincing.

First, Schniedewind argues "v. 18b...has no close compositional ties with the Manasseh narrative"[80]. But this conclusion is based on his idiosyncratic view that אֱלֹהָיו in v. 18 is ambiguous. He states, "it is unclear whether [אֱלֹהָיו] should be translated by 'his gods', 'his god' or 'his God' (namely Yahweh)"[81]. For good reason, there is no other scholar who has entertained such a reading[82]. Schniedewind's idiosyncratic reading of אֱלֹהָיו in v. 18 is unfounded for several reasons. Such a reading of אֱלֹהָיו does not agree with the use of this phrase elsewhere in the Chr's history which never concerns a god(s) other than Yahweh (2 Chr 20:30; 31:4; 32:21). Furthermore, the only traditions of prayers made by Manasseh are to Yahweh (see 2 Chr 33:12-13 and the apocryphal "Prayer of Manasseh"). The opening words of

---

78 William M. Schniedewind, "The Source Citations of Manasseh: King Manasseh in History and Homily", *VT* 41 (1991) 457.
79 *Ibid.,* 460.
80 *Ibid.,* 457.
81 *Ibid.*
82 For instance, Japhet understands Manasseh's prayer to אֱלֹהָיו to be part of what makes v. 18 a positive statement. She states, "v. 19 is basically a gloss to v. 18, intended to complement or even reverse *the 'positive only' statement of v. 18,* more in accord with the Deuteronomistic estimate of Manasseh" (1012, italics mine). For other scholars who do not see v. 18 as a reference to another god than Israel's, see Dillard, 269; and, Williamson, who considers the phrase "his prayer" part of the Chr's "favourite theological vocabulary" (395).

v. 18a (וְיֶתֶר דִּבְרֵי מְנַשֶּׁה) clearly complicate Schniedewind's view that the Chr is dependent on a source other than Kings in v. 18 even though he later carefully limits his view to the opinion that only v. 18b is from another source. Such a fragmentation of v. 18 is not compelling and appears to enter his argument simply because v. 18a clearly comes from 2 Kgs 21:17.

Schniedewind explains the use of וּתְפִלָּתוֹ in v. 19 as establishing a *Wiederaufnahme* which enables the Chr to interpret v. 18. However, appealing to this literary device to bracket the material between Manasseh's prayer to a putative pagan god, his view on v. 18, and the prayer to Yahweh in v. 19, is an uncustomary use of *Wiederaufnahme*. As Long states, *Wiederaufnahme* is generally concerned with "demark[ing] anachronies in the act of narrating, that is, points at which violations of story time (or primary sequentiality) were exploited to various effect"[83]. Schniedewind, however, does not suggest any such temporal function to this putative *Wiederaufnahme* in 2 Chr 33:18-19. וּתְפִלָּתוֹ in v. 18 has customarily been interpreted as a compositional link with Manasseh's prayer in v. 13. With remarkable inconsistency, Schniedewind permits וּתְפִלָּתוֹ in v. 19 to be one of the terms that shows this verse "is closely tied to the Chr's non-synoptic additions to 2 Kgs xxi" while such a link is disallowed for the identical form in v. 18.

Furthermore, the fact that Schniedewind analyses only one of the two doublets[84] in vv. 18-19 further complicates his thesis (see below for דברי חוזי/דברי החזים). His fragmentation of v. 18 appears to be a forced reading.

In conclusion, Schiedewind's view that v. 19 is a corrective of v. 18 is especially difficult because of his reading of אֱלֹהָיו, his treatment of וּתְפִלָּתוֹ as a *Wiederaufnahme*, his conjecture that Manasseh prayed to a pagan god(s), the fragmentation of v. 18, and because he addresses only one of the doublets in vv. 18-19.

Interestestingly, if Schniedewind's view were correct, then we would find further evidence to support our view that there was a literary

---

83   Burke O. Long, "Framing Repetitions in Biblical Historiography", *JBL* 106 (1987) 399.

84   We would not call either of the repetitions in 2 Chr 33:18-19 a *Wiederaufnahme*.

convention attached to the four-part citation pattern present in these regnal formulæ, i.e., Schniedewind attributes v. 18b to an unknown source which contains an extraposed nominal construction, הִנָּם, and an appellation. While this would be attractive to our treatment of the four-part citation pattern above, there are too many problems with his view to consider v. 18b as supporting such a literary convention.

It is more compelling to consider an interdependency between v. 18 and v. 19. Rather than Schniedewind's view that v. 19 corrects v. 18, these verses complement each other. In this manner these verses relate detailed information as well as summarising the Chr's novel history of Manasseh (see further below). This interrelation between v. 18 and v. 19 is marked by the two sets of doublets in vv. 18-19 (וּתְפִלָּתוֹ and דברי חוזי/דברי החזים) and the ellipted citation formula (without the citation base כְּתוּבִים) in v. 18 followed by the four-part regnal pattern in v. 19.

The Chr's standard composition technique among regnal source formulæ serves as the basis for identifying what are the unique characteristics of 2 Chr 33:18-19. In light of all of these formulæ, then, the aspects of 2 Chr 33:18-19 that need explaining are the Chr's use of two formulæ, the two sets of doublets, and the unique omission of כְּתוּבִים in what would otherwise be a regular regnal source formula in v. 18.

In light of our analysis, the exceptional nature of 2 Chr 33:18-19 is best accounted for by attributing it to the rephrasing of regnal source formulæ that the Chr undertakes in other pivotal pericopæ in his history (see Abijah and Joash above). The Chr begins his rewriting of the regnal source formula by repeating the opening words of his *Vorlage* וְיֶתֶר דִּבְרֵי מְנַשֶּׁה (cf. 2 Chr 33:18a and 2 Kgs 21:17a). But when he reaches the next clause וְכָל־אֲשֶׁר עָשָׂה, an expression that he always rephrases, he begins his own creative composition. Since Manasseh's prayer of repentance is the novel part of his history the Chr first emphasises this with וּתְפִלָּתוֹ which, contrary to Schniedewind, refers to v. 13 ("[Manasseh] prayed to him, and God received his entreaty, heard his plea, and restored him again to Jerusalem and to his kingdom. Then Manasseh knew that the LORD indeed was God"). In this way, v. 18 emphasises Manasseh's prayer of repentance, the distinctive aspect of the Chr's history in this chapter ("now the rest of the acts of Manasseh, his prayer to his God", v. 18a). V. 19, on the other hand, reconciles this novel feature of the Chr's account with his *Vorlage* ("all his sin and his faithlessness, the sites on which he built high places...before he humbled himself")[85].

The interdependency between vv. 18 and 19 appears to be marked in at least two ways. First, the ellipted formula in v. 18 is dependent on the plenary citation base in v. 19 which consists of all four elements. The second connection concerns the two sets of doublets (וּתְפִלָּתוֹ and דברי חוזי/דברי החזים).

There may be a third indication of dependency between vv. 18-19. Some scholars see an overlapping reference between the appellations used in these verses. Commenting on the repetition of "the words of seers", Williamson states, "comparison of these two verses suggests strongly that *the Chronicles of the Seers* are to be identified with *the Chronicles of the Kings,* since the latter are said to include *the words of the seers*"[86]. The inter-relatedness of v. 18 and v. 19 may suggest that "the chronicles of the seers" is providing a more detailed reference in the larger work "the chronicles of the Kings" where Manasseh's prayer of repentance, the Chr's novelty, can be located. Commenting on v. 19, Rudolph similarly concludes, "ergibt sich auch hier (vgl. 32 32), daß die ‚Worte seiner Seher' nur ein Sonderabschnitt der ‚Geschichte der Könige Israels'..., und nicht ein von ihr unabhängiges und neben ihr bestehendes Werk sind"[87].

Since 2 Chr 33:18-19 can be explained in terms of the Chr's rewriting of the source formulæ of other pivotal pericopæ this view is to be preferred over Schniedewind. The extent of the Chr's special rewriting of his *Vorlage* in 2 Chr 33:18-19 should be attributed to Manasseh's role as a type of post-exilic and restorationist Israel, and Manasseh's prayer is an integral part of this typology.

Concerning the three exceptional source regnal formulæ in Chronicles reviewed in this section we conclude that they agree with the Chr's observable compositional technique. Their exceptional nature is

---

85   Japhet, 1012.
86   Williamson, 395.
87   W. Rudolph, *Chronikbücher*, HAT (Tübingen: J.C.B.Mohr, 1955) 318.

first to be attributed to the pivotal role played by the narratives of Abijah, Joash, and Manasseh in his overall history. Secondly, the Chr rewrites the regnal source formula at the end of each of these pericopæ to stress his distinctive history. As a result, the typical background or off-line function of regnal source formulæ has been altered in these three cases.

B. Other Citation Bases with Non-Legal Referents

1. Introduction

The remainder of the occurrences of the passive participle of כתב√ which include non-legal referents encompass a diverse range of topics: laments, general histories, prophecies, genealogies, etc. These topics are also attributed to corpora with a diverse range of appellations. Notwithstanding these features, it will be seen that the majority of these constructions are related to the same distinctive four-part citation pattern of the regnal source formulæ above.

2. Laments

The citation base in 2 Chr 35:25 concerns the topic of laments.

ויקונן ירמיהו על־יאשיהו ויאמרו כל־השרים והשרות
בקינותיהם על־יאשיהו עד־היום ויתנום לחק על־ישראל
והנם כתובים על־הקינות (2 Chr 35:25)

Jeremiah also uttered a lament for Josiah, and *all the singing men and singing women* have spoken of Josiah in their laments [the meaningful referent] to this day; *they* made them [ir₂] a custom in Israel — they [ir₁] are written in the Laments (2 Chr 35:25).

2 Chr 35:25 is an example of how the four-part citation pattern observed in the regnal source formula could be adapted to include referents that did not include extraposed nominal phrases. In fact, 2 Chr 35:25 concerns a long anaphoric relation that is extended across three clauses.

Due to the distance between the citation base כְּתוּבִים (enlarged) and the referent ("laments"), two intermediate referents (ir₁ and ir₂) are used to signal the anaphoric relationship. It will be seen that this relationship could be confused without the use of these intermediate referents. Their use here, we maintain, reflects the desire to keep the relation between the citation base and the referent unmistakeable.

In our introductory example in Neh 10:35 (34), several scholars identified a referent that had nearly twice the amount of intervening material (seventeen forms instead of nine) as in 2 Chr 35:25 but without any sort of intermediate referents. This clearly does not discount the identification of such a referent in Neh 10:35 (34), but, at this point in our analysis, simply serves as a point of contrast. If the referent identified by these scholars in Neh 10:35 (34) is correct, then this would seem to suggest that the post-exilic community was not as concerned to cite the legal basis for their pledge in Neh 10 as the Chr was intent on referring to the lament in 2 Chr 35:25.

The relation between the citation base כְּתוּבִים in 2 Chr 35:25 and the referent differs slightly from the source formulæ. The referent קִינוֹת is a feminine plural noun while the participle and intermediate referents are inflected with masculine gender. While noteworthy, this observation is not problematic since, *"masculine suffixes (especially in the plural) are not infrequently used to refer to feminine substantives"*[88]. Furthermore, "this replacement of the feminine by the masculine (*genus potior*) is especially frequent in the later books, notably in the book of Chronicles"[89].

In 2 Chr 35:25, the Chr has identified the referent of the citation base with care. וַיִּתְּנוּם is a crucial form in making the anaphoric relation clear. Since the subject of this verb has to be כָּל־הַשָּׁרִים וְהַשָּׁרוֹת, the antecedent of the inseparable suffix must be קִינוֹת. In the next participial clause, in which the citation base occurs, the subject is no longer the singers. This change of subject is marked by ir₁. Without this suffix the singers would become a rival referent (e.g., "they [the singers] are written in the..."). Furthermore, ir₂ is essential for the

---

88   GK § 135 o (their emphasis).
89   JM, § 149b; see also DG § 1, *Rem.* 4.

identification of קִינוֹת as referent of this citation base as well. Without ir₂, the antecedent of ir₁ would be understood as the singers.

Consequently, the resumptive pronoun in הֵנָּם, its contiguous relation to the citation base כְּתוּבִים, and ir₂ are essential elements for the clear identification of the referent קִינוֹת. It may be suggested that these features reflect the intention to make the relation between the referent and the participle unmistakeable. Even if this is true, however, the type of development that will be observed among citation formulæ with legal referents in the non-synoptic post-exilic historiography is distinguishable from the quotation of laments in 2 Chr 35:25. Such a long anaphoric relation across three clauses will not be seen among the developed exegetical devices of the restoration era.

Despite the multitude of functions that have been attributed to והנה it is best to view the use of this form in 2 Chr 35:25 as being related to the form analysed in the regnal source formulæ[90]. As McCarthy has warned, והנה has a variety of functions "which parallel just about all the various kinds of 'clauses' listed in the syntax sections of our Hebrew grammars so one must always have an eye to the variety of meaning which [והנה] with various complementary forms may imply"[91]. According to McCarthy, והנה always maintains its own dramatic or emotional quality.

---

90 The categorisation of the uses of והנה has received a surprising amount of attention. For the uses of והנה categorised by D. J. McCarthy (excited perception, cause, occasion, conditional, concession, time, purpose, result, adversatives), see "The Uses of Wᵉhinneh in Biblical Hebrew", *Biblica* 61 (1980) 330-42. However, none of these uses detected by McCarthy corresponds to 2 Chr 35:25. Blau's view of והנה "als Verbindungsglied zwischen dem Adverb-Subjekt und dem Rest des Satzes", or copula, does not apply to 2 Chr 35:25 ("Adverbia als Psychologische und Grammatische Subjekte/Praedikate im Bibel Hebraeisch", *VT* 9 [1959] 133). For his conception of "surprise clauses" with והנה, see Andersen, 94-96. One should also note C. J. Labuschagne, "The Particle הֵן and הִנֵּה", *OTS* 18 (1973) 1-14, who does not note any distinctive use between הֵן and הִנֵּה except with verbs of observing and enquiring.

91 McCarthy, 341-42.

3. *"The Book of the Just"*

The next three citation bases ascribe material to "the Book of the Just". Two of these passages recount an episode associated with battle and all cite a referent in a similar way as the four-part citation pattern observed in the regnal source formulæ above. All three passages occur in the DtrH.

92 (Josh 10:13) ... הֲלֹא־הִיא כְתוּבָה עַל־סֵפֶר הַיָּשָׁר ...

This citation base differs from what we have already seen in that the pronoun is a third person feminine singular. However, unlike the intermediate referents that we have seen above, הִיא does not signal here an adnominal relation to the referent since there is not a satisfactory feminine nominal structure in the context. Rather, the pronoun הִיא in Josh 10:13 "refers in a general sense to the verbal idea contained in a preceding sentence (corresponding to our *it*)"[93]. *IBHS* refers to this use of the third feminine singular pronoun as a *neutrum,* i.e., "a grammatical element of vague or broad reference, often in Hebrew a feminine pronoun"[94]. Since Classical Hebrew is a masculine prior language, the use of a *neutrum* here is best understood as a deliberate marker to clarify what is being attributed to "the Book of the Just".

---

92   Read with MT. 𝕲 omits this citation base. A. G. Auld ("Joshua: the Hebrew and Greek Texts", *VTS* 30 [1979] 1-13) omits this construction on the speculation that an editor observed that "David's elegy over Saul and Jonathan is similarly introduced in 2 Sam. i 18" (13). However, most scholars accept the originality of the citation base (R. G. Boling and G. E. Wright, *Joshua,* AB [Garden City, NY: Doubleday, 1982] 285; T. C. Butler, *Joshua,* WBC [Waco, TX: Word Books, 1983] 107, 110; M. Woudstra, *Joshua,* NICOT [Grand Rapids, MI: Eerdmans, 1984] 174; V. Fritz, *Das Buch Josua,* HAT [Tübingen: J.C.B. Mohr, 1994] 111). Soggin also accepts the formula, but emends the negative interrogative inexplicably to לְ affirmative "surely", omitting the ה without a reason (*Le livre de Josué,* CAT [Paris: Delachaux & Niestlé Neuchatel, 1970] 285). Nevertheless, Soggin does indicate that there are several other omissions in vv. 16-27 by the LXX which further suggests that this formulation should be retained here.

93   GK § 135 p.

94   *IBHS,* 692, cf. 301. For the feminine pronoun used for unspecific reference, see DG § 1 *Rem. 3.*

Again we see that the use of a pronoun contiguous to the citation base is crucial to the identification of the referent. Apart from this contiguously placed *neutrum,* an extra-sentential relation between the participle כְּתוּבָה and the referent would not be established.

The use of a *neutrum* in Josh 10:13, however, has resulted in a lack of consensus concerning the identification of the extra-sentential referent. We will see, however, that this debate can be clearly resolved.

Keil, for instance, has identified the referent of the citation base in v. 13 as vv. 12-15, minus the exegetical device itself. In order to assess Keil's treatment, we list his identification of the referent below together with the citation base, which he excludes from the referent, in italics.

> On the day when the LORD gave the Amorites over to the Israelites, Joshua spoke to the LORD; and he said in the sight of Israel,
>   "Sun, stand still at Gibeon,
>   and Moon, in the valley of Aijalon."
>   And the sun stood still, and the moon stopped,
>   until the nation took vengeance on their enemies.
> *Is this not written in the Book of Jashar?*
> The sun stopped in midheaven, and did not hurry to set for about a whole day. There has been no day like it before or since, when the LORD heeded a human voice; for the LORD fought for Israel.
> Then Joshua returned, and all Israel with him, to the camp at Gilgal (Josh 10:12-15 [NRSV]).

Keil also contends that this referent is a literal quotation from "the Book of the Just"[95]. Keil's argument cannot be ignored since he has been followed recently by other scholars.

According to Keil, vv. 11 and 16 are closely associated (cf. נוס√) and have been composed by the author of Joshua. Vv. 12-15, he continues, form a parenthesis in Josh 10 and have been introduced, but not composed, by this same author. In addition to the repetition of נוס√, Keil gives two reasons for understanding Josh 10 in this manner. First, the opening words of v. 12 ("On the day when the LORD gave the

---

95 Carl F. Keil, *Commentary on the Book of Joshua,* trans. by J. Martin (Edinburgh: T. & T. Clark, 1857) 251-69; in German, *Josua, Richter und Ruth,* Biblische Commentar über die Prophetischen Geschictsbücher des Alten Testaments, zweite, verbesserte Auflage (Leipzig: Dörffling und Franke, 1874) 80-84.

Amorites over to the Israelites, Joshua spoke to the LORD; and he said in the sight of Israel, ...") "show that a different writer is speaking"[96]. Keil's main argument, however, concerns the events recounted in v. 15. Attributing v. 15 to the author of the material of chapter 10 is problematic for Keil and several other scholars[97]. Keil urges,

> the fifteenth verse...is unintelligible, unless we suppose it to form part of the quotation from the *Sepher Hayyashar*. And therefore in this verse we find the strongest proof that the quotation extends to v. 15 inclusive[98].

Since the south was not completely conquered until after v. 42, v. 15 cannot come from the hand of the single author of Josh 10. Therefore, v. 15 must be part of the material cited from "the Book of the Just". These arguments, according to Keil, prove that vv. 12-15 "is not the production of the author of the Book of Joshua, either wholly or in part, but is *word for word* an extract without alteration from the *Sepher Hayyashar*"[99].

Woudstra has recently addressed the problem that v. 15 has presented interpreters. He states,

> there is no unanimity among interpreters as to the precise point where the quotation from the book of Jashar (v 13b) begins and ends. Some believe that the reference to the source concludes the quote. Others believe that all of vv 12-15 is in effect a quotation from said book, with the exception, of course, of the reference to the book itself, which would be by the writer of Joshua. The second position appears most tenable and explains the sudden intrusion of v. 15[100].

While he entertains more than one option, in the end, Woudstra simply follows Keil.

In light of the exceptional nature of the view advocated by Keil and Woudstra, it is not difficult to see why other scholars have sought another route to explain the identification of the referent. Another referent is proposed by Alfrink who maintains that the referent is only

---

96 *Ibid.*, 252.
97 Keil cites various expositions including Calvin who have not been able to explain v. 15.
98 *Ibid.*, 253.
99 *Ibid.*, 252.
100 Woudstra, 174.

the poetic fragment in vv. 12b-13a[101]. Alfrink resolves the problem noted by Keil by placing v. 15 between vv. 42 and 43. Fritz, most recently, appears to be in agreement with Alfrink[102]. According to Fritz, v. 15 is probably taken over from v. 43 where it was originally positioned ("der Satz ist wahrscheinlich aus 43 übernommen"[103]).

While the use of a *neutrum* undoubtedly entails some sort of extra-sentential relationship, the present state of scholarship disagrees as to the identification of the referent of the citation base in Josh 10:13. Despite this lack of consensus, we maintain that the above debate can be resolved, although in an entirely different manner. First, the putative intrusion of v. 15 in chapter 10 can be otherwise explained. This involves the proper reading of Josh 10 which should be understood as constructed on a single topic: the defeat of the five king coalition in the south. Hence, Josh 10 consists of one literary scene or panel which is to be distinguished from a linear chronology. Accordingly, this reading is signalled by a striking example of *Wiederaufnahme* in v. 43 which precisely repeats v. 15:

וַיָּשָׁב יְהוֹשֻׁעַ וְכָל־יִשְׂרָאֵל עִמּוֹ אֶל־הַמַּחֲנֶה הַגִּלְגָּלָה (Josh 10:15)

וַיָּשָׁב יְהוֹשֻׁעַ וְכָל־יִשְׂרָאֵל עִמּוֹ אֶל־הַמַּחֲנֶה הַגִּלְגָּלָה (Josh 10:43)

The exact repetition of this sentence in v. 43 signals the resumption of the historical setting that was previously noted in v. 15. Hence, Josh 10 is correctly read as a single panel around the theme of the defeat of the south and not chronologically. V. 43 resumes the historical narrative at the last verse of chapter 10, thus concluding the section composed around the theme of the defeat of the southern kings. In keeping with the function of *Wiederaufnahme*, Josh 11 then continues from this perspective.

In light of the reading of Josh 10 as one literary scene, the identification of the referent becomes clearer. Once the seeming intrusiveness of v. 15 is explained by the use of *Wiederaufnahme*, there

---

101 B. J. Alfrink, *Josue* (Roermond en Maaseik: J. J. Romen & Zonen, 1952) 66.
102 Fritz, 111. In vv. 12-14, Fritz distinguishes between introductory material for the poetic fragment, a citation, a source, and a type of commentary (111).
103 *Ibid.*, 112.

then remains no reason for maintaining that vv. 12-15 is the referent. This observation removes the reason for considering the relation between the citation base and referent to be exceptional. Keil's view of v. 12a as part of the referent can also be dismissed since this is merely a short narrative introduction to the fragment (see e.g., Fritz). The final advantage of reading Josh 10 in this manner is that there is no need to reorder the text.

Hence, it appears clear that the poetic fragment (vv. 12b-13a) should be identified as the referent. Keil is probably correct to consider this a literal quotation since its good metre suggests that it has not undergone any alteration. The identification of the poetic fragment as the referent is further supported by the fact that every referent that is ascribed to "the Book of the Just" consists of poetry (see further below). The evidence suggests that this is a corpus of poetry about the heroic deeds of some of Israel's leaders.

Having resolved the identification of the referent, there are three features presented by the citation base in Josh 10:13 that should be highlighted. This is our first example of an extra-sentential relation between the citation base and the referent.

Secondly, this relation is signalled by the use of a *neutrum*. The feminine inflection of this literary convention of a *neutrum* stands out in the masculine prior language of Hebrew[104]. As we have seen before, this reflects an intention to make the relation between the referent and the citation base as clear as possible. If the citation formula occurred without a *neutrum* then the relation between the citation base and referent would be less clear. This extra-sentential relation between the citation base and the referent highlights the clarifying role of the resumptive pronoun in these formulæ. Furthermore, the contiguous relation between the citation base and *neutrum* is crucial for signalling this type of relation. Hence, our analysis shows that the four-part structure observed in the regnal source formulæ is a highly sophisticated citation device which is capable of adjusting to various types of referents and thus signalling different kinds of relations. Here the entire poetic

---

104 In general, Hebrew uses the masculine as "the prior gender". More specifically, the use of grammatical agreement of personal pronouns and their antecedents also follows this principle (GK §§ 144a, 122g, 135o, 132d, 145p, t, u; cf. *IBHS* § 6.5.3).

fragment in vv. 12b-13a is identified as the referent and so the nature of the relation that we have seen signalled by this citation base includes not only adnominal but also extra-sentential relations. As we saw in our analysis of regnal formulæ, the four-part citation pattern in Josh 10:13 functions as a sort of footnote.

Thirdly, as can be observed in 2 Chr 35:25 and Josh 10:13, the interchanging of הנה and the negative interrogative הלא in the second element of the citation pattern occurs *outside* of the regnal source formulæ. This clearly suggests that these other non-legal citation formulæ (2 Chr 35:25; Josh 10:13; further below) are related to the same literary convention observed above in the regnal source formulæ and that the differences between these formulæ are to be attributed to the types of relations that are required by the nature of the referent that is being cited. It is becoming increasingly difficult to maintain the view that these citation bases are not related or sophisticated literary devices.

The second citation of material from "the Book of the Just" occurs in 2 Sam 1:18.

$$\text{ויאמר ללמד בני־יהודה קֶשֶׁת הִנֵּה כְתוּבָה עַל־סֵפֶר}$$
$$\text{הַיָּשָׁר (2 Sam 1:18, MT) }^{105}$$

The constructions used in Josh 10:13 and 2 Sam 1:18 demonstrate that, like the references to "the Annals of the Kings", citations of "the Book of the Just" interchange the second element of the four-part citation pattern (i.e., הנה or the negative interrogative הלא). However, the lack of the resumptive pronoun with the emphatic particle הנה in MT is a departure from the manner in which we have observed these citation

---

105 𝔊ᴸ has Ισραηλ καὶ Ιουδα. 𝔊-ᴬᴹˢ omit קֶשֶׁת. For the most recent discussion of the textual problems and the argument that קֶשֶׁת was omitted by the LXX translators because it was unintelligible, see Hans Joachim Stoebe, *Das zweite Buch Samuelis,* KAT (Gütersloh: Gütersloher Verlagshaus, 1994) 90. A. A. Anderson similarly states, "'Bow' (קֶשֶׁת) is lacking in 𝔊ᴬ but is attested in other major versions. The omission may be due to the failure to understand the significance of קֶשֶׁת in this context" (*2 Samuel,* WBC [Dallas: Word Books, 1989] 12). For the manner in which the analysis of citation formulæ in the OT illuminates the text critical debate surrounding קֶשֶׁת, see below.

bases to operate. Perhaps, the distinctiveness of the singular feminine
antecedent of the participle in a language with the prior gender of the
masculine made this relation sufficiently clear. If this is so, it must be
stressed that this would then be the first occurrence of a citation base
with the four-part citation pattern in our examination that omits the
resumptive pronoun in this manner (cf. 2 Chr 13:22 and the Chr's
observable literary technique above).

On the other hand, there is another possibility that includes a
reconsideration of the pointing of the MT. The feminine singular
referent קֶשֶׁת and the consonantal text הנה of the MT present a unique
situation among all citation bases where the resumptive pronoun element
of the four-part citation pattern could easily be lost. Furthermore, the
standard citation pattern can be restored with the slight repointing of the
MT to הִנָּה which, we maintain, escapes the need to account for 2 Sam
1:18 as exceptional. The following points support such a repointing.

First, it must be recognized that only in the case of a referent that is
both a feminine singular as well as used in a citation base with הנה
(*contra* the negative interrogative ה in Josh 10:13) do the three letters of
this particle become ambiguous in meaning. In every regnal source
formulæ above where הנה is used as the second element in the four-part
citation pattern, the referent of the citation base requires a plural
resumptive pronoun. As a result, the four-part citation pattern normally
has הנם whose meaning could not be mistaken for the particle הִנָּה with
an inseparable suffix. Only with a feminine singular noun, such as we
have with קֶשֶׁת in 2 Sam 1:18, could the difference between using or
ignoring the four-part citation pattern not be reflected in the consonantal
text.

Secondly, the only way to come to an appreciation of the pattern of
these citation bases is by conducting the sort of study we are
undertaking. Insofar as this has never been done, there was no basis
for the Massoretes or anyone else to point the letters הנה in the manner
that we have seen is associated with these citation formulæ.

In light of the feminine singular referent קֶשֶׁת, the ambiguous letters
הנה in the citation base in 2 Sam 1:18, and the consistent use of a

resumptive pronoun in the four-part citation pattern studied above, we suggest that the citation in 2 Sam 1:18 should be repointed.

ויאמר ללמד בני־יהודה קֶשֶׁת הִנָּהּ כְּתוּבָה עַל־סֵפֶר הַיָּשָׁר

(2 Sam 1:18 [repointed])

We maintain that the evidence above now places the burden of proof on those who would advocate that הִנֵּה is to be retained in 2 Sam 1:18 as the only occurrence of the passive participle כתוב with הנה in a citation base without a resumptive pronoun[106].

Our study of citation bases in general and the repointing of 2 Sam 1:18 have a direct impact on the long and tortuous history of the text criticism of 2 Sam 1:18. Various scholars have reconstructed the text of 2 Sam 1:18, attempting to explain קֶשֶׁת, which is deemed difficult. Wellhausen supposed that בעלי קשת ("owners of bow") to be originally a marginal gloss in v. 6 to explain הפרשים ("the horsemen"). This gloss was later divided between v. 6 and v. 18 which, according to Wellhausen, were juxtaposed in opposite columns. By this one proposal, Wellhausen explained both problems that he saw in these

---

106 Our repointing of הִנֵּה to הִנָּהּ in 2 Sam 1:18 entails the occurrence of a third person feminine singular inseparable pronoun on a word which occurs 1,057 times (*THAT*, 506). As we have stated above, this is the only inseparable suffix which can become ambiguous in the four-part citation pattern with הנה. The masculine equivalent of our proposal is attested in the Old Testament only seven times (0.66%, הִנּוֹ thrice, הִנֶּנּוּ thrice, and הִנֵּהוּ once). In light of the predominance of the masculine gender in the Old Testament in general, one occurrence of the feminine הִנָּהּ to seven masculine appears to be proportionate to other feminine:masculine ratios.

In light of this repointing of 2 Sam 1:18, Williamson has suggested that a similar repointing could be proposed in Gen 18:9 which has been used as an example of the exceptional occurrence of a lacking pronoun. For instance, GK states, "sometimes...the pronoun referring to the subject is wanting, and the simple הִנֵּה takes the place of the subject and copula" (GK § 147b). Such a proposed repointing in Gen 18:9 would align this passage with normal usage and the masculine:feminine ratio is still in balance.

verses[107]. Even though it is ingenious, Wellhausen's proposal has not been followed because v. 6 has not been seen as difficult.

S. R. Driver considers the text of v. 18 to be suspicious and the occurrence of קֶשֶׁת as intrusive. Commenting on the use of קֶשֶׁת as a title for the Song, Driver states, "there is no analogy or parallel for such a usage in Hebrew; and קֶשֶׁת standing nakedly—not שִׁירַת הַקֶּשֶׁת, or even אֶת־הַקֶּשֶׁת—is not a probable designation of a song"[108]. Therefore, Driver makes "the assumption that 18ᵇ [הִנֵּה כְתוּבָה עַל־סֵפֶר הַיָּשָׁר] is misplaced, and was intended originally to follow 17"[109]. Driver's reordering of the text results in the identification of another referent, i.e., הַקִּינָה הַזֹּאת in v. 17. While Driver's view remains possible, we would resist a reconstruction that alters the referent of the citation base in this manner. We would first want to address the text of the MT in light of our examination of citation bases.

There is still no unanimity among contemporary scholars how to deal with קֶשֶׁת in 2 Sam 1:18. Recently, McCarter has challenged the view that קֶשֶׁת is the title of the song by arguing that the textual and translation "problem vanishes when it is recognized that [קֶשֶׁת], 'a bow,' is intrusive and can be struck from the text, a solution supported by the major witnesses to the Greek tradition"[110]. The problem with McCarter's argument is that he only considers the ramifications of his proposal for v. 18a and not the entire sentence. He has not addressed how his view results in a feminine singular participle כְּתוּבָה in v. 18b without an antecedent. When the entire sentence is in view, the feminine participle requires some feminine antecedent. Such a feminine

107 J. Wellhausen, *Der Text der Bücher Samuelis* (Göttingen: Vandenhoeck und Ruprecht's Verlag, 1871) 151.
108 S. R. Driver, *Notes on the Hebrew Text and the Topography of the Books of Samuel,* 2nd edn (Oxford: Clarendon Press, 1913) 233-34.
109 *Ibid.,* 234. The other necessary features of Driver's view include: וַיֹּאמֶר of v. 18 should introduce v. 19; and, בְנֵי יְהוּדָה קֶשֶׁת introduces v. 19. According to Driver, the remaining form לְלַמֵּד of v. 18a is "an awkward and inexplicable residuum" (234).
110 P. Kyle McCarter, *II Samuel,* AB (Garden City, New York: Doubleday & Co., 1984) 67.

singular noun is only found in קְשָׁת. As we saw above, Driver had to rearrange the text to establish הַקִּינָה הַזֹּאת in v. 17 as the referent of the citation base כְּתוּבָה in v. 18b. Hence, in contrast to McCarter, קְשָׁת is not intrusive but it or another feminine singular antecedent is in fact required by the feminine participle in v. 18b. Hence, we maintain that McCarter is mistaken when he states, "its retention spoils a shorter and problem-free text"[111].

In light of the problems with McCarter's view, it is not surprising that the discussion of קְשָׁת in 2 Sam 1:18 continues. Most recently, Stoebe has advocated the retention of קְשָׁת[112]. Commenting on the omission of קְשָׁת in the LXX, Stoebe states that it was deleted as unintelligible[113]. Our examination of the four-part citation pattern with non-legal referents appears to provide added weight to the view most recently stated by Stoebe. That is, קְשָׁת satisfies the first of the four-part structure of the citation formulæ we have been analysing.

Recently, Gordon has somewhat reluctantly advocated the omission of קְשָׁת "pending a better explanation of the MT"[114]. In light of the proposals that have been offered and the insight available from a study of citation bases, we submit that an explanation has been found which supports the retention of קְשָׁת in 2 Sam 1:18. Furthermore, the title קְשָׁת for this song (vv. 19-27) corresponds with "the fact that the word occurs in it somewhat prominently in v. 22"[115] as Driver states. Perhaps, it is best to understand קְשָׁת here as an appellative that has assumed the character of a proper name and thus is indefinite[116].

If our proposal is correct, 2 Samuel 1:18 perfectly agrees with the four-part citation pattern we have noted among forms with non-legal referents. Our analysis also supports the view that the LXX translators

---

111 *Ibid.,* 68.
112 H. J. Stoebe, *Das zweite Buch Samuelis,* KAT (Gütersloh: Gütersloher Verlagshaus, 1994) 90.
113 *Ibid.,* 90.
114 R. P. Gordon, *1 & 2 Samuel: A Commentary* (Exeter: Paternoster, 1986) 211.
115 Driver, 233.
116 GK § 125f, g.

did not render קְשֶׁת in their work because it was unintelligible. An appreciation for the originality of קְשֶׁת, however, can be supported by the examination of the four-part citation pattern.

A possible third reference to "the Book of the Just" in the Hebrew Scriptures leads us to another passage in the LXX. 3 Reigns 8:53a contains a citation formula (italics) that is not attested in the corresponding passage in the MT at 1 Kgs 8:12-13.

> Τότε ἐλάλησεν Σαλωμων ὑπὲρ τοῦ οἴκου, ὡς συνετέλεσεν τοῦ οἰκοδομῆσαι αὐτόν
> Ἥλιον ἐγνώρισεν [𝔊ᴸ ἔστησεν] ἐν οὐρανῷ κύριος,
> εἶπεν τοῦ κατοικεῖν ἐν γνόφῳ [𝔊ᴸ ἐκ γνόφου]
> Οἰκοδόμησον οἶκόν μου, οἶκόν ἐκπρεπῆ [𝔊ᴸ εὐπρεπῆ] σαυτῷ, τοῦ κατοικεῖν ἐπὶ καινότητος.
> *οὐκ ἰδοὺ αὕτη γέγραπται ἐν βιβλίῳ τῆς ᾠδῆς;* (3 Reigns 8:53a, LXX)

אָז אָמַר שְׁלֹמֹה
יְהוָה אָמַר לִשְׁכֹּן בָּעֲרָפֶל
בָּנֹה בָנִיתִי בֵּית זְבֻל לָךְ
מָכוֹן לְשִׁבְתְּךָ עוֹלָמִים (1 Kgs 8:12-13, MT)

The differences between these passages have proven to be a fruitful ground for research among scholars since Wellhausen. We agree with those scholars who consider the LXX to preserve a more original text than the MT and that the latter reflects the proper placement of this poetic fragment[117]. A more satisfactory metre is clearly preserved in the

---

117 The literature on the relation between 3 Reigns 8:53a and 1 Kgs 8:12-13 is immense.

For the view that 3 Reigns 8:53a contains midrashic exegesis, see Vladimir Peterca, "Ein midraschartige Auslegungsbeispiel zugunsten Salomos 1 Kön 8,12-13 - 3 Reg 8, 53a", *BZ* 31 (1987) 270-75. D. W. Gooding, "Problems of Text and Midrash in the Third Book of Reigns", *Textus* 7 (1969) 1-29; and *Relics of Ancient Exegesis: A Study of the Miscellanies in 3 Reigns 2* (Cambridge: Cambridge University Press, 1976).

For the preference of the LXX's sequence of the text, see Emmanuel Tov, "Some Sequence Differences Between the MT and LXX and Their Ramifications for the Literary Criticism of the Bible", *JNSL* 13 (1987) 151-60.

For the preference of the sequence of the MT, see most recently S. J. DeVries, *1 Kings*, WBC (Waco, Texas: Word Books, 1985) 117.

LXX. The citation base attested in 3 Reigns 8:53a must be original, it has recently been urged, because the translators "would never introduce this ancient rubric except from a Heb. *Vorlage*"[118]. Most scholars agree that the source mentioned in the citation base of the LXX (τῆς ᾠδῆς which attests to הַשִּׁיר) should be emended to הַיָּשָׁר (cf. Josh 10:13; 2 Sam 1:18). Only Noth suggests the opposite relation[119].

Even though this formula is a minus in the MT, the citation base in 3 Reigns 8:53a nevertheless bears witness to all of the same distinctive characteristics of the four-part citation pattern with the passive participle כָּתוּב and non-legal referents that we have previously analysed. Like

---

For the view that the original placement of the text is uncertain, see Stephen L. McKenzie, "1 Kings 8: A Sample Study into the Texts of Kings Used by the Chronicler and Translated by the Old Greek", *BIOSCS* 19 (1986) 28. McKenzie has recently produced a monograph on the composition of Kings (*The Problem With Kings: The Composition of the Books of Kings in the Deuteronomistic History*, *VTS* 42 [Leiden: E. J. Brill, 1991]; see R. P. Gordon's book review, *VT* 44 [1994] 135-36). As it pertains to our study, we must note that McKenzie's previous analysis of the relation between 1 Kings 8:12-13 and 3 Reigns 8:53a in *BIOSCS* has surprisingly not been incorporated into this later work despite the fact that it is listed in the bibliography and that a section is dedicated to 1 Kgs 8 (138-40). For a recent assessment of the debate of the textual traditions and families in Kings which are central to McKenzie's argument, see S. W. Holloway, "Kings, Book of 1-2", *ABD*, Vol. IV, 73-74.

For the view that the MT preserves a more original text than the LXX, see B. Stade, *The Books of Kings. Critical Edition of the Hebrew Text* (Leipzig: Leipzig & Co., 1904) 101-3; O. Loretz, "Der Torso eines kanaanäisch-israelitischen Tempelweihspruches in 1 Kg 8, 12-13", *UF* 6 (1974) 478-80.

In his recent study, Taylor attempts a new reading of the poetic fragment in 3 Reigns 8:53a (*Yahweh and the Sun: Biblical and Archaeological Evidence for Sun Worship in Ancient Israel*, JSOTS 111 [Sheffield: JSOT Press, 1993]). After a brisk treatment of the differences between the MT and LXX, Taylor considers the main problem of this fragment to be "the challenge of relating the fragment to its context" (138). He argues that the poetic fragment alludes to a "religio-historical relationship between Yahweh and the sun" which entails a sun cult at Gibeon. For the subsequent debate that has ensued from Taylor's study, see Steve A. Wiggins, "Yahweh: The God of Sun?", *JSOT* 71 (1996) 89-106; J. Glen Taylor, "A Response to Steve A. Wiggins, 'Yahweh: The God of Sun?'", *JSOT* 71 (1996) 107-19; Steve A. Wiggins, "A Rejoinder to J. Glen Taylor", *JSOT* 73 (1997) 109-12.

118 S. J. DeVries, 117.

119 M. Noth, *Könige*, BKAT (Neukirchen-Vluyn: Neukirchener Verlag des Erziehungsvereins, 1964-, issued in parts) 181-82.

Josh 10:13 and 2 Sam 1:18, 3 Reigns 8:53a appears to ascribe a referent to "the Book of the Just".

The Hebrew of 1 Kgs 8:12-13 has been reconstructed by scholars based on the LXX as follows[120]:

אז אמר שלמה

שמש הכין בשמים

יהוה אמר לשכן בערפל

בנה בניתי בית זבל לך

מכון לשבתך עולמים

הלא־היא כתובה על־ספר הישר

We have placed יהוה in the second stich so that it is in parallel with שמש[121].

The translation of 1 Kgs 8:12-13 when it is reconstructed on the basis of 3 Reigns 8:53a is as follows:

> Then Solomon said,
>> "The sun, He placed in the heavens,
>> The LORD said he would dwell in darkness;
>> I have in fact built for you an exalted house,
>> A place for you to dwell forever."
>> *Is it not written in the Book of the Just?*

---

120 For the poetic fragment listed here, see the reconstruction by Cheyne (*Origin of the Psalter* [London: Kegan Paul, Trench, Trübner & Co. Ltd., 1891] 212) in S. R. Driver, *An Introduction to the Literature of the Old Testament,* 9th edn (Edinburgh: T. & T. Clark, 1913) 192.

121 For the view that יהוה belongs in the second stich, see Taylor, 137. Others have suggested that יהוה should be at the end of the first stich functioning either as subject of the verb (C. F. Burney, *Notes on the Hebrew Text of the Books of Kings* [Oxford: Clarendon Press, 1903] 111; J. A. Montgomery, *The Books of Kings,* ICC [Edinburgh: T. & T. Clark, 1951] 190; Gray, 211-12; M. Rehm, *Das erste Buch der Könige: Ein Kommentar* [Wurzburg: Echter Verlag, 1979] 87; G. H. Jones, *1 and 2 Kings,* NCB [London: Marshall, Morgan & Scott Publ. Ltd., 1984] 196; S. J. DeVries, 113), or as a vocative at the end of the line (e.g., Wellhausen, *Die Composition des Hexateuchs und der historischen Bücher des alten Testaments,* 2nd edn [Berlin: Georg Reiner, 1889] 271; Noth, 168). But the positioning of יהוה at the end of the first stich substantially weakens an association between Yahweh and the sun that several scholars consider to be the motive behind the defective metre of the MT.

Hence, the citation base in 1 Kgs 8:13 (reconstructed) above is comparable to the one in Josh 10:13. Here we have a contiguously placed *neutrum* הִיא in the four-part citation pattern that marks a discourse relation to a poetic fragment excerpted from "the Book of the Just".

4. Genealogies

The same four-part citation pattern may also ascribe a referent to a source that contains genealogies. The use of such a citation base in 1 Chr 9:1 further demonstrates the manner in which this four-part pattern can manage various types of referents. In this case, the referent is much larger than those we have observed heretofore.

וכל־ישראל התיחשׂו והנם כתובים על־ספר מלכי ישראל
ויהודה (1 Chr 9:1a)

So all Israel was enrolled by genealogies — they are written in the Book of the Kings of Israel and Judah (1 Chr 9:1a).

Syntactically, the antecedent of the intermediate referent in הנם is כל־ישׂראל ("all Israel"). However, this nominal phrase is simply a semantic summary of the geneaologies listed in chapters 2-8 of 1 Chr[122]. In this respect, כל־ישׂראל is not the fully defined referent, but provides a summary of the seven chapters that are ascribed to "the Book of the Kings of Israel and Judah". This is an example of why we have designated כל among the elements that broaden the scope of a referent.

Another referent that is attributed to a literary collection of genealogies is located in Neh 7:5.

Then I found the Book of the Genealogy of those who came up first in which I found it had been written [ואמצא כתוב בו]: [geneaologies listed] (Neh 7:5ff.).

---

122 Scholars generally agree that this passage is the summary to chapters 2-8, "9 1a Unterschrift zu Kap. 2-8" (W. Rudolph, *Chronikbücher*, 83). Cf. Williamson, 86-87; Japhet, 206.

This does not appear to be directly related to the citation pattern we have
seen above but consists of the passive participle כָּתוּב with the verb
stem מצא. This construction occurs with both non-legal and legal
referents. Unlike the other forms we have examined, the citation base in
Neh 7:5 serves as a heading for the referent. However, just as we have
observed in the previous example in 1 Chr 9:1a, the referent is much
larger than those constructions we have addressed before this section on
genealogies. The citation base in Neh 7:5 introduces a referent that
consists of fifty-eight verses (Neh 7:6-63).

Another reference to a genealogical source occurs in Neh 12:23. As
with the regnal formula in 2 Chr 13:22, the second element of the four-
part citation pattern is not used in Neh 12:23.

בני לוי ראשי האבות כתובים על־ספר דברי הימים (Neh 12:23a)

The phrase ראשי האבות stands in apposition to the phrase בני לוי and
both comprise the referent which is contiguous to the citation base
כתובים.

5. The Book of Prophecies

The citation base in Jer 25:13 attributes a referent to a book of
prophecies.

> I will bring upon that land all My words [כל־דברי] which I have pronounced
> against it, all that is written in this book, which Jeremiah has prophesied
> against all the nations [כל־הכתוב בספר הזה אשר־נבא ירמיהו על־
> כל־הגוים] (Jer 25:13).

In order to identify the referent of this citation base we must look at both
the MT and LXX separately[123]. In Jer 25-31, the *Vorlage* of the LXX

---

123 The problem of the relation between the LXX and MT of Jer is an issue that has
    found little consensus among scholars. In general, it can be stated that the LXX
    "represents a shorter text than the MT. Vulg., Pesh., and Targ., on the other
    hand, are mostly in accord with MT" (William McKane, *A Critical and
    Exegetical Commentary on Jeremiah*, ICC, Vol. I [Edinburgh: T. & T. Clark,
    1986] xvi).

appears to preserve the more original sequence. Jer 25:14 LXX begins a series of prophetic oracles against foreign nations: Elam (25:14-20); Egypt (26:2-28); Babylon (27:1-28:64); Philistines (29:1-7); Edom (30:1-16); Ammon (30:17-22); Kedar (30:23-28); Damascus (30:29-33); Moab (31:1-44).

As is well-known, the MT indicates a different ordering of these chapters. The MT contains basically the same oracles against foreign nations in chapters 46-51. In order to clarify the relation between the citation base in 25:13 and the referent that is more than twenty chapters away, the MT glosses the rubric "that Jeremiah prophesied against all the nations". This latter phrase functions as an intermediate referent.

Though the problems of relating the text of the MT and the LXX are complex, in terms of the original location of the referent the LXX has perserved a sequence which appears to be more original. The *Vorlage* of the LXX appears to preserve an arrangement of the text that antedates that of the MT. Our understanding of the use of this citation base in the MT and the LXX is supported by McKane's magisterial work. Commenting on his own analysis, McKane states, "it follows from this exposition of Sept. that את כל הכתוב בספר הזה (v. 13) can only refer to the oracles against foreign nations contained in 25.14ff. (MT 46 ff.)"[124].

It is noteworthy to record Rudolph's recurring vacillation concerning the identification of the referents of citation bases. As he could not resolve which referent to identify in Neh 10:35 (34), Rudolph similarly entertains two referents in Jer 25:13. "According to Rudolph, 'all that is written in this book' refers either to the Source C collection of Jeremiah's words, or to chapters 1-20"[125].

---

124 *Ibid.*, 627.

125 *Ibid.*, 631-32; see Rudolph, *Jeremia,* HAT (Tübingen: J. C. B. Mohr, 1968) xviff., 159ff. Omitting vv. 12 and 14 as secondary insertions, Nicholson divides the statement "everything written in this book, which Jeremiah prophesied against all the nations" into two independent phrases. According to Nicholson, the first half concludes the discourse forming the conclusion of the first half of the book (*The Book of the Prophet Jeremiah Chapters 1-25* [Cambridge: University Press, 1973] 209, 211-12). The other half of this phrase originally introduced vv. 15-38 (212; see also his previous book, *Preaching to the Exiles: A Study of the Prose Tradition in the Book of Jeremiah* [Oxford: Blackwell, 1970] 34, 56-57).

We conclude that the form כל הכתוב in Jer 25:13 served as an introduction for all the oracles that originally followed it (see LXX 25:14-31:44). The referent is either six or six and a half chapters, one of the largest that we have noted. As a heading, we would not expect to find here the four-part formula or extraposition.

6. Official Correspondence

1 Kgs 21:11 introduces to our analysis a citation base in the form of a comparative clause introduced with כאשר (enlarged). While uncharacteristic of devices with non-legal referents, comparative citation bases are the most common form among citation bases with legal referents.

ויעשׂו (the elders of Naboth's town) . . . . כאשר שלחה אליהם איזבל
כאשר כתוב בספרים אשר שלחה אליהם (1 Kgs 21:11) [126]

In comparison to those forms above the salient feature of this citation construction is its capacity to mark adverbial qualifications (e.g., infinitive phrases, verbal clauses, etc.). The citation base כאשר כתוב may easily qualify narrated acts and does not have the functions of those constructions discussed above: the general use of regnal formulæ as a footnote; or the recounting of the act of citation marked by מצאא כתוב √.

Another novel feature concerns the intermediate referent עשׂה√ which is clearly central to the identification of the *meaningful* referent in this passage. עשׂה√ is not itself the referent since the citation signifies far more than that something was "done". In other words, עשׂה√ is an unsatisfactory antecedent and in fact functions as an intermediate referent. This view rests on the fact that the role of עשׂה√ in 1 Kgs 21:11 is more a syntactical than semantic device. Modern linguistic theory refers to this role as pro-form "do" or עשׂה√ [127]. In 1 Kgs 11,

---

126 Read with MT. 𝕲 ᴸ lacks the last clause.

127 For pro-forms in Classical Hebrew, see W. Richter, *Grundlagen einer althebräischen Grammatik, Bd. 13: III. Der Satz (Satztheorie)*, 20-21.

pro-form עשׂה√ relates to the meaningful referent located in vv. 9-10
("She wrote in the letters, 'Proclaim a fast, and seat Naboth at the head
of the assembly; seat two scoundrels opposite him, and have them bring
a charge against him, saying, "You have cursed God and the king".
Then take him out, and stone him to death'") while vv. 12-13 recount
the fulfilment of Jezebel's directives.

In BA, כתב√ is employed in Ezra 5:7 to introduce a report to
Darius.

> They [the leaders of the province of Beyond the River] sent him a report, in
> which was written as follows [וְכִרְנָה כְּתִיב בְּגַוֵּהּ]: "To Darius the king
> [לְדָרְיָוֶשׁ מַלְכָּא], all peace ..." (Ezra 5:7ff.).

כִּרְנָה ("thus, as follows") signals a discourse relation to the referent in
vv. 7b-17.

Another use of כתב√ in a citation base occurs in Ezra 6:2. Here it
introduces an official scroll that was stored in the fortress in Ecbatana.

> But it was in Ecbatana, the capital of the province of Media, that a scroll was
> found on which this was written [וְכֵן־כְּתִיב בְּגַוַּהּ]: "A record [דִּכְרוֹנָה]..."
> (Ezra 6:2ff.).

The pro-form כֵּן is used to mark the discourse relation to the referent in
vv. 2b-12. The distinctive introductory statement "a record [דִּכְרוֹנָה]"
in the referent in Ezra 6:2 suggests that this may have identified the
contents as an official decree.

7. Court Annals

Esth 6:2 concerns the attribution of a referent to a Persian literary
work: "the Book of the Records, the Annals" (v. 1; cf. Gordis). The
citation base in v. 2 differs in both form and function from the regnal
source formulæ we have analysed above.

> It was found written that [וַיִּמָּצֵא כָתוּב אֲשֶׁר] Mordecai had reported
> concerning Bigthana and Teresh, two of the king's eunuchs, who were

doorkeepers, that [אֲשֶׁר] they had conspired to assassinate King Ahasuerus (Esth 6:2).

Similar to the form with √מצא and כתוב in Neh 7:5, this construction is to be distinguished from the others that we have examined primarily in that it narrates the citation of material instead of presenting it as background information. As can be seen from Esth 6:1-2a ("On that night the king could not sleep, and he gave orders to bring 'the Book of Records, the Annals', and they were read to the king. It was found written how Mordecai...") the act of citation is part of the story line. While this construction does not become formulaic in the same sense as the four-part pattern above, these forms with √מצא and כתוב are only to be found in the non-synoptic post-exilic historiography (Neh 7:5; 8:14; 13:1; Esth 6:2[128]) in works that come from distinct provenances.

C. Conclusions regarding the Use of כָּתוּב with Non-Legal Referents

We will summarise all of the uses of כָּתוּב after addressing its use with legal referents. At this point, a brief statement should be made about how the examination above contributes to our understanding of the use of כָּתוּב in citation bases with legal referents. The vast majority of the forms above are in some way related to the four-part citation pattern used most frequently with the regnal source formulæ. Since it was used to cite a variety of topics and in literature from distinct provenances, this structure, we suggested, may have constituted a literary convention for marking off-line or tangential material. In contrast to its characteristic use observed above, the forms with legal referents never use the four-part citation pattern, or one of its adaptations. כָּתוּב citation bases with legal referents are used in distinguishable ways in the non-synoptic post-exilic historiography. The various uses of כָּתוּב citation bases with legal referents is best

---

128 Neh 7:5 entails a genealogical referent. Neh 8:14 and 13:1 have a legal referent (see below).

observed by a detailed analysis of the relevant forms to which we turn next.

III. כָּתוּב Citation Bases with Legal Referents

Considerable insight into the use of citation bases that employ the passive participle כָּתוּב for legal referents can be gleaned from an analysis of the syntactic constructions in which they occur. Certain semantic features of the passages that use these citation bases also repay attention. It appears that the citation bases with legal referents have undergone development in the course of time which departs from the use of the four-part citation pattern examined in the previous part of this chapter.

In the post-biblical period, the development of כַּכָּתוּב with legal referents appears to be indisputable (e.g., כַ in CD 19:1, see further below). In this section, we will attempt to demonstrate that the beginning of this development can be discerned within the Hebrew canon.

The citation bases with legal referents consist of either a relative construction, a comparative statement, or the form מצא√ כתוב already encountered in our analysis of non-legal referents. The use of the comparative constructions in citation bases (e.g., ככל־הכתוב, ככתוב, etc.) offer important insights into the development of the exegesis of the post-exilic period. The relative formulations (e.g., הכתוב) appear to reflect some of these features as well.

A. Relative Citation Bases with כָּתוּב

1. Relative Participles

The examples below represent the syntactic patterns among the citation bases that use a relative participle (passages listed in footnotes).

...כָּל־הָאָלָה הַכְּתוּבָה בַּסֵּפֶר הַזֶּה (Deut 29:19 [20]) 129

...כְּכֹל אָלוֹת הַבְּרִית הַכְּתוּבָה בְּסֵפֶר הַתּוֹרָה הַזֶּה (Deut 29:20 [21])

...מִצְוֹתָיו וְחֻקֹּתָיו הַכְּתוּבָה בְּסֵפֶר הַתּוֹרָה הַזֶּה (Deut 30:10)

...אֶת־דִּבְרֵי הַבְּרִית הַזֹּאת הַכְּתֻבִים עַל־הַסֵּפֶר הַזֶּה (2 Kgs 23:3) 130

All the citation bases in this category consist of a participle and an article
(enlarged above). As a result, these constructions attribute various
nominal constructions to another corpus.

There are three noteworthy issues regarding the relation between the
citation base and the referent in these passages. First, the antecedents of
these relative participles consist either of a construct chain of nouns or
two coordinated nouns. The syntactic nature of these nominal
constructions makes it difficult for a relative participle to agree with its
antecedent in every situation[131]. As a result, it appears that the

---

129 Deut 29:19 (20), 26 (27); 2 Chr 34:24 (see below).

130 2 Kgs 23:3 (with הזאת), 24; 2 Chr 34:31; Deut 28:58 (with כל and הזאת).

131 Even though a relative participle customarily agrees with its antecedent, scholars
differ on the best way to describe this relationship. Some describe it in terms of
attribution. Gordon states, "agreement in definiteness with the head appears on
the participle (in addition to agreement in gender and number...). Such
agreement is identical with the agreement that adjectives show" (Amnon Gordon,
"The Development of the Participle in Biblical, Mishnaic, and Modern Hebrew",
AL 8 [1982] § 2.5.1). *IBHS* also describes some relative participles in terms of
attribution (§ 37.5).

On the other hand, some scholars analyse this relation in terms of
apposition (DG § 112). Apposition is usually marked by agreement in
definitiveness (DG § 39) and the ability to transform the two components into a
nominal clause (JM § 131a; S. R. Driver, *Hebrew Tenses*, § 188).

More recently, Dyk has put forward a mediating position that is based on
modern linguistics. After surveying the definitions of GK and JM, she
concludes, "however defined, attribution and apposition are hard to distinguish
formally in Hebrew" (20). She also claims that the transformations above are
no longer satisfactory in light of modern linguistics (93-95). In light of these
considerations, she describes all appositive and attributive relations with the
overarching phrase "nominal adjunct with agreement restrictions". She states,
"the relationships of apposition and attribution will both be seen as a
modifications [*sic*] of the head, subject to agreement restrictions" (21). Dyk's

contiguous relation between the definite participle, which functions as the citation base, and the referent takes on greater significance.

Deut 30:10 contains the coordinated nominal phrase מצותיו וחקתיו before the relative participle הכתובה. The disagreement in number between the nominal phrase of two plural nouns and the singular participle is corrected in some ancient versions[132]. In the MT, however, the identification of the referent appears to be clear due to its contiguous relation to the citation base. In Deut 30:10, contiguity appears to be a more important factor than grammatical agreement.

In the other passages that use a relative participle, the referent consists of a construct chain of nouns. Grammatical agreement with such a compound nominal construction includes several considerations; most of these passages above fall within the range of agreement restrictions observed by grammarians[133].

In Deut 29:20 MT, the use of the two nouns of the same gender in the chain, however, results in some ambiguity as to the precise identity of the referent (cf. the passages listed with 2 Kgs 23:3 which consist of two nouns of different genders). In light of the context, this use of a relative participle does not appear to identify unequivocally either "the covenant" or "the curses of the covenant" as the referent. The referent of the citation base הכתובה initially seems to be identified as the *nomen*

---

analysis of the participle nevertheless supports the view that definite participles customarily agree with their head (for the relatively few passages that do not agree, see the participles that satisfy the code 16-----61- in Dyk, 236ff.).

We have chosen a pragmatic approach to this debate. That is, we have chosen to describe the features of agreement (definitiveness, number, and gender) between the participle and its nominal head rather than resolve the debate above.

132 Cf. ‏𝔖𝔗𝔗ᴶ‎.

133 When a construct chain of nouns occurs as the subject of a sentence, its agreement with the predicate may take more than one form. On one hand, when כל occurs in the *nomen regens*, agreement occurs with the genitive (GK § 146c). This agreement exists in Deut 29:19 (20), 26 (27) and 2 Chr 34:24. On the other hand, agreement may also occur between the relative participle and the *nomen regens* as in 2 Kgs 23:3 (with הזאת), 24, and 2 Chr 24:31. Both of these aspects of agreement pertain to Deut 28:58 (with כל and הזאת). GK § 146c does not account for construct chains with more than one noun after כל.

rectum בְרִית [134]. The agreement between these two forms, however, could simply be attributed to their juxtaposition[135]. If this is the basis for the inflection of הכתובה, then the entire construct chain is probably intended as the referent. In fact, some ancient versions have not read the antecedent as בְרִית. These versions render כתובה as a plural participle to agree with the *nomen regens* אֵלוֹת[136]. In light of other uses in this category (see Deut 29:19 [20] above), it appears that these versions have understood the entire construct chain as the intended referent of the citation base. Hence, Deut 29:20 (21) MT is an example of the way that the use of a relative participle as a citation base may not always result in the clear identification of a referent.

Despite a degree of ambiguity that results in some uses of a relative participle as a citation base, the contiguous relation between the citation base and the referent is always maintained. The presence of the demonstrative pronoun זֹאת in Deut 28:58 and 2 Kgs 23:3 does not negate the principle of contiguity in these passages. According to *IBHS*, "an attributive adjective directly modifies a substantive in such a way that the combined phrase functions as a single syntactic unit in the clause…"[137].

The second noteworthy feature of the relation between relative participles and their antecedents concerns an observation which stems from Dyk's analysis of the Hebrew participle. In her treatment of relative participles under the broader category of "the participle as nominal adjunct with agreement restrictions", Dyk observes that "there can be material intervening between the participle and the noun it modifies"[138]. For instance, Gen 46:27 contains a prepositional phrase that interrupts the relationship between the nominal head and the relative participle (both underlined).

---

134 This agreement appears to parallel the case of a predicate agreeing with a *nomen rectum* when it "represents the principal idea of the compound subject" (GK § 146 a).

135 See GK § 146 a n. 1.

136 See 𝔪 and 𝔖.

137 *IBHS*, § 14.3.1; cf. § 17.4.1.

138 Dyk, 95.

כל־הנפש לבית־יעקב הבאה מצרימה (Gen 46:27)

She comments, "a definite participle agrees with and modifies a distant N[oun]P[hrase] 'the soul'"[139]. In Gen 22:13, Gibson has observed an adverb intervening between an indefinite relative passive participle and its indefinite nominal head (איל אחר נאחז)[140]. Additionally, DG and *IBHS* note the poetic passages Psa 19:8-11 and 137:7[141]. JM similarly refers to occurrences of "loose apposition" (2 Kgs 14:7, 13)[142]. It is noteworthy that the agreement of definiteness, number, and gender appears to take on greater significance in order to establish the relationship between a relative participle and its antecedent.

From these observations, we can conclude that a contiguous relation between the relative participle and its antecedent is not a necessary feature in BH.

In general, it appears that when contiguity is not maintained between the relative participle and its antecedent, grammatical agreement between these two elements becomes more important. Conversely, as in the citation bases above, contiguity becomes more important when grammatical agreement cannot be unambiguously maintained. This situation appears to be relevant in our examination of כתוב in post-exilic historiography and leads us to our final point in this section.

Our third observation concerns the citation base in 2 Chr 34:24. Among the passages in this section, 2 Chr 34:24 is the only non-deuteronomistic passage[143]. In fact, according to Weinfeld, the participial expression את כל הכתוב בספר התורה הזה is "deuteronomic phraseology" and comprises part of the terms of the

---

139 *Ibid.*
140 DG §§ 112, 116a.
141 DG § 112; *IBHS*, § 37.5.
142 JM § 131m. והנה may also intervene between a definite noun and a modifying participle which, in Gen 24:30, McCarthy treats as a relative participle: "he went off to the man (who was) still standing (w^ehinneh ʿomed) with the camels by the well" (338, see also Gen 37:15; 41:1). McCarthy has shown that והנה has several functions "which parallel just about all the various kinds of 'clauses' listed in the syntax sections of our Hebrew grammars" while still maintaining its own dramatic or emotional quality (342).
143 2 Chr 34:31 is a synoptic passage with 2 Kgs 23:3.

category "observance of the law and loyalty to the covenant"[144]. In 2 Chr 34:24, the Chr rewrites his *Vorlage* in 2 Kgs 22:16 by introducing to his history a citation base with a relative participle of √כתב. The Chr's reworking of his *Vorlage* distinguishes the expression in 2 Chr 34:24 from Weinfeld's "deuteronomic phraseology".

כֹּה אָמַר יְהוָה הִנְנִי מֵבִיא רָעָה אֶל־הַמָּקוֹם הַזֶּה וְעַל־יֹשְׁבָיו אֵת
כָּל־דִּבְרֵי הַסֵּפֶר אֲשֶׁר קָרָא מֶלֶךְ יְהוּדָה (2 Kgs 22:16)

כֹּה אָמַר יְהוָה הִנְנִי מֵבִיא רָעָה עַל־הַמָּקוֹם הַזֶּה וְעַל־יוֹשְׁבָיו אֵת
כָּל־הָאָלוֹת הַכְּתוּבוֹת עַל־הַסֵּפֶר אֲשֶׁר קָרְאוּ לִפְנֵי
מֶלֶךְ יְהוּדָה (2 Chr 34:24)

The Chr rewrites דִּבְרֵי of his *Vorlage* with the more specific form הָאָלוֹת. But in this rephrasing, the Chr also introduces the citation base הַכְּתוּבוֹת. In light of the relation between the citation base and the referent in deuteronomistic literature observed above, it appears noteworthy that he uses the only occurrence of a feminine plural כתוב in the Hebrew Bible in order to make the relation between the citation base and the referent agree. Especially, as we have noted earlier, masculine suffixes are frequently employed for feminine antecedents[145], especially in the book of Chronicles[146]. Furthermore, the Chr also uses a contiguous relation between these elements which we have observed was not necessary (cf. Dyk and others).

The Chr's rewriting of this passage entails little else. Hence, the introduction of a citation base with the unique הַכְּתוּבוֹת, the contiguous placement of the relative participle to the antecedent, as well as the greater semantic detail of הָאָלוֹת appear to reflect a concern of the Chr. Here, the Chr gives more attention to this citation base with a legal referent than his *Vorlage*.

---

144 M. Weinfeld, *Deuteronomy and the Deuteronomistic School* (Oxford: Clarendon Press, 1972) 336, # 17b.
145 GK § 135 o.
146 JM § 149 b.

It is helpful to compare 2 Chr 34:24 to the long anaphoric relation between a citation base and a non-legal referent in 35:25. We observed there how the Chr used two intermediate referents to identify קִינוֹת as the term he was ascribing to a source. This non-legal referent can be contrasted with the citation base in 2 Chr 34:24 in two ways. First, the relation between the citation base and the legal referent is more succinct than with קִינוֹת in 2 Chr 35:25. Secondly, despite the characteristics of LBH, only the legal referent agrees with the feminine plural antecedent.

Even though the evidence so far is limited, we maintain that similar observations can be made among legal referents and the citation bases that use כתוב in the non-synoptic post-exilic historiography. Furthermore, the features associated with these forms suggest that כתוב was developed in the post-exilic era as an exegetical device. We suggest that the Chr, in 2 Chr 34:24, has used the contiguous relation between the definite participle and the referent (see Dyk), grammatical agreement (see deuteronomistic citations above in this section), and greater semantic detail in comparison to his *Vorlage* at 2 Kgs 22:16 to make the identification of the referent as unambiguous as possible.

2. כָּתוּב *in Relative Clauses*

There are only two occurrences of כָּתוּב used in a relative clause.

גַּם כָּל־חֳלִי וְכָל־מַכָּה אֲשֶׁר לֹא כָתוּב בְּסֵפֶר הַתּוֹרָה הַזֹּאת
יַעְלֵם יְהוָה עָלֶיךָ עַד הִשָּׁמְדָךְ (Deut 28:61)

וַתִּתַּךְ עָלֵינוּ הָאָלָה וְהַשְּׁבֻעָה אֲשֶׁר כְּתוּבָה בְּתוֹרַת מֹשֶׁה
(Dan 9:11)

The syntax of Dan 9:11 and Deut 28:61 is distinctive. Commenting on syndetic relative clauses, JM states, "in nominal clauses one finds especially a preposition with its noun, sometimes an adjective, rather rarely a participle"[147]. This citation base ascribes only nominal

---

147 JM §158 e.   According to Dyk's examination, there are fourteen out of the 3,144 (0.45%) passages in her study that agree with this syntactic environment.

constructions to another corpus. Like the previous passages we have
covered above, it is the contiguous position of these citation bases to
their antecedents that makes the identification of the referent clear. The
nature of these referents reflects the situation that we surveyed in
passages with a relative participle. Grammatical agreement between a
predicative participle and its antecedent also can be ambiguous at
times[148]. For instance, in Deut 28:61, the referent כָּל־חֳלִי וְכָל־מַכָּה is
qualified by the singular participle כתוב while the resumptive pronoun
is plural (יעלם).

Deut 28:61 is also the first example of a negative citation base.

B. Comparative Constructions With כָּתוּב

This category of exegetical devices significantly broadens the types
of relations that may exist between the citation base and the referent.
These citation bases mark adverbial, adnominal, and discourse relations.
Accordingly, the referent may consist of more than just the nominal
constructions that we have encountered among citation bases with legal
referents above.   In fact, it is this aspect of these comparative
constructions that has made the identification of the referent in citation
formulæ especially problematic. An analysis that focuses on the syntax
of all citation constructions appears to clarify many aspects of the way
these devices were used. Presumably, these citation bases were deemed
to have served a more precise function than is represented by the debates
that presently exist among scholars (see further below).

1. כָּתוּב in a Complex Comparative Sentence

Among legal citation bases with כָּתוּב, Dan 9:13a is the only
complex comparative sentence.

---

148 In addition to the references cited above, see GK § 146d; DG § 24.

כַּאֲשֶׁר כָּתוּב בְּתוֹרַת מֹשֶׁה אֵת כָּל־הָרָעָה הַזֹּאת בָּאָה
עָלֵינוּ (Dan 9:13a)

The citation base is כַּאֲשֶׁר כָּתוּב. Since כַּאֲשֶׁר marks a comparison between clauses[149], the identification of the referent is relatively straightforward. The referent is the main clause: "all this calamity has come upon us". The texts referred to appear to be Lev 26:14-39, Deut 28:15-68, and 29:18-28 (19-29)[150].

With the use of this comparative clause as the citation base, an adverbial relation has now been observed to exist between a citation base and a legal referent. The use of a comparative construction enables actions or behaviours to be compared, authorised, or based on the law.

Even though the bipartite sentence structure of a complex comparative sentence[151] means that the cited action in Dan 9:13a can be clearly established, there is not a contiguous relation between the citation base כַּאֲשֶׁר כָּתוּב and the referent.

2. כָּתוּב in Prepositional Phrases Introduced with כ

a. Jenni's Recent Summary of the Syntax of Comparative Statements

Constructions that use כָּתוּב in a prepositional phrase introduced with כ (e.g., כַּכָּתוּב) occur far more extensively as citation bases than the comparative clause examined in Dan 9:13a above. The recent work of Jenni has shown that these two comparative constructions must be considered together. The aim of Jenni's analysis of the preposition כ is to create an exhaustive semantic coding[152]. Despite the semantic focus

---

149 Seybold, *TWOT,* Vol. VII, 2; in German, *TWAT,* Bd. IV, 2. See also Jenni, 30, 133; DG § 119; JM § 174.
150 Donner, 232.
151 JM § 174.
152 Introducing the scope of his research, Jenni states, "Diese Aktualisierung der ‚Grundbedeutung' je nach den involvierten Kategorien von Korrelaten im einzelnen aufzuzeigen und zu klassifizieren, ist die Hauptaufgabe der vorliegenden lexikalischen Untersuchung" (*Ibid.,* 12). The full scope of Jenni's

of his work, Jenni offers an introductory section on the syntax of the various expressions and constructions that are formed with the preposition כְּ. This syntactic analysis is doubtless the most thorough treatment of comparative structures to date in BH[153]. However, as we will see, this important syntactic treatment must be expanded in order to advance the present assessment of citation formulæ among scholars. In order to accomplish this task, we must first review the important groundwork that Jenni has provided.

In his analysis, Jenni draws an analogy between the comparative clauses introduced with כַּאֲשֶׁר (e.g., Dan 9:13) and the prepositional phrases with כְּ (e.g., the ככתוב citation bases below). Jenni treats these under the heading "Vergleichssätze und deren Verkürzungen"[154]; excepting one passage, every occurrence of כתוב in a prepositional phrase introduced with כְּ is categorised under this heading. Jenni draws an analogy between these two constructions based on the following point. He states,

> das mit כְּ gebildete Präpositionale[155] jeweils nicht mehr als Prädikatskern, sondern nur als modale Angabe erscheint, gilt gemeinsam, daß das Vergleichspräpositionale immer mit einem ganzen Vergleichssatz gleichwertig ist[156].

Based on this view of the equivalency of a *Vergleichspräpositionale* (e.g., ככתוב in our present chapter) and a comparative clause

---

project concerns all the monoconsonantal prepositions in three volumes.

153 Jenni describes this part of his treatment as a somewhat eclectic syntax based on the work of W. Richter and P. von Polenz (*Ibid.*, 26, n. 86).

154 *Ibid.*, 30-31, see also 130-37. According to Jenni, constructions that include כֹל (e.g., ככל־הכתוב) are included under this heading as well.

155 In the category "Vergleichssätze und deren Verkürzungen", Jenni uses the linguistic term "Präpositionale" to refer to the abbreviations of a comparative clause with כַּאֲשֶׁר. These forms are introduced by the preposition כְּ and have a complement in the form of an abstract noun (e.g., כמצות, see further below), an infinitive (e.g, כשמע), or a passive participle (ככתוב, 2 Kgs 23:21) (see *Ibid.*, 30-31, 187). For a discussion of this term as it pertains to comparative constructions as a whole, see *Ibid.*, 12.

156 *Ibid.*, 30.

introduced with כַּאֲשֶׁר, Jenni proceeds to compare the function and form of these two constructions. He continues,

> Die Umstandsbestimmung *fungiert* als verkürzte Formulierung eines ganzen Vergleichssatzes und läßt sich jederzeit auf einen solchen zurückführen, wobei die fehlenden Satzglieder aus dem Hauptsatz zu erschließen sind. Umgekehrt ausgedrückt: Werden zwei Sachverhalte in einem Vergleichssatzgefüge mit Hauptsatz und Nebensatz verknüpft, wobei der mit כַּאֲשֶׁר eingeleitete Vergleichs-(Neben)satz eine voll ausformulierte, durch אֲשֶׁר nominalisierten Proposition zur Erklärung der Hauptproposition beiträgt, können unter bestimmten Umständen ein oder mehrere Konstituenten des Vergleichssatzes in den Hintergrund gedrängt bzw. eingespart werden[157].

According to Jenni, the *Vergleichspräpositionale* כככתוב should be understood as an abbreviated, or ellipted, version of the כַּאֲשֶׁר clause of a complex comparative sentence; both constructions are equivalent in function and theoretically in form.

There are some examples of this equivalence of כככתוב to a comparative clause among the citation bases in this chapter which demonstrate Jenni's insight.

וַיְצַו הַמֶּלֶךְ אֶת־כָּל־הָעָם לֵאמֹר עֲשׂוּ פֶסַח לַיהוָה אֱלֹהֵיכֶם
כַּכָּתוּב עַל סֵפֶר הַבְּרִית הַזֶּה (2 Kgs 23:21)

In 2 Kgs 23:21, the form of an entire comparative clause (כַּאֲשֶׁר ...כָּתוּב) can be reconstructed from כַּכָּתוּב. In this passage, the function of כַּכָּתוּב is equivalent to the comparative clause introduced with כַּאֲשֶׁר כָּתוּב. Therefore, in 2 Kgs 23:21, the referent of the citation base כַּכָּתוּב is the main clause עֲשׂוּ פֶסַח לַיהוָה אֱלֹהֵיכֶם like Dan 9:13a above. The only disagreement between scholars concerning this citation base is whether only Deut 16:1-8 is referred to here[158], or whether Exod 12:21-27 and v. 47 are in view as well[159]. Insofar as 2 Kgs 23:23 ("but in the eighteenth year of King Josiah, this Passover

---

157 *Ibid.*, emphasis mine.
158 E.g., Donner, 227.
159 E.g., DeVries, 625.

was observed to the LORD in Jerusalem") states that the Passover was kept in Jerusalem, the recently discovered deuteronomic law is most likely in view here.

However, there appear to be some clear examples where כַּכָּתוּב does not *function* as the equivalent of a כַּאֲשֶׁר clause of a complex comparative sentence. In other words, the syntactic summary of *Vergleichspräpositionalen* provided in Jenni's semantic analysis of comparative statements has limits and is, as he indicated, in need of further research.

b. An Overview of the Types of Syntactic Relations of כַּכָּתוּב

כַּכָּתוּב does not always qualify a main clause. Immediately below, we will list some passages that show ways in which Jenni's provisional syntactic assessment of the function of a *Vergleichspräpositionale* can be expanded. Jenni states that he hopes his syntactic treatment of comparative statements will lead someday to a full elaboration of the syntactic possibilities and conditions under which a prepositional phrase introduced with כְּ can occur[160]. While we do not presume to have such a goal in mind, the lack of consensus regarding the use of citation bases cannot be advanced without exploring the field of inquiry to which Jenni refers.

With the intent to shed some light on the debate surrounding the use of citation bases, we propose to examine the various syntactic relations that a prepositional phrase introduced with כְּ may have. Toward this end, we will first present some examples where כַּכָּתוּב (and its form with כל[161]) qualifies a sentence constituent other than a main clause. It appears that we should understand and describe the characteristics of the contexts of these passages that enable scholars to agree on the identity of these referents. This approach will be instrumental for our subsequent treatment of passages that do not concern the simplest of comparative

---

160 Jenni, 26. Seybold (*TWOT*, Vol. VII, 2; in German, *TWAT*, Bd. IV, 2) and
    other grammarians treat only the simplest of constructions.
161 See n. 154.

constructions. We will then attempt to show how this approach can illuminate the debated passages and perhaps establish guidelines that can then be applied beyond the issue of citation bases.

We will initially present a total of six passages, including 2 Kgs 23:21 above, that we believe establish at least four types of functions that כַּכָּתוּב may have with its syntactic environment. Then, we will proceed in this chapter to treat the remainder of the *Vergleichspräpositionalen* with כָּתוּב.

In 2 Chr 35:26, כַּכָּתוּב (enlarged) does not function as a comparative clause in a complex sentence.

וְיֶ֫תֶר דִּבְרֵי יֹאשִׁיָּהוּ וַחֲסָדָיו כַּכָּתוּב בְּתוֹרַת יְהוָה וּדְבָרָיו
הָרִאשֹׁנִים וְהָאַחֲרֹנִים הִנָּם כְּתוּבִים עַל־סֵפֶר
מַלְכֵי־יִשְׂרָאֵל וִיהוּדָה (2 Chr. 35:26-27)

Scholars agree that the referent of this citation base is the preceding form חֲסָדָיו[162].

The syntactic and semantic characteristics of the context, we maintain, significantly illuminate the reason why the identification of the referent in 2 Chr 35:26 is beyond any reasonable doubt. More importantly, this example illuminates the relevant issues for resolving some of the disputed occurrences below. First, כתוב is embedded in a series of coordinated extraposed nominal constructions. The sentence structure of extraposition sets the function of כתוב apart from the core of the sentence that contains the predicative participle כְּתוּבִים and the resumptive pronoun. This positioning of כתוב in an extraposed phrase demonstrates that this citation base does not function as a כאשר clause in a complex comparative sentence.

---

162 Japhet, 1058; Donner, 230-31; Williamson, "History", 29; Rudolph, 333. Only Goettsberger claimed otherwise (*Die Bücher der Chr oder Paralipomenon,* Die Hl. Schrift des AT [Feldmann-Herkenne, 1939]). Successfully countering this claim, Rudolph states, "v. 26b will allgemein sagen, daß Josias fromme Taten dem Gesetz entsprachen, und nicht, daß er sich in seinen Maßnahmen nach dem neugefundenen Gesetz richtete ..., was der vorausgehenden Darstellung widerspräche (s. bei 34 3 ff.)" (Rudolph, *Chronikbücher,* 333).

Secondly, the consideration of the semantic nature of the three extraposed nominal constructions points to another factor that affects the identification of the referent. Of the three extraposed nominal constructions, חֲסָדָיו is the most detailed nominal (cf. יֶתֶר דִּבְרֵי יֹאשִׁיָּהוּ and דְּבָרָיו). חֲסָדָיו is best understood as an elaboration of "the rest of the deeds of Josiah". Thus, the referent of this citation is introduced with a *waw-explicativum*[163].

The Chr's rephrasing is also noteworthy. The Chr has replaced the phrase כָּל־אֲשֶׁר עָשָׂה (2 Kgs 23:28), which he always rewrites, with the entire phrase וַחֲסָדָיו כַּכָּתוּב בְּתוֹרַת יְהוָה. It is also this citation base and referent that accounts for the most meaningful part of the Chr's rewriting in these verses. This rewriting of his *Vorlage* is reminiscent of that observed in 2 Chr 34:24 which centred around the greater semantic detail of the referent and the introduction of the citation base הכתובות.

The use of ככתוב in 2 Chr 35:26 demonstrates that a combination of semantic and syntactic features may have to be considered to identify the referent in these types of comparative constructions. Furthermore, the contiguous placement is central to the function of ככתוב for two reasons. On one hand, the grammatical agreement between a relative citation and its referent observed above is not possible for a citation base that is a prepositional phrase. On the other hand, ככתוב in any other position in 2 Chr 35:26 would result in the identification of another referent in this passage. The careful positioning of such citation bases will be of greater significance below among the more disputed passages.

2 Chr 35:26 is an example of ככתוב with a nominal referent and a contiguous relation to a noun.

Another use of כתוב that Jenni places under his category "Vergleichssätze und deren Verkürzungen" that does not qualify either a main clause or a noun (or nominal phrase) occurs in 2 Kgs 22:13 and 2 Chr 34:21.

---

163 GK § 154 a N (b).

עַל אֲשֶׁר לֹא־שָׁמְעוּ אֲבֹתֵינוּ עַל־דִּבְרֵי הַסֵּפֶר הַזֶּה
לַעֲשׂוֹת כְּכָל־הַכָּתוּב עָלֵינוּ (2 Kgs 22:13)

עַל אֲשֶׁר לֹא־שָׁמְרוּ אֲבוֹתֵינוּ אֶת־דְּבַר יְהוָה
לַעֲשׂוֹת כְּכָל־הַכָּתוּב עַל־הַסֵּפֶר הַזֶּה (2 Chr 34:21)

The semantic characteristics of these passages indicate that the *Vergleichspräpositionale* כְּכָל־הַכָּתוּב functions in yet another way. Note that in each passage a positive statement ("to do according to everything that is written...") is embedded in a negative clause ("our fathers have not listened to/observed the words of...")[164]. It appears clear that the negative clause is not what is being ascribed to another corpus. Therefore, the referent is the infinitive לַעֲשׂוֹת. Since it does not qualify the main clause, the prepositional phrase כְּכָל־הַכָּתוּב does not function as a subordinate clause in a complex comparative sentence as Jenni's syntactic summary states.

Insight can also be gleaned from the syntax of these passages. In 2 Kgs 22:13/2 Chr 34:21, כְּכָל־הַכָּתוּב does not qualify the nearest finite verb or verbal clause. Rather, the semantics— the positive and negative propositions—indicate that כְּכָל־הַכָּתוּב qualifies only the abutting infinitive phrase. Since כְּכָל־הַכָּתוּב is an adverbial construction and thus could qualify more than one constituent in the sentence, it is not surprising that its placement beside the infinitive לַעֲשׂוֹת is part of what makes its function intelligible. This use of כְּכָל־הַכָּתוּב entails the qualification of a contiguous infinitive. Again, with a prepositional phrase which cannot have grammatical agreement with its referent and which may signal various types of qualifications (adverbial, adnominal, or discourse relations [see below]), its contiguous placement to the sentence constituent it qualifies appears to be a major consideration in determining its scope of modification. This point is not a truism in the discussion of Hebrew syntax as chapter one, and the many debates below, demonstrate.

---

164 Jenni observes this point in passing (135, n. 44), but it has not affected his syntactic treatment.

The Chr's rephrasing of his *Vorlage* in 2 Chr 34:21 again indicates his marked interest in citation bases. The Chr has repositioned הסּפר הזה from describing what the fathers had disobeyed in 2 Kgs 22:13 to a reference to a corpus in 2 Chr 34:21. He also emphasises that it was the word of the LORD that had been disobeyed. In fact, it is the Chr's rephrasing of his *Vorlage* that results in a citation formula in 2 Chr 34:21. In 2 Kgs 22:13, כְּכָל־הַכָּתוּב is not used to ascribe anything to a corpus, but only to describe the expected behaviour of the Israelites. Only 2 Chr 34:21 ascribes a referent explicitly to a corpus (cf. עלינו of his *Vorlage* is rewritten to על־הספר הזה).

In Josh 1:8, כְּכָל־הַכָּתוּב appears to function in a similar fashion.

לֹא־יָמוּשׁ סֵפֶר הַתּוֹרָה הַזֶּה מִפִּיךָ וְהָגִיתָ בּוֹ יוֹמָם וָלַיְלָה
לְמַעַן תִּשְׁמֹר לַעֲשׂוֹת כְּכָל־הַכָּתוּב בּוֹ כִּי־אָז תַּצְלִיחַ אֶת־דְּרָכֶךָ
וְאָז תַּשְׂכִּיל (Josh 1:8)

The contents of the final כִּי clause appear to relate what the logical (אָז) outcome was for having observed everything that was written (לַעֲשׂוֹת כְּכָל־הַכָּתוּב) in the law. Thus, the citation base qualifies the infinitive.

Another example of a ככתוב citation base that qualifies yet another kind of sentence constituent occurs in 2 Chr 30:18.

כִּי־אָכְלוּ אֶת־הַפֶּסַח בְּלֹא כַכָּתוּב (2 Chr 30:18)

בְּלֹא כַכָּתוּב is a modal adverbial construction[165] that describes the manner in which the unclean worshippers ate the passover. Grammarians have analysed בְּלֹא in slightly different ways. Commenting on passages like 2 Chr 30:18 that use בְּלֹא in a manner that the rendering "without" does not capture, Kropat states, "die Präposition בְּ bleibt vollständig selbständig und tritt in ihren

---

[165] Kropat distinguishes this use of בלא from its temporal use "before" (§ 11).

verschiedensten Funktionen vor derartige Wortzusammensetzungen"166. Even though König treats it as a synonym of אַיִן, his rendering of בְּלֹא in 2 Chr 30:18 ("ohne dass es gemäss der Schrift war"167) agrees with the view of Kropat above that בְּ remains independent in this word-combination in 2 Chr 30:18. If בְּ is independent, then, in 2 Chr 30:18, it governs the ellipted clause לֹא כַּכָּתוּב (= לֹא הָיָה כַּכָּתוּב). From this perspective, the identification of the referent is simply the negative particle לֹא.

Hence, a prepositional phrase introduced with בְּ may qualify a contiguous particle. Once again, apart from the contiguous relation between the citation base and the referent another understanding of the sentence constituent that is qualified by ככתוב would result.

In contrast to Jenni's syntactic summary of forms introduced by כְּ, ככתוב functions in more ways than as a כאשר clause in a complex comparative sentence. ככתוב has been shown to qualify either a clause, an infinitive, a noun, or a negative particle. In order to ease our analysis below, we will refer to these relations between a citation base and its referent as:

Type I (one clause);
Type II (an infinitive or infinitival phrase);
Type III (a noun or nominal phrase); or
Type IV (any particle).

We will need to expand this analysis below, especially when we observe that discourse relations are possible for some כאשר citation bases. In the cases above, both adnominal and adverbial relations were marked by ככתוב.

By considering the context of these uses of ככתוב, we have attempted to reveal the various semantic and syntactic issues that make the identification of these referents clear. These observations should

---

166 *Ibid.* Kropat also discounts the view that בְּלֹא always constitutes the preposition "without" (so Müller § 430 2b).
167 König, III, § 402r.

illuminate our consideration of the passages over which scholars have continually disagreed.

c. An Expanded Analysis of the Types of Relations of כַּכָּתוּב

We are now in a position to address the uses of כַּכָּתוּב which include more complex relations to their referents. These uses of כַּכָּתוּב generally consist of a more elaborate relation to the referent than those above. Some examples of כַּכָּתוּב below will still be related to those above, but we will also note ways in which our observations need to be extended further. Considering the ways that scholars have treated these citation bases will facilitate the extension of Jenni's syntactic treatment of "Vergleichssätze und deren Verkürzungen". After consideration of the passages below, we will draw concluding remarks regarding the overall use of כַּכָּתוּב.

There are two uses of כַּכָּתוּב in Josh 8:30-34. כַּכָּתוּב functions in a new way in v. 31, while its use in v. 34 is debated.

In Josh 8:31, כַּכָּתוּב is used in conjunction with the citation base כַּאֲשֶׁר צִוָּה מֹשֶׁה (both enlarged). Hence, these two forms must be treated together. Such occurrences we have designated as "compound citation bases". The entire complex sentence concerns vv. 30-31a.

אָז יִבְנֶה יְהוֹשֻׁעַ מִזְבֵּחַ לַיהוָה אֱלֹהֵי יִשְׂרָאֵל בְּהַר עֵיבָל
כַּאֲשֶׁר צִוָּה מֹשֶׁה עֶבֶד־יְהוָה אֶת־בְּנֵי יִשְׂרָאֵל
כַּכָּתוּב בְּסֵפֶר תּוֹרַת מֹשֶׁה מִזְבַּח אֲבָנִים שְׁלֵמוֹת אֲשֶׁר
לֹא־הֵנִיף עֲלֵיהֶן בַּרְזֶל (Josh 8:30-31a)

Then Joshua built an altar to the LORD, the God of Israel, in the mountain of Ebal, as Moses the servant of the LORD had commanded the sons of Israel, as it is written in the book of the law of Moses: an altar of uncut stones, on which no man had wielded an iron tool (Josh 8:30-31a).

ככתוב is related to its context in two different manners. Rather than functioning as a comparative clause (Type I), ככתוב stands in apposition to the previous citation base כַּאֲשֶׁר צִוָּה מֹשֶׁה168. The referent of this latter citation base with √צוה is the main clause in v. 30 (Type I). ככתוב, however, adds to the first formula the concept that the commandment of Moses was written in the book of the law. The addition of the ככתוב citation formula may signify a need felt by the historian to strengthen the authority of the written corpus by correlating it with the figure of Moses (see further below).

At the same time, כַּכָּתוּב בְּסֵפֶר תּוֹרַת מֹשֶׁה introduces another referent in v. 31aβ. In this case, the referent is a paraphrase of Deut 27:5-6169. However, there is not a contiguous relation between ככתוב and the referent which is a nominal phrase followed by a subordinate clause. The colon in the rendering above best reflects the manner in which ככתוב introduces the referent. Rather than marking an adverbial or adnominal relation, ככתוב signals a relation to the discourse.

Since the citation base ככתוב is related to its context in two different ways, the dual function of ככתוב in Josh 8:31 is perhaps best understood as a Janus170 usage. In Josh 8:31, the complement of כ has two relations to its context171. Thus, in addition to a single adnominal or adverbial relation in a sentence, ככתוב may also have a dual relation to its context. In the present case, this consists of both a discourse and an appositive relation. At a later point in this study, we will see that it is noteworthy that such a Janus function for ככתוב occurs in the DtrH.

In his essay „Wie geschrieben steht", Donner refers to the debate regarding the scope of the reference of ככל-הכתוב in Josh 8:34.

וְאַחֲרֵי־כֵן קָרָא אֶת־כָּל־דִּבְרֵי הַתּוֹרָה הַבְּרָכָה וְהַקְּלָלָה
כְּכָל־הַכָּתוּב בְּסֵפֶר הַתּוֹרָה (Josh 8:34)

Comparing his view to Noth, Donner states, "Fraglich ist allenfalls, ob

---

168 On clausal apposition, see DG §§ 146, 147.
169 Cf. Exod 20:25-26.
170 We have adopted this term from a suggestion made by Prof. Williamson.
171 See W. Richter, *Bd. 10*, 31.

ein genereller oder ein spezieller Hinweis vorliegt"[172]. This debate
concerns whether this citation base refers to "all the words of the law",
or the appositive phrase "the blessing and the curse". Donner maintains
that the referent should be restricted to the latter. It appears that he
understands the significance of כֹל in the citation base to refer to the
blessings and the curses distributed throughout Deut. He concludes that
the texts referred to are Deut 11:29 and chapters 27-28 (especially
27:12f.). If Donner is correct, then the citation base in Josh 8:34 has a
contiguous relation to the referent. Furthermore, by the use of
apposition, the referent, according to this view, would consist of greater
semantic detail than its environment. If this view is correct, then the
function of ככתוב would be similar to 2 Chr 35:26 (Type III).

The debate, however, is broader than Donner indicates. At least
some scholars consider the referent to have a wider reference.
Commenting on the scope of reference for this citation base, DeVries
states, "the 'all' in Josh 8:34 is explicated in v. 35, which implies that
the entire Mosaic law, not just the blessings and curses, was read to the
people (cf. Neh 8:1-3, 18)"[173]. DeVries' attempt to explain כֹל in terms
of the context of Josh 8 appears more plausible than Donner's position.
However, DeVries' view does not appear to have fully considered the
context. The כֹל in the citation base is perhaps to be first understood in
relation to the previous one in the direct object כָּל־דִּבְרֵי הַתּוֹרָה. In
light of these considerations, it does not appear that either of these views
adequately explains the כֹל in the citation base. Noth and most recently
Fritz argue for a broad reference based on the view that the appositive
phrase is secondary (see below)[174]. However, there appears to be more
to the use of כְּכָל־הַכָּתוּב in v. 34 than any of these scholars have
appreciated.

---

172 Donner, 226.
173 DeVries, 624, n. 14.
174 M. Noth, *Das Buch Josua*, 2nd edn, HAT (Tübingen: J. C. B. Mohr, 1953) 52;
    V. Fritz, *Das Buch Josua*, 95, 97. For the view that "'the blessing and the
    curse' are not later additions…, but belong to the conclusion of the making of
    every covenant in the ancient N. E.", see Soggin, 226, cf. 250.

The comparison of Josh 8:30ff. and Deut 27 appears to indicate a way forward. The following observations suggest that both the direct object and the appositive phrase could be understood as the referent. If this view is correct, then the identification of the referent would in part be based on the striking parallels that exist between these two passages. First, both Josh 8:30ff. and Deut 27 concern the covenant renewal at the mountains of Ebal and Gerizim. Secondly, as we have already seen, Josh 8:31 also contains a quotation of Deut 27:6 to explain the manner in which the altar was to be constructed.

In Josh 8:34, there are two more specific aspects that correspond to Deut 27. First, the stipulation to write out "all the words of this law" (Deut 27:3, 8) on stones is satisfied in Josh 8:32. The direct object אֶת־כָּל־דִּבְרֵי הַתּוֹרָה in Josh 8:34 appears to be a verbatim reference to this stipulation in Deut 27:3, 8 (אֶת־כָּל־דִּבְרֵי הַתּוֹרָה הַזֹּאת), excepting the demonstrative adjective. Secondly, the appositive phrase הַבְּרָכָה וְהַקְּלָלָה in Josh 8:34 corresponds to the stipulation in Deut 27:12-13 in a similar manner ("When you have crossed over the Jordan, these [tribes] shall stand on Mount Gerizim for the blessing…. And these [tribes] shall stand on Mount Ebal for the curse [הַקְּלָלָה]…." [NRSV, also 11:29]).

In light of the relationship between these chapters, it appears that the referent of כְּכָל־הַכָּתוּב in Josh 8:34 should be understood as terms stemming directly from Deut 27. Like v. 31, v. 34 entails what is nearly a literal reference to Deut 27. This marked correspondence appears to make less attractive the view that the appositive phrase is secondary (see Noth and Fritz). If this view is correct, then the citation base in Josh 8:34 marks an adnominal relation to a contiguous nominal phrase "all the words of the law, 'the blessing and the curse'" (Type III).

Further examination of these pericopæ shows that Joshua is presented as having departed from other stipulations in Deut 27. If this is true then despite the marked correspondences between Josh 8:30ff. and Deut 27, it is difficult to substantiate the use of the citation base "according to *everything* that was written" in Josh 8:34.

Note the manner in which Josh 8:30ff. departs from the stipulations in Deut 27. First, Joshua appears to have usurped the role of the

Levites in reading "the curse". While Deut 27:14 stipulates that the Levites shall read "the curse", it is Joshua who reads them to the people "according to the law of Moses" (Josh 8:34). This reading by Joshua appears to contradict the stipulations of Deut 27 dramatically since the Levites were carrying the ark (Josh 8:33) and thus available to read "the curse" according to Deut 27:14.

Secondly, according to Deut 27:11-14, the assembly was to consist of the twelve tribes of Israel paralleling the twelve curses (Deut 27:15ff.). In Josh 8:35, however, aliens are included in the gathering as well. The manner in which Josh 8 departs from the stipulations of Deut 27 has more in common with the imperfect obedience that characterised Israel during the conquest rather than the view espoused in Josh 8:34 that "everything had been done as it was written".

Even though the relation between Deut 27 and Josh 8 has informed our understanding of the possible referents in Josh 8:34, we cannot claim to have as yet fully explained the use of כְּכָל־הַכָּתוּב.

Jenni offers yet another understanding of כְּכָל־הַכָּתוּב in Josh 8:34. His treatment complements our observations above regarding the relation between Deut 27 and Josh 8:30ff. This is the only occurrence of כתוב in a *Vergleichspräpositionale* that Jenni does not categorise under his heading "Vergleichssätze und deren Verkürzungen". Rather than viewing this expression as functioning in a way related to a comparative clause, Jenni considers it to be a statement that makes a comparison to the object of the main clause. Without realising that Josh 8:30ff. departs significantly from Deut 27, Jenni has analysed the citation base in Josh 8:34 in a way that clarifies the situation above. According to Jenni's view, כְּכָל־הַכָּתוּב indicates another way to understand the object that Joshua read ("Objektvergleiche"). Relating this to our analysis means that even though כְּכָל־הַכָּתוּב in Josh 8:34 appears to be a citation base in form, it does not function in such a way at all. If this view of Jenni is correct, then this would help explain not only the lack of consensus among scholars above but also the relation between Deut 27 and Josh 8:30ff. that made the use of a citation base with כל difficult to explain.

As it turns out, this use of כְּכָל־הַכָּתוּב is distinguishable from every other use of this phrase in the Hebrew Bible. The reconstruction of the ellipted elements of the comparison appears to be the best way to demonstrate that כתוב does not function as a citation base in Josh 8:34.

$$\text{כְּ(דִבְרֵי) כָל־הַכָּתוּב בְּסֵפֶר הַתּוֹרָה}^{175}$$

...[Joshua] read all the words of the law, the blessing and the curse, like [the words of] all that is written in the book of the law (Josh 8:34).

This reconstruction shows that כְּכָל־הַכָּתוּב merely describes a second time the object that was read. The reconstructed form כְּדִבְרֵי כָל־הַכָּתוּב demonstrates the reason for not treating כתוב in Josh 8:34 as a citation base. This reading of Josh 8:34 matches other uses of כתוב in the deuteronomistic literature.

First, as with כְּ(דִבְרֵי) כָל־הַכָּתוּב in Josh 8:34, the phrase כְּכָל־הַכָּתוּב in 2 Kgs 22:13 does not function as a citation base, i.e., it does not ascribe a referent to a source. In fact, the Chr rephrases his *Vorlage* at this point in order to make כְּכָל־הַכָּתוּב function as a citation base in 2 Chr 34:21. Secondly, this reading of Josh 8:34 results in repetition (see above) which is characteristic of the deuteronomistic literature (see Rooker and Weinfeld below).

The distinction between a citation formula that attributes a referent to another source and the use of כְּכָל־הַכָּתוּב in Josh 8:34 is significant. While our observations concerning the similarities between Deut 27 and Josh 8:30ff. are still valid, the correspondences we have noted between these two chapters do not require כְּכָל־הַכָּתוּב to function as a citation base. In fact, we have observed reasons why a citation base would be inappropriate at this point: Joshua usurped the role of the Levites as defined in Deut 27:14; and the assembly included more than the twelve tribes that Deut 27:12-13 stipulated.

---

175 For an example of his syntactic category "Objektsvergleiche", Jenni gives Ps 2:9 "כִּכְלִי יוֹצֵר תְּנַפְּצֵם 'wie (man) Töpfergeschirr (zerschmeißt) magst du sie zerschmeißen'" (31). The formula for reconstructing under the general category "Sprechakt wie Sprechvorlage/Sprechmuster" is "x redet wie die Worte des y" and this is the reason for דברי above (102-3).

Hence, in Josh 8:30ff., the use of כָּתוּב introduces two features to our analysis. In v. 31, ככתוב has a Janus use, and כְּכָל־הַכָּתוּב in v. 34 does not function as a citation base even though in form it resembles one. These uses in Josh 8:30ff. appear to reflect the period before כתוב became a developed exegetical device. Since our focus is on citation bases we will not categorise this use of a comparative construction. Its analysis is nevertheless important since it shows that not every deuteronomistic use of כתוב in a *Vergleichspräpositionale* functions as a citation base.

There is no unanimity among scholars on how to interpret the citation base (enlarged) in 1 Kgs 2:3.

אָנֹכִי הֹלֵךְ בְּדֶרֶךְ כָּל־הָאָרֶץ וְחָזַקְתָּ וְהָיִיתָ לְאִישׁ
וְשָׁמַרְתָּ אֶת־מִשְׁמֶרֶת יְהוָה אֱלֹהֶיךָ לָלֶכֶת בִּדְרָכָיו לִשְׁמֹר חֻקֹּתָיו
מִצְוֹתָיו וּמִשְׁפָּטָיו וְעֵדְוֹתָיו כַּכָּתוּב בְּתוֹרַת מֹשֶׁה לְמַעַן תַּשְׂכִּיל
אֵת כָּל־אֲשֶׁר תַּעֲשֶׂה וְאֵת כָּל־אֲשֶׁר תִּפְנֶה שָׁם (1 Kgs 2:2-3)

On one hand, Fishbane considers this to be a "literal" citation of a single regulation though he does not state the specific passage or the referent in the context that he has in mind[176]. In contrast to Fishbane, several scholars maintain that this citation base signals some sort of broad reference to legal regulations. These scholars, however, disagree on the identification of this corpus. For example, DeVries claims, "Solomon's obligation alluded to in 1 Kgs 2:3 is nothing less than the performance of the entire Pentateuch"[177]. Donner, however, considers this citation base to indicate a general reference to Deuteronomy[178]. It remains unclear what any of these scholars understand as the referent. However, a referent can be deduced from the analysis of Jenni who classifies 1 Kgs 2:3 as a *Vergleichspräpositionale* that functions as a subordinate clause in a complex comparative sentence (Type I).

A consideration of the syntax and semantics of this passage, however, appears to show that ככתוב does not qualify any clause in

---

176 Fishbane, 106, cf. 385.
177 DeVries, 625.
178 Donner, 226.

this verse[179]. First, if we read כתוב in this manner (Type I) then the referent consists of a tautological statement (שָׁמַרְתָּ...לִשְׁמֹר) which, one might expect, would be avoided. Secondly, this finite verb is construed with two other forms (...וְשָׁמַרְתָּ...וְהָיִיתָ וְחָזַקְתָּ) that together form one complex directive to Solomon. Even though a comparative clause can qualify more than one clause (see the analysis of צוה√ in the next chapter), there is not to our knowledge a scholar who reads כתוב as qualifying this complex directive[180]. Consequently, כתוב does not appear to function as a comparative clause (Type I).

This points to a use of כתוב related to the passages that qualify the nearest verbal sentence constituent. Initially this view would support the qualification of the contiguous infinitive phrase introduced by לִשְׁמֹר (Type II)[181]. In context, however, such a conclusion appears less satisfactory than considering the referent to be comprised of the two infinitive phrases לָלֶכֶת בִּדְרָכָיו לִשְׁמֹר חֻקֹּתָיו מִצְוֹתָיו וּמִשְׁפָּטָיו וְעֵדְוֹתָיו.

There are two main criteria that make the identification of this referent more plausible than those reviewed above. First, the two infinitive phrases appear to function together as one composite statement to explain the reason for the directives. Perhaps this view of the referent is further suggested by the fact that both of these sentence constituents consist of the same part of speech. Secondly, the legal language that both infinitive phrases include appears to link them together semantically. Weinfeld notes that both of these infinitive phrases consist of deuteronomistic phraseology for "observance of the law and loyalty to the covenant"[182]. It appears best to conclude that the referent of כתוב consists of both infinitive phrases (Type II).

Once the referent has been identified in 1 Kgs 2:3, then the determination of the cited legal texts becomes clearer. The first infinitive

---

179 Jenni, 30-31, 171.
180 Neither has anyone considered the initial participial clause as the sentence element modified by כתוב.
181 So Gray, 97.
182 Weinfeld, 333-34, ## 6, 6a, and 338, #21f.

phrase refers to various texts in Deut (6:7; 8:6; 10:12; 11:19, 22; 19:9; 26:17; 28:9; 30:16). On the other hand, the second infinitive phrase is a summary of the law in general.

Finally, it is noteworthy to observe the repetitive nature of the legal nouns in the last infinitive phrase. The referents of the post-exilic period, it will be observed, do not generally consist of such a repetitive nature.

2 Kgs 14:6/2 Chr 25:4 use a compound citation base to mark the referent and a quotation. This construction entails the following forms: ככתוב, אשר צוה 183, and לאמר184 (all enlarged).

וְאֶת־בְּנֵי הַמַּכִּים לֹא הֵמִית כַּכָּתוּב בְּסֵפֶר תּוֹרַת־מֹשֶׁה
אֲשֶׁר־צִוָּה יְהוָה לֵאמֹר לֹא־יוּמְתוּ אָבוֹת עַל־בָּנִים וּבָנִים לֹא־
יוּמְתוּ עַל־אָבוֹת כִּי אִם־אִישׁ בְּחֶטְאוֹ יָמוּת   (2 Kgs 14:6/2 Chr 25:4185)

In this compound citation base, ככתוב has only one relation to the context (*contra* the Janus use of ככתוב in the composite citation in Josh 8:31). The referent of ככתוב is the main clause (Type I). The quotation of Deut 24:16 is indicated by לאמר186. The Chr simply follows his *Vorlage* here. This contrasts with the occurrences of ככתוב that he has introduced in the non-synoptic material.

The remaining uses of ככתוב occur in the non-synoptic post-exilic historiography.

There is no consensus among scholars regarding the meaning of the citation bases in Ezra 3:2-4.

וַיָּכִינוּ אֶת־מִזְבַּח אֱלֹהֵי יִשְׂרָאֵל לְהַעֲלוֹת עָלָיו עֹלוֹת

---

183 As with כתוב, so we will address the various constructions in which צוה is used in a citation.

184 For לאמר as a citation device, see Fishbane, 106.

185 Read with 𝔊ᴸ cf. 2 Kgs 14:6.

186 DeVries, 625; Donner, 227. For the view that a more original form of Deut 24:16 was the basis of 2 Kgs 14:6, see Fishbane, 341. According to Fishbane, "Most probably, the original formulation of Deut. 24:16 was solely concerned to prohibit vicarious substitutions in capital cases, or their gross extension to blood relatives".

כַּכָּתוּב בְּתוֹרַת מֹשֶׁה אִישׁ־הָאֱלֹהִים (Ezra 3:2b)

וַיַּעֲשׂוּ אֶת־חַג הַסֻּכּוֹת כַּכָּתוּב וְעֹלַת יוֹם בְּיוֹם
בְּמִסְפָּר כְּמִשְׁפַּט דְּבַר־יוֹם בְּיוֹמוֹ (Ezra 3:4)

Some scholars read ככתוב in v. 2 as qualifying the context in a broad
manner. Referring to Ezra 3:1-3, Shaver states, "this first step toward a
restored religious community was taken, we are told, כתוב בתורת־
מֹשֶׁה (v. 2)"187. Commenting on the first steps made to reinstitute the
cult in vv. 1-6, Rudolph states, "alles genau nach dem ‚Gesetz Moses'
(2b)"188. Kidner's view is similar, but he accounts for both כתוב
citation bases in v. 2 and v. 4. Concerning the new start of this
community in vv. 1-6a, Kidner states, "we read of all being done *as it is
written...as it is written*"189. In terms of our analysis, it appears that
Kidner understands these as compound citations which qualify the entire
paragraph. If this is correct, then these two כתוב bases mark a
relation to the discourse.

The view that one or both of these כתוב citation bases in Ezra 3
has a wide scope of reference to the prevailing context does not appear
to be well-founded. First, all of the citation bases above are integrated
into the sentence structure of each passage. They also are not used with
any element to indicate that they refer beyond their respective sentences
(e.g., כל, pro-form עשׂה√, a summary statement, a rubric, etc.). The
fact that the scholars who treat these bases in this manner all arrive at
differing conclusions, further suggests that this approach yields
unsatisfactory results.

Secondly, none of these scholars account for the citation base
כְּמִשְׁפַּט in v. 4b190. In fact, the use of these three formulations is
distinct from the *compound* citation bases covered in the
deuteronomistic literature. In the latter, when citation bases were used
in close proximity to each other they were syntactically linked together

187 Shaver, 82.
188 Rudolph, *Esra und Nehemia,* 31.
189 Kidner, 46.
190 This formula will be treated separately in chapter 4 below.

to form a compound construction. In Ezra 3, none of these citation
bases are connected to form such a construction. Each of these bases in
v. 2 and v. 4 should be understood as having a specific scope of
reference. The use of independent citation bases in close proximity may
be an indication of a development of the use of exegetical devices in the
post-exilic community. For the use of the disjunctive clause in v. 4b to
distinguish the two citation bases in v. 4, see our treatment of כְּמִשְׁפָּט
in chapter 4 below.

Thirdly, the view of some scholars that everything had been done
according to the law does not agree with the account in Ezra 3:1-6. For
instance, the omission of a reference to the observance of the great Day
of Atonement on the tenth of Tishri suggests that everything had not
been done according to the law. Rudolph argues that this problem can
be overcome by noting that the observance of the Day of Atonement
presupposes the existence of the temple (Lev 16:7, 12ff., 33). Since
only an altar has been constructed by the time of the tenth of Tishri, the
Day of Atonement could not be observed[191].

Ezra 3:4-6, however, suggests that even though a complete
observance was impossible, a limited observance of the Day of
Atonement did occur. It is indicated that "all the sacred festivals of the
LORD" had been observed from the first day of Tishri. V. 6 ("from the
first day of the seventh month they began to offer burnt offerings to the
LORD"), however, restricts the observance at these festivals to the
presentation of burnt offerings. This restriction to the burnt offerings
agrees with the fact that only the altar had been reconstructed. While
certainly the entire legislation of the Day of Atonement could not be
observed without a sanctuary and a mercy seat, the text of Ezra 3:1-6
appears to require that the burnt offerings of the Day of Atonement were
satisfied. That is, the burnt offering of Lev 16:24 ("And he
shall...come forth and offer his burnt offering and the burnt offering of
the people, and make atonement for himself and for the people") appears
to have been fulfilled. These burnt offerings do not require anything
more extensive than the altar.

---

191 For the view that the regulations for the Day of Atonement are a very late
    addition to the law (i.e., after the time of the composition of Ezra-Neh), see
    Roland DeVaux, *Ancient Israel: Its Life and Institutions,* 2nd edn, trans. by
    John McHugh (London: Darton, Longman and Todd Ltd., 1965) 507-10.

This limited observance of the law is due to the period of transition in the early days of the restoration. The limited observance of the law, however, is a different assessment than that represented by the scholars above. The readings of these citation bases by the scholars above do not address the problem that the contents of Ezra 3:1-6 simply do not fulfill all aspects of the law for the seventh month. Hence, it appears that the law was observed to the extent that it was practicable without a complete cult.

Most importantly, when the citation bases in Ezra 3:2 and 4 are read as precise exegetical devices that pinpoint specific points of the observance of the law, the need to explain the apparent reference to the celebration of the Great Day of Atonement dissipates.

Other scholars have read these exegetical devices with a small scope of reference as we suggest. However, there are still disagreements among this second group of scholars regarding the use of citation bases in Ezra 3:1-6.

Some read כככתוב in Ezra 3:2 as qualifying the main clause (Type I). These scholars understand the construction of the altar to be the act that was accomplished according to the law. Among these scholars, however, there is disagreement concerning which pentateuchal tradition is in view here. On one hand, DeVries states, "the formula as found in Ezra 3:2 pertains to the altar of burnt offering referred to in Exod 27:1-8; 38:1-7"[192]. If DeVries is correct, then the citation base in Ezra 3:2 indicates that the altar was constructed with acacia wood and with horns on its corners, overlaid with bronze and accompanied with various implements. On the other hand, Clines claims that "the altar would have been rebuilt of unhewn stones, according to the law of Moses (Exod. 20:25; cf. Dt. 27:6; 1 Mac. 4:47)"[193].

Another referent altogether has been understood by those who read the infinitive phrase לְהַעֲלוֹת עָלָיו עֹלוֹת as the deed authorised by

---

192 DeVries, 625. One should disregard DeVries' analysis of Ezra 3:2 as "a covenant to put away foreign wives" with the citation formula כַּתּוֹרָה (621, n. 8). DeVries is obviously referring to Ezra 10:1-3.

193 Clines, 65; see also Blenkinsopp, 97. Gunneweg understands the construction of the altar yet never specifies the legal basis (70-73).

כתוב 194. According to this view, the deed authorised by ככתוב is
the offering of burnt sacrifices. Our syntactic analysis so far supports
this reading. That is, ככתוב does not qualify the entire sentence, but
only the nearest verbal form(s) (Type II).

The latter view appears to be supported on other grounds as well.
For instance, the fact that the writer has not distinguished between the
two traditions of altar construction in the law indicated by DeVries and
Clines above, suggests that this is not the act he intends to be authorised
by ככתוב. Presumably, the writer would have been aware of both
traditions and would have wanted to relate which one had been followed
if the construction of the altar was the intended referent. The additional
qualification "the altar of the God of Israel" also does not clarify which
tradition was followed and is probably to be attributed to the fact that the
altar was at the site of the first temple. The altar may have been built
according to one of these traditions but it appears that the intent of the
author in using the citation base is to show rather that the burnt offerings
had been properly observed (cf. Ezra 3:5-6). Consequently, there is no
need to resolve the debate between DeVries and Clines195.

In v. 2, we conclude that the referent is לְהַעֲלוֹת עָלָיו עֹלוֹת (Type
II). This referent does not appear to have a specific regulation in view
but refers to the law in a general manner. As Ezra 3:3-6 attests, this
altar would be used for various sorts of offerings (Succoth, new moon,
regular burnt offerings, all the sacred festivals, etc.). If this view of the
referent is correct, then the legal texts to which Ezra 3:2 refers are those
concerned with burnt offerings in general.

Based on this view, the exegetical process marked by ככתוב in
Ezra 3:2 is characterised by the observance of the law to the extent that it
was practicable (see our discussion of the Day of Atonement). The
exegetes of this community, thus, did not consider the impossibility of

---

194 Ryle, 39; Donner, 227-28. Donner suggests that Deut 27:6 is the text behind
Ezra 3:2, stressing that העלה עליו עלות ליהוה "kommt in Verbindung
mit einem Altar innerhalb des Pentateuch nur Dt 27,6 vor" (227).

195 Perhaps altar construction could not be accomplished ככתוב in any respect. In
light of the circumstances of these exiles, either of these traditions of altar
construction may have been difficult to manage.

fulfilling some aspects of a law as a basis for being unfaithful to what could be observed.

In Ezra 3:4, the referent of ככתוב is the main clause וַיַּעֲשׂוּ אֶת־חַג הַסֻּכּוֹת (Type I). The עשׂה√ does not function as a pro-form since with חַג it denotes festive celebration ("to hold festive celebration")[196]. The most significant feature of this citation base is that ככתוב occurs without any subsequent reference to the cited corpora (e.g., "in the law of Moses"). In fact, the use of such appellations of corpora are deuteronomic. Weinfeld lists "this law", "this book of the law", "the law of Moses", and "the book of the law of Moses" among the deuteronomic phraseology associated with "observance of the law and loyalty to the covenant"[197]. Since this citation base occurs without these appellations only in the non-synoptic post-exilic historiography, the independent use of ככתוב appears to be another development of this exegetical device.

The texts referred to by ככתוב in Ezra 3:4 appear to be both Num 29:12-38 and Deut 16:13-15. Donner suggests Deut 16:13 because "nur dort und nirgendwo anders ist das Laubhüttenfest Akkusativobjekt zum Verbum ‚machen, veranstalten' (עשׂה)"[198]. However, the use of the distinctive phrase בְּמִסְפָּר כְּמִשְׁפַּט in both Num 29:12-38 (seven times) and Ezra 3:4b suggests that the influence of both pentateuchal texts can be detected in Ezra 3:4. Since כמשפט and ככתוב in v. 4 do not form a compound citation base, we will address the former formula in a subsequent chapter.

Another disputed passage concerns the proclamation in Neh 8:15b[199]. The function of ככתוב appears to be limited to the proclamation stated in v. 15b (see further below). Scholars agree that

---

196 L. Koehler and W. Baumgartner, *The Hebrew and Aramaic Lexicon of the Old Testament,* trans. and ed. by M. E. J. Richardson *et al.,* vol. I (Leiden: E. J. Brill, 1994) 289.

197 Weinfeld, 339, ## 23, 24.

198 Donner, 228.

199 Neh 8:14-15a contains another citation construction (מצא כתוב אשר... וַאֲשֶׁר) that will be treated after we finish treating the citation bases that occur in a *Vergleichspräpositionale.*

Lev 23 is the text being reflected on in Neh 8:14f. since Num 29 docs not refer to the seventh month or the assembly on the eighth day[200].

צְאוּ הָהָר וְהָבִיאוּ עֲלֵי־זַיִת וַעֲלֵי־עֵץ שֶׁמֶן וַעֲלֵי הֲדַס
וַעֲלֵי תְמָרִים וַעֲלֵי עֵץ עָבֹת לַעֲשֹׂת סֻכֹּת כַּכָּתוּב (Neh 8:15b)

There are at least three ways that scholars have treated ככתוב (enlarged). Two of these views appear to read ככתוב as qualifying the clauses introduced with the two imperatives ("go out to the hills and bring").

Some scholars understand the referent of ככתוב to be "the command to collect branches to make booths"[201]. Discounting any influence from Lev 23:40, Shaver states, "since no other text in the Hebrew Bible even contains the command to collect branches, let alone with the stated purpose of building booths, we must conclude that if the Chronicler had a specific text in mind as his authority, that text is no longer extant"[202]. Consequently, he declares that this command has not been preserved in the Hebrew Bible[203]. Williamson has observed that Shaver's view runs counter to what is generally deemed to be the expansionistic nature of the law.

Most recently, Donner has offered a vastly different explanation of ככתוב in Neh 8:15. Even though he admits that there are several parallels between Lev 23 and Neh 8:15, Donner observes that the exact contents of the proclamation are not located in this legal text. He understands the referent to entail the different species of branches as well as the command to build booths. Donner prefers to explain these differences between the proclamation and the law in terms of the author's carelessness or his (faulty) memory. He states, "ein genauer Vergleich von Neh 8,15 mit Lev 23,40 ergibt allerdings, daß der Chronist den Leviticustext nicht ganz genau, sondern etwas sorglos — aus dem Gedächtnis? — zitiert hat"[204]. If Donner is correct that the

---

200 Most recently, Donner, 228; Gunneweg, 116.
201 Shaver, 127. See also Rudolph, 151; Houtman, 104-5; Ackroyd, 297.
202 Shaver, 102-3.
203 *Ibid.*, 127; see also Gunneweg, 116.
204 Donner, 228.

differences between the proclamation and the law are to be attributed to the author's carelessness or his (faulty) memory, then this has serious ramifications for our assessment of the exegetical process of the community. While Donner's view is of course possible, it is surprising that he does not address the other ways that scholars have sought to explain this use of the citation base. Thus, the burden of proof rests on Donner to demonstrate that other views are implausible.

A third group of scholars understands the referent to be לַעֲשׂת סֻכֹּת (Type II)[205]. This view, which is supported by our syntactic examination, does not attribute to the law the command to collect branches or the various species of branches stated earlier in this verse. These scholars understand the command to make booths to be implicit in the directive to live in such structures in Lev 23:42. Referring to Lev 23:40-43, Clines argues,

> Ezra would doubtless have argued that what the law implied it also commanded. Why else would boughs have been gathered at the festival of booths except to make booths?[206]

Rather than concluding that Neh 8:15b is an indication of a law that was not preserved or the carelessness of an exegete, this referent indicates that the authority of the law extends to its obvious implications.

Rather than being part of the referent, the remainder of the proclamation consists of a contemporary interpretation of the requirements of Lev 23 by the post-exilic community. This interpretation entailed the command to go out and collect the various species of branches listed. Thus, the proclamation is comprised of a reference to the law and a contemporary interpretation. This suggests that the mention of different species of branches may best be attributed to the types that were plentiful enough to supply the required amount for the assembly[207].

---

205 √עשׂה ("to construct") here clearly does not function as a pro-form.

206 Clines, 187. Similarly Blenkinsopp, 292. For the view that this interpretation process was "an etymological exegesis of the noun 'booths'", see Fishbane, 111. For a critique of this position, see Williamson, "History", 30.

207 For the view that Neh 8:15ff. suggests that the proclamation also contained a summons to Jerusalem, see Williamson, *Ezra, Nehemiah,* 295. Since this would have been deduced only from Deut 16:15, he concludes that this is an indication of "Scripture interpreting Scripture" (Lev 23:40ff. and Deut 16:15).

The citation base in Neh 8:15b is another example of the shortened form of ככתוב without a subsequent reference to its source (e.g., בְּתוֹרַת מֹשֶׁה). ככתוב marks a Type II qualification as well. Summarising the other noteworthy features of the exegetical process here, we note that: the referent consists of a direct implication from the law; a reference to the law is accompanied by its interpretation; and a contiguous relation exists between the citation base and the referent. The fact that a referent may be comprised of an inference of the law can be contrasted with the quotations that we observed in the deuteronomistic literature. Some of these features may be part of the development in the use of ככתוב and Scripture.

The various referents that scholars have understood in Neh 10:35 (34) have already been introduced in chapter one as an example of the present state of scholarship concerning citation bases. At this point in our study, certain observations can be made regarding this verse. First, in light of all the referents that have been attributed to ככתוב in this passage, it is surprising that only Rudolph has considered a Type I qualification for this citation base. It will be recalled, however, that even Rudolph does not unequivocally defend this position. A consideration of the other sentences we have observed that are comprised of a finite verb and two infinitive phrases with a subsequent citation base appears to inform the way to read ככתוב in Neh 10:35 (34). This final positioning of the citation base so far in our study has never qualified the finite verb. Therefore, Rudolph's supposition, which has not been followed, that the entire complex act of Neh 10:35 (34) may constitute the referent appears to have little support (Type I).

It is arguable whether dismissing the above reading of ככתוב (Type I) entirely eliminates the view that the wood offering is the referent. Since אֶת־קָרְבַּן־הָעֵצִים is the implied direct object of the first infinitive phrase ("to bring it [the wood offering]..."), some might claim that the identification of this sentence constituent as the referent would still support the view that the citation base authorises the wood offering from the law.

Neh 10:35 (34), however, has other syntactic features which are worthy of further attention. In Neh 10:35, there are three adverbial phrases ("according to our fathers' households, at fixed times, year by year") between the first infinitive phrase (לְהָבִיא לְבֵית אלהינו) and the second one (לְבַעֵר עַל־מִזְבַּח יהוה אלהינו). Note that all interpreters agree that these adverbial phrases qualify the previous infinitive phrase ("to bring it [the wood offering] to the house of our God"). Hence, it appears that if the writer wanted the wood offering to be the referent of the citation base, then he would have placed ככתוב somewhere in this series of adverbial phrases. In fact, he would have had to place it as the initial adverbial phrase in order to ascribe only "the wood offering" to the law. For instance, had he placed it as the fourth in this series of adverbial phrases, then the referent would consist of the entire complex act of "the wood offering according to our fathers' households, at fixed times, year by year".

Consideration of the second infinitive phrase appears further to support the view that each infinitive phrase with its respective indirect object is qualified by its own adverbial construction(s). That is, ככתוב is placed in respect to the second infinitive phrase in the same manner as the three adverbial phrases are to the first infinitive phrase (Type II). Perhaps, the diagram below best represents our point:

וְהַגּוֹרָלוֹת הִפַּלְנוּ עַל־קֻרְבַּן הָעֵצִים הַכֹּהֲנִים הַלְוִיִּם וְהָעָם
לְהָבִיא [וְאֶת־קֻרְבַּן הָעֵצִים] לְבֵית אֱלֹהֵינוּ
↑ לְבֵית־אֲבֹתֵינוּ לְעִתִּים מְזֻמָּנִים שָׁנָה בְשָׁנָה
לְבַעֵר [וְאֶת־הָעֵצִים] עַל־מִזְבַּח יְהוָה אֱלֹהֵינוּ
↑ כַּכָּתוּב בַּתּוֹרָה (Neh 10:35)

Even if we analyse the semantic relation between these two infinitive phrases as we did with other Type II passages, there still appears to be no basis for considering "the wood offering" as part of the referent[208]. These two infinitive phrases relate two different propositions and do not have a corresponding semantic nature. In fact, our analysis suggests that if "the wood offering" was to be defended as the referent, then the

---

208 On this view, both infinitive phrases would then be the referent.

second infinitive phrase would have to be included as well. But there is not a scholar who defends such a position.

We conclude then that ככתוב in Neh 10:35 qualifies only לְבַעֵר [וְאֶת־הָעֵצִים] עַל־מִזְבַּח יְהוָה אֱלֹהֵינוּ (Type II). The syntax and semantics of this verse support the qualification of only the contiguous infinitive phrase.

Our analysis supports the view of the legal development in Neh 10:35 first articulated by Clines as "the creation of facilitating law"[209]. He describes this category as the "establishment of machinery for carrying out a prescription; thus 10:35...enables the law of Leviticus 6:1-6, that fire should burn continually on the altar, to be carried out"[210]. Two levels of the exegetical process are observable in Neh 10:35. The reference to the law is made by the second infinitive phrase while the remainder of the verse refers to the means adopted by the post-exilic community to ensure this legal requirement was satisfied. Williamson has referred to these two features of the exegetical process as "text and interpretation"[211].

At this point in our study, Neh 10:35 appears to provide particular insight into the use of prepositional phrases introduced with כ. As we have already suggested, the position of such phrases is crucial for properly identifying what they qualify. These constructions have the capability to mark a range of adverbial and adnominal relations. In a VSO language like Hebrew, prepositional phrases have mobility in the sentence. The characteristics of these constructions appear to require that they be strategically placed so that the relation to the qualified element is intelligible. We have indicated the way that the semantics of certain passages may be part of what establishes the scope or limits of the qualification. The three adverbials that qualify the first infinitive phrase in Neh 10:35 (34), suggest that the principle of the contiguous placement of adverbial constructions may be interrupted only by another adverbial construction. It has seemed necessary to treat these issues in order to advance the present state of scholarship on ככתוב as well as

---

209 Clines, "Nehemiah 10", 112.
210 *Ibid.*
211 Williamson, "History", 28-29.

other citation bases and formulæ. It does not appear to be the case that such syntactic and semantic issues have been considered by Semitists to be relevant to the identification of the referents of citation bases, or even to comparative statements in general.

Neh 10:37 (36) contains another citation base (enlarged) that is debated among scholars.

וְאֶת־בְּכֹרוֹת בָּנֵינוּ וּבְהֶמְתֵּינוּ כַּכָּתוּב בַּתּוֹרָה וְאֶת־בְּכוֹרֵי בְקָרֵינוּ
וְצֹאנֵינוּ לְהָבִיא לְבֵית אֱלֹהֵינוּ לַכֹּהֲנִים הַמְשָׁרְתִים בְּבֵית אֱלֹהֵינוּ
(Neh 10:37)

Shaver considers ככתוב above to mark the provision of the first fruits[212]. Such an indentification of the referent here is surprising insofar as the obligation to provide the first fruits is in v. 36 (35) while the citation base ככתוב occurs in v. 37 (36) which is concerned with the firstborn. Shaver does not support his reading of ככתוב which appears doubtful. Even though the pledge in Neh 10:29ff. does contain some uncommon syntactic features, the syntax in this list of obligations is not so unwieldy as to permit Shaver's view[213].

Donner, referring to such passages as Deut 12:6 and 15:19 that use בקר and צאן exclusively, appears to understand the entire direct object ("the first-born of our sons and of our cattle, and the first-born of our herds and our flocks") as the referent of ככתוב[214]. While Donner's assertion remains possible, another view of the referent appears to be more plausible.

Some scholars understand ככתוב to qualify only the first nominal phrase in v. 37 (36) (Type III). For instance, Blenkinsopp states, "it is

---

212 Shaver, 89, see also 84.

213 For the view that the first direct object is to be read with "unto the house of the LORD" in v. 36b, see G. Brin, "The Firstling of Unclean Animals", *JQR* 68 (1978) 2. The semantic nature of the first two sets of direct objects in v. 37a, however, suggests that they are coordinated by *waw-copulativum*. Hence, Brin's view should not be followed (see further below on the placement of ככתוב in v. 37).

214 Donner 231-32. Clines may also understand the referent in this manner ("Nehemiah 10", 113).

noticeable…that the qualification 'as prescribed in the law' refers only to sons and livestock generically, distinguishing these from the cattle and sheep which are destined for sacrifice"[215]. Williamson has provided a sound basis for supporting this general view of the referent, but he shows that there is more to this interpretation than Blenkinsopp has indicated. Williamson has shown that the placement of ככתוב in Neh 10:37 corresponds with the distinction drawn between the firstborn sons and animals (בהמה) at Num 18:15 and 17[216]. According to this view, ככתוב has the force of designating בהמה as the "unclean animals" in Num 18:15. This reading corresponds with our Type III use of ככתוב which reflects the precise scope with which this citation base may be used in the post-exilic era. Once again, the contiguous placement of the citation base attributes only the first noun phrase to the law. As in 2 Chr 35:26f. ("Now the rest of the deeds of Josiah, *even his acts of piety* as it is written in the law of the LORD, and his acts…"), only one of a series of nominal phrases is attributed to the law in v. 37 (36).

As we have seen in other places, Neh 10:37 (36) demonstrates the great adaptability that ככתוב has to be strategically positioned in order to distinguish a referent from its context.

Recent treatments of 2 Chr 23:18 have only expanded the range of referents that have been defended for כַּכָּתוּב here.

וַיַּעֲמֵד יְהוֹיָדָע פְּקֻדֹּת בֵּית יְהוָה בְּיַד הַכֹּהֲנִים הַלְוִיִּם אֲשֶׁר חָלַק דָּוִיד
עַל־בֵּית יְהוָה לְהַעֲלוֹת עֹלוֹת יְהוָה כַּכָּתוּב בְּתוֹרַת מֹשֶׁה בְּשִׂמְחָה
וּבְשִׁיר עַל יְדֵי דָוִיד (2 Chr 23:18)

According to most scholars, ככתוב should be read as qualifying the infinitive phrase לְהַעֲלוֹת עֹלוֹת יְהוָה (Type II)[217].

This view has been recently challenged by three scholars. According to this emerging new position, ככתוב qualifies the main clause (Type I). For instance, Shaver understands the act that is

---

215 Blenkinsopp, 318. DeVries, 625.

216 Williamson, *Ezra, Nehemiah*, 337; and, "History", 28.

217 Japhet, 836; Williamson, *1 and 2 Chronicles*, 318; and, "History", 28; DeVries, 625; Fishbane, 106, 213; Curtis, 431-32.

authorised by the citation base to be "the restoration of the Yahwistic temple personnel and sacrificial ritual"[218]. Contrasting his view against that of Williamson, Donner states, "die Formel ‚wie geschrieben steht' an dieser Stelle…einfach an den Sachverhalt erinnert, daß der Opferdienst nach dem Zeugnis der ganzen Thora Aufgabe der Priester war; vgl. Num 18, 5.7. Dt 33,10 u. ö."[219]. Dörrfuß also views this citation base as emphasising that the arrangement of the cult was in the written law[220]. However, according to his view, the citation base was part of a "Mosaic" redaction of the early second century B.C. to correct the idealised image of the Davidic kingdom and the cult.

Shaver and Donner do not defend their position so it is difficult to know the basis for their identification of the referent concerning the restoration of the cult. Furthermore, there appears to be no contextual, syntactic or other reason for accepting this reading of כתוב (Type I). An issue that appears to challenge this view of ככתוב is that there is another finite verb that is in closer proximity to the citation base than the first form in the passage. In light of what we have observed, this issue would have to be addressed if we are to accept the recent views of Shaver and Donner. These scholars could attempt to defend their view on linguistic grounds (Topic/Comment), but, as we have shown in chapter one, such an approach makes these exegetical devices unnecessarily arbitrary. In light of our growing syntactic analysis, we conclude that the burden of proof rests on those who advocate the view that ככתוב should not be read with a Type II qualification (see below on Dörrfuß).

The ramifications of this debate are significant. 2 Chr 23:18 is a passage that usually surfaces in the assessment of the Chr's view toward his authorities. In recent years, there has been no shortage of proposals concerning the significance of 2 Chr 23:18 on this issue. DeVries argues that 2 Chr 23:18 is one of the passages in the book where the relation between Mosaic and Davidic authority can be seen to be complementary. The reestablishment of the burnt offerings,

---

218 Shaver, 77.
219 Donner, 229; see also Rudolph, 273.
220 Ernst Michael Dörrfuß, *Mose in den Chronikbüchern Garant theokratischer Zukunftserwartung*, BZAW 219 (Berlin: Walter de Gruyter, 1994) 202.

according to DeVries, was fulfilled based on the rule of Moses, while the arrangement of the Levites and their liturgy was authorised by David[221].

Dörrfuß also considers Mosaic and Davidic authority to be distinguishable, but rather than seeing them as complementary they are in his view antithetic. According to his view, the Mosaic redaction of Chronicles in the early second century B.C. was a correction of the idealised portrayal of the Davidic kingdom and the cult in Jerusalem. In this editorial work, Moses becomes the surety of a theocratic hope for the future of this dominated Jewish community. In 2 Chr 23:18, ככתוב בתורת משה was inserted as part of this Mosaic redaction in order to stress the establishment of the cult according to the written law. In this way, according to Dörrfuß, the Mosaic redaction forms an antithesis to the glorification of David in 2 Chr 23:18[222].

A vastly different assessment of the relation between these authorities is given by Shaver. He argues, "2 Chron. 23:18 so entwines Davidic and Mosaic authority that one must conclude that for the Chronicler a distinction between what was required by David and what by Moses was non-existent--or at least not important"[223]. This view can be maintained only by reading ככתוב with a large scope of reference which Shaver does not justify. We have observed Shaver's unwieldy reading of ככתוב elsewhere, but such a view of the syntax of Vergleichspräpositionalen is not supported by our analysis. His view of the relation of these authorities does not fit with the general picture of the Chr's history, i.e., a large part of Chronicles is dedicated to the enduring significance of David to the post-exilic generation (highlights include 1 Chr 3; 23-27; 28:11-19; 2 Chr 8:14-15).

Our research supports the position of DeVries on 2 Chr 23:18. While Dörrfuß's view remains possible, it does not appear to us that the Mosaic references have been part of a systematic redactional process or that David and the cult are portrayed idealistically (e.g., 1 Chr 21:1-17)[224]. Furthermore, Sweeney has astutely observed that "Dörrfuß's

---

221 DeVries, 634.
222 Dörrfuß, 202.
223 Shaver, 118.
224 Dörrfuß excludes the reference to Moses in 1 Chr 5:29.

literary-critical conclusions concerning the secondary additions of references to Moses presuppose the fundamental Wellhausenian dichotomy between priest and prophet or priest and monarch that is increasingly questioned in current studies concerning the social roles of leadership figures in ancient Judean and Near Eastern societies"[225].

According to our analysis, the expressions עַל יְדֵי דָוִיד ("according to the order of David") and ככתוב בתורת משה distinguish between Davidic and Mosaic authority in 2 Chr 23:18. In this manner, the expression used for David functions much like a citation base. Once again, in the post-exilic era, such expressions may be used in close proximity without forming a composite construction. This specific marking of authority in 2 Chr 23:18 complements our analysis of ככתוב which is emerging as a developed exegetical device with a much more specific scope of reference than many scholars have attributed to it. From a syntactic point of view, it is difficult to see how these two prepositional phrases can be read in another way without understanding them as being completely arbitrary in their relation to their respective contexts.

The referent of ככתוב consists of a summary of all the burnt offerings of the law. These references to authority in 2 Chr 23:18 are part of the Chr's rewriting of Jehoiada's reestablishment of the cult. As we have observed elsewhere, the Chr takes more interest in citation bases than his *Vorlage*. In 2 Chr 23:18, he also carefully marks traditional authorities since both expressions have their own referent ("to offer burnt offerings to the LORD, *as it is written in the law of Moses*, with rejoicing and with singing, *according to the order of David*", NRSV). The referent of ככתוב is the contiguous infinitive phrase (Type II).

In 2 Chr 30:5, ככתוב appears to qualify the nearest clause (Type I).

$$\text{כִּי לֹא לָרֹב עָשׂוּ כַּכָּתוּב} \quad \text{(2 Chr 30:5)}$$

The referent includes only לָרֹב עָשׂוּ [226]. This referent consists of an

---

225 Marvin A. Sweeney, book review, *JBL* 116 (1997) 338.
226 For the view that לָרֹב should be rendered as "often" (JPS), see Japhet, 940-41.

obvious implication from Deut 16:1-8[227]. This citation base in 2 Chr 30:5 is one of the uses of ככתוב in the non-synoptic post-exilic historiography which are not followed by a reference to a source. These two features (a referent consisting of an obvious implication from the law and the use of ככתוב without a following statement referring to a corpus) are emerging as features of a developed exegetical device. 2 Chr 30:5 also attests the use of a citation base to mark aspects of the law that were not being observed. The Chr has introduced this citation base in his history (see below).

The most recent treatment of the citation base in 2 Chr 31:3 has attributed a new referent to ככתוב.

וּמְנָת הַמֶּלֶךְ מִן־רְכוּשׁוֹ לָעֹלוֹת לְעֹלוֹת הַבֹּקֶר וְהָעֶרֶב וְהָעֹלוֹת
לַשַּׁבָּתוֹת וְלֶחֳדָשִׁים וְלַמֹּעֲדִים כַּכָּתוּב בְּתוֹרַת יְהוָה   (2 Chr 31:3)

Donner concludes that the referent of ככתוב is the king's contribution for the burnt offerings[228]. Donner reads ככתוב as qualifying the entire sentence (Type I). At this point in our study, there appears to be little ground for this view. While a complex comparative sentence may at times possess a non-verbal main clause, this is uncommon. We have also shown that the bipartite information structure of a sentence (Topic/Comment), to which Donner could appeal, is unhelpful for determining the referent of citation bases (see chapter one). We will return to another weakness in Donner's position after we review an alternative view of the referent.

The majority of scholars have read this passage as referring to the detailed list of offerings לְעֹלוֹת הַבֹּקֶר וְהָעֶרֶב וְהָעֹלוֹת לַשַּׁבָּתוֹת וְלֶחֳדָשִׁים וְלַמֹּעֲדִים[229]. The most significant contextual issue appears

---

227 Japhet states, "in the present text we find no actual literal allusions to the law as phrased in Deut. 16" (941).

228 Donner, 230.

229 Japhet, 964; Shaver, 126, cf. 90-91; Williamson, *1 and 2 Chronicles,* 373-74; Fishbane, 106, 112, n. 21. DeVries identifies the referent as "the various [עֹלוֹת] mentioned, not to the king's gift (*contra,* Rudolph...)" (625, n. 18). Rudolph, however, holds the same view as DeVries. Rudolph states, ככתוב "bezieht sich nicht auf 3aα, sondern auf die Opfer' (304).

to be that this phrase stands in apposition to לְעֹלוֹת which immediately precedes this list [230]. We have previously observed the referent of ככתוב being embedded in a series of specific nominal forms (2 Chr 35:26; Neh 10:37) in post-exilic writing. It should also be noted that even though this referent is a long and *detailed* list it is not the lengthy and *repetitive* one observed in the deuteronomistic literature (1 Kgs 2:3). A referent that is more specific than its head noun, whether by apposition or *waw-explicativum*, constitutes a use of ככתוב (Type III). Hence, the majority view appears to be correct.

Now that we have identified the referent we can return to Donner's treatment of this citation base. He attempts to identify "the king's contribution" by the following argument. Commenting on Rudolph's view of the referent ("the sacrifices", v. 3aα), Donner states, "das ist syntaktisch möglich, wenn auch nicht sicher zu erweisen"[231]. In his identification of the referent, Donner commits a non-sequitur. It simply does not follow that "the king's contribution" is established as the correct referent by claiming that the alternative is only syntactically possible. In contrast to Donner, we have identified reasons for the view maintained by Rudolph and many others.

The Chr's addition of the citation base and the detailed referent in 2 Chr 31:3 is related to some of his central concerns in his history. In 2 Chr 31:2ff., Hezekiah restores the cult that had been shut down by Ahaz (28:24-25)[232]. Williamson has shown how the Chr has depicted Hezekiah's provision for burnt offerings and the cult on the basis of Solomon's institution of the temple (8:12-15). With this kind of rewritten history, the Chr has provided a model for his community which is largely based on the golden age of Israel before the division into the northern and southern kingdoms. Furthermore, his introduction of the detailed referent and the citation base suggest that he is stressing the fact that faithfulness to the cult cannot be divorced from Israel's written tradition. The text referred to in 2 Chr 31:3 appears to be Num 28-29.

---

230 Strictly speaking we would expect the preposition ל on הָעֹלוֹת, the middle form in the list (cf. GK § 131h).
231 Donner, *ibid.*
232 Williamson, 373; Japhet, 963.

In 2 Chr 35:12, a considerable number of referents have been attributed to ככתוב (enlarged).

וַיָּסִירוּ הָעֹלָה לְתִתָּם לְמִפְלַגּוֹת לְבֵית־אָבוֹת לִבְנֵי הָעָם
לְהַקְרִיב לַיהוָה כַּכָּתוּב בְּסֵפֶר מֹשֶׁה וְכֵן לַבָּקָר (2 Chr 35:12)

Some scholars read ככתוב as qualifying the main clause (Type I). For instance, Shaver states, "in v. 12 it is said that the burnt offerings were set apart to be offered 'as it is written...'"[233]. However, Shaver also appears to read ככתוב in yet another manner. Commenting on vv. 11-12, he states, "the priests sprinkled the blood 'as it is written in the book of Moses' (ככתוב בספר מֹשֶׁה, vv. 11-12)"[234]. We observe in Shaver another example of how a scholar has identified more than one referent in the examination of a citation base.

Fishbane, like Shaver's second view, maintains that all of the events associated with the paschal sacrifice in vv. 11-12a were performed according to the law[235]. According to these scholars, ככתוב qualifies vv. 11-12a. Their reading of the citation base entails a qualification of three clauses. In light of these readings of ככתוב, Shaver and Fishbane conclude that there is no pentateuchal basis for the act authorised by this citation base.

Other scholars have read ככתוב as qualifying the contiguous infinitive phrase[236]. We have encountered this general sentence structure above (finite verb and two infinitive phrases with the citation base following the second infinitive phrase). In 2 Chr 35:12, it appears to be significant that the two infinitives relate to separate propositions and that each introduces an infinitive phrase. It appears that the forms ככתוב and לַיהוָה are placed in respect to לְהַקְרִיב as the forms לְמִפְלַגּוֹת לְבֵית־אָבוֹת לִבְנֵי הָעָם are placed to the first infinitive in the sentence (see Neh 10:35 [34]). Consequently, this latter group of

---

233 Shaver, 115.
234 *Ibid.*, 116.
235 Fishbane, 137.
236 Japhet, 1052; Williamson, "History", 29; Rudolph, 327.

scholars is correct to identify לְהַקְרִיב [אֶת־הָעֹלָה] לַיהוָה as the referent (Type II).

2 Chr 35:12 consists of a reference to the law as well as its interpretation. Lev 3 is the text in mind here (cf. the distinctive use of √קרב and √סור in 2 Chr 35:12 and Lev 3). The interpretation in v. 12 consisted of the fatty pieces[237] of the passover lambs being presented as a burnt offering according to Lev 3, while, according to Japhet, it appears that the Levites also replaced the role of the laymen[238].

The Chr has concentrated several כָּתוּב citation bases at the end of his history in a manner that emphasises the importance of the authority of Israel's written tradition for his day. In this regard, the Chr focuses on the Passover celebrations of Hezekiah and Josiah in the final chapters of his history. The Chr marks the imperfect observance of Passover under Hezekiah with two negative uses of ככתוב (2 Chr 30:5, 18). In contrast to these two citation bases in 2 Chr 30, the Chr emphasises the great success of a Passover celebration during Josiah's reign. The Chr achieves this contrast in part by employing two positive forms of this same citation base (35:12, 26). In v. 12, כַּכָּתוּב בְּסֵפֶר מֹשֶׁה indicates that the burnt offerings had been fulfilled according to the written traditions. In light of the way the Chr has used כָּתוּב in these two accounts of a Passover celebration, it is not surprising that the Chr also rewrites the summary of Josiah's reign with חסדיו ככתוב (2 Chr 35:26).

The importance of the written tradition is marked with another כָּתוּב citation base earlier in the Chr's narrative of Josiah. After hearing the reading of the law book that had just been discovered, the Chr presents Josiah as using the citation base כְּכָל־הַכָּתוּב. Like the two negative citation bases in Hezekiah's Passover, this form marks Israel's shortcomings with respect to the written tradition ("the wrath of the LORD that is poured out on us is great, because our ancestors did

---

237 JPS renders the beginning of this verse as "they removed the parts to be burnt...". For the translation of עלה as "(fatty) parts", see Japhet, 1052, and Rudolph, 327.
238 Japhet, 1052.

not…act *according to all that is written* in this book"). The Chr presents
Josiah as the key figure of his generation who restored the written
traditions in Israel. Josiah takes a pledge to adhere to the book of the
law (34:29ff.). As a result of Josiah's leadership, all Israel and Judah
observed a Passover that was unsurpassed in the history of the
monarchy ("No passover like it had been kept in Israel since the days of
the prophet Samuel; none of the kings of Israel had kept such a passover
as was kept by Josiah, by the priests and the Levites, by all Judah and
Israel who were present, and by the inhabitants of Jerusalem", 2 Chr
35:18, NRSV). The Chr has presented Josiah as a model of faithfulness
to the written tradition. In light of the Chr's use of the כָּתוּב citation
bases above, his rewriting of the regnal source formula becomes all the
more understandable (i.e., "his acts of piety *as it is written*", 2 Chr
35:26). The Chr's presentation of Hezekiah's Passover with negative
citation bases makes the conformity to the legal traditions in Josiah's
day even more prominent. In his rewriting of the account of Josiah,
part of what the Chr appears to be emphasising is the importance of the
observance of the written authority for his community. The Chr even
cites the *written* authority of David and Solomon in v. 4 ("And prepare
yourselves by your fathers' households in your divisions, according to
the writing of David king of Israel and according to the writing of his
son Solomon"). As we will see below, there are even more citation
bases in the Chr's treatment of Josiah's reign.

In BA, the sole occurrence of the noun כְּתָב in a comparative
citation base has elicited a number of proposals[239]. Scholars have
frequently considered this form together with several of those above.

וַהֲקִימוּ כָהֲנַיָּא בִּפְלֻגָּתְהוֹן וְלֵוָיֵא בְּמַחְלְקָתְהוֹן עַל־עֲבִידַת בֵּית
אֱלָהָא דִּי בִירוּשְׁלֶם כִּכְתָב סְפַר מֹשֶׁה (Ezra 6:18)[240]

Several scholars understand the referent of כִּכְתָב to be the appointment
of priests and Levites in their various divisions and courses. Since

---

239 Ezra 7:22 states that the decree of Artaxerxes was not limiting the amount of
    salt, in contrast to the other supplies that were to be provided by the treasures of
    the province according to prescribed limits.
240 Read with 𝕲^L, 𝕾.

David is the founder of these divisions (1 Chr 23-26), scholars have sought various ways to explain the apparent attribution of these measures to סֵפֶר מֹשֶׁה.

Some scholars maintain that Ezra 6:18 demonstrates that the law book of the post-exilic author contained legislation concerning the organisation of the priests and Levites in the cult[241]. Houtman uses this verse to support the conclusion that "the law-book which the books of Ezra and Nehemiah suppose cannot be identified with the Pentateuch or a part of it"[242]. Drawing an analogy to the Temple Scroll of Qumran, Houtman suggests that the law book presupposed by Ezra-Nehemiah was one of the law codes that existed beside the Pentateuch before the latter was canonised. In contrast to Houtman, Shaver uses Ezra 6:18 to conclude that the Chr's "Torah book appears to be more than the canonical Pentateuch, in which case, at least for the Chronicler, the canonization of the Torah had not yet occurred"[243]. Williamson has observed that the process described here by Shaver runs contrary to what is customarily seen as the expansionistic nature of the law in Israel[244]. Blenkinsopp suggests that the occasion for the reorganisation of the cultic attendants was the "Passover which, like that of Josiah, had to be carried out in conformity with Mosaic law (2 Chron. 35:6)"[245].

Another group of scholars explains this apparent attribution of Davidic directives to the law in terms of the origin of Ezra 6:18. Some scholars who believe the Chr is largely responsible for Ezra-Nehemiah conclude that Ezra 6:18 indicates that there was another author for Ezra 6:16-18[246]. Williamson, who does not consider the Chr responsible for Ezra-Nehemiah, suggests that the ascription of these divisions or courses to "the book of Moses" in Ezra 6:18 is similar in some respects to the work of a pro-priestly reviser of Chronicles. This reviser wrote a generation after the Chr and had been under the influence of the twenty-

---

241 Houtman, 104; Shaver, 118, 127.
242 Houtman, 111.
243 Shaver, 128, see also 83 and n. 15.
244 For his critique of Houtman's view, see Williamson, *Ezra, Nehemiah,* 288.
245 Blenkinsopp, 131.
246 Clines, *Ezra, Nehemiah, Esther,* 96; Fensham, 94-95.

four course organisation of the priesthood[247]. Due to some similarities between the work of this reviser and Ezra 6:18, Williamson suggests that "it is very probable that the author of Ezra 1-6 comes from the same circle as the later pro-priestly reviser of Chronicles"[248].

According to Rudolph and DeVries, the explanation is to be found elsewhere. If the Chr is the author of Ezra 6:18, then they conclude that he is referring here to David's arrangements despite what appears to be a reference to the law[249]. This view, however, does not appear to be the most plausible approach to the passage.

At least one scholar has understood כִּכְתָב in a manner that does not include ascribing the Davidic organisation of the priests and Levites to the law of Moses. Haag states, "according to Ezr. 6:18, the service of God in the temple was restored 'according to the prescription...of the book of Moses'"[250]. If Haag is correct, then the referent of כִּכְתָב is עֲבִידַת בֵּית אֱלָהָא דִּי בִירוּשְׁלֶם . In connection with this view, Williamson has offered an alternative to his approach above. He also suggests that the citation base כִּכְתָב may qualify only "the service of God"[251].

Our research suggests that Haag has read כִּכְתָב in the most plausible manner. In terms of our analysis the referent would be דִּי בִירוּשְׁלֶם ("which is in Jerusalem" = "the service of the house of God which is in Jerusalem"). In order to read כִּכְתָב as attributing the Davidic organisation of the Levites and the priests to the Mosaic law, one must disregard this referent as the closest clause to the citation base. Based on our analysis, there does not appear to be a reason for reading כִּכְתָב as qualifying anything other than the nearest predication (Type I).

This view also agrees with two characteristic uses of כַּכָּתוּב in the non-synoptic post-exilic historiography. First, Haag's view results in the contiguous placement of this citation base beside its referent.

---

247 Williamson, "The Origins of the Twenty-Four Priestly Courses", *VTS* 30 (1979) 251-68.

248 Williamson, *Ezra, Nehemiah*, 84.

249 Rudolph, 61; DeVries, 625, n. 22.

250 Haag, *TDOT,* Vol. VII, 382; in German, *TWAT,* Bd. IV, 397.

251 Williamson, "History", 36 n. 2.

Secondly, the referent consists of an obvious implication of the law from the perspective of the post-exilic community דִּי בִירוּשְׁלֶם (i.e., "at the place that the LORD will choose" becomes "Jerusalem"). According to this view, the referent is based on Deut 12:14-15 ("Take care that you do not offer your burnt offerings at any place you happen to see. But only at the place that the LORD will choose in one of your tribes—there you shall offer your burnt offerings and there you shall do everything I command you" [see also 12:5, 18; 31:11]).

The context also appears to support this referent. Since Ezra 6:13ff. is concerned with the completion and dedication of the Temple, the use of a citation base with a referent that underlines that the cult has been restored at its proper location appears to fit the context better than a reference to the arrangement of the cultic attendants.

Regarding the relation between Mosaic and Davidic authority in the post-exilic community, Ezra 6:18 attests, according to our analysis, that these sources were distinguished by the post-exilic community, as DeVries has already suggested in 2 Chr 23:18 (*contra* Shaver). In contrast to DeVries' view, however, the authority of Moses could at times be stressed over that of David[252]. In Ezra 6:18, both authorities are represented as complementing each other. The exegetical process in Ezra 6:18 reflects the manner in which the law could be supplemented by subsequent revelation (cf. David's plan of the Temple, 1 Chr 28:19).

C. כָּתוּב √מצא Citation Bases with Legal Referents

Scholars have considered this expression to be a type of legal citation base[253]. We have already covered this construction in our analysis of non-legal referents (Neh 7:5; Esth 6:2). As we noted there this expression is used to recount the citation process. The legal referents of this citation base are always marked with אֲשֶׁר[254]. The referents employed with this formulation are larger than the post-exilic exegetical devices just analysed. In this respect, this citation formula is

---

252 E.g., Dörrfuß.
253 Fishbane, 109-10; Blenkinsopp, 291.
254 For אֲשֶׁר as a citation construction, see Fishbane, 106.

more like the deuteronomistic forms. The citation base מצאָ√ כָּתוּב marks a paraphrase of Deut 23:4-6 in Neh 13:1b.

וְנִמְצָא כָתוּב בּוֹ אֲשֶׁר לֹא־יָבוֹא עַמֹּנִי וּמֹאָבִי בִּקְהַל הָאֱלֹהִים
עַד־עוֹלָם (Neh 13:1b)

אֲשֶׁר has a contiguous relation to the referent.

In Neh 8:14-15a, two separate referents are marked (אֲשֶׁר...וַאֲשֶׁר).

וַיִּמְצְאוּ כָּתוּב בַּתּוֹרָה אֲשֶׁר צִוָּה יְהוָה בְּיַד־מֹשֶׁה אֲשֶׁר
יֵשְׁבוּ בְנֵי־יִשְׂרָאֵל בַּסֻּכּוֹת בֶּחָג בַּחֹדֶשׁ הַשְּׁבִיעִי וַאֲשֶׁר יַשְׁמִיעוּ
וְיַעֲבִירוּ קוֹל בְּכָל־עָרֵיהֶם וּבִירוּשָׁלַ͏ִם (Neh 8:14-15a)

Most scholars agree that the first reference is to Lev 23:42. Williamson has rightly, in our view, drawn attention to the influence of Lev 23:2 and 4 on Neh 8:15a[255]. These verses require that a proclamation be given pertaining to the appointed festivals in Lev 23. Clines and Blenkinsopp consider the call to be implied in Lev 23:40ff.[256] Torrey refers to this verse as reflecting the Chr's shoddy practice of citation, but he does not supply any evidence to support his view[257]. This citation base is also a compound construction (אֲשֶׁר צִוָּה יְהוָה בְּיַד מֹשֶׁה). Like Neh 13:1 above, this citation base has relatively large referents when compared to other post-exilic exegetical devices. In light of our analysis above the large referents of the מצאָ√ כָּתוּב citation base may suggest that the *Vergleichspräpositionale* כָּתוּב citation bases in the non-synoptic post-exilic historiography were the focus of development as exegetical devices, perhaps because of their syntactic nature. That is, only these latter exegetical devices could: mark both adnominal and adverbial relationships; and be scrupolously positioned throughout a sentence. The most striking aspect of this formula (מצאָ√ כָּתוּב...אֲשֶׁר...[וַאֲשֶׁר]) is that its use is restricted to the post-exilic historiography in Nehemiah and Esther. However, the evidence

---

255 Williamson, *Ezra, Nehemiah,* 293-95.
256 Clines, 187; Blenkinsopp, 292.
257 Torrey, 277 n. g.

for כָּתוּב √מצא citation bases is too slim to clearly associate it with the same kind of development of exegetical devices observed elsewhere. The use of this citation base for both legal (Neh 8:14-15a; 13:1) and non-legal (official genealogies [Neh 7:5]; court annals [Esth 6:2]) referents may suggest that they were all authoritative documents of the community.

IV. Conclusions regarding the Use of כָּתוּב in Citation Bases with Non-Legal and Legal Referents

The four-part citation pattern that is used exclusively for non-legal referents is attested over an extended period of time and appears to stem from distinct provenances. This citation pattern can be used to qualify a range of referents. It may either qualify a nominal construction or signal a discourse relation by means of the *neutrum* הִיא or the lexeme כֹּל. The size of the referent has ranged from an extraposed noun to several chapters of Hebrew text (1 Chr 2-8). We also observed various configurations of intermediate forms that pointed to a meaningful referent in the context. A series of intermediate referents could mark an anaphoric relation three clauses away. While the four-part pattern typically functions as a footnote to provide background information we also noted places where the Chr took advantage of its concluding position to emphasise his distinctive message in his rewrite of the Abijah, Joash, and Manasseh pericopæ[258].

---

258 In light of our analysis, the following picture is emerging concerning the literary collections that are referred to by various appellations in the Old Testament. First, there appears to be at least one corpus of material that can be referred to by more than one title (e.g., "the Annals of the Kings of Judah/Israel/Judah and Israel"). At the same time, however, other collections are consistently referred to by one title. For example, "The Book of the Just" appears to contain significant poetic accounts of Israel's heroes and leaders (the upright). Jeremiah 25:13 (MT and G) refers to a book that contains oracles against foreign nations. It appears that this refers to what was indeed a separate collection of literature at one time on the topic of Jeremiah's prophecies against foreign nations. At least part of this collection of literature appears to have been included in MT (chapters 46-50) and in the LXX (25:14ff.). We have also seen

The citation base מצא√ כָּתוּב has distinctive features. First, they occur exclusively in the non-synoptic post-exilic historiography. Secondly, they have the unique function of recounting the act of citation in a narrative. They provided a helpful point of contrast to the *Vergleichspräpositionale* with legal referents in the non-synoptic post-exilic historiography.

The occurrences of both of these forms (the four-part pattern and מצא√ כָּתוּב) in distinctive provenances might suggest that they reflect literary conventions known in more than one location. The use of the four-part citation pattern for various types of non-legal referents (regnal, historical, genealogical, etc. topics), together with the interchangeability of its second element among such topics, appeared to further support such a literary convention. It is interesting to observe that the MT has not retained features of citation bases in 2 Sam 1:18 and Jer 25:13, while the LXX has preserved an entire four-part citation pattern in 3 Reigns 8:53a.

We have noted a number of features associated with the use of כָּתוּב in citation bases in the non-synoptic post-exilic historiography. These observations appear to support the view that כָּתוּב has been developed into a sophisticated exegetical device for the citation of legal referents in the post-exilic period. This development stands in contrast to the use of כָּתוּב with non-legal referents. The development of כָּתוּב in citation bases with legal referents continues into the post-biblical literature, but it takes a new direction[259]. In light of our analysis, the

---

evidence that a subsection within a larger work can be referred to by what appears to be a sub-title (see 2 Chr 33:18-19).

259 It appears that CD, 4QFlor, and 1QS all reflect various developments of the use of citation bases of the biblical era. This development can be attributed to at least two factors. First, the use of the participle in post-biblical Hebrew undergoes marked development (for this, see A. Gordon, "The Development of the Participle in Biblical, Mishnaic, and Modern Hebrew", *Afroasiastic Linguistics* 8 [1982] 121-79; M. H. Segal, *A Grammar of Mishnaic Hebrew* [Oxford: Clarendon, 1927] 156; J. W. Dyk and E. Talstra, "Computer-Assisted Study of Syntactical Change, the Shift in the Use of the Participle in Biblical and Post-Biblical Hebrew Texts", in *Spatial and Temporal Distributions, Studies*

development of כָּתוּב as an exegetical device, which is evident in the post-biblical period, appears to have begun within the OT.

We will further summarise our syntactic observations as well as the developed features of non-synoptic post-exilic exegetical devices with legal referents in a separate chapter below after all citation bases have been examined.

---

in language variation offered to Anthonij Dees on the occasion of his 60th birthday, P. van Reenen and K. van Reenen-Steins eds. [Amsterdam: John Benjamins, 1988], 49-62; E. Qimron, *The Hebrew of the Dead Sea Scrolls* [Atlanta: Scholars Press, 1986] 76). Secondly, the development of, for instance, ככתוב to כל appears to concern its use as an exegetical device. An analysis of the novel phrases in the post-biblical period should consider the influence of these factors on the following forms: כִּי כֵן כָּתוּב [1QS 5:15; CD 11:18]; כִּי כָּתוּב [CD 11:20]; אֲשֶׁר כָּתוּב [4QFlor 1:15-16; CD 7:10; 19:7]; אֲשֶׁר הָיָה כָּתוּב [CD 11:3]; כָּתוּב [CD 5:1, 10; 9:5]; כל [CD 19:1]). At the same time, the citation base כאשׁר כתוב is still used in the later period (1QS 5:17; 8:14; 4QFlor 1:2, 12; CD 7:19) while ככתוב is not. However, our present concern is to examine the full-range of citation bases within the OT (forms with כתוב, כרת, כמשפט, כמצות, כתורה , etc.) as a basis for the examination of this latter period.

Chapter 3: Citation Bases with √צוה and מִצְוָה

In this chapter, we will analyse the citation bases that employ √צוה or מִצְוָה in either relative or comparative constructions. The examination of these forms suggests an impetus for some of the developments we have observed among citation bases.

I. Relative Citation Bases with √צוה

In constrast to כָּתוּב, √צוה never occurs in a citation base in the form of a definite relative participle (e.g., הַמְצַוֶּה). The relative construction אֲשֶׁר צוה√, however, is used far more extensively than it was with כָּתוּב. Among these occurrences there are several functions and forms of citation bases that we have not yet encountered in our examination. The relative citation base אֲשֶׁר צוה√ also has an uneven distribution in the OT.

The following analysis is organised according to the main forms of the relative citation base אֲשֶׁר צוה√. This construction may, of course, be employed alone as the independent relative citation base. This basic citation base, however, is not infrequently construed with other forms (e.g., terms, phrases, or one or more exegetical devices) that in various ways affect the relation between the base and the referent. Each of these larger constructions will be introduced after we have reviewed the independent relative citation base with אֲשֶׁר צוה√.

A. The Forms of the Independent Relative Citation Base with צוה√

The verb stem in the relative construction אֲשֶׁר צוה√ may take the form of either a participle or a finite verb.

1. The Participial Form

אֲשֶׁר צוה√ occurs several times in the form of a participle (enlarged below), as in Deut 4:40.

וְשָׁמַרְתָּ אֶת־חֻקָּיו וְאֶת־מִצְוֹתָיו אֲשֶׁר אָנֹכִי מְצַוְּךָ הַיּוֹם (Deut 4:40a)

Even though it occurs fifteen times in the OT, this participial form is used exclusively in Deuteronomy[1]. Excepting one passage, the referent of these citation bases always consists of a nominal phrase that summarises various laws that are represented as having been given to Israel by the LORD. In every passage, Moses is the antecedent of אָנֹכִי and is represented as the earthly agent of the LORD.

In Deut 30:16 MT, a unique relation exists between the referent and the citation base which stands at the head of the verse. The relative citation base is substantivised as the subject of the sentence in v. 16a; the predicate (italicised) consists of three successive infinitive phrases.

אֲשֶׁר אָנֹכִי מְצַוְּךָ הַיּוֹם *לְאַהֲבָה אֶת־יְהוָה אֱלֹהֶיךָ לָלֶכֶת*
בִּדְרָכָיו וְלִשְׁמֹר מִצְוֹתָיו וְחֻקֹּתָיו וּמִשְׁפָּטָיו וְחָיִיתָ וְרָבִיתָ וּבֵרַכְךָ
יְהוָה אֱלֹהֶיךָ בָּאָרֶץ אֲשֶׁר־אַתָּה בָא־שָׁמָּה לְרִשְׁתָּהּ (Deut 30:16)

> What I am commanding you today is to love the LORD your God, to walk
> in his ways, and to observe his commandments, statutes, and ordinances,
> then you shall live and become numerous, and the LORD your God will
> bless you in the land that you are entering to possess (Deut 30:16).

The referent of this substantivised citation base is the predicate. Note that the adverbial phrase הַיּוֹם is part of the relative citation base. Hence, the entire substantivised phrase is placed beside the referent.

---

1   Deut 4:2 (twice; two citation bases), 40; 6:6; 7:11; 8:11; 10:13; 11:13, 27, 28; 27:4, 10; 28:13 (מִצְוֹת יְהוָה אֱלֹהֶיךָ); 30:11, 16 (see below).

But unlike others in this category, the relative marker of the citation base is not contiguous to the referent.

Some avoid this irregular citation base and sentence by reconstructing a full conditional protasis (אִם תִּשְׁמַע אֶל מִצְוֹת יְהוָה אֱלֹהֶיךָ) to the beginning of v. 16a. This reconstruction is supported only by 𝔊2. Even if this reconstruction is warranted, the ellipsis of the referent would still make the use of אֲשֶׁר √צוה in Deut 30:16 unique[3].

2. *The Form* אֲשֶׁר √צוה *with a Finite Verb*

The relative citation base אֲשֶׁר √צוה may also occur in the form of a finite verb. These forms have a wider distribution than the participial constructions above even though they are still not uniformly dispersed throughout the OT.

The finite form of אשר √צוה (enlarged) occurs in Gen 3:11.

וַיֹּאמֶר מִי הִגִּיד לְךָ כִּי עֵירֹם אָתָּה הֲמִן־הָעֵץ אֲשֶׁר צִוִּיתִיךָ
לְבִלְתִּי אֲכָל־מִמֶּנּוּ אָכָלְתָּ (Gen 3:11)

As above, this independent citation base customarily marks an adnominal relation to the referent. These constructions at times ascribe only a single concept (e.g, "tree") to a source. However, a resumptive pronoun may reintroduce the referent in the relative clause in order to provide further information ("from which I commanded you not to eat [from it/מִמֶּנּוּ]").

---

2   S. R. Driver, *Deuteronomy*, ICC, 2nd edn (Edinburgh: T. & T. Clark, 1902) 332. See also J. Hempel, *BHS*, cf. 11:27. Weinfeld does not reconstruct this clause (337, #18).

3   It seems unlikely that the protasis with its introductory אִם particle would be ellipted or omitted in a conditional sentence. It is not clear how a complex conditional sentence is to be understood in Deut 30:16 without an introductory אִם in the protasis. It is a far more common feature of Hebrew conditional statements to have a suppressed apodosis (Koehler *et al.*, vol. I, 58), thus giving אִם the force of "not" (see also R. C. Steiner, "Ancient Hebrew", in *The Semitic Languages,* ed. by R. Hertzon [London: Routledge, 1997] 169).

This type of citation base is concentrated in the law and deuteronomistic writings[4]. The DtrH accounts for twenty-three of these passages while it occurs seven times in Jeremiah. The book of Jeremiah is, of course, extensively influenced by deuteronomic thought[5] so it is not surprising that it is the only prophetic material before the post-exilic era that attests this form. This form of citation base is attested throughout the law (fourteen occurrences) while it is used six times (14.0%) in post-exilic writings. These post-exilic passages are best considered after we have reviewed some of the exceptional passages in the law and the deuteronomistic material[6].

There are some passages where a non-contiguous relation exists between the citation base and the referent. In Num 34:13, another relative clause (italics) interrupts the relation between the citation base and הָאָרֶץ (both enlarged).

וַיְצַו מֹשֶׁה אֶת־בְּנֵי יִשְׂרָאֵל לֵאמֹר זֹאת הָאָרֶץ *אֲשֶׁר תִּתְנַחֲלוּ אֹתָהּ בְּגוֹרָל* אֲשֶׁר צִוָּה יְהוָה לָתֵת לְתִשְׁעַת הַמַּטּוֹת וַחֲצִי הַמַּטֶּה (Num 34:13)

A similar non-contiguous relation exists between the citation base and the referent in 2 Kgs 17:15.

---

4   Gen 3:11; Exod 32:8; 36:5; Lev 7:35-36, 37-38; Num 34:13; Deut 4:13; 6:17, 20; 9:12, 16; 13:6; 28:45; 31:29; Josh 1:13; 7:11; 22:5; 23:16 (the meaningful referent is בְּרִית יְהוָה אֱלֹהֵיכֶם); Judg 2:20; 3:4; 1 Sam 2:29; 13:13; 21:3; 1 Kgs 2:43; 8:58; 11:11; 13:21; 2 Kgs 17:15; 18:6; Jer 7:23; 11:3-4; 13:6; 35:14 (the meaningful referent is דִּבְרֵי יְהוֹנָדָב בֶּן־רֵכָב), 16; 50:21; 51:59; Zech 1:6; Mal 3:22; Lam 2:17; Neh 1:7; 8:1; 1 Chr 16:40; 22:13.

5   For recent examinations of the deuteronomic tradents in Jeremiah, see Winfried Thiel, *Die deuteronomistische Redaktion von Jeremia 1-25*, WMANT 41 (Neukirchen-Vluyn: Neukirchener Verlag, 1973); and, *Die deuteronomistische Redaktion von Jeremia 26-45*, WMANT 52 (Neukirchen-Vluyn: Neukirchener Verlag, 1981); W. McKane, *Jeremiah*, ICC, 2 Vols (Edinburgh: T. & T. Clark, 1986, 1996); J. Gordon McConville, *Judgment and Promise: An Interpretation of the Book of Jeremiah* (Leicester: Apollos, 1993); and, *Grace In The End: A Study in Deuteronomic Theology*, SOTBT (Grand Rapids, Michigan: Zondervan, 1993).

6   Henceforth, the term "deuteronomistic" will be used to describe the contents of both the DtrH as well as the book of Jer.

In 1 Sam 21:3, two relative clauses have been coordinated together to qualify הַדָּבָר. The second of these subordinate clauses is the citation base which is not juxtaposed to the referent (both enlarged).

וַיֹּאמֶר דָּוִד לַאֲחִימֶלֶךְ הַכֹּהֵן הַמֶּלֶךְ צִוַּנִי דָבָר וַיֹּאמֶר אֵלַי אִישׁ
אַל־יֵדַע מְאוּמָה אֶת־הַדָּבָר אֲשֶׁר־אָנֹכִי שֹׁלֵחֲךָ וַאֲשֶׁר צִוִּיתִךְ
וְאֶת־הַנְּעָרִים יוֹדַעְתִּי אֶל־מְקוֹם פְּלֹנִי אַלְמוֹנִי (1 Sam 21:3)

Among the uses of the citation base אֲשֶׁר צוה√ with a finite verb in the law and the deuteronomistic writings there are three occurrences of a non-contiguous relation between the citation base and the referent.

Having reviewed it in the law and the deuteronomistic literature (DtrH and Jer), we may now compare the use of this form of the relative citation base in the post-exilic material. Among the six post-exilic uses of this form, there are no comparable non-contiguous relations between citation formulæ and referents; Mal 3:22 is unique among these forms (see further below). In half of these passages (Neh 8:1; 1 Chr 16:40; 22:13) the most noteworthy observation concerns the fact that they entail no significant difference from the contiguous forms above. The citation base in Neh 1:7, which also consists of a contiguous relation, will be treated in conjunction with our discussion of the citation base in v. 8 (see below).

The remaining post-exilic uses of this finite formulation, however, are worthy of more detailed attention here. These citation bases in Zech 1:6 and Mal 3:22 may be related to the "temple tradition" of preaching and teaching as described by Mason. If this is correct then such a link to this temple tradition may provide a plausible Sitz im Leben for the general development of citation bases that we have observed in the non-synoptic post-exilic historiography. We hope to demonstrate the plausibility of this view while at the same time slightly extending the observations made by Mason. In order to relate our analysis of citation bases to this wider concern we must review Mason's analysis of Zech 1:1-6.

Recently, Mason has developed von Rad's analysis of "Levitical

Sermons" in Chronicles[7]. Von Rad identified speeches in the non-synoptic material of Chronicles that share various thematic and stylistic features. One of the characteristic elements of these speeches concerns the citation of or allusion to earlier legal or prophetic sayings. After a re-examination of von Rad's analysis and an expression of his dissatisfaction with the form-critical classification "Levitical Sermons"[8], Mason has demonstrated that several of the features of these homilies in 1 and 2 Chronicles can also be found in other post-exilic "addresses". By these addresses, according to Mason, the faithful were encouraged, instructed, warned, and exhorted. Describing the general features common to these addresses in the post-exilic material, Mason states, "these passages...do evince many characteristics of 'preaching' and show remarkable continuity of theme and method"[9].

According to Mason, there are "striking parallels"[10] of themes and literary devices between Zech 1:1-6 and some of the homiletic addresses in Chronicles. The salient themes common to both Zech 1:1-6 and these post-exilic addresses concern: a warning based on the disobedience of their fathers ("do not be like your ancestors", v. 4a; see also vv. 4c, 5a and v. 6, and the message to the prophet in v. 2)[11]; a call to faithfulness and repentance ("return to me", v. 3b; see also v. 4b); and, a challenge to hear the present Word of God ("thus says the LORD of hosts", v. 3b).

---

7   R. Mason, *Preaching the Tradition: Homily and Hermeneutics after the Exile* (Cambridge: Cambridge University Press, 1990). G. von Rad, "The Levitical Sermon in I and II Chronicles", in *The Problem of the Hexateuch and Other Essays,* trans. by E. W. T. Dicken (Edinburgh and London: Oliver & Boyd, 1966) 267-80; in German, "Die Levitische Predigt in den Büchern der Chronik" in *Festschrift für Otto Proksch* (Leipzig: J. C. Hinrichs'sche Buchhandlung, 1934) 113-24; then in, *Gesammelte Studien zum Alten Testament* (Munich: Kaiser, 1958); see also D. L. Petersen, *Haggai & Zechariah 1-8,* OTL (London: SCM Press, 1985).

8   See also D. Mathias, "'Levitische Predigt' und Deuteronomismus", *ZAW* 96 (1984) 23-49; R. Braun, *1 Chronicles,* WBC (Waco, TX: Word Books, 1986) xxiv-xxv.

9   Mason, 200.

10   *Ibid.,* 204.

11   Other addresses that highlight this theme include 2 Chr 28:9; 29:6, 9; 30:7-8. We will return to the address in 2 Chr 30:7-8 when we reach that form of citation base below.

Secondly, Mason has demonstrated that Zech 1:1-6 shares certain modes of expression with the addresses in Chronicles. These include such stylistic features as the three rhetorical questions in vv. 5f., the illustration of a point by alluding to history (vv. 2, 4ff.), a play on words (שוב√ between Zech 1:4 and 2 Chr 30:6-9)[12], and, most important for our analysis, an appeal to or citation of Scripture[13].

It is this last characteristic element of these "addresses" that we wish to consider in light of our analysis of the citation base אֲשֶׁר צוה√ in Zech 1:6. We must, however, review Mason's treatment of the reference to Scripture in this homily fragment before relating it to our study. Mason concentrates his analysis of the citation of or allusion to earlier "Scripture" on Zech 1:4. In this verse, a reference is made to what "the former prophets" had proclaimed. Mason demonstrates how the phrase "the former prophets" is similarly employed in 2 Chr 20:20 to refer to Isa 7. He also shows how other terminology is shared between Jer 25:4-5 (הָרָעָה מַדַּרְכּוֹ and שׁוּבוּ־נָא) and Zech 1:4 (הָרָעִים מַדְּרְכֵיכֶם and שׁוּבוּ נָא). In this way, both Zech and Jer referred to "the horatory role of the prophets"[14]. This reference to the earlier prophets in Zech 1:4, according to Mason, appears

> to stand in a tradition, no doubt given powerful impetus by the Babylonian exile, which served to underscore the authenticity and relevance of the words of those prophets who were understood to have predicted it. This tradition sees in the present, post-exilic situation a time of renewal of God's grace in the offer of a new covenant and so an opportunity to learn from the sins of the previous generations, who were seen to have occasioned the judgement[15].

---

12   For the view that Zech 1:6 and 2 Chr 30:6-9 are not related to each other and that שוב√ in 2 Chr 30 refers merely to a geographical return to the land, see Petersen, 117.

       For the fourfold repetition of שוב√ in vv. 3-6 as a "literary vehicle for contrasting the stubborn spirit of the preexilic age with the more compliant spirit of the postexilic era", see C. L. Myers and E. M. Myers, *Haggai, Zechariah 1-8* (New York: Doubleday, 1987) 99.

13   Mason emphasises these last three features in v. 4.

14   Mason, 201. Jeremiah was no less a preacher of the law than Zechariah (E. W. Nicholson, *Preaching to the Exiles,* 49ff.). Our point here is that there is a distinctive use of a citation base in the homiletic fragment in Zech 1:1-6.

15   Mason, 202.

Mason is undoubtedly correct. The vindication of the traditions in light of 587/6 B.C. and the Babylonian exile surely was instrumental in the adoption of this terminology by those in the exilic and post-exilic periods. More generally, the evidence that Mason has marshalled to connect Zech 1:1ff. to the addresses of the temple tradition repays attention.

The strength of Mason's treatment of the reference to previous "Scripture" ("citing or alluding to 'Scripture'") in Zech 1:1ff. is his concentration on the use of terminology in v. 4. However, it appears that something more can be said regarding the citation of Scripture in Zech 1:1-6. The use of citation bases in this homily extends beyond v. 4 to include v. 6 as well. Once we have addressed all forms in this study, it will become clear that certain forms and functions of citation bases characterise the law and the deuteronomistic literature. What Mason's analysis has not noted is that some of the uses of citation bases that are common in the post-exilic literature have been developed in the restoration period. Not only do several types of citation bases and associated features cease or subside dramatically after the DtrH, but some exegetical devices are used in novel ways in the non-synoptic post-exilic historiography.

At this point we refer to the citation base in Zech 1:6 (enlarged).

אַךְ דְּבָרַי וְחֻקַּי אֲשֶׁר צִוִּיתִי אֶת־עֲבָדַי הַנְּבִיאִים הֲלוֹא
הִשִּׂיגוּ אֲבֹתֵיכֶם וַיָּשׁוּבוּ וַיֹּאמְרוּ כַּאֲשֶׁר זָמַם יְהוָה צְבָאוֹת
לַעֲשׂוֹת לָנוּ כִּדְרָכֵינוּ וּכְמַעֲלָלֵינוּ כֵּן עָשָׂה אִתָּנוּ (Zech 1:6)

Another point of similarity between Zech 1:6 and those addressed by Mason concerns the form of the citation base as well as its function within the overall homiletic fragment. What has not been previously observed is how two of the characteristic features of these addresses are combined in v. 6: the citation base occurs in a rhetorical question ("but did not My words and My statutes, which I commanded My servants the prophets, overtake your fathers?"). What appears even more noteworthy is the way these two characteristic features of these addresses function in the overall homiletic fragment. The force that results from placing a citation base, which reinforces the authority of the recently vindicated legal tradition, in the form of a rhetorical question, a feature already identified by Mason, is to elicit a response from the audience. In order that this combination may achieve the greatest effect, the citation base and the rhetorical question are placed at the concluding and climactic part of the homily in Zech 1:6.

Notice the similarities between the function of this citation base in v. 6 and Mason's description of such devices in the addresses from Chronicles. Regarding the common traits among these chronistic addresses, Mason concludes,

> the addresses are marked by many of the characteristics of preaching. They often quote, or refer to, a text of "Scripture" which is presumably regarded as authoritative by speakers and hearers alike. They expound some theological truth about God and they call for immediate and lively response to this truth, either by way of encouragement, rebuke or exhortation[16].

We maintain that Mason's description of the citation of and allusion to Scripture in Chronicles as a summons for an "immediate and lively response" is precisely the way that the citation base framed in a rhetorical question functions in Zech 1:6.

Hence, we would simply add the citation base in 1:6 to the observations that Mason has already made regarding the reference to "Scripture" elsewhere in Zech 1:1-6. That is, the reference or allusion to Scripture in Zech 1:1-6 is not limited to the terminology that Mason has unraveled in v. 4 ("the former prophets", מִדַּרְכֵיכֶם הָרָעִים and שׁוּבוּ נָא), but also entails the use of a citation base that is cast in the form of a rhetorical question in v. 6.

The citation base in Zech 1:6 (perhaps Hag 1:1ff. as well[17]) is part of a more sophisticated use of exegetical devices than those we have

---

16 *Ibid.*, 257.
17 In his study, Mason has related Hag 1:1ff. to the Levitical Sermons analysed by von Rad. For instance, note the rhetorical question in Haggai's address in 1:4 and the play on words in v. 6, and, in v. 3, the construction בְּיַד־חַגַּי הַנָּבִיא לֵאמֹר, a veritable citation base. Note that this form is also construed with הַנָּבִיא. It does not appear to be a mere coincidence that this reference to authority introduces a rhetorical question which is intended to evoke a response from the audience in a comparable fashion as we have observed above. In light of the other features in this fragment and the same period (520 B.C.), this citation expression may be related to Mason's "preaching the tradition".

examined in the law, the deuteronomistic literature, and Jer. In addition
to ascribing a referent to a source, the citation base in Zech 1:6 has also
become a powerful homiletic device that has been formulated
presumably to elicit a response from an audience to the recently
vindicated legal and prophetic traditions.

We hope to have added further weight to Mason's already
compelling expansion of von Rad's thesis regarding Zech 1:1ff. In the
final analysis, Mason concludes that the data seem "to provide strong
evidence to support the hypothesis that the influence common to them all
was a general pattern of preaching and teaching which was familiar from
the practice of the second temple"[18]. It appears that the formation of
such a preaching phenomenon would best be understood as having been
based on the vindication of the legal and prophetic traditions some time
after the fall of Jerusalem. We will return to Zech 1:6 after
consideration of the form in Mal 3:22 and other citation bases below.

The other post-exilic use of אֲשֶׁר צוה√ that repays attention in this
category occurs in Mal 3:22. This passage is part of another address
(3:22-24) that Mason has convincingly related to the addresses studied
by von Rad in Chronicles. Before we review its relevance to the
hypothesis of post-exilic homilies, we must treat one exceptional feature
of this passage. In Mal 3:22, אֲשֶׁר צוה√ occurs in Hebrew poetry
which is not typical of citation bases in any period or category (cf. Jer
50:21; Lam 2:17). In terms of the continuum between Hebrew poetry
and prose[19], Mal 3:22 appears to be more closely related to the former
than the latter[20].

זִכְרוּ תּוֹרַת מֹשֶׁה עַבְדִּי אֲשֶׁר צִוִּיתִי אוֹתוֹ
בְחֹרֵב עַל־כָּל־יִשְׂרָאֵל חֻקִּים וּמִשְׁפָּטִים (Mal 3:22)

---

18 *Ibid.*, 258.
19 J. Kugel, *The Idea of Biblical Poetry* (New Haven: Yale University Press, 1981).
20 Recently R. L. Smith described Malachi generally as "free verse" noting that German scholars usually considered Malachi related to poetry (*Micah - Malachi*, WBC [Waco, Texas: Word, 1984] 301; cf. RSV, NEB, JB). Smith renders 3:22-24 in poetry.

Note that the final noun phrase (חֻקִּים וּמִשְׁפָּטִים) is difficult to account for if the verse is read prosaically ("at Horeb, for all Israel, statutes and ordinances"). But if read according to the conventions of poetry, then the citation base and the referent (both enlarged) have simply been placed in parallel to each other. Though the evidence of citation bases in metre is slim, this latter reading appears to be the best option.

More significantly, the use of the citation base in Mal 3:22 appears to be associated with "the preaching of the tradition" as we observed in Zech 1:6. Mason broadly associated Mal 3:22-24 (4:4-6) with "the role of the good preacher" he detected in Chronicles, Haggai, and Zechariah. Describing 3:22-24, Mason concludes, "the proclamation stresses God's grace in the past and the promise of victory in the future, but these are stressed in such a way as to bring out the challenge to the hearers to live worthily of their past and their future calling"[21].

Though its redaction history is debated[22], there is nevertheless general agreement among some scholars of how Mal 3:22-24 functions. Smith describes the motivation of his redactor in a way that recalls Mason's view of "the good preacher". Commenting on the challenge put forth in 3:22ff. by a legalist, Smith states, "he seeks to call attention to the fact that the triumph described in the preceding verses can be realised only through Israel's strict and loyal adherence to the law of Moses"[23]. In his description of the editorialising of Mal 3:22-24,

---

21   *Ibid.,* 241.

22   Some view it as a correction by a legalist in connection with the final redaction of the Book of the Twelve (R. L. Smith, 340; Rudolph, 291-93; Fishbane, 524). McKenzie and Wallace consider the apocalyptic view of 3:13-21 as secondary and distinct from the Malachi material (S. L. McKenzie and H. N. Wallace, "Covenant Themes in Malachi", *CBQ* 45 [1983] 549-63). J. M. P. Smith considers v. 22 an isolated marginal note from some later legalist who missed any express mention of the Mosaic law in the book (H. G. Mitchell, J. M. P. Smith and J. A. Bewer, *A Critical and Exegetical Commentary on Haggai, Zechariah, Malachi and Jonah,* ICC [Edinburgh: T. & T. Clark, 1912] 81). Childs argues that Mal 3:22 and vv. 23-24 are two appendices and that to consider them as a corrective to something expressed in the book is to misunderstand the canonical process. According to Childs, these appendices were attached as a control, not an attack, on the prophet's message (B. S. Childs, *Introduction to the Old Testament as Scripture* [London: SCM Press, 1979] 495).

23   J. M. P. Smith, 81.

Childs demonstrates how these verses share some of the same features that Mason has identified among addresses concerned with "the preaching of the tradition". According to Childs,

> The effect of identifying Malachi's eschatological prophet with Elijah was [in part] to describe theologically the condition of the addressee through this typological analogy. The appendix served to equate the hearers of Malachi's prophecy — along with future generations — with the disobedient, vacillating people [of Elijah's day] whose national allegience to the God of their fathers was in danger of being dissolved[24].

Both Smith and Childs attribute a horatory role to Mal 3:22 which is based on the view that the hope for the future of the Malachi's audience was inextricably connected with Israel's past. Though his treatment of Mal 3:22-24 is brisk, Mason links it to "the good preacher" he noted elsewhere in the post-exilic addresses.

The similarities between Mal 3:22 and the addresses concerned with preaching the tradition are deeper than Mason has suggested. We would add to Mason's comments the fact that the citation base in v. 22 is used in a similar way to the one noted in Zech 1. Like Zech 1:6, the citation base in Mal 3:22 is construed with an irreal mood of expression, here an imperative ("remember the law of Moses!"), that is intended to evoke a response from the audience. The function of the citation base in Mal 3:22 framed in a non-indicative expression is to elicit a response from the audience by appealing to a past authority that has been recently vindicated by Israel's history. We will observe another imperative of √זכר in conjunction with a post-exilic citation base below that also appears to be related to the homilies in Zech 1 and Mal 3. There are other features that Mal 3:22 shares with the post-exilic addresses that may be related to the tradition of preaching observed by Mason.

We will return to both Zech 1:6 and Mal 3:22 below. What we have observed above is the manner in which a citation base can be used in connection with a question or an imperative to give added force to one's appeal for a response. The vindication of the legal and prophetic traditions, both referred to in Zechariah and Malachi, by the events of the sixth century B.C. would lend great weight to such appeals.

---

24 Childs, 496.

Hence, there appears to be a basis for the hypothesis that the development of at least some of the citation bases in the post-exilic period was associated with the wider phenomenon of "the preaching of the tradition". While the common features among a number of post-exilic addresses may loosely be connected with the development of citation bases, the degree to which such phenomena are connected with the temple is less certain.

The sudden decline in the use of √צוה אֲשֶׁר after DtrH and Jer (see further below) suggests that something had changed in the use of this form after the mid-sixth century B.C. (i.e., the *terminus ad quem* of the DtrH). The fact that the construction in Zech 1:6 already exhibits some of the novelties that are observable among post-exilic citation bases suggests that the development of these forms preceded the relaunch of the building of the Temple of Zerubbabel in 520 B.C. Perhaps the disappointment of the initial return immediately following Cyrus' decree in 538 B.C. resulted in contemplation of the legal and prophetic traditions that had been vindicated by the turbulent history of Judah in the earlier part of the sixth century. This could have been the impetus for the development of citation bases that is now observable in Zech 1:6 as well as subsequent post-exilic literature (see further below). It is reasonable to conclude that the marked change in the use of citation bases between the deuteronomistic and the post-exilic literature is integrally related with the tumultuous events of the sixth century. There appears to be nothing inconsistent with attributing the development of citation bases to the early post-exilic period. Such a period of reflection and contemplation appears to be a plausible hypothesis (e.g., Zech 1:2-6) which has the added advantage of explaining both the sudden drop-off in the deuteronomistic citation bases after the 550s and the novel uses that characterise the non-synoptic post-exilic material beginning in 520 B.C. The fall of Jerusalem and the temple, the Babylonian exile, and the limited success of the initial wave of returnees would have restored great confidence in the legal and prophetic traditions among some in the early post-exilic setting. Perhaps a development in exegetical devices beginning in, or during, the 520s could explain the many novelties associated with citation bases with legal referents in the restoration period[25].

Perhaps such a preaching of the tradition is a plausible Sitz im Leben for the development of citation bases that we have observed in the non-synoptic post-exilic historiography. We will return to this hypothesis and related concerns below as we treat other addresses in the post-exilic historiography that use citation bases in a distinctive way.

B. The Forms of the Independent Citation Base Construed with Other Terms

When it is used in conjunction with another term, אֲשֶׁר צוה√ may occur in the form of a participle or a finite verb.

1. The Participial Form

a. The Independent Citation Bases with כֹּל

Like the participial constructions reviewed above, these citation bases are not uniformly distributed in the OT. In some cases, these bases refer to a more meaningful referent in the context. כֹּל appears in the referent of the participial construction in two different forms.

The first form of these expressions occurs when כֹּל is part of the referent (enlarged).

---

25 While there is much disagreement concerning the time when the sources of the Pentateuch were finally brought together, there are not a few scholars who view the sources as exilic or pre-exilic. Two recent works represent the range of views in Pentateuchal criticism (see E. W. Nicholson, *The Pentateuch in the Twentieth Century: The Legacy of Julius Wellhausen* [Oxford: Clarendon Press, 1998]; and R. N. Whybray, *The Making of the Pentateuch: A Methodological Study,* JSOTS 53 [Sheffield: Sheffield Academic Press, 1987]). My thesis is not dependent on dating the Pentateuch before 520 B.C. since the authoritative law in the underlying sources would still constitute a resource from which exegesis and interpretation could proceed.

כָּל־הַמִּצְוָה אֲשֶׁר אָנֹכִי מְצַוְּךָ הַיּוֹם תִּשְׁמְרוּן לַעֲשׂוֹת
לְמַעַן תִּחְיוּן וּרְבִיתֶם וּבָאתֶם וִירִשְׁתֶּם אֶת־הָאָרֶץ אֲשֶׁר־נִשְׁבַּע
יְהוָה לַאֲבֹתֵיכֶם (Deut 8:1)

Similarly to what we saw above, this participial form occurs exclusively in Deut[26]. Insofar as all of these participial constructions occur with הַיּוֹם throughout 4:40-30:16, one could surmise that, in the final form of the text, the most meaningful referent for the citation base in 8:1 consists of this entire series of chapters. Hence, these citation bases that include כֹּל in the referent appear to have a greater scope of reference than the independent participial forms presented earlier.

Another unique feature of the relation between the citation base and the referent can be observed among these forms that include כֹּל. In Deut 19:9, the common hendiadys phrase תִּשְׁמֹר לַעֲשׂוֹת has been interrupted by the direct object. Since this results in a non-contiguous relation between the citation base and the referent ("the entirety of this commandment") an inseparable resumptive pronoun (3fs) is used with the infinitive construct to relate the citation base to the most meaningful referent in the sentence.

כִּי־תִשְׁמֹר אֶת־כָּל־הַמִּצְוָה הַזֹּאת לַעֲשֹׂתָהּ אֲשֶׁר אָנֹכִי מְצַוְּךָ
הַיּוֹם (Deut 19:9a)

In this respect, the citation base in Deut 19:9 has a non-contiguous relation to the most meaningful referent in the sentence.

When the referent consists entirely of כֹּל, the entire construction is substantivised. In contrast to those above that refer to a referent in the context, this substantivised construction results in a referent which varies in length. This construction is also limited to Deuteronomy[27]. In Deut 12:11, the substantivised citation base כָּל־אֲשֶׁר אָנֹכִי מְצַוֶּה אֶתְכֶם

---

26   Deut 8:1; 11:8, 22; 12:28; 13:1, 19; 15:5; 19:9; 27:1; 28:1, 14, 15; 30:8. Deut 6:2 has this form, but it is also part of a larger construction (see further below).

27   Deut 12:11, 14; 18:18.

(enlarged) is defined later in the verse in the form of a lengthy noun phrase (italics).

וְהָיָה הַמָּקוֹם אֲשֶׁר־יִבְחַר יְהוָה אֱלֹהֵיכֶם בּוֹ לְשַׁכֵּן שְׁמוֹ שָׁם שָׁמָּה
תָבִיאוּ אֵת כָּל־אֲשֶׁר אָנֹכִי מְצַוֶּה אֶתְכֶם עוֹלֹתֵיכֶם וְזִבְחֵיכֶם
מַעְשְׂרֹתֵיכֶם וּתְרֻמַת יֶדְכֶם וְכֹל מִבְחַר נִדְרֵיכֶם אֲשֶׁר
תִּדְּרוּ לַיהוָה (Deut 12:11)

כֹל substantivises the citation base and thus broadens the meaning of the referent ("all that I am commanding you") beyond those observed in the independent form of this construction.

The use of the participial forms, with or without כֹל, only in Deuteronomy is striking. Since he does not analyse how these constructions function as citation bases, Weinfeld lists all of these participial forms of אֲשֶׁר צוה√ together[28]. He also does not find any comparable forms outside of Deuteronomy.

b. The Independent Citation Base with אֵת

The nominalisation of the citation base אֲשֶׁר צוה√ may also occur with אֶת־. The only participial form occurs in Exod 34:11a ("what I am commanding you today").

שְׁמָר־לְךָ אֵת אֲשֶׁר אָנֹכִי מְצַוְּךָ הַיּוֹם (Exod 34:11a)

The meaningful referent consists of the covenant renewal in vv. 12-26.

2. *The Finite Verb Form*

The independent form of the citation base אֲשֶׁר צוה√ may be construed with certain words or phrases that affect its function.

---

28 Weinfeld, 356, # 7.

a. The Independent Citation Base with a Negative Particle

The use of "strange fire" (אֵשׁ זָרָה) by Nadab and Abihu provides an occasion for the use of a negative citation base (enlarged).

וַיִּקְחוּ בְנֵי־אַהֲרֹן נָדָב וַאֲבִיהוּא אִישׁ מַחְתָּתוֹ וַיִּתְּנוּ בָהֵן אֵשׁ
וַיָּשִׂימוּ עָלֶיהָ קְטֹרֶת וַיַּקְרִבוּ לִפְנֵי יְהוָה אֵשׁ זָרָה
אֲשֶׁר לֹא צִוָּה אֹתָם (Lev 10:1)

Such negative citation bases occur exclusively in the deuteronomistic material (DtrH and Jer) and in the law[29].

b. The Independent Citation Base with כֹּל

כֹּל may constitute part of the referent.

וַיַּגֵּד מֹשֶׁה לְאַהֲרֹן אֵת כָּל־דִּבְרֵי יְהוָה אֲשֶׁר שְׁלָחוֹ
וְאֵת כָּל־הָאֹתֹת אֲשֶׁר צִוָּהוּ (Exod 4:28)

This form is well-attested and is used exclusively in the deuteronomistic material (DtrH and Jer) and in the law[30].

As before, when כֹּל constitutes the entire head noun, the whole expression is nominalised. Jeremiah's calling is a good example of the way this form may be substantivised to refer to a great expanse of material.

וַיֹּאמֶר יְהוָה אֵלַי אַל־תֹּאמַר נַעַר אָנֹכִי כִּי עַל־כָּל־אֲשֶׁר
אֶשְׁלָחֲךָ תֵּלֵךְ וְאֵת כָּל־אֲשֶׁר אֲצַוְּךָ תְּדַבֵּר (Jer 1:7)

---

29 Lev 10:1; Deut 17:3; 18:20; Jer 7:31; 19:5; 29:23. Jer 32:35 has this same negative relative citation base. Despite having the same form this citation base functions like a comparative clause and will be treated separately below.

30 Exod 4:28; 19:7; 35:29; Lev 8:36 (see further in comparative section on Lev 8); Deut 4:23; 5:33; Josh 4:10; 8:35 (a phrase consisting of a partitive construction מִכֹּל אֲשֶׁר־צִוָּה מֹשֶׁה); 11:15 (see 8:35); 22:2b; 1 Kgs 15:5 (see Josh 8:35); 2 Kgs 21:8b; Jer 11:8; 26:2; 35:8.

The distribution of this form is very similar to those treated immediately above[31].

In Deut 18:18, the substantivised citation base with כל signals a referent that is never defined ("I will raise up a prophet from among their countrymen like you, and I will put My words in his mouth, and he shall speak to them all that I command him [כָּל־אֲשֶׁר אֲצַוֶּנּוּ]").

2 Chr 33:8 is the only occurrence of this construction in the post-exilic historiography. This citation base, however, is part of the synoptic material in the Chr's history.

אִם־יִשְׁמְרוּ לַעֲשׂוֹת כְּכֹל אֲשֶׁר צִוִּיתִים... (2 Kgs 21:8)

אִם־יִשְׁמְרוּ לַעֲשׂוֹת אֵת כָּל־אֲשֶׁר צִוִּיתִים... (2 Chr 33:8)

In light of the distribution of the constructions we have examined so far in this chapter, it is not surprising that a citation base that cannot be attributed to the creativity of the Chr has a form that is common to the deuteronomistic literature and the law.

c. The Independent Citation Bases with אֵת

There are more occurrences of אֲשֶׁר צוה√ nominalised with a finite verb.

וּבְבֹא מֹשֶׁה לִפְנֵי יְהוָה לְדַבֵּר אִתּוֹ יָסִיר אֶת־הַמַּסְוֶה
עַד־צֵאתוֹ וְיָצָא וְדִבֶּר אֶל־בְּנֵי יִשְׂרָאֵל אֵת אֲשֶׁר יְצֻוֶּה (Exod 34:34)

The use of this finite form with אֵת is restricted to the law and the DtrH[32].

---

31 Exod 7:2; 25:22; 31:6; 35:10; 36:1; 38:22; Josh 1:18; 22:2; Judg 13:14; 1 Kgs 11:38; 2 Kgs 18:12; Jer 1:7, 17; 26:8; 32:23; Job 37:12; 2 Chr 33:8.
32 Exod 34:34; Lev 9:5; Josh 9:24; 1 Sam 13:14; 1 Kgs 11:10.

d. The Independent Citation Base with Pro-Form עשׂה√

Pro-form עשׂה√ is another element that may be used in conjunction with these citation bases. Such formulations generally signal a referent that is larger than many of those previously addressed in this chapter.

וַיִּקְבְּרוּ אֶת־עַצְמוֹת־שָׁאוּל וִיהוֹנָתָן־בְּנוֹ בְּאֶרֶץ בִּנְיָמִן
בְּצֵלָע בְּקֶבֶר קִישׁ אָבִיו וַיַּעֲשׂוּ כֹּל אֲשֶׁר־צִוָּה הַמֶּלֶךְ
וַיֵּעָתֵר אֱלֹהִים לָאָרֶץ אַחֲרֵי־כֵן (2 Sam 21:14)

The form in 2 Sam 21:14 uses both כל and pro-form עשׂה√ to link with the more meaningful referent in vv. 5-6. Hence, pro-form עשׂה√ has the added capability to signal a meaningful referent several verses away. The other passage with pro-form עשׂה√ in this section is Josh 1:16. The meaningful referent here is located in vv. 11-15.

3. Conclusions

The referent governed by an independent citation base is typically enlarged by using one of the above elements. In general, the referent tends to be larger than the independent form of the citation base. Sometimes the referent is undefined and limitless in scope. The referent may also at times be located in the distant context. Among the terms we have seen used with these constructions, only the negative particle לֹא does not affect the relation between the citation base and the referent.

C. Compound Citation Bases

The participial form never occurs as a compound citation base. The relative construction אֲשֶׁר צוה√ with a finite verb, however, occurs in various forms as a compound citation base.

1. The Most Common Compound Citation Base

The most common form of a compound citation base consists of the relative citation base אֲשֶׁר צוה√ with the DD marker לֵאמֹר[33]. This compound citation base occurs four times in the OT (Gen 3:17; 2 Sam 7:7; Ezra 9:11; Neh 1:8)[34].

These compound citation bases function in a distinguishable manner from the other forms of אֲשֶׁר צוה√ we have examined heretofore. This formulation introduces a quotation or paraphrase of material. For instance, in constrast to the independent citation base אֲשֶׁר צוה√ in Gen 3:11 that marks the referent "the tree" (see above), the compound form in v. 17 is used in order to quote a prior command.

$$\text{וּלְאָדָם אָמַר כִּי־שָׁמַעְתָּ לְקוֹל אִשְׁתֶּךָ וַתֹּאכַל מִן־הָעֵץ}$$
$$\text{אֲשֶׁר צִוִּיתִיךָ לֵאמֹר לֹא תֹאכַל מִמֶּנּוּ (Gen 3:17)}$$

The most satisfying referent of this entire compound citation base is not הָעֵץ, the head noun of אֲשֶׁר, because לֵאמֹר introduces the quotation of the previous command ("you shall not eat from it", italics). This exact command was stated in Gen 2:17:

$$\text{וּמֵעֵץ הַדַּעַת טוֹב וָרָע לֹא תֹאכַל מִמֶּנּוּ (Gen 2:17)}$$

2 Sam 7:7 quotes the LORD in a similar fashion.

The two compound citation bases that occur in the post-exilic historiography (Ezra 9:11; Neh 1:8) are used in a related but more sophisticated manner. This use of the compound citation base אֲשֶׁר צוה√...לֵאמֹר in Ezra 9:11 and Neh 1:8 distinguishes them from the earlier uses of this form in Gen 3:17 and 2 Sam 7:7. The formulations may in fact be related to "the preaching of the tradition" treated above.

In both Ezra 9:11 and Neh 1:8, אֲשֶׁר צוה√...לֵאמֹר introduces a paraphrase of the law as part of a more elaborate phenomenon. Only in these two passages is this compound citation base used in the course of

---

33   For treating the DD marker לֵאמֹר as a citation device, see Fishbane, 106.

34   The form in 1 Chr 17:6 is used attributively to describe judges ("whom I commanded"), and thus does not function as a citation base. The forms in 2 Kgs 14:6/2 Chr 25:4 (read with 𝔊 which does not attest כִּי) describe a person as well as being construed with כַּכָּתוּב (see chapter 2).

a prayer to introduce a recitation of God's law through His "servant(s)";
these servants are either the prophets (Ezra 9:11), or Moses (Neh 1:8).

וְעַתָּה מַה־נֹּאמַר אֱלֹהֵינוּ אַחֲרֵי־זֹאת כִּי עָזַבְנוּ מִצְוֹתֶיךָ אֲשֶׁר צִוִּיתָ
בְּיַד עֲבָדֶיךָ הַנְּבִיאִים לֵאמֹר
(Ezra 9:10-11a) [a quote of the law]

זְכָר־נָא אֶת־הַדָּבָר אֲשֶׁר צִוִּיתָ אֶת־מֹשֶׁה עַבְדְּךָ לֵאמֹר
(Neh 1:8) [a quote of the law]

Mason has already suggested extending von Rad's category of
"Levitical Sermons" to post-exilic *addresses* concerned with the
preaching and teaching of the tradition (see our treatment of Zech 1:6
and Mal 3:22 under the independent form of this citation base). The
evidence of Ezra 9:11 and Neh 1:8 may suggest that there was a
complementary phenomenon concerned with "praying the tradition", a
category recently examined by Boda[35]. The evidence appears
significant enough to entertain the possibility that the prayers in Ezra 9
and Neh 1, *addresses* to God, could be related to the tradition of
addresses identified by Mason. It does not seem improbable that two
types of addresses associated with the worshipping community might be
related. Could there have been a complementary "praying the tradition"
alongside Mason's "preaching the tradition" which consisted of the
same or comparable features?

The prayers in which these compound citation bases are
incorporated (Ezra 9:6ff.; Neh 1:5ff.) share many of the characteristic
elements of the addresses identified by Mason. Furthermore, the

---

35   M. Boda, *Praying the Tradition: The Origin and Use of Tradition in Nehemiah
9*, BZAW 277 (Berlin: DeGruyter, 1999). After his traditio-historical analysis
of Neh 9, Boda concludes that the prayer therein substantially antedates the
reforms of Ezra and Nehemiah: "One element unique to Neh 9 provided an
initial clue to the precise historical provenance of Neh 9: clear connections to
Zech 1 and 7-8. By examining Neh 9 in its literary context it was demonstrated
that the prayer originated prior to the work of Ezra and Nehemiah. Pursuing this
more closely, the early Persian period was identified as the most likely candidate.
Within this era the period immediately preceding the ministry of Haggai and
Zechariah was favoured, but the period after the disappearance of Zerubbabel but
before Ezra could not be discounted" (197). While seeking to build on the
strengths of Mason's compelling method above, we hope to demonstrate the
value of Boda's category "praying the tradition".

compound constructions in Ezra 9:11 and Neh 1:8 appear to have much in common with the citation bases we have already analysed in Zech 1:6 and Mal 3:22. Viewed together, this evidence suggests that the prayers in Ezra 9:6ff. and Neh 1:5ff. may be related to the addresses Mason described as "preaching the tradition".

First, both of these prayers share certain themes with the addresses concerned with "preaching the tradition". The following themes are noteworthy: the negative example of Israel's ancestors is clearly expressed (Ezra 9:7; Neh 1:6-7, 2 Chr 30:7); the themes of שוב√ (Ezra 9:14; Neh 1:9; Zech 1:3 [twice], 4, 6; Mal 3:24; 2 Chr 15:4; 29:10; 30:6 [twice], 8, 9 [thrice]) and פְּלֵיטָה "remnant" (Ezra 9:8, 13, 14, 15; Neh 1:2; 2 Chr 30:6); and, the LORD's extension of grace and compassion (2 Chr 30:9 [חַנּוּן וְרַחוּם יְהוָה]; Ezra 9:9 [חֶסֶד]36; Neh 1:5 [חֶסֶד]).

Secondly, the devices used in these two prayers in Ezra 9:6ff. and Neh 1:5ff. have parallels in the addresses concerned with "preaching the tradition". Ezra's prayer includes three rhetorical questions (Ezra 9:10, 14a, b). The illustration of a point by reference to history occurs in both prayers (vv. 7, 13; Neh 1:6). Both prayers, of course, also include at least one citation base (Ezra 9:11; Neh 1:8). An independent relative citation base צוה√ אֲשֶׁר occurs in Neh 1:7 as well37. In light of our study of citation bases we need to address all of these forms in detail.

The three citation bases in Ezra 9:11 and Neh 1:7-8 are reminiscent of those in Zech 1:6 and Mal 3:22. The similarities among these two groups of citation bases concern both their terminology and function. All of the citation bases in these addresses (Ezra 9:11; Neh 1:7, 8; Zech 1:6; Mal 3:22) are construed with עֶבֶד-language.

> ...which you have commanded by your *servants* the prophets, saying...(Ezra 9:11).

> ...which you did command your *servant* Moses (Neh 1:7).

> ...remember the word which you did command your *servant* Moses, saying...(Neh 1:8).

---

36   See also Ezra 9:13, 15.

37   We deferred our discussion of the citation base in Neh 1:7 above so that it could be considered with the compound citation base in Neh 1:8.

...which I commanded my *servants* the prophets...(Zech 1:6).

...remember the law of Moses my *servant*, even the statutes and ordinances which I commanded... (Mal 3:22).

In Neh 1:5-11, עֶבֶד occurs seven times (vv. 6 [twice], 7, 8, 10, 11[twice]). In fact, the similarities between Mal 3:22 and Neh 1:7-8 are especially striking. The most noteworthy features include: the imperative √זכר, the citation bases אֲשֶׁר צִוִּיתָ √צוה , the עֶבֶד-language, and identical legal terminology (highlights enlarged).

...וְלֹא־שָׁמַרְנוּ אֶת־הַמִּצְוֺת וְאֶת־הַחֻקִּים

וְאֶת־הַמִּשְׁפָּטִים אֲשֶׁר צִוִּיתָ אֶת־מֹשֶׁה עַבְדֶּךָ

זְכָר־נָא אֶת־הַדָּבָר אֲשֶׁר צִוִּיתָ אֶת־מֹשֶׁה עַבְדְּךָ

לֵאמֹר (Neh 1:7-8a)

זִכְרוּ תּוֹרַת מֹשֶׁה עַבְדִּי   אֲשֶׁר צִוִּיתִי אוֹתוֹ

(Mal 3:22) חֻקִּים וּמִשְׁפָּטִים   בְחֹרֵב עַל־כָּל־יִשְׂרָאֵל

The similarity between "preaching the tradition" and "praying the tradition" also extends to the function of these citation bases. The compound citation base in Ezra 9:11a and the paraphrase of legal passages that it introduces (vv. 11b-12) emphasise the law in connection with two rhetorical questions ("after all that has come upon us...shall we break your commandments and intermarry...? Would you not be angry with us until you destroy us without remnant or survivor?"). The convergence of these devices toward the end of these addresses results in a powerful summons to the audience to respond in faithfulness. Hence, Ezra's public prayer to the LORD not only possesses the exhortatory force of a homily, but this citation base is also used with two rhetorical questions which occur at the close of an address in order to elicit a faithful response from the assembly. The citation base, the referent, and a rhetorical question in Zech 1:6 also functioned to evoke a response at the climax of an address. In both passages the community responds (Ezra 10:1ff.; Zech 1:6b). The relations between the use of citation bases in the prayer in Ezra 9:6-15 as well as the homily fragment in Zech 1:1-6, demonstrate how the phenomena of preaching and prayer may have been related to each other.

Nehemiah's prayer is not a *public* address and understandably lacks any homiletical element. But making due allowance for this *private* address to God, it is noteworthy that after the compound citation base with its characteristic paraphrase of legal passages Nehemiah ends his prayer with a series of requests ("...be attentive...give success...grant...mercy...", vv. 10-11). Nehemiah closes this address waiting for a response. The use of the formulation in Nehemiah's prayer is broadly comparable to the way that a citation base was used to elicit a response from an audience in the examples of "preaching the tradition" above.

Another point of comparison between these passages concerns the common view of the relation between the legal and prophetic traditions. Regarding Zech 1:6, Mason states, "it is interesting that the prophetic word is now becoming regarded as authoritative teaching on a par with Torah, for that is what the paralleling of the legal term 'statutes'...with my words must imply"[38]. The citation base in Malachi also associates the legal and prophetic traditions. Similar to Zech 1:6, Mal 3:22ff. links the command to remember the law in the post-exilic age with the coming prophet who is typified as the great Elijah of the prophetic tradition. The citation base in Ezra 9:11ff. also links the law with the prophetic tradition. Note that the citation base which refers to what had been entrusted to the prophets ("... your commandments which you gave by your servants *the prophets* saying...") introduces a paraphrase from several legal texts. In Neh 1:7 and 8, Moses, the prototypical prophet (Deut 18:15ff.), is cited.

Though the evidence is admittedly slim, a case might be made for associating the prayers in Ezra 9:6ff. and Neh 1:5ff. with the tradition of preaching Mason has proposed. That is, "preaching the tradition" may be expanded to include addresses concerned with "praying the tradition".

---

38 See also Mason's translation of Elliger's view that this is a step toward the canon (290 n. 17; see Elliger, *Die Propheten Nahum, Habakuk, Zephanja, Haggai, Sacharja, Maleachi,* ATD [Göttingen: 1964] 101).

2. Other Compound Citation Bases

The other compound citation bases that occur with the relative formulation אֲשֶׁר צוה√ are never repeated. The most noteworthy feature of these citation bases is that they occur exclusively in the deuteronomistic literature.

The forms that may be construed with אֲשֶׁר צוה√ as a compound citation base include: כְּדְבַר כְּכָל־הַתּוֹרָה (Josh 1:7; 2 Kgs 17:13); כְּכָל־הַדְּבָרִים הָאֵלֶּה אֲשֶׁר צִוָּה הַמֶּלֶךְ (Josh 8:27); and יְהוָה (Jer 38:27). אֲשֶׁר צוה√ may even take a tautological form (e.g., כְּכָל־הַמִּצְוָה אֲשֶׁר צִוִּיתִי אֶתְכֶם [Deut 31:5]; see also 26:13)[39]. We will refer to 2 Kgs 17:34 later since the dominant construction used in this passage is the comparative citation base.

D. Rubric - "A Distinct Literary Convention"

A third use for the relative citation base אֲשֶׁר צוה√ in the form of a finite verb is as part of a rubric. Meier states, "a typical identifying feature of a rubric is the verbless phrase, 'This is the law/words/blessing (which)…'"[40]. A rubric is "a distinct literary convention" that has a "titular character" and provides a "descriptive title"[41]. Meier describes the specific role of a rubric by comparing its function with that of a DD marker. He states that a DD marker "integrates a statement into a literary continuum without summarizing its content, a rubric summarizes the content of a quotation with little attention to integrating the quotation into a larger context"[42]. Rubrics may assume an independent or a compound form.

---

39 Both of these constructions in Deut will be treated below in the section on comparative citation bases.
40 Meier, 22.
41 *Ibid.*, 21.
42 *Ibid.*, 23.

1. The Independent Rubric

When it is part of a rubric the relative citation base אֲשֶׁר צוה√ functions in yet more ways than we have previously observed. For instance, this "literary convention" may either introduce (Exod 16:16, 32; 35:1; Num 30:2; 31:21) or conclude (Lev 8:5; 9:6; 27:34; Num 30:17; 36:13; Deut 28:69) a referent. Furthermore, these referents take several different forms and sizes. As can be seen from the passages above, these independent rubrics occur exclusively in the law.

In Exod 16:16, an independent form of a rubric (enlarged) introduces a referent which consists of the rest of the verse (italicised).

זֶה הַדָּבָר אֲשֶׁר צִוָּה יְהוָה לִקְטוּ מִמֶּנּוּ אִישׁ לְפִי אָכְלוֹ
עֹמֶר לַגֻּלְגֹּלֶת מִסְפַּר נַפְשֹׁתֵיכֶם אִישׁ לַאֲשֶׁר בְּאָהֳלוֹ תִּקָּחוּ
(Exod 16:16)

Exod 16:16 has a relatively short referent for an independent rubric.

Independent rubrics typically occur with much larger referents. Repetition also frequently occurs among these constructions.

For instance, the rubric in Deut 28:69 governs the entire chapter that it concludes.

אֵלֶּה דִבְרֵי הַבְּרִית אֲשֶׁר־צִוָּה יְהוָה אֶת־מֹשֶׁה לִכְרֹת
אֶת־בְּנֵי יִשְׂרָאֵל בְּאֶרֶץ מוֹאָב מִלְּבַד הַבְּרִית אֲשֶׁר־כָּרַת אִתָּם
בְּחֹרֵב (Deut 28:69; referent = vv. 1-68)

In Num 36:13, the rubric serves as a detailed title for a much larger referent.

אֵלֶּה הַמִּצְוֹת וְהַמִּשְׁפָּטִים אֲשֶׁר צִוָּה יְהוָה בְּיַד־מֹשֶׁה אֶל־בְּנֵי
יִשְׂרָאֵל בְּעַרְבֹת מוֹאָב עַל יַרְדֵּן יְרֵחוֹ (Num 36:13)

The rubric includes all of v. 13. The information provided by this entire non-verbal sentence is what enables us to determine the referent. The titular nature of the rubric restricts the referent to, in this case, those commands that were related to Israel on the plains of Moab by the Jordan opposite Jericho (בְּעַרְבֹת מוֹאָב עַל יַרְדֵּן יְרֵחוֹ). This is a recurring phrase throughout a large portion of Numbers (22:1; 26:3, 63; 31:12; 33:48, 50; 35:1). An examination of these phrases suggests that the referent of the rubric in Num 36:13 is the section 26:1-36:13[43]. Not only is this one of the largest referents that we have observed, but the rubric in Num 36:13, the last verse in the book, also functions as a summary statement.

Similarly, the last verse of Leviticus appears to function as a concluding rubric for the entire book.

אֵלֶּה הַמִּצְוֹת אֲשֶׁר צִוָּה יְהוָה אֶת־מֹשֶׁה אֶל־בְּנֵי יִשְׂרָאֵל בְּהַר סִינָי

(Lev 27:34; referent = the entire book of Lev)

Uniquely, the referent in Num 30:3-15 is governed by two rubrics located in vv. 2 and 17. It is consistent with the passages we have observed that a summarising rubric that concludes the referent generally has a fuller titular character.

זֶה הַדָּבָר אֲשֶׁר צִוָּה יְהוָה (Num 30:2)

אֵלֶּה הַחֻקִּים אֲשֶׁר צִוָּה יְהוָה אֶת־מֹשֶׁה בֵּין אִישׁ לְאִשְׁתּוֹ בֵּין־אָב
לְבִתּוֹ בִּנְעֻרֶיהָ בֵּית אָבִיהָ (Num 30:17)

The use of two rubrics for one referent is an example of the repetition that we will see is generally characteristic of the citation bases in the law and the deuteronomistic literature.

The most outstanding features of these independent rubrics concern their exclusive use in the Pentateuch, their size, the relatively large referents that they govern, and, to a lesser degree, repetition.

2. Compound Rubrics

Rubrics may also consist of a compound form. The DD marker לֵאמֹר is the form that is most frequently used with the relative citation base in a rubric. The use of לֵאמֹר transforms the function of the independent rubric with which it is construed. According to Meier, "a rubric may easily be transformed into a DD marker by appending a subordinate clause that closes with לֵאמֹר or by employing the phrase

---

43   The use of this phrase in Num 22:1 does not appear to be related to the rubric in 36:13.

within a narrative proper"[44]. However, the compound citation base is not simply a DD marker since a rubric, which provides a descriptive title, is part of this construction. This compound rubric is used only to introduce a referent and it is also restricted to the law[45].

The compound rubric that occurs in Deut 6:1-2 is the largest introduction that entails a rubric we have encountered. Rather than using לאמר, this rubric is construed with the citation base צוה√ אֲשֶׁר in the form of a participle. In Deut 6:1-2, both of these forms of the rubric (enlarged below) function together to introduce the referent.

וְזֹאת הַמִּצְוָה הַחֻקִּים וְהַמִּשְׁפָּטִים אֲשֶׁר צִוָּה יְהוָה
אֱלֹהֵיכֶם לְלַמֵּד אֶתְכֶם...לִשְׁמֹר אֶת־כָּל־חֻקֹּתָיו וּמִצְוֹתָיו
אֲשֶׁר אָנֹכִי מְצַוְּךָ אַתָּה... (Deut 6:1-2)

This rubric introduces the referent in vv. 3-25. The identification of this referent would not be clear apart from the information that is related in the compound rubric in vv. 1-2. Note that the title of this rubric in v. 1 includes a reference to life in Palestine ("in the land where you are going ...") which is the only indication that the referent includes vv. 10ff. There are also various legal terms repeated in this cumbersome introduction to the referent.

E. צוה√ אֲשֶׁר Functioning as a Comparative Clause

There are a handful of passages where צוה√ אֲשֶׁר functions like a comparative clause[46]. These citation bases govern a range of elements. Three of these constructions (Exod 34:18; Num 4:49; Deut 17:3) qualify one clause (Type I). Jer 32:35 is a negative formulation ("which I had not commanded them"). This citation base, however, qualifies only the contiguous infinitive phrase (Type II; enlarged).

---

44 Meier, 22.
45 Exod 35:4 (referent = vv. 5-19); Lev 17:2 (referent = vv. 3-7, cf. v. 8); Num 36:6a (referent = vv. 6b-9).
46 GK § 161b.

וַיִּבְנוּ אֶת־בָּמוֹת הַבַּעַל אֲשֶׁר בְּגֵיא בֶן־הִנֹּם לְהַעֲבִיר אֶת־בְּנֵיהֶם

וְאֶת־בְּנוֹתֵיהֶם לַמֹּלֶךְ אֲשֶׁר לֹא־צִוִּיתִים (Jer 32:35a)

אֲשֶׁר צוה√ is never used as a comparative clause in the post-exilic literature.

Lastly there are several uses of אֲשֶׁר צוה√ which do not attribute a referent to another source and thus do not enter our examination[47].

F. Conclusions

In this chapter, the forms we have studied have been overwhelmingly concentrated in the law and the deuteronomistic literature. Among the few occurrences of these citation bases in the non-synoptic post-exilic literature, five of the eight citation bases were observed to function in a distinctive manner. Furthermore, these citation bases (Ezra 9:11; Neh 1:7-8; Zech 1:6; Mal 3:22) may be related to the vindication of the legal and prophetic traditions after the fall of Jerusalem and the experience of exile.

Excursus: Genre

The distribution of the forms and functions of citation bases in the law, the deuteronomistic material, and the post-exilic literature cannot be attributed simply to the difference in literary genres. For instance, many forms common in the legal material were also observed in the deuteronomistic historiography and the prose sections of Jeremiah. Since the non-synoptic post-exilic historiography does not customarily reflect these deuteronomistic forms, one cannot conclude that a certain construction is typical of biblical historiography. Hence, the differences appear to be

---

47   When the antecedent of אֲשֶׁר is יוֹם the expression functions as a temporal statement (Num 15:23; Deut 32:46; 2 Sam 7:11; Neh 5:14; 1 Chr 17:10). In Gen 18:19, לְמַעַן אֲשֶׁר צוה√ introduces a purpose statement. In Deut 2:37, the form כֹּל אֲשֶׁר־צִוָּה יְהוָה אֱלֹהֵינוּ is used in a locative sense and does not attribute a referent to another source. In other places (Num 34:29; Lam 1:10; 1 Chr 17:6), one of the forms addressed above is substantivised to describe a group of people who had been commanded to fulfil some task (e.g., "those whom the LORD commanded").

due to other factors (the development of citation bases, SBH and LBH; etc.; see below).

II. Comparative Citation Bases with צוה√ and מִצְוָה

A. Introduction

Both צוה√ and מִצְוָה are used more extensively in comparative citation bases than the corresponding forms with כָּתוּב. Consequently, our analysis of the comparative clause כַּאֲשֶׁר צוה√ and the *Vergleichspräpositionale* כְּמִצְוַה below will advance our provisional assessment of Jenni's view that these sentence constituents are equivalent in function. The following analysis will also provide a broader context to understand the syntactic functions that we observed above for כַּכָּתוּב. After analysing the following comparative citation bases, we will be able to judge more accurately whether the range of functions observed for כַּכָּתוּב is unique to it, or whether it is consistent with the *Vergleichspräpositionale* כְּמִצְוַה.

Whatever the evidence will indicate, the analysis of these comparative constructions will not only advance our emerging assessment of Jenni's theory of the equivalent functions of these two comparative constructions, but it will also provide a broader basis for evaluating the use of *Vergleichspräpositionalen* as citation formulæ in the post-exilic period.

B. Comparative Clauses with צוה√

In this section, we will demonstrate the different ways that the citation base כַּאֲשֶׁר צוה√ is employed.

1. The Independent Form of √צוה כַּאֲשֶׁר

a. Citation Bases that Qualify One Clause

As we have observed before, a comparative clause may qualify a single clause (Type I). The main clause (enlarged) is usually the contiguous clause.

וַיָּמָל אַבְרָהָם אֶת־יִצְחָק בְּנוֹ בֶּן־שְׁמֹנַת יָמִים
כַּאֲשֶׁר צִוָּה אֹתוֹ אֱלֹהִים (Gen 21:4)

This type of relation between the citation base and the referent occurs throughout the Old Testament[48], but, following the distribution pattern of relative citation bases in this chapter, it is concentrated in the law and the deuteronomistic material. There are only two uses in the post-exilic historiography.

There are some deviations from the standard form in Gen 21:4 above which provide a background for our consideration of the two post-exilic citation bases. Among the Type I passages that occur outside of the post-exilic historiography, there is one use of the citation base כַּאֲשֶׁר √צוה that qualifies an ellipted clause. Since the command and the fulfillment statement occur in close proximity to each other, the latter may consist of only an ellipted clause. The command is given in Num 26:2.

שְׂאוּ אֶת־רֹאשׁ כָּל־עֲדַת בְּנֵי־יִשְׂרָאֵל מִבֶּן עֶשְׂרִים
שָׁנָה וָמַעְלָה לְבֵית אֲבֹתָם כָּל־יֹצֵא צָבָא בְּיִשְׂרָאֵל (Num 26:2)

---

48 Gen 21:4; Exod 16:24; 23:15; Lev 9:21; 10:18; Num 1:19 (referent v.18); 2:33; 3:42, 51; 20:9; 31:7, 41; Deut 4:5; 5:32; 6:25; 10:5b; 12:21; 20:17; 24:8b; Josh 11:20; 13:6; 14:2; 21:8; Ezek 37:10; Esth 2:20; Ezra 4:3. Lev 10:15 most likely belongs in this category; however, the referent may consist of vv. 12-15 (for the use of כַּאֲשֶׁר √צוה to modify more than one clause, see below). The participial form of this construction is rare (Num 32:25).

Take a census of all the congregation of the sons of Israel from twenty
years old and upward, by their fathers' households, whoever is able to go
out to war in Israel (Num 26:2).

This directive is fulfilled in v. 4. The observance of this command is
marked with a citation base (italics) but the referent (compare the
enlarged material in both v. 2 and v. 4) has been ellipted.

מִבֶּן עֶשְׂרִים [————————ellipted material————————]
(Num 26:4) ... *שָׁנָה וָמָעְלָה כַּאֲשֶׁר צִוָּה יְהוָה אֶת־מֹשֶׁה וּבְנֵי יִשְׂרָאֵל*

Num 26:4 is the only occurrence of an ellipted apodosis in a complex
comparative sentence with √צוה. However, this ellipsis appears to be
at least comparable to a feature Steiner observes among conditional
clauses.

Omission of the apodosis is permissible in contexts which allow the
hearer to reconstruct it. When the speaker lays out two antithetical
alternatives in conditional form, the apodosis of the first conditional may
be omitted if it is the one preferred by the speaker and requires no further
action[49].

Based on Num 26:4, a similar situation appears to exist among complex
comparative sentences. The main clause of the complex comparative
sentence need only consist of enough material so as to make its
reconstruction obvious from the context.

כַּאֲשֶׁר צוה√ may also qualify a command in the form of an
infinitive absolute phrase[50]. Such a usage occurs twice among the ten
commandments.

שָׁמוֹר אֶת־יוֹם הַשַּׁבָּת לְקַדְּשׁוֹ כַּאֲשֶׁר צִוְּךָ יְהוָה
(Deut 5:12) אֱלֹהֶיךָ

The entire command in v. 12a appears to be the referent (cf. Exod 20:8).
The infinitive absolute used as an imperative supplies the predication for

---

49   R. C. Steiner, 169.
50   For the emphatic imperative in the form of an infinitive absolute, see GK § 113
     bb and n. 2.

the sentence (cf. the other imperatives and negative commands in Deut 5:7ff.). Thus, the role of the infinitive absolute in this sentence corresponds to that of a finite verb (i.e., the imperative שָׁמֹר; Type I) and not an infinitive construct (Type II). The citation base in Deut 5:16 also qualifies an infinitive absolute phrase.

Both Deut 5:32 and 6:25 include citation bases that qualify a hendiadys statement (enlarged) that consists of the two verb stems √שמר and √עשה ("to diligently observe").

וּשְׁמַרְתֶּם לַעֲשׂוֹת כַּאֲשֶׁר צִוָּה יְהוָה אֱלֹהֵיכֶם אֶתְכֶם לֹא תָסֻרוּ
יָמִין וּשְׂמֹאל (Deut 5:32)

וּצְדָקָה תִּהְיֶה־לָּנוּ כִּי־נִשְׁמֹר לַעֲשׂוֹת אֶת־כָּל־הַמִּצְוָה הַזֹּאת
לִפְנֵי יְהוָה אֱלֹהֵינוּ כַּאֲשֶׁר צִוָּנוּ (Deut 6:25)

Since these two verb stems function together to form a hendiadys statement, the citation base cannot be considered to qualify merely the infinitive construct with √עשה (Type II).

In addition to the uncustomary features just reviewed, there are two other citation bases in this section that appear to be used in an undeveloped manner.

In Lev 9:21, we have another use of a citation base where all of the details of the command that is ostensibly being cited are not observed. The legal tradition in Lev 7:32-34 requires that the breast and thigh of the elevation offering be given to the priests perpetually. In contrast to this legislation, Lev 9:21 states that Aaron raised these portions of the sacrifice as "an elevation offering to the LORD".

וְאֵת הֶחָזוֹת וְאֵת שׁוֹק הַיָּמִין הֵנִיף אַהֲרֹן תְּנוּפָה לִפְנֵי יְהוָה
כַּאֲשֶׁר צִוָּה מֹשֶׁה (Lev 9:21)

Like the use of the citation bases in Josh 8:30ff., there is dissonance between what Lev 9:21 represents as the observance of the law and the cited legal basis. Such dissonance between a command and a fulfilment statement has been observed only in the law and the deuteronomistic literature. This appears to be part of the undeveloped use of citation bases. Milgrom may be correct to suggest that the change from כַּאֲשֶׁר

צִוָּה יְהוָה in v. 10 to כַּאֲשֶׁר צִוָּה מֹשֶׁה in v. 21 might suggest that Aaron's deed stems from the initiative of Moses and not the LORD[51]. But even if Milgrom is correct, this would still distinguish the reference to Mosaic authority in Lev 9:21 from those in the post-exilic historiography. Such dissonance between commands and their alleged fulfilment is consistent with our view above that the veracity of the legal and prophetic traditions was embraced in a distinctive manner after the fall of Jerusalem, the Babylonian exile, and the limited success of the initial returns after the decree of Cyrus in 538 B.C.

Another undeveloped use of citation bases among these Type I constructions in the law concerns the placement of these forms. The citation base in Deut 12:21 qualifies only one clause (Type I). However, in Deut 12:21b, a relative clause (enlarged below) causes there to be a non-contiguous relation between the referent ("then you may slaughter of your herd and flock") and the citation base ("as I have commanded you").

וְזָבַחְתָּ מִבְּקָרְךָ וּמִצֹּאנְךָ אֲשֶׁר נָתַן יְהוָה לְךָ כַּאֲשֶׁר
צִוִּיתִךָ (Deut 12:21b)

In the other passages in this category, we have not observed a non-contiguous relation to exist between the citation base and referent.

Note that all these exceptional forms of the simple Type I qualification are restricted to the law.

In light of the use of this citation base in the law and the deuteronomistic material, we will now address the two post-exilic citation bases that qualify the immediate clause (Type I). The two occurrences of this formulation in post-exilic literature are used to refer to commands given in the reconstruction period. The form in Ezra 4:3 cites an order of Cyrus of Persia. This citation base does not qualify the entire complex sentence, but only the contiguous כִּי clause (Type I).

וַיֹּאמֶר לָהֶם זְרֻבָּבֶל וְיֵשׁוּעַ וּשְׁאָר רָאשֵׁי הָאָבוֹת לְיִשְׂרָאֵל
לֹא־לָכֶם וָלָנוּ לִבְנוֹת בַּיִת לֵאלֹהֵינוּ כִּי אֲנַחְנוּ יַחַד נִבְנֶה לַיהוָה
אֱלֹהֵי יִשְׂרָאֵל כַּאֲשֶׁר צִוָּנוּ הַמֶּלֶךְ כּוֹרֶשׁ מֶלֶךְ־פָּרָס (Ezra 4:3)

---

51   Milgrom, *Leviticus 1-16*, AB (London: Doubleday, 1991) 586.

We are assured that the citation base (enlarged) qualifies only the subordinate clause introduced with כִּי (italics) for at least two reasons. First, in Ezra 4:3, only the subordinate clause ("but we alone will build to the LORD, the God of Israel") corresponds to Cyrus' edict in Ezra 1:1-4 to which the citation base refers. Secondly, כִּי introduces an adversative clause after a negation and is thus distinguished from the preceding material[52]. Hence, in contrast to Deut 12:21 (above), Ezra 4:3 qualifies the contiguous subordinate clause and not the main clause or the entire complex sentence[53].

Esth 2:20 contains the second post-exilic citation base in this section. The use of some of the citation bases in Esther is related to the literary artistry of this book. Part of this artistry in Esther concerns the use of ironic phrases to indicate dramatic reversals of fortune in the narrative. More than one pair of citation bases in Esther are part of this phenomenon. The first pair occurs in Esth 2:20 and 4:17 (see 3:12 and 8:9 below)[54]. In Esth 2:20 and 4:17, two citation bases (enlarged) are used to indicate a transfer of authority in connection with the ironic reversal of the fate of Israelites in Susa.

אֵין אֶסְתֵּר מַגֶּדֶת מוֹלַדְתָּהּ וְאֶת־עַמָּהּ כַּאֲשֶׁר צִוָּה עָלֶיהָ
מָרְדֳּכַי וְאֶת־מַאֲמַר מָרְדֳּכַי אֶסְתֵּר עֹשָׂה כַּאֲשֶׁר הָיְתָה
בְאָמְנָה אִתּוֹ (Esth 2:20)

---

52 For "Adversativsätze mit כִּי nach Negation", see Walter Gross, "Satzfolge, Satzteilfolge und Satzart als Kriterien der Subkategorisierung hebräischer Konjunktionalsätze, am Beispiel der כִּי-Sätze untersucht", in *Text, Methode und Grammatik: Wolfgang Richter zum 65. Geburtstag,* Walter Gross et al. (Sankt Ottilien: EOS, 1991) 108.

53 In order to maintain such distinctions between uses of comparative citation bases, it appears best to address the types of relations between comparative citation bases and referents in terms of the number of clauses modified. This has the advantage of not compounding the presentation of the material by classifying according to the sentence type (simple, compound, complex), especially since a complex sentence may entail several subordinate clauses. Moreover, compound sentences in a chain language like Hebrew would be difficult to define to the satisfaction of all scholars.

54 Though it will be categorised according to its specific form below, Esth 4:17 must be discussed with 2:20.

וַיַּעֲבֹר מָרְדֳּכָי וַיַּעַשׂ כְּכֹל אֲשֶׁר־צִוְּתָה עָלָיו אֶסְתֵּר (Esth 4:17)

In 2:20, Esther is depicted as the one who had always obeyed the authority of Mordecai from her childhood. At this point in the narrative, she maintains her commitment to conceal her Jewish identity just as Mordecai had instructed her (2:10). Esth 2:20 becomes a base for some of the ironic reversals in chapter 4. The dramatic force of this reversal culminates in 4:16-17. Here Esther dramatically expresses her new commitment to reveal her Jewish identity which in turn results in the delivery of the Israelites in Susa.

A reversal of authority also occurs between Mordecai and Esther at this point in the narrative. At this climax in the narrative, all of these reversals (Esther's identity, Jewish destiny, and the Hebrew who has authority to give directions) converge and are interwoven with great skill and effect. It is noteworthy that Esther's renowned statement in v. 16 ("Go gather all the Jews..., and hold a fast on my behalf...; I and my maids [will do likewise]. After that I will go to the king, though it is against the law; and if I perish, I perish") is the referent of the citation base (v. 17) and that all of these reversals pivot on these two verses. Esther's declaration states her resolve to disclose her identity which is instrumental for overturning the fate of the Jewish community. Furthermore, the citation base in v. 17 marks the reversal of authority between Mordecai and Esther. In contrast to the narrative up to this point, Esther now directs Mordecai. Note that the ironic switch to Esther as the one who commands her uncle is made even more forceful with the form of the citation base in 4:17 ("So Mordecai went away and did everything [כֹל] just as Esther had commanded him").

Hence, the citation bases in Esther 2:20 and 4:17 are part of the sophisticated literary structure that is concerned with the central reversals in the book of Esther: Esther's identity (non-Jewish or Jewish); the fate of the Jewish community (death or life); and the Jewish person who gives commands in the narrative (Mordecai or Esther)[55].

---

55   For the most recent examinations of the literary artistry of Esther, see Frederic W. Bush, *Ruth, Esther,* WBC (Dallas, Texas: Word, 1996); and, Charles V. Dorothy, *The Books of Esther: Structure, Genre and Textual Integrity,* JSOTS 187 (Sheffield: Sheffield Press, 1997).

Bush similarly describes the reversal of authority between Mordecai and Esther.

> The narrator begins his characterization of her quite indirectly, for she is not given an independent introduction in the story but is presented as Mordecai's ward, a role the narrator maintains for her even when she becomes queen (as the repeated note in 2:10, 20 that she continued to obey Mordecai indicates)[56].

> This is dramatically changed, however, in the exchange with Mordecai (4:4-17; cf. Clines...). In one moving and surprising dialogue she is transformed from the pretty young thing who has been more object than agent, and the dutiful ward who is always obedient, into Queen Esther, one of the two leaders of the Jewish community[57].

Describing Esther's pivotal words in 4:16 and their relation to the reversal of authority, Bush states,

> This is the turning point in Esther's development. Heretofore, though queen, she was nevertheless fully under Mordecai's authority as his ward. Now she is the one who sets the conditions and gives the commands. Indeed, in his closing narrative summary 4:17, the narrator sets up a striking contrast. In v. 8 it was Mordecai who *ordered* Esther to go to the king in order to plead with him on behalf of her people. Here he reports "Mordecai did exactly as Esther had *ordered* him"[58].

As we have already observed, the theme of Mordecai's commands to Esther is developed earlier in 2:10 and 20. The use of the citation base with כל and the pro-form √עשׂה in 4:17 makes the switch to Esther's authority in the community even more thorough, especially since the referent of this citation base expresses Esther's resolve which is the pivot for several of the key reversals in the book.

Hence, the pair of citation bases in Esth 2:20 and 4:17 is inextricably connected to the sophisticated literary structure that is at the heart of the book of Esther.

---

56 Bush, 319.
57 *Ibid.*, 320.
58 *Ibid.*, his emphasis.

b. Citation Bases that Qualify More Than One Clause

So far in this chapter we have observed various comparative clauses that qualify a single clause (Type I). We now turn our attention to explore the other ways that a כַּאֲשֶׁר comparative clause may function. So far in our study of comparative constructions, both in the form of a clause and a prepositional phrase, we have encountered examples where the referent consists of either one clause (Type I) or some smaller sentence constituent (Types II, III, etc.). Immediately below, we will introduce examples of כַּאֲשֶׁר √צוה citation bases that qualify referents which consist of more than one clause. Since these types of construction appear to mark the salient difference between the customary functions of a comparative clause and a *Vergleichspräpositionale*, we will categorise these larger roles with Arabic letters (e.g., Type A, B, etc.) and not Roman numerals. This final point remains to be demonstrated, but we introduce the distinction at this point so as to clarify our discussion below.

i. Citation Bases that Qualify Two Clauses

A single כַּאֲשֶׁר √צוה comparative clause may qualify two clauses; this can be demonstrated in at least three different ways. First, a citation base may at times be used to fulfil a command that has been recounted in the previous context. When this is the case, the correspondence between the command and its fulfilment in the same pericope verifies that the citation base qualifies both clauses. For example, the deed authorised in Num 31:47 is based on the directive stated in v. 30. The degree of correspondence between these two verses is so extensive that it appears needless to highlight it.

וּמִמַּחֲצִת בְּנֵי־יִשְׂרָאֵל תִּקַּח אֶחָד אָחֻז מִן־הַחֲמִשִּׁים מִן־הָאָדָם
מִן־הַבָּקָר מִן־הַחֲמֹרִים וּמִן־הַצֹּאן מִכָּל־הַבְּהֵמָה וְנָתַתָּה אֹתָם
לַלְוִיִּם שֹׁמְרֵי מִשְׁמֶרֶת מִשְׁכַּן יְהוָה (Num 31:30)

וַיִּקַּח מֹשֶׁה מִמַּחֲצִת בְּנֵי־יִשְׂרָאֵל אֶת־הָאָחֻז אֶחָד
מִן־הַחֲמִשִּׁים מִן־הָאָדָם וּמִן־הַבְּהֵמָה וַיִּתֵּן אֹתָם לַלְוִיִּם שֹׁמְרֵי
מִשְׁמֶרֶת מִשְׁכַּן יְהוָה כַּאֲשֶׁר צִוָּה יְהוָה אֶת־מֹשֶׁה (Num 31:47)

The correspondence between these two verses indicates that the referent in v. 47 consists of both clauses ("from the Israelites' half Moses took one [√לקח] of every fifty, both of persons and of animals, and gave [√נתן] them to the Levites who had charge of the tabernacle of the LORD; as the LORD had comanded Moses", NRSV).

The Type A citation bases that have this sort of correlation between a command and its fulfilment occur exclusively in the law and the deuteronomistic literature[59].

A second way that √צוה כַּאֲשֶׁר can be shown to qualify two clauses is when there is a synonymous or complementary relation between them. In Josh 11:12, the two initial clauses are concerned with the concept of subjugation (√לכד and √נכה, enlarged).

וְאֶת־כָּל־עָרֵי הַמְּלָכִים־הָאֵלֶּה וְאֶת־כָּל־מַלְכֵיהֶם לָכַד יְהוֹשֻׁעַ
וַיַּכֵּם לְפִי־חֶרֶב הֶחֱרִים אוֹתָם כַּאֲשֶׁר צִוָּה מֹשֶׁה עֶבֶד
יְהוָה (Josh 11:12)

Though the command for Joshua's actions cannot be located in the immediate context or in one specific verse elsewhere, it appears that both clauses are the fulfilment of various passages in the law (e.g., Num 37:50-53; Deut 7:2; 20:16-17). There is no significant difference in the distribution of these citation bases in the Old Testament and those treated immediately above[60].

A third way of identifying passages that belong in this subcategory occurs when a comparative clause introduced with √צוה כַּאֲשֶׁר

---

59 Gen 7:9 (referent = vv. 7-9a, cf. vv. 1ff.); 47:11 (referent = v. 11, cf. v. 6, command by Pharoah); Num 31:47 (referent = v. 47, cf. v. 30); 1 Sam 17:20 (referent = the two immediate finite verbs which do not form a hendiadys statement, cf. vv. 17-18, command by Jesse); Jer 13:5b (referent = v. 5a, cf. v. 4). Commands are typically given by the God of Israel or his servant Moses unless otherwise noted above. Josh 10:40 (referent = v. 40, cf. Deut 1:7-8) is best presented here in order to limit our categories even though the command is not in the immediate context.

60 Exod 39:1c (not a pro-form √עשׂה, referent = v. 1a-b); Deut 1:19b (referent = v. 19a), 41c (referent = v. 41b); Josh 11:12c (referent = v. 12a-b, cf. 9:24; 10:40; Num 33:52-53; Deut 7:2; 20:16-17).

qualifies two coordinated clauses that are semantically dependent upon one another. In Josh 8:33b, the semantic dependence between the two preceding non-verbal clauses ("half of them are in front of Mount Gerizim and half of them are in front of Mount Ebal") requires that the כַּאֲשֶׁר clause qualifies both statements.

חֶצְיוֹ אֶל־מוּל הַר־גְּרִזִים וְהַחֶצְיוֹ אֶל־מוּל הַר־עֵיבָל כַּאֲשֶׁר
(Josh 8:33b) צִוָּה מֹשֶׁה עֶבֶד־יְהוָה לְבָרֵךְ אֶת־הָעָם יִשְׂרָאֵל בָּרִאשֹׁנָה

Josh 8:33b appears to be the only occurrence of two clauses that are semantically dependent upon each other.

The lack of a verb stem in the referent is not a common syntactic occurrence among such comparative citation bases and may be related to the other outstanding features we noted in Josh 8:30ff. in our treatment of כַּכָּתוּב. As we observed there, the deeds in v. 33 that are stated to have been accomplished according to the law (Deut 27) were not in fact followed in every detail despite the high concentration of citation bases in these few verses. This formed part of the basis for concluding that the use of כָּתוּב citation bases in Josh 8:30ff. was undeveloped. It is not surprising, then, to discover another uncharacteristic feature associated with the כַּאֲשֶׁר צוה√ citation in v. 33b. What we can add to our previous discussion of vv. 30ff is that the non-verbal referent in v. 33bα is rare among comparative citation bases.

In these three different manners, we have demonstrated that comparative clauses can qualify two clauses (Type A). It is striking that the distribution of these citation bases is restricted to the law and deuteronomistic literature. Such a Type A function for a comparative construction has not been observed among *Vergleichspräpositionale* studied so far in our examination. If this continues to be the case in examples to be analysed below, then this may be an indication that this *Vergleichspräpositionale*, an abbreviation of the larger comparative clause according to Jenni[61], is employed when a smaller scope of qualification is desired.

---

61 Jenni, 30-31, cf. 130f.

In fact, the difference between the qualification ranges of *Vergleichspräpositionalen* and comparative clauses is much more diverse than what is suggested by the Type A passages above.

ii. Citation Bases that Qualify Three Clauses

A comparative clause can also qualify three clauses (Type B). Compare the command in Exod 34:1-2 to the fulfilment statement with citation base in v. 4.

וַיֹּאמֶר יְהוָה אֶל־מֹשֶׁה פְּסָל־לְךָ שְׁנֵי־לֻחֹת אֲבָנִים כָּרִאשֹׁנִים
וְכָתַבְתִּי עַל־הַלֻּחֹת אֶת־הַדְּבָרִים אֲשֶׁר הָיוּ עַל־הַלֻּחֹת הָרִאשֹׁנִים
אֲשֶׁר שִׁבַּרְתָּ ׃ וֶהְיֵה נָכוֹן לַבֹּקֶר וְעָלִיתָ בַבֹּקֶר אֶל־הַר סִינַי
וְנִצַּבְתָּ לִי שָׁם עַל־רֹאשׁ הָהָר (Exod 34:1-2)

וַיִּפְסֹל שְׁנֵי־לֻחֹת אֲבָנִים כָּרִאשֹׁנִים וַיַּשְׁכֵּם מֹשֶׁה בַבֹּקֶר
וַיַּעַל אֶל־הַר סִינַי כַּאֲשֶׁר צִוָּה יְהוָה אֹתוֹ (Exod 34:4)

The close proximity of the command and the fulfilment statement, as well as the marked correspondence of terms (see especially the highlights above), clearly indicate that the citation base in v. 4 qualifies the three preceding clauses in this verse (עלה√, שכם√, and פסל√). Hence, the כַּאֲשֶׁר clause of a complex comparative sentence may qualify three clauses (Type B). The citation base כַּאֲשֶׁר צוה√ functions in this manner only in the law and the deuteronomistic literature[62].

iii. Citation Bases that Qualify Four Clauses

There are two examples of a כַּאֲשֶׁר צוה√ comparative clause qualifying four clauses (Type C)[63]. One way to establish that כַּאֲשֶׁר

---

62   Exod 34:4b β (referent = 4a-b α, cf. vv. 1-3); Num 15:36b (referent = v. 36a, cf. v. 35); Jer 17:22 (referent = v. 22, cf. Exod 20:10; 31:14; etc.).

63   Gen 7:16 (see below); Lev 9:10b (referent = vv. 9b-10a, cf. 4:6, 7, 17, 18, 25, 30; etc.).

צוה√ may qualify four clauses can be observed in Gen 7:13-16. The first four clauses in these verses have בוא√ as the finite verb. In context, the consecutive use of the same verb stem appears to make the citation base in v. 16b (italicised) qualify all four of the previous clauses that contain בוא√ (enlarged). Note that בוא√ occurs twice in v. 16a, and once each in vv. 13 and 15. V. 14 is a parenthetical list of the various animals that accompanied Noah's family in v. 13.

בָּא נֹחַ...וַיָּבֹאוּ אֶל־נֹחַ אֶל־הַתֵּבָה שְׁנַיִם שְׁנַיִם...וְהַבָּאִים
זָכָר וּנְקֵבָה מִכָּל־בָּשָׂר בָּאוּ כַּאֲשֶׁר צִוָּה אֹתוֹ אֱלֹהִים
וַיִּסְגֹּר יְהוָה בַּעֲדוֹ (Gen 7:13-16)

The use of four בוא√ in the immediate context appears to link these clauses together pragmatically.

Comparing the citation base in Lev 9:10 with various commands (4:6, 7, 17, 18, 25, 30; etc.) suggests that the four clauses preceding it are all qualified by the comparative clause. Lev 9:10 along with Gen 7:16 attest to a Type C function for a comparative clause. Such a function for a comparative citation base with צוה√ is limited to the law.

iv. A Citation Base that Qualifies Five Clauses

There is one example of כַּאֲשֶׁר צוה√ qualifying five clauses (Type D) among citation bases addressed in this chapter. A series of five imperatives which are all based upon the authority of יהוה constitutes the referent of כַּאֲשֶׁר צוה√ in Lev 9:7. Note the five imperatives (enlarged) that are coordinated to each other in Lev 9:7.

וַיֹּאמֶר מֹשֶׁה אֶל־אַהֲרֹן קְרַב אֶל־הַמִּזְבֵּחַ וַעֲשֵׂה אֶת־חַטָּאתְךָ
וְאֶת־עֹלָתֶךָ וְכַפֵּר בַּעַדְךָ וּבְעַד הָעָם וַעֲשֵׂה אֶת־קָרְבַּן
הָעָם וְכַפֵּר בַּעֲדָם כַּאֲשֶׁר צִוָּה יְהוָה (Lev 9:7)

The fact that these imperatives and the citation base together constitute
the direct discourse introduced by וַיֹּאמֶר מֹשֶׁה אֶל־אַהֲרֹן also supports
the view that all five clauses are qualified by this comparative clause.

v. Citation Bases that Qualify a "Paragraph"

Several other כַּאֲשֶׁר צוה√ citation bases mark even larger referents
but by other means. In Exod 39, 40 and Lev 8, several of these
formulæ have been construed together to result in a function that is
something more than just the qualification of one or more clauses
(Types I, A, B, etc.).

כאשר צוה יהוה את־משה (Exod 39:1, 5, 7, 21, 26, 29, 31)

כאשר צוה יהוה את־משה (Exod 40:19, 21, 23, 25, 27, 29, 32)

כאשר צוה יהוה את־משה (Lev 8:4, 9, 13, 17, 21, 29)

כל־הדברים אשר־צוה יהוה ביד־משה (Lev 8:36)[64]

This threefold septenary structure throughout Exod 39-Lev 8 begs for
an explanation. It is not surprising that the recognition of such a
distinctive arrangement of comparative clauses affects their function.
Most recently, Milgrom has offered an explanation which will lead to
our description of how these citation bases are functioning. Based on
his analysis of Leviticus 8, Milgrom states,

> the refrain *ka'aser siwwa YHWH* appears seven times in this chapter (vv 4, 9,
> 13, 17, 21, 29, 36 [enlarged] [*sic*]) and seven times in the accounts that describe
> the manufacture of the priestly vestments (Exod 39:1-31) and the assembling of
> the Tabernacle (Exod 40:17-38). This refrain subdivides the chapter into seven
> coherent sections...and constitutes the scaffolding upon which Lev 8 was
> constructed[65].

---

64 Though not strictly part of our discussion of comparative citation bases here,
    this citation base in Lev 8:36 must be addressed in conjunction with these other
    forms (see below).
65 Milgrom, 499.

According to Milgrom, the final citation base in v. 36 has been enlarged
in order to have כל־הדברים as its antecedent[66]. This enlarged form,
thus, serves as a concluding form for the three sections in Exod 39, 40
and Lev 8. With reference to all three sections, Milgrom suggests, "the
three pericopes containing this sevenfold formula (Exod 39; 40:17-33;
Lev 8) may at one time have been consecutive"[67].

From his view of the scaffolding provided by these citation bases,
Milgrom proceeds to reconstruct the original structure of Lev 8.
According to Milgrom, vv. 3-5 and 10-11 of Lev 8 are secondary
additions of P_2 which have disturbed the original chiastic form of this
chapter. By restoring this chiastic structure (A [vv. 1-2]; B [vv. 6-9, 12-
13]; X [vv. 14-29]; B′ [v. 30]; A′ [vv. 31-36]) the consecration rites in
vv. 14-29 are reestablished "as the center and pivot of the chapter"[68].

Milgrom's view of the original chiasm in Lev 8, however, appears
to unnecessarily undermine the sevenfold structure of this chapter as
well as its relation to Exod 39 and 40. For instance, if כאשר צוה יהוה
את־משה in v. 4 is secondary, as Milgrom asserts, then the septenary
structure of Lev 8, which is the basis for relating this chapter to the
distant chapters in Exod, is lost. Milgrom's attempt to substitute this
lacuna in his reconstruction of Lev 8 with כַּאֲשֶׁר צֻוֵּיתִי[69] of v. 31 as
the original element of the septenary structure appears to be a forced

---

66 *Ibid.*, 542.
67 *Ibid.*, 543. The use of this "scaffolding" in these chapters, however, may also
    permit Lev 1-7 to be an original part of the scaffolding. These laws appear to fit
    in well with the overall theme of these chapters: Exod 39 (the making of the
    sacred vestments); Exod 40:17-33 (the setting up of the tabernacle); Lev 1-7
    (legislation for the cultic offerings); and Lev 8 (ordination of Aaron and his
    sons). Since Exod 40:1-16, 34ff., which may be secondary, gives an ending to
    the book it is possible that these verses were introduced when the law code was
    divided into five parts and that the three-fold septenary structure in Exod 39-Lev
    8 antedates the division of the Pentateuch.
68 *Ibid.*, 544.
69 Read passive צֻוֵּיתִי with 𝕲, 𝕾, 𝕮 as in v. 35; 10:13 (G. Quell, *BHS*).

attempt to arrive at a chiasm. The citation base used in v. 31 is not the recurring phrase כאשר צוה יהוה את־משה [70] of the scaffolding.

Though his view of the original structure of Lev 8 is unhelpful, Milgrom's view regarding the three-fold septenary structure is compelling. These citation bases, thus, function not only as devices to attribute a referent to another source but also as a scaffolding device for these chapters.

Once כאשר צוה יהוה את־משה has been observed as a scaffolding device in these chapters, it then becomes evident that some of these comparative clauses qualify more clauses than what can be determined from simply a syntactical point of view. The observation that כַּאֲשֶׁר צוה√ functions as a scaffolding device is a pragmatic consideration. Regarding their position in the overall "scaffolding", each of these citation bases has been placed at the end of a segment of material (e.g., a "paragraph").

Each of these citation bases qualifies the paragraph that it concludes; this is a discrete function (Type α). Since each paragraph consists of a certain number of clauses these comparative clauses can also be categorised like others in our examination (e.g., Type B, C, etc.). For example, a comparative clause with a Type αE function is the concluding statement in a paragraph that includes six clauses qualified by כאשר צוה יהוה את־משה . In Lev 8, the largest of these functions concerns the citation base in v. 29 which qualifies eight verses, or seventeen clauses (Type αP; referent = vv. 22-29a). The citation base in v. 9 concludes a paragraph that consists of twelve clauses (Type αK; referent = vv. 6-9a). The other citation bases in Lev 8 occur in: v. 13b (Type αJ; referent = vv. 10-13a); v. 17b (Type αJ; referent = vv. 14-17a); and, v. 21b (Type αI; referent = vv. 18-21a). V. 4 has the pro-form עשה√ so it differs in this respect from the others in Lev 8 (referent = vv. 2-4).

---

70   In light of the structural and lexical symmetry between these three pericopes, we would expect a similar chiastic structure in the others as well, but such a structure does not seem likely in Exodus 39 or 40:17ff.

The use of the כַּאֲשֶׁר צִוָּה יהוה אֶת־מֹשֶׁה citation base as a qualifying statement for an entire paragraph applies to Exod 39 as well. In this chapter, there are several occurrences of √עשׂה "to make (vestments for priests)" which do not function as pro-forms. The citation bases in vv. 1 and 7 qualify two clauses (Type αA; referents = v. 1 and vv. 6-7 respectively). The other citation bases in Exod 39 occur in: v. 5 (Type αD; referent = vv. 2-5); v. 31 (Type αB; referent = vv. 30-31); v. 29 (Type αI, referent = vv. 27-29); and, v. 26 (Type αC; referent = vv. 22-24). The referent for Exod 39:21 is the largest and consists of eighteen clauses (vv. 8-21; Type αQ[71]).

The citation bases in 40:23, 25, and 27 qualify two clauses (Type αA; referents are vv. 22-23, 24-25, 26-27 respectively). The other citation bases in Exod 40 occur in: v. 29 (Type αB; referent = vv. 28-29); v. 32 (Type αC; referent = vv. 30-32); and vv. 19 and 21 (Type αF; referents are vv. 17-19, 20-21 respectively).

The use of the כַּאֲשֶׁר √צוה citation base as a scaffolding device is limited to these chapters in Exodus and Leviticus.

2. כַּאֲשֶׁר √צוה *Used with Broadening Terms*

כַּאֲשֶׁר √צוה may also be used in conjunction with various terms which generally affect the relation between the citation base and the referent. This results in a vast range of referents for the forms below, some even larger than those just analysed. These forms concern the use of כֹּל, √היה, and various pro-forms.

a. כַּאֲשֶׁר √צוה and כֹּל

כֹּל is frequently used to govern relatively larger referents than is possible in citation bases without this term.

---

71 This enumeration of clauses would be increased if we had not considered vv. 10b-13a a single complex sentence.

וַיֹּאמֶר מֹשֶׁה אֶל־בְּנֵי יִשְׂרָאֵל כְּכֹל אֲשֶׁר־צִוָּה יְהוָה אֶת־מֹשֶׁה
(Num 30:1)

For instance, this statement in Num 30:1 functions as a summary for the referent in chapters 28-29. Most of these forms that use כֹּל are concentrated in the deuteronomistic literature[72].

The post-exilic uses of this citation base repay attention. As we have recently observed, part of the literary artistry of Esther entails the use of citation bases in the narrative. The second pair of citation bases used in this manner occurs in Esth 3:12 ("according to everything that Haman commanded") and 8:9 ("according to everything that Mordecai commanded"). The forms common to both of these passages are so extensive it is perhaps best to list them with the citation bases enlarged.

וַיִּקָּרְאוּ סֹפְרֵי הַמֶּלֶךְ בַּחֹדֶשׁ הָרִאשׁוֹן בִּשְׁלוֹשָׁה עָשָׂר יוֹם בּוֹ
וַיִּכָּתֵב כְּכָל־אֲשֶׁר־צִוָּה הָמָן אֶל אֲחַשְׁדַּרְפְּנֵי־הַמֶּלֶךְ וְאֶל־הַפַּחוֹת
אֲשֶׁר עַל־מְדִינָה וּמְדִינָה וְאֶל־שָׂרֵי עַם וָעָם מְדִינָה וּמְדִינָה כִּכְתָבָהּ
וְעַם וָעָם כִּלְשׁוֹנוֹ בְּשֵׁם הַמֶּלֶךְ אֲחַשְׁוֵרֹשׁ נִכְתָּב וְנֶחְתָּם בְּטַבַּעַת הַמֶּלֶךְ
(Esth 3:12)

וַיִּקָּרְאוּ סֹפְרֵי־הַמֶּלֶךְ בָּעֵת־הַהִיא בַּחֹדֶשׁ הַשְּׁלִישִׁי הוּא־חֹדֶשׁ
סִיוָן בִּשְׁלוֹשָׁה וְעֶשְׂרִים בּוֹ וַיִּכָּתֵב כְּכָל־אֲשֶׁר־צִוָּה מָרְדֳּכַי
אֶל־הַיְּהוּדִים וְאֶל הָאֲחַשְׁדַּרְפְּנִים־וְהַפַּחוֹת וְשָׂרֵי הַמְּדִינוֹת אֲשֶׁר מֵהֹדּוּ
וְעַד־כּוּשׁ שֶׁבַע וְעֶשְׂרִים וּמֵאָה מְדִינָה מְדִינָה וּמְדִינָה כִּכְתָבָהּ וְעַם
וָעָם כִּלְשֹׁנוֹ וְאֶל־הַיְּהוּדִים כִּכְתָבָם וְכִלְשׁוֹנָם (Esth 8:9)

In fact, the correspondence between these two verses is only part of the close relation that exists between Esth 3:12-15 and 8:9-16. In the latter set of verses, Haman's edict to annihilate the Jewish community is neutralised by Mordecai's decree which enables the Israelites to defend themselves. The narrator marks this development by using the same

---

72   Num 30:1; Deut 1:3 (part of introduction); 26:14 (√עשה is not a pro-form here, but this verb with כֹּל marks general obedience); Josh 4:10; 2 Sam 9:11; 2 Kgs 21:8 (hendiadys); Jer 35:10 (√עשה is not a pro-form here, see Deut 26:14), 18 (see v. 10); Esth 3:12; 8:9; 1 Chr 6:34. The participial form of this כֹּל construction is rare (Deut 30:2).

form of the citation base in both verses. It is hard to surpass Bush's description of the significance of this ironic reversal.

> Given the immutability of Persian law, it has not been possible simply to rescind Haman's edict. What Mordecai has been able to do is write and promulgate a counteredict that gives the Jews specific royal permission to defend themselves by destroying any and all who attack them[73].

The citation bases in Esth 3:12 and 8:9 mark the ironic reversal of authority between Haman and Mordecai. This reversal of authority is further developed in Esth 9:3. Here the list of officials in 3:12 and 8:9 is rearranged so that כָּל־שָׂרֵי הַמְּדִינוֹת ("all the princes of the provinces") is at the head of the list and verse. This alteration is due to the fact that the account is now narrated from the viewpoint of the Jewish community[74]. The effects of the reversal of authority marked by the citation base in 8:9 are completed by this final change in perspective of the Jewish populace.

It is not surprising that both of these citation bases have the same referent יִכָּתֵב (Type I). As we have seen before, the use of these constructions in Esther is part of the literary artistry at the heart of the book. Even though they cite Persian, and not Jewish, law, these citation bases may reflect another way these constructions were developed in the post-exilic era. For instance, it will be recalled that in Esth 10:2 a non-legal referent was cited with the distinctive syntactic form found repeatedly in DtrH and the Chr's history. The development of a citation base as an element in a broad and sophisticated literary structure of a book may be attributable to the development of citation bases in the post-exilic period.

The other use of the citation base in this category in the post-exilic historiography occurs at 1 Chr 6:34 (49).

וְאַהֲרֹן וּבָנָיו מַקְטִירִים עַל־מִזְבַּח הָעוֹלָה וְעַל־מִזְבַּח הַקְּטֹרֶת
לְכֹל מְלֶאכֶת קֹדֶשׁ הַקֳּדָשִׁים וּלְכַפֵּר עַל־יִשְׂרָאֵל כְּכֹל אֲשֶׁר צִוָּה
מֹשֶׁה עֶבֶד הָאֱלֹהִים (1 Chr 6:34 [49])

---

73   Bush, 454.

74   See H. Bardke, *Das Buch Esther,* KAT (Gütersloh: G. Mohn, 1963) 381; followed by Bush, 462.

The use of כֹל in both the citation base and the final indirect object shows that the contiguous infinitive phrase does not constitute the referent by itself (Type I)[75]. Hence, the entire main clause is qualified by this citation base. This is a noteworthy passage since we have seen a number of examples of a sentence structure comprised of a finite verb, one or more infinitive phrase(s), and a concluding comparative citation base. When a *Vergleichspräpositionale* was used as the comparative citation base with כָּתוּב in the non-synoptic post-exilic historiography, it consistently qualified the infinitival portion (Type II) of the sentence. By contrast, the comparative clause in 1 Chr 6:34 (49) qualifies a relatively larger referent as we would expect for a citation base that uses כֹל. It is not entirely clear, however, whether the use of a כַּאֲשֶׁר citation base here was employed so that the entire sentence would be qualified. All we can say is that a *Vergleichspräpositionale* was not used here for a Type I qualification.

b. כַּאֲשֶׁר צוה√ and the Impersonal היה√

היה√ inflected in the third feminine singular may have the impersonal force "it". This impersonal היה√ (3fs) represents the subject of the verb that is expressed elsewhere in the context[76] (cf. feminine *neutrum* used in citation formulæ with כָּתוּב above). This occurs once in connection with the inquiry made by the daughters of Zelophehad in Num 27:11.

וְאִם־אֵין אַחִים לְאָבִיו וּנְתַתֶּם אֶת־נַחֲלָתוֹ לִשְׁאֵרוֹ הַקָּרֹב אֵלָיו
מִמִּשְׁפַּחְתּוֹ וְיָרַשׁ אֹתָהּ וְהָיְתָה לִבְנֵי יִשְׂרָאֵל לְחֻקַּת מִשְׁפָּט
כַּאֲשֶׁר צִוָּה יְהוָה אֶת־מֹשֶׁה (Num 27:11)

---

75 לְכַפֵּר does not appear to be introduced by *waw-explicativum* GK § 154 n. 1 (b).
76 GK § 144b.

היה√ (3fs) points to the referent in vv. 8-11a which contains a reinterpretation of the laws of inheritance. Since Zelophehad had died without any sons, his daughters sought a reinterpretation of these laws so that the property of their father would not revert to another tribe or family. In Num 27, the reference to the previous legal tradition of inheritance in vv. 3-4[77] is stated separately from their reinterpretation in vv. 8-11a. This contemporary reinterpretation enabled Zelophehad's surviving daughters to receive their father's inheritance. This distinction between a past legal tradition and its contemporary reinterpretation is similar to the introduction of the wood offering in Neh 10:35 (34). The main difference between these two reinterpretations of the former legal tradition is that the one in the post-exilic historiography is far more succinct.

c. Pro-Forms with כַּאֲשֶׁר Citation Bases

A comparative clause frequently qualifies a main clause that includes a pro-form. Four different pro-forms may be used with this citation base; they virtually always point to a meaningful referent in the context.

i. Pro-Form עשׂה√

a) The Independent Form of כַּאֲשֶׁר צוה√ with Pro-Form עשׂה√

Num 31:31 uses this citation base.

וַיַּעַשׂ מֹשֶׁה וְאֶלְעָזָר הַכֹּהֵן כַּאֲשֶׁר צִוָּה יְהוָה אֶת־מֹשֶׁה (Num 31:31)

The referent for the citation base in Num 31:31 consists of the LORD's various instructions to Moses and Eliezer concerning the distribution of the booty from the Midianite war (vv. 26-30). The majority of these pro-

---

77   E.g., Exod 18:15-19; Lev 24:12-13; Num 15:34.

forms mark several verses. This form of a citation base occurs most frequently in the law[78].

There is one exceptional form among these passages. In Deut 34:9, √עשה is not related to any group of verses that elucidate its meaning.

וִיהוֹשֻׁעַ בִּן־נוּן מָלֵא רוּחַ חָכְמָה כִּי־סָמַךְ מֹשֶׁה אֶת־יָדָיו עָלָיו
וַיִּשְׁמְעוּ אֵלָיו בְּנֵי־יִשְׂרָאֵל וַיַּעֲשׂוּ כַּאֲשֶׁר צִוָּה יְהוָה אֶת־מֹשֶׁה
(Deut 34:9)

Consequently, this form appears to have an abstract referent ("what the LORD commanded Moses")

There is one occurrence of this form in the post-exilic historiography. In light of its distribution in the Old Testament, it is not surprising that the Chr's use of this citation base with the pro-form √עשה is due to his dependence on his *Vorlage*.

וַיַּעַשׂ דָּוִד כֵּן כַּאֲשֶׁר צִוָּהוּ יְהוָה (2 Sam 5:25a)

וַיַּעַשׂ דָּוִיד כַּאֲשֶׁר צִוָּהוּ הָאֱלֹהִים (1 Chr 14:16a)

Hence, 1 Chr 14:16a does not reflect the type of citation bases that originated in the post-exilic period.

b) Pro-Form √עשה with כֹּל

כֹּל may also be used with the כַּאֲשֶׁר citation base with the pro-form √עשה.

וַיַּעַשׂ נֹחַ כְּכֹל אֲשֶׁר־צִוָּהוּ יְהוָה (Gen 7:5)

The referent signalled by the pro-form √עשה in Gen 7:5 consists of vv. 1b-4. The distribution of the citation bases that employ both of these

---

78 Lev 16:34b (referent = v. 34a); 24:23 (referent = v. 23a); Num 20:27 (referent = vv. 24-26); 27:22 (referent = vv. 18-21); 31:31 (referent = vv. 26-30); Deut 34:9 (abstract referent); 2 Sam 13:29 (referent = v. 28); 1 Chr 14:16 (referent = vv. 14-15).

features is concentrated in the law and the deuteronomistic material[79]. There are three occurrences of this form in the post-exilic historiography.

The use of a pro-form עשׂה√ in a post-exilic citation base is exceptional. As we have previously noted above, however, the citation base in Esth 4:17 plays a pivotal role in the intricate literary structure of the book of Esther. If it was desired to have all of the dramatic reversals of the book of Esther converge on the pivotal statement, then there appears to have been no better way to refer to Esther's words in v. 16 than with a pro-form. At any rate, the pro-form used with this post-exilic citation base appears to be rare. The main consideration of the four citation bases with צוה√ in Esther has been the literary artistry of the book. The development of citation bases in Chronicles, Ezra, and Nehemiah, however, is distinguishable from the use of such exegetical devices in Esther.

There are two other post-exilic occurrences of a citation base with the pro-form עשׂה√ and כֹל. In 2 Chr 23:8, the Chr has adopted the construction from his *Vorlage* (Type I).

וַיַּעֲשׂוּ שָׂרֵי הַמֵּאִיוֹת כְּכֹל אֲשֶׁר־צִוָּה יְהוֹיָדָע הַכֹּהֵן (2 Kgs 11:9a)[80]

וַיַּעֲשׂוּ הַלְוִיִּם וְכָל־יְהוּדָה כְּכֹל אֲשֶׁר־צִוָּה יְהוֹיָדָע הַכֹּהֵן (2 Chr 23:8a)

In the referent of v. 8a, however, the Chr has altered the phrase "the captains of hundreds" of his *Vorlage* to "the Levites and all Judah" in keeping with his interest in these latter groups.

The Chr may alter his *Vorlage* in order to more clearly define the scope of the qualification of the comparative clause. In 2 Chr 7:17, the Chr similarly rewrites his *Vorlage*, omitting בְּתָם־לֵבָב וּבְיֹשֶׁר, in order to introduce an infinitive construct with *waw-explicativum*.

---

79   Gen 7:5 (referent = vv. 1b-4); Exod 31:11b (referent = v. 11a); Deut 26:14 (referent = both vv. 13-14); 2 Kgs 11:9 (referent = vv. 5-8); 16:16 (referent = v. 15); Jer 35:10 (referent = vv. 8-9); 36:8 (referent = vv. 5-7); 50:21 (referent = vv. 2-46); Ezek 9:11 (referent = v. 4); Ruth 3:6 (referent = vv. 3-4); Esth 4:17 (see also the discussion of Esther 2:20 above); 2 Chr 7:17 (see below); 23:8a (referent = 8b-11, cf. vv. 4-7).

80   Qere הַמֵּאוֹת.

וְאַתָּה אִם־תֵּלֵךְ לְפָנַי כַּאֲשֶׁר הָלַךְ דָּוִד אָבִיךָ בְּתָם־לֵבָב וּבְיֹשֶׁר
לַעֲשׂוֹת כְּכֹל אֲשֶׁר צִוִּיתִיךָ חֻקַּי וּמִשְׁפָּטַי תִּשְׁמֹר (1 Kgs 9:4)

וְאַתָּה אִם־תֵּלֵךְ לְפָנַי כַּאֲשֶׁר הָלַךְ דָּוִיד אָבִיךָ וְלַעֲשׂוֹת כְּכֹל אֲשֶׁר
צִוִּיתִיךָ וְחֻקַּי וּמִשְׁפָּטַי תִּשְׁמוֹר (2 Chr 7:17)

The referent is לַעֲשׂוֹת (Type II). The Chr has used *waw-explicativum*
in order to distinguish the citation base and the referent from the context
more clearly than in his *Vorlage*.

c) Conclusions

There are only two citation bases with pro-form עשׂה√ that originate
in the post-exilic era; both of these devices occurred with כֹּל. The
citation base in Esth 4:17 has a dual function while the Chr gives
prominence to a Type II qualification for the one in 2 Chr 7:17. One
feature associated with developed citation bases in the post-exilic period
is the use of *waw-explicativum* to ease the identification of the referent
(2 Chr 7:17).

ii. Pro-Form כֵּן

a) The Independent Form of כַּאֲשֶׁר צוה√ with Pro-Form כֵּן

The most common pro-form in these כַּאֲשֶׁר צוה√ citation bases is
כֵּן. The use of this particle together with a comparative clause concerns
what some call a correlative construction. Within this complex
sentence, כֵּן is the word that signals a relationship to the more
meaningful referent outside of the correlative construction. There are

basically two different manners in which these correlative structures with כֵּן may appear[81].

First, the correlative construction may itself constitute a complex sentence.

כַּאֲשֶׁר צִוָּה יְהוָה אֶת־מֹשֶׁה כֵּן עָשׂוּ בְּנוֹת צְלָפְחָד (Num 36:10)

In Num 36:10, the pro-form כֵּן refers to the more meaningful referent in vv. 5-9.

These correlative constructions that constitute a sentence are never used in the post-exilic historiography[82]. They are one of several cumbersome citation bases that occur in the law and in the deuteronomistic material.

Summarising his research on the particle כֵּן, M. J. Mulder concludes, "unsere Untersuchungen der Partikel *kn* haben deutlich gezeigt, daß *kn* eine anaphorische Function hat und viel in Vergleichungen o.ä. benutzt wird"[83]. Mulder's statement is generally

---

81 König attempted to make the following fine distinction among correlative constructions. König states, "zu diesen [subordinirten] Sätzen gehören nicht die mit ‚wie-so' (oä.) eingeleiteten Sätze, so lange dieselben das Gleichgewicht zweier Qualitäten, also eine Correlation…anzeigen wollen. Allerdings wenn das ‚so' nur eine verdeutlichende oder pleonastische Zusammenfassung des ‚wie'-Satzes ist, gehört letzterer zu den subsidiären Sätzen" (*Ibid.*, § 378b, p. 546). König, however, offers no examples of his latter category and it is questionable whether this is necessary or helpful. For instance, even when the same verb stem is used in both correlates (e.g., כַּאֲשֶׁר עָשָׂה כֵּן יֵעָשֶׂה לּוֹ [Lev 24:19]; כַּאֲשֶׁר יִתֵּן מוּם בָּאָדָם כֵּן יִנָּתֶן בּוֹ [Lev 24:20]; etc.) these correlates do not appear to be pleonastic, i.e., in both of the כֵּן clauses above invaluable information is still conveyed by the Niphal verb stems and the prepositional phrases.

For the view that כַּאֲשֶׁר — כֵּן constructions can be analysed as subordinate clauses, see Richter, Bd. III, 190-92.

82 Gen 50:12 (referent = vv. 13, cf. 49:29-32; 50:5-9); Exod 7:10 (referent = v. 9b), 20 (referent = v. 19); Num 8:22 (referent = vv. 21-22, see the citation base in v. 20 for vv. 6ff.); 36:10 (referent = vv. 6b-9); Josh 4:8a (referent = v. 8b); 14:5a (referent v. 5b); 2 Sam 5:25 (referent = vv. 23b-25).

83 M. J. Mulder, "Die Partikel כֵּן im Alten Testament", *OTS* 21 (1981) 226.

true for these correlative citation bases since the majority of them conclude their respective referents. However, the correlative constructions in Gen 50:12, Josh 4:8a, and 14:5a introduce the referent and thus have a cataphoric function.

The second type of correlative citation base (enlarged) is governed by a main clause with the pro-form √עשה.

$$\text{וַיַּעֲשׂוּ כָּל־בְּנֵי יִשְׂרָאֵל כַּאֲשֶׁר צִוָּה יְהוָה אֶת־מֹשֶׁה}$$
$$\text{וְאֶת־אַהֲרֹן כֵּן עָשׂוּ (Exod 12:50)}$$

More so than those immediately above, this second type of correlative construction functions consistently as a concluding ballast to a series of complex commands or, in one case, a single comprehensive directive (e.g., "You shall speak all that I command you"; Exod 7:2a). Such citation bases occur in the law and Josh 11:15[84].

The syntactic construction of a correlative clause governed by another clause appears to be especially associated with √צוה and √עשה. Concerning correlative constructions in narrative texts, M. J. Mulder states, "das Pf. *swh* findet man öfter hinter *k'sr* und das Pf. *'sh* hinter *kn* (Ex. vii 6; xii 28,50; xxxix 43 usw.)..."[85]. In SBH, it appears that correlative constructions are also associated with citation bases.

Williamson has observed that these constructions possess a Janus quality since, in addition to their being treated as a correlative sentence constituent governed by another clause, they may be read as expanded complex comparative sentences (i.e., main clause—comparative clause with an additional כֵּן clause). The Janus quality of this construction results in a statement that stresses the referent by repeating and reflecting on the fulfilment of the previous commands (e.g., "they did it...thus they did it"). Perhaps this is why this cumbersome citation base typically functions as a concluding ballast. These correlatives also correspond to what we observed among the rubrics where citation

---

84   Exod 7:6 (referent = v. 2); 12:28 (referent = vv. 1-27), 50 (referent = vv. 43-49); 39:43a (referent = vv. 32-41) Num 17:26 (referent = v. 25); Josh 11:15 (see below).

85   Mulder, 209.

constructions that conclude referents tend to be larger than those that introduce material.

Even though the correlative construction in Exod 7:6 summarises 6:28-7:5, the referent for this citation base is placed in v. 2. Citation bases with legal referents in the distant context have not been observed in Chronicles, Ezra, or Nehemiah. Another non-contiguous relation occurs between the citation base in Exod 39:43 and its large referent in vv. 32-41.

The correlative citation base (enlarged) in Josh 11:15 is used in conjunction with a partitive construction construed with דָּבָר (italicised) which could, in one respect, be considered a citation construction ("a word from everything that the LORD commanded Moses").

כַּאֲשֶׁר צִוָּה יְהוָה אֶת־מֹשֶׁה עַבְדּוֹ כֵּן־צִוָּה מֹשֶׁה אֶת־יְהוֹשֻׁעַ
וְכֵן עָשָׂה יְהוֹשֻׁעַ לֹא־הֵסִיר *דָּבָר* מִכֹּל אֲשֶׁר־צִוָּה יְהוָה
אֶת־*מֹשֶׁה* (Josh 11:15)

This correlative construction includes a second כֵּן clause. Josh 11:15 does not appear to function as a concluding ballast.

b) Pro-Form כֵּן and כֹּל

The latter type of correlative structure may also be construed with כֹּל in the כַּאֲשֶׁר clause.

וַיַּעֲשׂוּ בְּנֵי יִשְׂרָאֵל כְּכֹל אֲשֶׁר צִוָּה יְהוָה אֶת־מֹשֶׁה כֵּן עָשׂוּ (Num 1:54)

This complex sentence concludes the referent in vv. 17-53. These forms occur exclusively in the law[86]. The majority of these formulations conclude a referent (contra Exod 40:16).

---

86   Gen 6:22 (see below); Exod 39:32b (referent = v. 32a); 40:16 (referent = vv. 17-33, introductory); Num 1:54 (referent = vv. 17-53); 2:34a (referent = v. 34b, כֵּן used twice); 8:20 (referent = vv. 6-19); 9:5b (referent = v. 5a).

Gen 6:22 contains a construction that demonstrates how several of the elements that may be construed with citation bases can converge on one form.

וַיַּעַשׂ נֹחַ כְּכֹל אֲשֶׁר צִוָּה אֹתוֹ אֱלֹהִים כֵּן עָשָׂה (Gen 6:22)

The features associated with the citation base in Gen 6:22 include: the correlative construction; כֹל; the pro-forms עשׂה√ and כֵּן; a non-contiguous relation between the citation base and the meaningful referent; a relatively large referent (vv. 14-21); and the general cumbersomeness of this form. There is a strong tendency for such features to occur in the law and the deuteronomistic literature. The convergence of all of these features on one citation base, as in Gen 6:22, is unattested in the post-exilic historiography.

iii. Other "Pro-Forms"

The correlative construction may rarely substitute כֵּן with another element. In Exod 29:35, כֹּה functions in this manner.

וְעָשִׂיתָ לְאַהֲרֹן וּלְבָנָיו כָּכָה כְּכֹל אֲשֶׁר־צִוִּיתִי אֹתָכָה שִׁבְעַת
יָמִים תְּמַלֵּא יָדָם (Exod 29:35)

In this case, the referent consists of 28:1-29:34[87]. Exod 29:35 is the only example of this form, but it functions as a concluding ballast like many of the other citation bases with pro-forms.

In Exod 16:34, וֹ (enlarged) appears to function as a substitute for the כֵּן of a correlative construction.

כַּאֲשֶׁר צִוָּה יְהוָה אֶל־מֹשֶׁה וַיַּנִּיחֵהוּ אַהֲרֹן לִפְנֵי הָעֵדֻת לְמִשְׁמָרֶת
(Exod 16:34)

The referent is in v. 33.

---

[87] Though כֹּה may have a cataphoric function (e.g., כֹּה אָמַר יהוה), Mulder is correct to describe it more generally as a "‚deiktisch'...weil es sich auf Daseiendes bezieht und so eine Identität betont" (227).

d. Non-Recurring Forms

There are a few passages which are not easily classified since a number of issues converge upon them. As a result, they do not consist of any recurring forms (see Num 30:1; 32:35; Deut 30:2; Jer 11:4). There appears little value in addressing the details of these forms aside from the observation that none of them occur in the post-exilic historiography[88].

3. Compound Citation Bases

Various compound citation bases are also possible with כַּאֲשֶׁר צוה√ which may be used with: כַּכָּתוּב (Josh 8:31); כִּדְבַר־נֵּר (2 Sam 24:19); כִּדְבַר יְהוָה (1 Chr 15:15); or כְּמִשְׁפָּטָם (1 Chr 24:19). Josh 4:10 even uses two צוה√. In light of the distribution of such forms in our study, we must address the two compound citation bases that occur in the post-exilic historiography.

The Chr emphasises the importance of faithfulness to the legal traditions in his extensive rewriting of the transport of the ark to the central sanctuary in 2 Sam 6:13ff. He accomplishes this in two stages. First, the Chr makes one important change in his representation of the first attempt. The Chr treats the Levites as being responsible for the abandonment of the first attempt. The Chr's addition of "the Levites" in 1 Chr 15:12 had simply been referred to in his *Vorlage* as "those who bore the ark of the LORD [נֹשְׂאֵי אֲרוֹן־יְהוָה]" (2 Sam 6:13). The reason that the Levites are to be faulted, according to the Chr, is due to their lack of the observance of the law. This transgression of the legal tradition is made explicit with the use of a negative citation base in 1 Chr 15:13 ("because you [the Levites] did not carry it at the first, the LORD our God made an outburst on us, for we did not seek Him according to

---

88 The expression כַּאֲשֶׁר צוה√ in the Pual (e.g., "as he was commanded") does not ascribe a directive to another person or source and thus does not enter our inquiry (Lev 8:31 [Read with 𝕲, 𝕾, 𝕿]; Num 3:16; Ezek 12:7; 24:18; 37:7).

the ordinance [כַּמִּשְׁפָּט דְּרַשְׁנֻהוּ כִּי־לֹא]"). The Chr's representation of
this attempt in terms of the failure of the Levites to conduct the return of
the ark in keeping with the legal tradition enables him to present the
initial failure as an antitype which becomes an important basis for what
follows.

The other way that the Chr stresses the significance of observing the
law concerns his rewriting of the second attempt. In order to clearly
indicate the reason for the success of the second attempt, the Chr
employs two citation bases (enlarged) which are followed by the
additional phrase "on their shoulders with the poles" (italics) in 1 Chr
15:15. This latter phrase alludes to the legislation in Exod 25:13-15,
37:3-5, Num 4:11, and 7:9 [89]. Furthermore, this phrase together with
the compound citation demonstrates that the observance of the law by
the Levites was the central reason that the ark ever came to its rightful
place according to the Chr.

$$\text{וַיִּשְׂאוּ בְנֵי־הַלְוִיִּם אֵת אֲרוֹן הָאֱלֹהִים כַּאֲשֶׁר צִוָּה}$$
$$\text{מֹשֶׁה כִּדְבַר יְהֹוָה בִּכְתֵפָם בַּמֹּטוֹת עֲלֵיהֶם (1 Chr 15:15 }^{90}\text{)}$$

His use of a compound form here stands out among the other citation
bases we have analysed in his history. The reason for this exceptional
form may be attributed to his concern that the cult in Jerusalem in his
day be established and maintained according to the law[91]. Even though
there was no ark in the second temple, the Chr uses the installation of
the ark at the central sanctuary as an occasion to stress faithful cultic
observance, but, in order to do so, he has presented a considerable

---

89   Only Japhet argues that "the words 'as Moses had commanded'…do not refer the
     reader to any specific precept or to any given text found in the Pentateuch, but
     only state that the transfer was carried out with legal precision, in full
     conformity with the will of God, as expressed in the Mosaic command" (302).
     She bases this view on the lack of "literal correspondence between the manner of
     carrying the ark and the practice established in the Pentateuch" (*Ibid.*). However,
     later exegetes do not always quote laws verbatim and frequently paraphrase or
     allude to legal stipulations.

90   Read with MT. 𝔊 reads כְּכָתוּב, but see 2 Chr 35:3.

91   For the view that faithfulness to the customs of the Temple and its cult was a
     significant bond providing the post-exilic community with an important link
     with pre-exilic Israel, see Williamson, *1 and 2 Chronicles,* 28; Braun, xxixff.

rewrite of his *Vorlage*. The Chr has employed three citation bases throughout this account in order to emphasise the point that the cult needed to be established upon the observance of the law by the Levities. The extent of the rewrite signals that faithfulness to the legal traditions is no small concern of the Chr even though it appears he has used a compound citation base in v. 15.

There remains the possibility that the two citation bases in v. 15 are to be understood as having independent referents and thus agree with the general use of these forms elsewhere in the non-synoptic portions of the Chr's history. According to this view, the phrase "with the poles on their shoulders", the crucial point of conformity to the law, is introduced by כִּדְבַר יְהוָה while the previous כַּאֲשֶׁר צִוָּה מֹשֶׁה citation base qualifies the preceding clause (Type I). If this view is correct, it would agree with what we have seen to be generally true of the comparatively smaller qualification ranges of *Vergleichspräpositionalen* over against comparative clauses. We have also observed only *Vergleichspräpositionalen* functioning with qualifications smaller than Type I.

The Chr uses another compound citation base (enlarged) in 1 Chr 24:19.

$$\text{אֵלֶּה פְּקֻדָּתָם לַעֲבֹדָתָם לָבוֹא לְבֵית־יְהוָה כְּמִשְׁפָּטָם}$$
$$\text{בְּיַד אַהֲרֹן אֲבִיהֶם כַּאֲשֶׁר צִוָּהוּ יְהוָה אֱלֹהֵי}$$
$$\text{יִשְׂרָאֵל} \quad (1 \text{ Chr } 24:19)$$

These had as their appointed duty in their service to enter [לָבוֹא] the house of the LORD according to the procedure established for them by their ancestor Aaron, as the LORD God of Israel had commanded him (1 Chr 24:19).

Even though the Chr rarely introduces a compound citation base, the function of this expression is characteristic of the *Vergleichspräpositionalen* we have observed in the non-synoptic post-exilic historiography. The referent of this compound citation base does not include the initial non-verbal predicate ("these were their offices for their ministry") since the text clearly attributes the twenty-four divisions of the sons of Eleazar and Ithamar to the falling of the lot ("David, with Zadok of the sons of Eleazar and Ahimelech of the sons of Ithamar,

divided them according to their offices for their ministry", v. 3).
Therefore, this compound citation base qualifies only the infinitive
phrase ("to enter in the house of God"; Type II). The compound
citation bases in the law and deuteronomistic literature have generally
qualified Type I or larger sentence constituents, especially when they
included at least one comparative clause introduced with כַּאֲשֶׁר as in 1
Chr 24:19. Hence, even though the *form* in 1 Chr 24:19 is one that is
rare in the non-synoptic material in Chronicles, the *function* of this
citation construction reflects the greater restrictiveness of the
Vergleichspräpositionalen we have studied in the non-synoptic post-
exilic historiography.

4. Conclusions regarding the Comparative Citation Bases Introduced with כַּאֲשֶׁר

In light of the evidence of this chapter, there appears to be a strong
tendency for independent comparative clauses with צוה√ to qualify one
or more clauses, especially those in the law and the deuteronomistic
literature (Type I, A, B, etc.). Some of these forms may even qualify
an entire paragraph when they are used as a scaffolding device (e.g.,
Type αP). When they are construed with certain terms (e.g,. כֹּל,
various pro-forms, היה√, etc.) the scope of reference is customarily
expanded. Some of these latter citation bases even qualify entire books
(e.g., Lev) or indicate an unrestricted referent. There were also various
unconventional uses of these independent comparative clauses (e.g, the
dissonance between the law ostensibly cited and its fulfilment). These
observations together with the fact that only two Type II qualifications
can be located for כַּאֲשֶׁר צוה√ (1 Chr 24:19, a compound citation base;
2 Chr 7:17, a citation base with כֹּל and *waw-explicativum*)
provisionally demonstrate that this comparative clause is more likely to
govern larger sentence constituents than the *Vergleichspräpositionalen*
treated with כָּתוּב. What remains, of course, is to determine whether
the breadth of functions we have observed for comparative clauses is
also characteristic of כְּמִצְוָה. The fact that these two כַּאֲשֶׁר צוה√
clauses occur in Chronicles may reflect the development of citation

bases. Admittedly, the citation base in 1 Chr 15:15 does not align in either form or function with the development we have otherwise observed in the non-synoptic post-exilic historiography. Despite this exceptional case, the general trajectory appears to be toward the development of some citation bases with legal referents.

Jenni maintains that the meaning of comparative clauses is unaffected by כֹל which only increases their syntactic range[92]. While Jenni's observation remains generally true, it is interesting that one of the two examples of a Type II qualification among the כַּאֲשֶׁר clauses above is construed with כֹל. Perhaps this is another indication of the Chr's use of citation bases with qualifications that are more restricted than those we have observed to characterise the law and the deuteronomistic literature.

Regarding the distribution of these forms in this chapter, we have observed that the use of citation bases is concentrated in the law and deuteronomistic material (DtrH and/or Jer). In fact, some forms have been exclusively attested in the law.

C. Vergleichspräpositionalen with מִצְוָה

1. Introduction

In stark contrast to the distribution of the forms already analysed in this chapter, the citation bases in the form of a *Vergleichspräpositionale* with מִצְוָה below are concentrated in the post-exilic historiography. Furthermore, the relatively few occurrences of this form that exist outside of this literature use features we have seen to be associated with the citation bases in the law and the deuteronomistic material (e.g., Type A qualifications, compound citation bases, repetition). Consequently, the first distinction to be made among these citation bases concerns those forms which occur outside of the post-exilic historiography.

---

92   Jenni, 19-20.

2. *The Deuteronomistic Literature*

Vergleichspräpositionalen with מִצְוָה in the deuteronomistic
literature (Deut 26:13; 31:5; 2 Kgs 17:34) are used in ways that are most
consistent with those we have previously examined in the law and the
DtrH. For instance, all three of these passages include a compound
citation base. So far in our study, compound citation bases tend to
occur outside of the post-exilic historiography. In fact, all three of these
are construed with a form of אֲשֶׁר צוה√ and, as a result, form a
tautological construction. This type of repetition has not been observed
among the post-exilic citation bases.

Furthermore, both of the compound citation bases (enlarged) in
Deut 31:5 and 26:13 also employ כֹּל. This is another feature that does
not tend to occur among non-synoptic post-exilic citation bases.

וּנְתָנָם יְהוָה לִפְנֵיכֶם וַעֲשִׂיתֶם לָהֶם כְּכָל־הַמִּצְוָה אֲשֶׁר צִוִּיתִי
אֶתְכֶם (Deut 31:5)

וְאָמַרְתָּ לִפְנֵי יְהוָה אֱלֹהֶיךָ בִּעַרְתִּי הַקֹּדֶשׁ מִן־הַבַּיִת וְגַם נְתַתִּיו לַלֵּוִי
וְלַגֵּר לַיָּתוֹם וְלָאַלְמָנָה כְּכָל־מִצְוָתְךָ אֲשֶׁר צִוִּיתָנִי לֹא־עָבַרְתִּי
מִמִּצְוֺתֶיךָ וְלֹא שָׁכָחְתִּי (Deut 26:13)

There are even more undeveloped forms and functions used in these two
passages.

In Deut 31:5, the meaningful referent of כְּכָל־הַמִּצְוָה is indicated
by the pro-form עשׂה√. However, this referent is not in the immediate
context as has usually been the case. Rather, the meaningful referent is
located more than twenty chapters away at Deut 7:1-6. Thus, in
addition to the other features we have observed in this form, the citation
base in Deut 31:5 has the most distant referent marked by the pro-form
עשׂה√ that we have encountered so far in our examination.

The use of the citation base in Deut 26:13 agrees with yet another
one of the features that have been emerging as generally undeveloped.
The referent of this citation base entails two clauses (Type A; cf. v. 12).

Since we have already noted several examples of a comparative
clause with a Type A qualification, this *Vergleichspräpositionale* in Deut

26:13 shows that Jenni's theory concerning the functional equivalence between these two comparative constructions can be observed in several passages. Up to this point in our analysis, we have observed that both a comparative clause and a *Vergleichspräpositionale* may qualify an infinitive phrase (Type II), a single clause (Type I), or two clauses (Type A). This clearly relates to the problem we have introduced in chapter one. But a satisfactory answer to the problem introduced there needs to consider which type of qualification is most characteristic of each of these comparative citation bases. As we continue we must note other uses of the *Vergleichspräpositionale* that may correspond to the types of qualification we have observed among comparative clauses. In this manner, we shall be able to assess the degree to which these two comparative sentence constituents are functionally equivalent. So far, our study suggests that *Vergleichspräpositionalen* tend to qualify Type I and smaller sentence constituents while comparative clauses introduced with כַּאֲשֶׁר tend to qualify Type I and larger referents. In the post-exilic historiography, in the case of a sentence with a finite verb and one or more infinitives, the citation bases in the form of a *Vergleichspräpositionale* always qualified the contiguous form(s).

Several undeveloped features have converged on the two deuteronomistic citation bases above. In fact, the formulation in 2 Kgs 17:34 consists of the most complex compound citation base in the Old Testament (the five constructions are enlarged below).

וְאֵינָם עֹשִׂים כְּחֻקֹּתָם וּכְמִשְׁפָּטָם וְכַתּוֹרָה וְכַמִּצְוָה
אֲשֶׁר צִוָּה יְהוָה אֶת־בְּנֵי יַעֲקֹב (2 Kgs 17:34)

Other undeveloped features of citation bases also occur in 2 Kgs 17:34: the referent is signalled with the pro-form עשׂה√; and the repetitive use of terms in citation bases. In keeping with his overall use of citation bases, the Chr does not employ this formulation in his history.

We refer to Rooker's thesis *Biblical Hebrew in Transition* in connection with this outstanding citation base in 2 Kgs 17:34, even though his conclusions apply to several other passages in our examination. Rooker states, "the Chronicler is…more economic in his use of language, writing only what is necessary and avoiding the repetition of the earlier"[93]. Rooker also concludes that this lack of repetition characterises the age of the Chronicler in general. He states, "in LBH there was an apparent tendency toward brevity which resulted in the avoidance of repetition"[94]. If Rooker is correct, then the lack of repetition in the citation bases of the post-exilic historiography (cf. the repetition of legal terminology in 2 Kgs 17:34) appears to be attributed more to the changes in LBH than to the development of citation bases.

Other studies of the developments of BH[95] also pertain to our study. It appears, however, that the bulk of the features we are observing has not been associated with the differences between SBH and LBH. This at least suggests that the reason there are differences between SBH and LBH citation bases with legal referents is to be attributed to some other factor. The use of citation bases in homilies and prayers which saw in the history of the sixth century a vindication of the legal and prophetic traditions could indicate an impetus for the development of citation bases with legal referents. This development would be the result of a greater concern to restore the traditions to Israel. The sustained use of the distinctive four-part citation pattern with various non-legal referents throughout the DtrH, Chronicles, and Esther further highlights the changes observed among forms with legal referents. The evidence at this point suggests that there was a development of some citation bases with legal referents in the post-exilic period. Elliger and Mason have referred to the early post-exilic era as the time when a move toward canonisation was made[96]. If these

---

93   M. F. Rooker, *Biblical Hebrew In Transition: The Language of the Book of Ezekiel*, JSOTS 90 (Sheffield: Sheffield Academic Press, 1990) 116.

94   *Ibid.*, 115.

95   S. R. Driver, *Introduction*, 539; Kropat, 58-59; Williamson, *Israel in the Books of Chronicles* (Cambridge: University Press, 1977) 37-59; Throntveit, "Linguistic Analysis and the Question of Authorship in Chronicles, Ezra and Nehemiah", *VT* 32 (1982) 201-16. The observations of Driver and Kropat will arise in our treatment of another citation base in a following chapter. The features that we have noted do not correlate with those that can be attributed to the influence of Aramaic on Hebrew (Polzin, *Late Biblical Hebrew: Toward An Historical Typology of Biblical Hebrew Prose*, HSM 12 [Missoula, Montana: Scholars Press, 1976] 61ff.).

96   Commenting on the relation between the legal and prophetic traditions in Zech 1:6, Elliger states, "but while the fathers, the object of the preaching, and the prophets, the subject of the preaching, no longer exist, the content of the

scholars are correct, then the development of exegetical tools to cite the literature that was growing in authority should not be surprising.

3. The Post-Exilic Historiography

The *Vergleichspräpositionalen* with מִצְוָה that occur in the post-exilic literature divide into two general categories. The Chr's references to a contemporary monarch with the citation base כְּמִצְוַת הַמֶּלֶךְ are distinguishable from the references to legal and cultic authorities with כְּמִצְוַת מֹשֶׁה or כְּמִצְוַת דָּוִיד in the post-exilic historiography (see further below). In fact, the references to the authority of the מֶלֶךְ have more in common with the comparative citation bases in the deuteronomistic literature above.

a. The Citation of the מֶלֶךְ with כְּמִצְוָה

In 2 Chr 29:15, the citation base refers foremost to the authority of king Hezekiah.

וַיַּאַסְפוּ אֶת־אֲחֵיהֶם וַיִּתְקַדְּשׁוּ וַיָּבֹאוּ כְמִצְוַת־הַמֶּלֶךְ
בְּדִבְרֵי יְהוָה לְטַהֵר בֵּית יְהוָה (2 Chr 29:15)

This citation base is used in a manner that is most consistent with those in the deuteronomistic material above. First, כְּמִצְוַת־הַמֶּלֶךְ בְּדִבְרֵי יְהוָה qualifies the two italicised clauses in v. 15 (cf. v. 5; Type A). Such a Type A qualification for a *Vergleichspräpositionale* has been observed only in Deut 26:13. Unlike the form in Deut 26:13, however, this *Vergleichspräpositionale* occurs without the broadening term כל. Hence, 2 Chr 29:15 is the first clear example that supports Jenni's view of the equivalent functions of the two comparative citation bases in our examination of constructions that qualify more than one clause.

---

preaching does, i.e., the prophetic word of God to which the present generation can and must pay heed. With these words, the concept of an Old Testament Canon is heralded" (Elliger, 101; Mason's translation, 290, n. 17).

Secondly, even though בְּדִבְרֵי יְהוָה does not technically agree with the construction we are studying, its use with כְּמִצְוַת־הַמֶּלֶךְ in 2 Chr 29:15 does resemble a compound citation base. Insofar as this is the case, this compound device would be yet another similarity with the features associated with undeveloped citation bases.

More significantly, the entire phrase כְּמִצְוַת־הַמֶּלֶךְ בְּדִבְרֵי יְהוָה grounds the king's authority in his relation with the LORD, probably stemming from the king's special relation as God's "son" established at his coronation (Psa 2). However, full consideration of the contexts may indicate that the Chr's reference to the authority of the monarch is a subsidiary concern to his use of citation formulæ with legal or cultic referents. In vv. 5-11, the Chr has introduced another homily which includes certain characteristic elements. Williamson has bolstered previous analyses of this homily by identifying the phrase בְּדִבְרֵי יְהוָה in v. 15 as the "inspired speaker" element of the Levitical Sermon in vv. 5ff. However, despite its association with a Levitical Sermon this reference to the authority of the king is characteristically deuteronomistic (a Type A qualification and a compound citation base). This is another indication that the Chr's concern for legal and cultic authority is more central to his history than the representation of the authority of the monarchy.

Another citation of the monarch occurs in the Levitical Sermon in 2 Chr 30:6ff. As in 2 Chr 29:15, this reference to the authority of the monarchy has much in common with the undeveloped citation bases.

וַיֵּלְכוּ הָרָצִים בָּאִגְּרוֹת מִיַּד הַמֶּלֶךְ וְשָׂרָיו בְּכָל־יִשְׂרָאֵל וִיהוּדָה
וּכְמִצְוַת הַמֶּלֶךְ לֵאמֹר בְּנֵי יִשְׂרָאֵל שׁוּבוּ אֶל־יְהוָה אֱלֹהֵי אַבְרָהָם
יִצְחָק וְיִשְׂרָאֵל וְיָשֹׁב אֶל־הַפְּלֵיטָה הַנִּשְׁאֶרֶת לָכֶם מִכַּף
מַלְכֵי אַשּׁוּר (2 Chr 30:6)97

First, כְּמִצְוַת הַמֶּלֶךְ forms a compound citation base with לֵאמֹר (enlarged). Secondly, this use of כְּמִצְוַת הַמֶּלֶךְ is unique insofar as it is placed outside the main clause, which is part of the referent, in a way

_____

97 Read וכמצות with MT (cf. several MSS have ובמ׳, while 𝔊𝔒 attest כמ׳ [Rudolph, BHS]).

that we have not observed among *Vergleichspräpositionalen* that are
used as citation bases. The deed that is authorised by this citation base
appears to be best summarised as "the reading aloud of the king's edict
while the couriers travelled throughout Israel and Judah". Thus, the
compound citation base כְּמִצְוַת הַמֶּלֶךְ לֵאמֹר and the referent are non-
contiguous. One feature that has characterised undeveloped
constructions is the non-contiguous relation between the citation base
and referent.

The כְּמִצְוַת הַמֶּלֶךְ citation base in 2 Chr 35:10 is employed in a
way that is similar to several of those observed above in the law and the
deuteronomistic literature.

וַתִּכּוֹן הָעֲבוֹדָה וַיַּעַמְדוּ הַכֹּהֲנִים עַל־עָמְדָם וְהַלְוִיִּם עַל־מַחְלְקוֹתָם
כְּמִצְוַת הַמֶּלֶךְ (2 Chr 35:10)

In this non-synoptic passage, the referent of כְּמִצְוַת הַמֶּלֶךְ consists of
the two preceding clauses with כון√ and עמד√ (cf. vv. 4-6; Type A).
The identification of this referent is based on the king's command in vv.
3-6, especially vv. 4-5 ("prepare yourselves [כון√]…and stand [עמד√]
in the Holy Place…" [NEB]).

Based on 2 Chr 29:15, 30:16, and 35:10, the citation base כְּמִצְוַת
הַמֶּלֶךְ in the Chr's history appears to be used in a manner that is most
consistent with the forms in the law and the deuteronomistic material.

The last use of כְּמִצְוַת הַמֶּלֶךְ in Chronicles (2 Chr 35:16) does not
disagree with the view that this citation base is employed in an
undeveloped manner. The authority of Josiah is referred to in 2 Chr
35:16 (enlarged).

וַתִּכּוֹן כָּל־עֲבוֹדַת יְהוָה בַּיּוֹם הַהוּא לַעֲשׂוֹת הַפֶּסַח
וְהַעֲלוֹת עֹלוֹת עַל מִזְבַּח יְהוָה כְּמִצְוַת הַמֶּלֶךְ
יֹאשִׁיָּהוּ (2 Chr 35:16)

In order properly to relate this citation of Josiah's authority to the uses
of *Vergleichspräpositionale* that refer to the law, we must consider the
structure of this sentence. This passage entails the sentence structure

that has led to the greatest range of scholarly opinion regarding the function of *Vergleichspräpositionalen*: one finite verb; and one or two infinitive phrases followed by a citation base. In such sentences, it will be recalled that כַּכָּתוּב with legal referents always qualified the contiguous infinitive phrase(s) (Type II) in the post-exilic historiography. However, the referent of the כְּמִצְוַת הַמֶּלֶךְ citation base in 2 Chr 35:16 includes the remainder of the sentence (Type I; cf. Josiah's commands in vv. 3-6). Josiah's commands in 2 Chr 35:4 and 6 support this identification of the referent particularly ("make preparations [כוּן√]... slaughter the passover lamb [הַפֶּסַח]... and on behalf of your kindred make preparations [הָכִינוּ]"). Hence, the use of כַּכָּתוּב with legal referents in the post-exilic historiography (Type II) is distinct from the way that כְּמִצְוָה is employed when citing the authority of Josiah in 35:16. The qualification of the entire clause (Type I) is a function common to both *Vergleichspräpositionalen* and comparative clauses. Jenni's view of the equivalent functions of these two sentence constituents finds most of its support in Type I qualifications. We now address the use of כְּמִצְוָה for legal and cultic authorities.

b. The Citation of Legal and Cultic Authorities with כְּמִצְוָה

In rewriting 1 Kgs 9:25, the Chr adds a citation base that refers to the authority of Moses (enlarged).

וְהֶעֱלָה שְׁלֹמֹה שָׁלֹשׁ פְּעָמִים בַּשָּׁנָה עֹלוֹת וּשְׁלָמִים עַל־הַמִּזְבֵּחַ
אֲשֶׁר בָּנָה לַיהוָה וְהַקְטֵיר אִתּוֹ אֲשֶׁר לִפְנֵי יְהוָה וְשִׁלַּם אֶת־הַבָּיִת
(1 Kgs 9:25)

וּבִדְבַר־יוֹם בְּיוֹם לְהַעֲלוֹת כְּמִצְוַת מֹשֶׁה לַשַּׁבָּתוֹת וְלֶחֳדָשִׁים
וְלַמּוֹעֲדוֹת שָׁלוֹשׁ פְּעָמִים בַּשָּׁנָה בְּחַג הַמַּצּוֹת וּבְחַג הַשָּׁבֻעוֹת
וּבְחַג הַסֻּכּוֹת (2 Chr 8:13)

The citation base qualifies the infinitive (Type II) and has a contiguous relation to the referent. By introducing this citation base into his history, the Chr provides a more comprehensive statement concerning the offering practices of Solomon[98].

In 2 Chr 35:15, a reference is made to the authority of David and the supervisors of the cultic musicians (cf. 1 Chr 25:6; 28:13; enlarged).

וְהַמְשֹׁרֲרִים בְּנֵי־אָסָף עַל־מַעֲמָדָם כְּמִצְוַת דָּוִיד וְאָסָף
וְהֵימָן וִידֻתוּן חוֹזֵה הַמֶּלֶךְ (2 Chr 35:15a)

The act authorised by the citation base ("according to the command of David, Asaph, Heman, and Jeduthun the king's seer") is related in the non-verbal clause ("the singers, the sons of Asaph, were also at their stations"; Type I; cf. 1 Chr 25). The *Vergleichspräpositionale* in 2 Chr 35:15a functions in the clause in which it occurs (*contra* the מֶלֶךְ citation bases). In contrast to this Type I qualification, the reference to the authority of Josiah in 2 Chr 35:16 did not restrict its scope of qualification to the nearest verb stem.

In Neh 12:45, David and Solomon are cited as authorities.

וַיִּשְׁמְרוּ מִשְׁמֶרֶת אֱלֹהֵיהֶם וּמִשְׁמֶרֶת הַטָּהֳרָה וְהַמְשֹׁרְרִים
וְהַשֹּׁעֲרִים כְּמִצְוַת דָּוִיד וּשְׁלֹמֹה בְנוֹ (Neh 12:45)[99]

Even though the Hebrew of this verse is awkward[100], the citation base qualifies the contiguous clause (Type I).

4. *Conclusions for* Vergleichspräpositionalen

It is important to compare the two Type I qualifications in 2 Chr 35:15 and Neh 12:45 we have just observed to the other uses of

---

98 Williamson, 232.

99 Read the conjunction ו before שלמה with several MSS and versions (contra MT).

100 There are a variety of views taken by scholars on the significance of the phrase "and the singers and the gatekeepers". Clines understands it as a secondary addition by an editor after the Chr. Batten understands this phrase as the subject of the verb in v. 45. Most scholars, however, consider the subject of this verb to be the antecedent "the priests and Levites" in v. 44 (Myers, 205; Fensham, 258; Williamson, 384; Blenkinsopp, 350).

Vergleichspräpositionalen. The scope of qualification of these citation bases is more restricted than all of those forms that referred to הַמֶּלֶךְ in the Chr's history observed above. This is especially clear regarding the passages that use a *Vergleichspräpositionale* with a Type A qualification (2 Chr 29:15; 35:10) or a non-contiguous relation (30:6). It will be recalled that these references to the monarch shared several features with the deuteronomistic citation bases. Furthermore, the only Type II qualification, the characteristic use of כַּכָּתוּב in the non-synoptic post-exilic historiography, was attested with a legal referent (2 Chr 8:13). This relatively more restricted range of qualification for citation bases with legal referents can also be detected in the one Type I use as well (2 Chr 35:16). Type I functions are the most common qualification shared between the two comparative citation bases in our examination, so a nuanced approach is required. In 2 Chr 35:16, the Type I qualification includes one finite verb and two infinitives. In 2 Chr 35:15, the Type I qualification is limited to the nearest predicate which is a simple sentence. In this way, the use of *Vergleichspräpositionalen* with מִצְוָה with legal and cultic referents has more in common with the use of כַּכָּתוּב with legal referents in the post-exilic historiography. Both of these citation bases have a more resticted scope of qualification in the post-exilic historiography for legal and cultic referents. The restricted range of *Vergleichspräpositionalen* in this literature consists of Type I (simple sentence) and smaller qualifications; they always consist of contiguous referents.

III. Conclusions

In this chapter, we have shown that some functions, forms, and features of exegetical devices are more likely to appear with the √צוה and מִצְוָה citation bases that occur outside of the non-synoptic post-exilic literature. Conversely, several of these citation bases with legal and cultic referents in the post-exilic historiography are consistent with the development we have previously observed. In Esther, citation bases were developed in conjunction with the literary artistry of that book. In Zechariah, Ezra, Nehemiah, and Malachi, a select number of citation bases appear to have evolved into sophisticated exegetical and homiletical devices. The sustained use of the distinctive syntactic structure used with non-legal referents in our chapter on כָּתוּב (an extraposed noun; a particle with a resumptive pronoun; a form of the passive participle √כתב; and a literary corpus) appears to attach further significance to the changes among citation bases with legal referents. In connection with this, it is interesting to observe that the Chr's citation of the authority of the monarch with the form מִצְוַת הַמֶּלֶךְ has more in common with the forms that are concentrated in the law and deuteronomistic literature than his own reference to the legal and cultic authorities.

One of the developments among post-exilic citation bases with legal referents suggested a Sitz im Leben which could explain the changes that we have observed. We suggested that there was nothing inconsistent with positing a development in citation bases with legal referents in the early Persian era. This development of citation bases could have easily been the result of seeing the vindication of the legal and prophetic traditions in light of the events of the sixth century B.C. These events — the fall of Jerusalem, the temple, and the Davidic dynasty, the Babylonian exile, and the limited success of the initial return after Cyrus' decree — led to a growth in the authority ascribed to these traditions. This vindication of the legal and prophetic traditions may have been the impetus for the development of these exegetical tools to refer to the traditions of the fathers. We have also seen these developed citation bases to be used as homiletical devices to elicit a response from an audience. This development of citation bases, the evidence has suggested, was probably done unwittingly and is best understood as a result of the new care given to the law. Such a development is attractive to posit since there is such a drastic change in the use of citation bases with legal referents after *ca.* 550 B.C.

Chapter 4: Citation Bases with √שפט and מִשְׁפָּט

Our remaining discussion of citation bases will proceed much more efficiently for several reasons. First, we have already encountered the main forms and functions that are used in these constructions. Secondly, we have also treated some of the formulations that this chapter addresses in our previous examination of compound citations bases. Finally, √שפט and מִשְׁפָּט occur in citation bases much less frequently than the terms treated above.

I. √שפט and מִשְׁפָּט in Relative Citation Bases

√שפט is never used as a citation base in the form of a definite relative participle (i.e., הַשֹּׁפְטִים). In fact, there is only one occurrence of a relative citation base in the form of a finite verb (enlarged).

וַיִּשְׁמְעוּ כָל־יִשְׂרָאֵל אֶת־הַמִּשְׁפָּט אֲשֶׁר שָׁפַט הַמֶּלֶךְ (1 Kgs 3:28a)

The only noteworthy aspect of this formulation is the tautological expression ("the judgment which the king had handed down"). At this point in our examination, we have seen such tautological citation bases to be characteristically employed in the law and deuteronomistic material. Hence, the use of the construction in 1 Kgs 3:28a is consistent with the distribution of other tautological citation bases we have examined throughout the OT.

II. √שפט and מִשְׁפָּט in Comparative Citation Bases

A. √שפט and מִשְׁפָּט in a Comparative Clause

Both of the terms √שפט and מִשְׁפָּט occur in clauses introduced with כַּאֲשֶׁר, but none of these forms functions as a citation base[1].

B. מִשְׁפָּט in *Vergleichspräpositionalen*

The most common form of construction in this chapter consists of מִשְׁפָּט in a *Vergleichspräpositionale*. Unlike the other citation bases analysed in previous chapters, there is no distinctive distribution of these constructions in the OT. It remains, of course, to be seen whether there are any differences in the way that they are used throughout the OT. These forms may be used as independent citation bases, or they may be employed in conjunction with another term or citation base. Like כָּתוּב above, the semantic range of מִשְׁפָּט is broad enough (e.g., "ordinance, custom, habit") for it to be used with both non-legal and legal referents.

1. Non-Legal Referents

So far in our examination the citation bases with non-legal referents have not reflected the development we have observed among those with legal referents. It will be recalled that such development in citation bases with legal referents appears to have emerged by 520 B.C. This section will further illuminate the significance of the four-part citation pattern observed with כָּתוּב for non-legal referents which was unaffected by this development in exegetical devices.

---

1   Ezek 20:36; 35:11; 2 Chr 22:8. Somewhat exceptionally כַּאֲשֶׁר in Isa 26:9 governs the non-verbal clause כַּאֲשֶׁר מִשְׁפָּטֶיךָ לָאָרֶץ.

a. *Vergleichspräpositionalen* with a Non-Legal Referent that Qualify One Clause

i. Independent Citation Bases

כְּמִשְׁפָּט may qualify one clause with a range of non-legal meanings. For instance, the "practice" or "custom" of the Sidionians (כְּמִשְׁפַּט צֹרֹנִים) is cited in Judg 18:7. Their tradition was to "dwell in safety".

וַיֵּלְכוּ חֲמֵשֶׁת הָאֲנָשִׁים וַיָּבֹאוּ לַיְשָׁה וַיִּרְאוּ אֶת־הָעָם אֲשֶׁר־בְּקִרְבָּהּ
יוֹשֶׁבֶת־לָבֶטַח כְּמִשְׁפַּט צֹרֹנִים שֹׁקֵט וּבֹטֵחַ וְאֵין־מַכְלִים
דָּבָר בָּאָרֶץ יוֹרֵשׁ עֶצֶר וּרְחֹקִים הֵמָּה מִצִּדֹנִים וְדָבָר אֵין־לָהֶם
עִם־אָדָם (Judg 18:7)

This citation base qualifies only the contiguous appositive clause ("those dwelling in safety"; Type I). The referent is limited to this appositive statement since it is the only element of the prevailing context to which the people of Laish are compared. This identification of the referent is made clear by the elaboration on the secure lifestyle of the inhabitants of Laish in v. 7b ("quiet and unsuspecting; for there was no ruler humiliating them for anything in the land, and they...had no dealings with anyone").

This deuteronomistic citation base with a non-legal referent has a similar use as the post-exilic constructions with legal referents that distinguish two exegetical horizons (i.e., a reference to a text and its reinterpretation). We have observed before the capacity of a *Vergleichspräpositionale* to succinctly identify the source of a referent as well as permit a place in the same passage for an exegetical comment. It appears noteworthy that a *Vergleichspräpositionale* is used to distinguish two statements in the DtrH with a non-legal referent (see below). The reference to a legal tradition is accompanied with its reinterpretation in Num 27:1-11, but this exegetical process is marked in another way. The reinterpretation of the laws of inheritance for the daughters of Zelophehad in Num 27 was conveyed with undeveloped features and consisted of several verses.

כְּמִשְׁפָּט is employed in 2 Kgs 17:33 to refer to the custom of foreign nations (enlarged).

אֶת־יְהוָה הָיוּ יְרֵאִים וְאֶת־אֱלֹהֵיהֶם הָיוּ עֹבְדִים כְּמִשְׁפַּט הַגּוֹיִם
אֲשֶׁר־הִגְלוּ אֹתָם מִשָּׁם (2 Kgs 17:33)

The antithetical relation between the two initial clauses ("they feared the LORD *but* served their own gods according to the custom of the nations", v. 33a) assures us that כְּמִשְׁפַּט הַגּוֹיִם qualifies only the contiguous clause (italics; Type I). The antithetical relation between the first two clauses is a semantic consideration that facilitates the identification of the referent.

The citation base כַּמִּשְׁפָּט in 2 Kgs 11:14 (enlarged) is employed to refer to an Israelite tradition.

וַתֵּרֶא וְהִנֵּה הַמֶּלֶךְ עֹמֵד עַל־הָעַמּוּד *כַּמִּשְׁפָּט* וְהַשָּׂרִים
וְהַחֲצֹצְרוֹת אֶל־הַמֶּלֶךְ וְכָל־עַם הָאָרֶץ שָׂמֵחַ וְתֹקֵעַ בַּחֲצֹצְרוֹת
וַתִּקְרַע עֲתַלְיָה אֶת־בְּגָדֶיהָ וַתִּקְרָא קֶשֶׁר קָשֶׁר (2 Kgs 11:14)

כַּמִּשְׁפָּט refers to the custom of the king standing beside a pillar. The significance of this act is not clearly stated in 2 Kgs 11 though it appears to indicate to Athaliah that Joash, whose position she had previously usurped (vv. 1-3), had just been anointed and received as Judah's true king (Type I; cf. v. 12). Knoppers correctly explains Joash's standing by the pillar by referring to the same deed performed by Josiah. Josiah "journeys to the temple to ratify the covenant (2 Kgs 23:2) and stands 'by the pillar' (2 Kgs 23:3)"[2]. Athaliah's reaction to Joash's standing by the pillar ("she tore her clothes and cried, 'Treason! Treason!'", v. 14b) agrees with the significance given to this act in Josiah's account. The referent is introduced with a disjunctive clause. However, it appears that this disjunctive clause does not distinguish this non-legal referent from its context as we will observe among the exegetical devices that use this form to cite the legal traditions. That is, the use of וְהִנֵּה here merely introduces the object of √ראה (i.e., "she saw that the

---

2   G. N. Knoppers, *Two Nations Under God: The Deuteronomistic History of Solomon and the Dual Monarchies. Volume 2: The Reign of Jeroboam, the Fall of Israel and the Reign of Josiah,* HSM 53 (Atlanta, Georgia: Scholars Press, 1994) 162. Gray states, "it was customary...for the king on such solemn appearances to the people to stand by one of the pillars, cf. 23.3..." (J. Gray, *I & II Kings,* OTL [London: SCM Press LTD, 1964] 521).

king was standing…")[3]. Although some of the features associated with developed citation bases were associated with כְּמִשְׁפָּט in Judg 18:7, the use of a disjunctive clause in connection with a *Vergleichspräpositionale* citation base in 2 Kgs 11:14 is not always concerned with distinguishing the referent from its context in the DtrH.

In 2 Chr 30:16a, כְּמִשְׁפָּט appears to mark the habit or practice of the priests and Levites (e.g., "they took their accustomed posts…", NRSV)[4].

$$\text{וַיַּעַמְדוּ עַל־עָמְדָם כְּמִשְׁפָּטָם כְּתוֹרַת מֹשֶׁה אִישׁ־הָאֱלֹהִים}$$
(2 Chr 30:16)

כְּמִשְׁפָּטָם does not have a legal referent (e.g., "they took their posts according to their ordinance"). In fact, כְּמִשְׁפָּטָם does not attribute a referent to another source. We will return to this passage in our treatment of כתורה below since, according to our view, this latter form is the only citation base in 2 Chr 30:16. Despite its form, כְּמִשְׁפָּטָם in 2 Chr 30:16 does not function as a citation base.

All of these uses of כמשפט with a non-legal referent qualify one clause (Type I) and are concentrated in the law or the DtrH[5].

ii. Pro-Form עשׂה√

There are only three occurrences of כמשפט with the pro-form עשׂה√. Two of these forms occur in Ezekiel and qualify one clause (Type I)[6].

$$\text{וּכְמִשְׁפְּטֵי הַגּוֹיִם אֲשֶׁר סְבִיבוֹתֵיכֶם לֹא עֲשִׂיתֶם}$$ (Ezek 5:7b)

---

3   For the use of והנה to mark the object of ראה√, see JM §§ 126bN, 177 (cf. Gen 24:63; 33:1; 37:25).
4   Japhet, 950.
5   Gen 40:13; Exod 21:9; Judg 18:7; 2 Kgs 11:14; 17:33.
6   Ezek 5:7; 11:12.

We have previously addressed 2 Kgs 17:34 as the most complex compound citation base in the OT. But it has been left until this chapter to indicate that כְּמִשְׁפָּט is used twice in this verse. Only the first citation base (enlarged) has a non-legal referent.

עַד הַיּוֹם הַזֶּה הֵם עֹשִׂים כַּמִּשְׁפָּטִים הָרִאשֹׁנִים (2 Kgs 17:34a)

The meaningful referent for this pro-form √עשׂה is located in vv. 32-33.

Though the evidence is limited, there is nothing about these uses of pro-form √עשׂה that disagrees with the distribution of broadening terms in the OT we have observed in this study.

b. *Vergleichspräpositionalen* with a Non-Legal Referent that Qualify
    Two Clauses

There are three examples of כְּמִשְׁפָּט with non-legal referents that qualify two clauses (Type A). In Josh 6:15, כַּמִּשְׁפָּט הַזֶּה has the meaning "according to the same practice" referring to certain behaviour in the foregoing context.

וַיְהִי בַּיּוֹם הַשְּׁבִיעִי וַיַּשְׁכִּמוּ כַּעֲלוֹת הַשַּׁחַר וַיָּסֹבּוּ אֶת־הָעִיר
כַּמִּשְׁפָּט הַזֶּה שֶׁבַע פְּעָמִים רַק בַּיּוֹם הַהוּא סָבְבוּ אֶת־הָעִיר
שֶׁבַע פְּעָמִים (Josh 6:15)

The two preceding clauses with √שׁכם and √סבב are qualified by this *Vergleichspräpositionale*. כַּמִּשְׁפָּט הַזֶּה refers to the manner in which the priests and the armed men had previously marched around Jericho in vv. 12-13. The majority of vv. 12-13 is concerned with the manner in which the Israelites were to circuit (√סבב) Jericho on the seventh day, but these verses also entail the statement that "Joshua rose early [√שׁכם] in the morning" (v. 12). The two contiguous clauses that employ these verb stems are the act that is cited by כַּמִּשְׁפָּט הַזֶּה .

In 1 Kgs 18:28, the citation base (enlarged) also qualifies two clauses.

וַיִּקְרְאוּ בְּקוֹל גָּדוֹל וַיִּתְגֹּדְדוּ כְּמִשְׁפָּטָם בַּחֲרָבוֹת
וּבָרְמָחִים עַד־שְׁפָךְ־דָּם עֲלֵיהֶם (1 Kgs 18:28)

It appears best to understand all of the cultic behaviour of these Baal worshippers ("they cried with a loud voice and cut themselves") as constituting the practice that is cited by כְּמִשְׁפָּטָם (Type A).

There is evidence of both of these deeds being performed on Baal's behalf in inscriptions. In *CTA* 1.5-6, El and Anat mourn for Baal, who they mistakenly think has died, in a manner that is analogous to the Baal worshippers in the Elijah narrative[7]. Presumably the deeds of El and Anat reflect the worship of the members of the Baal cult. In mourning, El cuts his flesh and cries out. It is stated:

> he scraped (his) skin with a stone, with a flint for a razor he shaved (his) side-whiskers and beard; he harrowed his collar-bone, he ploughed (his) chest like a garden, he harrowed (his) waist like a valley. He lifted up his voice and cried: "Baal is dead!" (*CTA* 1.5.VI.14ff.).

Anat is depicted as behaving in a similar manner in response to what she thought was Baal's corpse (*CTA* 1.6.I.2ff.). *CTA* appears to illuminate the behaviour of the cultic worshippers of Baal. This text clearly supports reading the citation base in 1 Kgs 18:28 with a Type A qualification[8].

כְּמִשְׁפָּט in Psa 119:132 appears to qualify both of the imperatives at the beginning of the line.

פְּנֵה־אֵלַי וְחָנֵּנִי כְּמִשְׁפָּט לְאֹהֲבֵי שְׁמֶךָ (Psa 119:132)

---

7   See J. C. L. Gibson, *Canaanite Myths and Legends,* 2nd edn (Edinburgh: T. & T. Clark, 1977) 14ff.

8   There is dispute over the identification of the Baal that Jezebel worshipped. According to Day, "there is every reason to believe that Jezebel's Baal was in fact Baal-Shamem, [a] Tyrian deity who is in fact identical with the Baal attested elsewhere in the OT" ("Baal (Deity)", *ABD*, Vol. 1, 548). Regarding Baal-Shamem, Röllig concludes that "there are no references to him in the classical books of the OT" ("Baal-Shemem", *DDD,* 287). Röllig reserves a place for allusions to Baal-Shamem only in Dan (8:13; 9:27).

The psalmist refers to the reliable habit of the LORD to "turn to…and be gracious to [him]" (Type A).

With non-legal referents, כְּמִשְׁפָּט does not mark Type A qualifications in the post-exilic historiography.

c. A *Vergleichspräpositionale* with a Non-Legal Referent that Qualifies a Noun

The *Vergleichspräpositionale* in 1 Kgs 5:8 (4:28) qualifies only the contiguous noun (Type III).

וְהַשְּׂעֹרִים וְהַתֶּבֶן לַסּוּסִים וְלָרָכֶשׁ יָבִאוּ אֶל־הַמָּקוֹם אֲשֶׁר
יִהְיֶה־שָּׁם אִישׁ כְּמִשְׁפָּטוֹ (1 Kgs 5:8 [4:28])

This prepositional phrase marks the responsibilities of each official who came to Solomon's table to provide for the horses "each according to his charge [אִישׁ כְּמִשְׁפָּטוֹ]" (NRSV). While this passage is useful in understanding the range of qualifications for *Vergleichspräpositionalen*, we realise that the use of כְּמִשְׁפָּטוֹ in 1 Kgs 5:8 (4:28) does not clearly ascribe a referent to another source.

d. Conclusions

The evidence for כמשפט above differs from the previous forms with non-legal referents in this examination. On the one hand, כמשפט does not take a distinctive form or function like the four-part citation pattern with כָּתוּב. On the other hand, it does not occur exclusively in the post-exilic historiography as does the citation base √מצא כָּתוּב. While the form כמשפט with a non-legal topic was attested in the post-exilic historiography (2 Chr 30:16a) it did not attribute a referent to a source. When it was used with an undeveloped feature of citation bases (i.e., a pro-form, a Type A qualification) כמשפט did not occur in the post-exilic literature in which we have previously observed developed exegetical devices. Some of these forms, however, had uses comparable to the developed citation bases in the post-exilic historiography (i.e., Type III). The use of a *Vergleichspräpositionale* with a disjunctive clause proved to be a superficial similarity. In general, the evidence of כמשפט with non-legal referents is mixed. The most noteworthy aspect in this section is that the use of כמשפט with non-legal referents drops-off dramatically in the post-exilic literature associated with developed citation bases. This shift in usage may be related to the development of citation bases with legal referents that we have observed with other forms in this study. We now turn to the use of כמשפט with legal referents.

2. *Legal Referents*

a. Independent Citation Bases

i. *Vergleichspräpositionalen* that Qualify One Clause

כמשפט with a legal referent may qualify a single clause (Type I). These forms are distributed throughout the OT[9].

With the form in Num 15:24 (enlarged), there is a non-contiguous relation between the citation base and the referent (italics).

וְהָיָה אִם מֵעֵינֵי הָעֵדָה נֶעֶשְׂתָה לִשְׁגָגָה וְעָשׂוּ כָל־הָעֵדָה פַּר
בֶּן־בָּקָר אֶחָד לְעֹלָה לְרֵיחַ נִיחֹחַ לַיהוָה וּמִנְחָתוֹ וְנִסְכּוֹ
כַּמִּשְׁפָּט וּשְׂעִיר־עִזִּים אֶחָד לְחַטָּת (Num 15:24)

Then, if it [the sin] is done unintentionally, without the knowledge of the congregation, that *all the congregation shall offer one bull for a burnt offering,* as a soothing aroma to the LORD, with its grain offering, and its

---

9   Exod 21:31; 26:30; Lev 5:10 (not a pro-form √עשׂה, "to prepare a burnt offering"); Num 15:24 (see below); Psa 119:149, 156; 1 Chr 6:17 (32); 15:13 (a negative citation base); 2 Chr 4:7 (see below); 8:14 (see below); 35:13 (see below). The *Vergleichspräpositionale* in Ezek 42:11 does not function as a citation base.

libation, according to the ordinance, and one male goat for a sin offering
(Num 15:24).

The laws referred to in Num 15:24 are the regulations for the sin
offering in Lev 4[10]. Note that the forms closest to the citation base
regard grain and drink offerings (נֶסֶךְ and מִנְחָה) and that these are not
referred to in Lev 4. Even the burnt offering as a "pleasant aroma"
(לְרֵיחַ נִיחֹחַ) is referred to in Lev 4 in connection with the offering
made on behalf of the individual (v. 31) and not the congregation as in
Num 15:24[11]. In fact, the only thing that can be claimed to have been
accomplished according to Lev 4 in Num 15:24 is the burnt offering
itself. In Num 15:24, the forms contiguous to the citation base are not
in fact to be ascribed to the source that is being cited here. Such a non-
contiguous relation between the citation base and the referent in the law
is consistent with the distribution of the undeveloped features of
exegetical devices in the OT.

2 Chr 8:14 consists of the type of complex sentence (a finite verb,
one or more infinitive phrases, and a citation base in the form of a
Vergleichspräpositionale) that has proven to be the most controversial
syntactic environment for scholars to agree on the identification of a
referent of a citation base.

וַיַּעֲמֵד כְּמִשְׁפַּט דָּוִיד־אָבִיו אֶת־מַחְלְקוֹת הַכֹּהֲנִים עַל־עֲבֹדָתָם
וְהַלְוִיִּם עַל־מִשְׁמְרוֹתָם לְהַלֵּל וּלְשָׁרֵת נֶגֶד הַכֹּהֲנִים לִדְבַר־יוֹם
בְּיוֹמוֹ וְהַשּׁוֹעֲרִים בְּמַחְלְקוֹתָם לְשַׁעַר וָשָׁעַר כִּי כֵן מִצְוַת
דָּוִיד אִישׁ־הָאֱלֹהִים (2 Chr 8:14)

---

10   For example, Fishbane states, "it must be noted that a detailed comparison of
the sequence and language of the two sources under review (Lev. 4 and Num. 15:
22-9), such as that undertaken by A. Toeg, conclusively demonstrates that Num.
15: 22-9 is based on Lev. 4: 13-21, 27-31: for not only can one observe a
precise terminological correspondence in the consecution of these two sets of
legal materials (cf. Lev. 4: 13 and Num. 15: 22-24aα; Lev. 4: 14 and Num. 15:
24aβ-bβ; Lev. 4: 20b and Num. 15: 25-6; Lev. 4: 27a and Num. 15: 27a; Lev 4:
28b and Num. 15: 27b; and Lev. 4: 31b and Num. 15: 28), but, more
importantly, Num. 15: 22-9 is characterized by a variety of exegetical
expansions which supplement the skeletal frame which it shares with Lev. 4"
(191; see A. Toeg, "Numbers 15: 22-31 – a Halakhic Midrash", *Tarbiz* 40 [1960-
61] 1-20). See also Budd, xviii.

11   The offering of a goat in Lev 4:22 is for a ruler and not the congregation.

This passage supports the emerging view of this examination that the
Vergleichspräpositionale citation bases with legal referents in the non-
synoptic portions of Chronicles, Ezra, and Nehemiah[12] have been
placed more carefully than those used elsewhere (cf. Num 15:24, for
example, immediately above). The reason the position of comparative
statements — both כַּאֲשֶׁר statements and *Vergleichspräpositionalen* —
is so important is because between them they can qualify a tremendous
range of referents (e.g., Type IV [a particle], Type I [a single clause],
Type D [five clauses] and Type α [a "paragraph"]). כַּאֲשֶׁר clauses
customarily mark a Type I or larger qualification; a
Vergleichspräpositionale generally has a Type I or smaller qualification.
These comparative statements cannot be inflected to agree with a
referent. It is their placement that is key to the identification of the
referent. The construction in 2 Chr 8:14 shows another aspect of the
placement of a citation base in the form of a *Vergleichspräpositionale* in
the non-synoptic post-exilic historiography.

    2 Chr 8:14 is an important passage that needs to be compared with
the several passages that consist of a finite verb, an infinitive phrase(s),
and a comparative citation base. The placement of the
Vergleichspräpositionale citation base is especially key in these types of
sentences. Among the passages with these elements, the citation base
has consistently qualified the infinitive phrase(s) (Type II); such a
qualification has been indicated by its contiguous placement to this
sentence constituent. Unlike these examples, כְּמִשְׁפַּט דָּוִיד־אָבִיו in 2
Chr 8:14 is placed beside the finite verb of the complex sentence. This
placement of the *Vergleichspräpositionale* means that the referent is not
limited to the infinitive but entails the entire sentence (Type I; cf. 1 Chr
23-27). In the non-synoptic portions of Chronicles, Ezra, and
Nehemiah, the *Vergleichspräpositionalen* we have examined have been
carefully positioned as exegetical devices. This principle is not a truism
as the debates reviewed throughout this study clearly demonstrate.

---

12   The development of such forms in Esther is related to the literary artistry of this
     book.

It appears that there was greater concern to mark the scope of qualification of certain citation bases in the form of a *Vergleichspräpositionale* in the post-exilic period.

2 Chr 35:13 appears to be another example of the way that the Chr places a *Vergleichspräpositionale* (enlarged) in order to distinguish one portion of a passage as a specific point of legal observance.

וַיְבַשְּׁלוּ הַפֶּסַח בָּאֵשׁ כַּמִּשְׁפָּט וְהַקֳּדָשִׁים בִּשְּׁלוּ בַּסִּירוֹת
וּבַדְּוָדִים וּבַצֵּלָחוֹת וַיָּרִיצוּ לְכָל־בְּנֵי הָעָם (2 Chr 35:13)

The placement of the citation base beside this first clause ("they roasted the Passover animals on the fire") is because it is the only act that is being ascribed to the law in v. 13 (cf. Exod 12:8-9). This appears to be the reason why the second clause in 2 Chr 35:13 is not introduced with a conversive form, but consists of a disjunctive clause ("while the sacred offerings they cooked in pots")[13]. In contrast to the positioning of the citation base in Num 15:24, which is beside forms not related to the source cited there, the contiguous forms in 2 Chr 8:14 and 35:13 further support the view that the placement of certain citation bases is distinctive in the non-synoptic portions of Chronicles, Ezra, and Nehemiah.   The history recounted in v. 13b ("they boiled the holy things in pots, in kettles, in pans, and carried them speedily to all the lay people") stem from the events specific to Josiah's Passover. That is, the events in v. 13b are not to be attributed to the law, but are to be understood as facilitating measures that enabled the law to be observed. In this compound sentence, it appears that the reason for using the following disjunctive clause was to show that the כַּמִּשְׁפָּט has a Type I qualification. The *Vergleichspräpositionale* in 2 Chr 35:13 shows how the referent could be distinguished by the positioning of this construction together with a disjunctive clause.

---

13 For a general typology of disjunctive clauses, see T. O. Lambdin, *An Introduction to Biblical Hebrew* (New York: Charles Scribner's Sons, 1971) § 132. For a thorough examination of these Hebrew clauses, see Francis I. Andersen, *The Sentence in Biblical Hebrew* (The Hague: Mouton, 1974).

ii. A *Vergleichspräpositionale* that Qualifies Two Clauses

There is only one independent כְּמִשְׁפָּט citation base with a legal referent that qualifies two clauses (Type A). In Lev 9:16, both clauses are qualified by כְּמִשְׁפָּט (enlarged).

וַיַּקְרֵב אֶת־הָעֹלָה וַיַּעֲשֶׂהָ כַּמִּשְׁפָּט (Lev 9:16)

The referent of Lev 9:16 entails both the presentation (√קרב) and the making (√עשׂה is not a pro-form) of the offering according to Lev 1:2-10, 4:13-17 and 6:2-6[14].

iii. A *Vergleichspräpositionale* that Qualifies an Infinitive Phrase

In 2 Chr 4:19b-22, a list of items that Solomon made for the house of God is given. In v. 20, the lampstands with their lamps of pure gold are qualified by a subsequent infinitive phrase that states the manner in which they were to be arranged ("to burn in front of the inner sanctuary"; cf. Exod 27:20-21; 25:31ff.). The citation base כַּמִּשְׁפָּט (enlarged) that occurs in this list qualifies only the lampstands and golden lamps mentioned in v. 20 and not the other items listed in v. 19.

וְאֶת־הַמְּנֹרוֹת וְנֵרֹתֵיהֶם לְבַעֲרָם כַּמִּשְׁפָּט לִפְנֵי הַדְּבִיר זָהָב סָגוּר (2 Chr 4:20)

The resumptive pronoun on the infinitive לְבַעֲרָם can only refer to the two preceding nominal forms in v. 20 (Type II). The nouns in the same list in v. 19b are not referred to because they do not consist of material that was to be burnt (i.e., "the golden altar", "the tables"). The identification of the referent for the citation base in 2 Chr 4:20 is another example of the manner in which semantics can play a role in determining the referent of a comparative citation base. It is important to note that the Chr limits the observance of the law in this verse to the positioning of the lamps in Solomon's Temple ("in front of the inner sanctuary").

---

14   Fishbane emphasises the passages in chapters 4 and 6 (209).

In discussing the identification of this referent (Type II), it is especially noteworthy to observe the Chr's rephrasing of his *Vorlage*.

וְאֶת־הַמְּנֹרוֹת חָמֵשׁ מִיָּמִין וְחָמֵשׁ מִשְּׂמֹאול לִפְנֵי הַדְּבִיר זָהָב

סָגוּר (1 Kings 7:49)

The Chr has introduced the citation base "as prescribed" and the phrase "their lamps of pure gold to burn them". By comparing 1 Kgs 7:49 to his history, one can observe how the Chr has eliminated the aspect of his *Vorlage* that does not conform to the law ("five on the south side and five on the north"). Since the regulations in Exod 25 and 27 pertain to only one lamp, there was, of course, no legislation for five to be placed on the right and the left of the inner sanctuary. By rewriting his *Vorlage* in this manner, the Chr's use of this citation base in 2 Chr 4:20 represents the legal conformity of the lamps in the Solomonic Temple to the greatest extent possible. This emphasises his concern for the cult of his day to be grounded in the ancient traditions.

This identification of a referent from a list of forms is comparable to the use of ככתוב in the list of the firstborn in Neh 10:37, and the extraposed nominal phrase in 2 Chr 35:26.

iv. כְּמִשְׁפָּטָם that Qualifies a Noun Phrase

We have presented Type I, II, and A uses first since these are the most frequently attested qualifications of the comparative statements in this category of legal referents. These uses also provide the background for understanding all minor functions such as the qualification of a noun or a nominal phrase (Type III).

Num 29:1-6 concerns the offerings that are to be made at the Festival of Trumpets on the first day of the seventh month. While vv. 2-5 describe the special offerings to be made on the occasion of the Festival of Trumpets, v. 6 refers to those sacrifices that are part of the monthly and daily cycle. The regular offerings are listed in v. 6a (enlarged) and they are the referent of כְּמִשְׁפָּטָם (italics) in v. 6b.

מִלְּבַד עֹלַת הַחֹדֶשׁ וּמִנְחָתָהּ וְעֹלַת הַתָּמִיד וּמִנְחָתָהּ

וְנִסְכֵּיהֶם כְּמִשְׁפָּטָם לְרֵיחַ נִיחֹחַ אִשֶּׁה לַיהוָה (Num 29:6)

The referent of this *Vergleichspräpositionale* consists of a compound noun phrase (Type III) which is placed in a contiguous relation to the citation base. The entire nominal phrase is the referent and there is no particularisation in this series of nouns (see Num 29 below).

The form כְּמִשְׁפָּטָם is used in 2 Chr 4:7 which includes an inseparable third masculine plural suffix.

וַיַּעַשׂ אֶת־מְנֹרוֹת הַזָּהָב עֶשֶׂר כְּמִשְׁפָּטָם וַיִּתֵּן בַּהֵיכָל חָמֵשׁ
מִיָּמִין וְחָמֵשׁ מִשְּׂמֹאול (2 Chr 4:7)

The observance of the law in v. 7 is limited to the fact that the lampstands were made (√עשׂה "to construct" is not a pro-form) of gold. It appears that the Chr has used the suffix ם- on the citation base ("according to their [the מְנֹרוֹת] ordinance") to limit what he was attributing to the law. The antecedent of the inseparable suffix is מְנֹרוֹת[15].

There is an important difference between the use of this citation base here and those we have observed with inseparable suffixes on כמשפט. Previously the inseparable suffixes represented a person to whom a referent was being attributed. For example, in 1 Kgs 18:28, כְּמִשְׁפָּטָם was used instead of כְּמִשְׁפַּט נְבִיאֵי הַבַּעַל. The inseparable suffix in this case represents a human source, i.e., "the prophets of Baal".

In contrast to this situation, the Chr has affixed the inseparable suffix to the form in 2 Chr 4:7 to distinguish, not the source, but the referent: מְנֹרוֹת. If the Chr had used the form כְּמִשְׁפָּטָם without the inseparable suffix, then he would have been attributing to the law a stipulation for ten golden מְנֹרוֹת. By affixing the inseparable suffix to the citation base, the Chr avoids attributing עֶשֶׂר to the law. In Exod 25 and 27, there is, of course, only one lampstand in the tabernacle.

---

15 In LBH, masculine suffixes are frequently employed for feminine antecedents (GK § 135 o), especially in Chronicles (JM § 149 b).

v. The Citation Base בְּמִסְפָּר כַּמִּשְׁפָּט and Succoth

As with the citation base כַּאֲשֶׁר צוה√ which served as a scaffolding device in Exod 39, 40, and Lev 8, the seven occurrences of כמשפט in Num 29 are best treated together.

In Num 29:12ff., the offerings for the Festival of Succoth are given. After the requirements for the first day of the festival are stated in vv. 13-16, vv. 17ff. continues to list the detailed offerings for each successive day of the festival. Throughout the lists of offerings for the second to seventh days (vv. 17-34), a set phrase is repeated every three verses. The main alterations throughout these verses concern the day of the festival ("second", "third", etc.) and the number of bulls ("twelve", "eleven", etc.), i.e., the number of bulls offered was to be decreased by one as each day of the festival passed. In vv. 35-38, the offerings detailed for the concluding eighth day of Succoth alters this pattern slightly (cf. the summary citation at Lev 8:36). In the section concerned with the offerings of the second to eighth days of Succoth (vv. 17ff.), the citation base כמשפט occurs seven times. We will list only the portion of these passages which directly concerns the use of these constructions.

וּ)מִנְחָתָם וְנִסְכֵּיהֶם לַפָּרִים לָאֵילִם וְלַכְּבָשִׂים בְּמִסְפָּרָם כַּמִּשְׁפָּט
(Num 29:18, 21, 24, 27, 30)

וּמִנְחָתָם וְנִסְכֵּהֶם לַפָּרִים לָאֵילִם וְלַכְּבָשִׂים בְּמִסְפָּרָם כְּמִשְׁפָּטָם
(Num 29:33)

מִנְחָתָם וְנִסְכֵּיהֶם לַפָּר לָאַיִל וְלַכְּבָשִׂים בְּמִסְפָּרָם כַּמִּשְׁפָּט
(Num 29:37)

Throughout Num 29:12-38, כַּמִּשְׁפָּט is governed by the prepositional phrase בְּמִסְפָּרָם. The citation base כַּמִּשְׁפָּט qualifies only the contiguous nominal phrase מִסְפָּרָם: "their [the previous list of offerings] number according to the ordinance" (Type III). The form in v. 33 repeats the inseparable suffix. On the second day of the festival, for example, this list is: "twelve bulls, two rams, fourteen male lambs onc year old without defect; and their grain offering and their libations for the bulls, for the rams and for the lambs" (vv. 17b-18a). Unlike the use of *Vergleichspräpositionale* citation bases in the non-synoptic post-exilic historiography, the entire list is the meaningful referent.

The similar phrase בְּמִסְפָּר כַּמִּשְׁפָּט is used as a citation base twice in the post-exilic historiography in connection with the celebration of Succoth. The entire phrase בְּמִסְפָּר כַּמִּשְׁפָּט is used as a citation base in Ezra 3:4 and 1 Chr 23:31 to refer to the Succoth regulations in Num 29:12ff.[16] Without the inseparable suffix in either of these terms, the entire expression בְּמִסְפָּר כַּמִּשְׁפָּט functions as a *Vergleichspräpositionale* citation base for the observance of Succoth.

וַיַּעֲשׂוּ אֶת־חַג הַסֻּכּוֹת כַּכָּתוּב וְעֹלַת יוֹם בְּיוֹם בְּמִסְפָּר כְּמִשְׁפַּט
דְּבַר־יוֹם בְּיוֹמוֹ (Ezra 3:4)

This citation base qualifies only the contiguous nominal phrase "daily burnt offerings" (Type III)[17]. עוֹלָה is not governed by עשׂה√ and appears to introduce an ellipted clause. At any rate, it is the sentence structure of a disjunctive clause which eases the identification of the referent. This is especially important in Ezra 3:4, since two citation bases, each with its own referent, occur in close proximity. In striking contrast to the occurrence of two citation bases in a single passage in the law and deuteronomistic literature, כמשפט and ככתוב do not form a compound citation base.

---

16 Fishbane points out that there is an extended cross-reference between Ezra 3:3b-5 and Num 28-29 (the text behind v. 3b is Num 28:1-8, v. 4 is Num 29:1-38 and v. 5 is Num 28:11-29:38). Commenting on Ezra 3:3b-5, Fishbane states, "Num. 28-9 has...been 'used' historiographically to give a synopsis of post-exilic piety and conformity to the Pentateuchal laws of sacrifice" (Fishbane, 112, n. 21). He describes this as a "lapidary" cross-referencing of material. Donner considers that the Succoth legislation in Num 29:12-38 is referred to by בְּמִסְפָּר כְּמִשְׁפַּט. DeVries' analysis regarding the identification of the reference text in the Pentateuch is confusing. On one hand, he considers the citation base in Ezra 3:4 to refer to Lev 23:33-43 and Num 29:12-38 (625); in another place he claims only Num 29:12-28 (*sic*) (623, n. 12).

17 I.e., this nominal phrase is introduced with the noun עֹלָה that governs the adverbial statement יוֹם בְּיוֹם.

The Chr's use of this citation base in 1 Chr 23:30-31 appears to show that it is used in a manner that we have seen to be characteristic of the non-synoptic post-exilic historiography.

וְלַעֲמֹד בַּבֹּקֶר בַּבֹּקֶר לְהֹדוֹת וּלְהַלֵּל לַיהוָה וְכֵן לָעָרֶב
וּלְכֹל הַעֲלוֹת עֹלוֹת לַיהוָה לַשַּׁבָּתוֹת לֶחֳדָשִׁים וְלַמֹּעֲדִים
בְּמִסְפָּר כְּמִשְׁפָּט עֲלֵיהֶם תָּמִיד לִפְנֵי יְהוָה (1 Chr 23:30-31)

The association of בְּמִסְפָּר כְּמִשְׁפָּט with the burnt offerings in Num 29 indicates that the referent is comprised of only the contiguous infinitive phrase ("to offer all burnt offerings to the LORD, on the sabbaths, the new moons, and the fixed festivals in the number set by the ordinance concerning them, continually before the LORD"; Type II). Thus, the phrase does not qualify the two infinitive phrases in v. 30 ("[the Levites are] to stand every morning to thank and to praise the LORD, and likewise at evening"). As we have seen before, the use of a *Vergleichspräpositionale* as a citation base in the non-synoptic post-exilic historiography does not generally mark unwieldy referents. Rather than governing all three coordinated infinitive phrases, the citation base qualifies only the abutting one.

The phrase used in Num 29, Ezra 3:4b, and 1 Chr 23:30-31 could also be shortened to כַּמִּשְׁפָּט and still refer to the Succoth legislation. In Neh 8:18, the regulation for a solemn assembly on the eighth day of Succoth is cited by כַּמִּשְׁפָּט. The referent (enlarged) appears to be a direct quotation from Num 29:35.

בַּיּוֹם הַשְּׁמִינִי עֲצֶרֶת תִּהְיֶה לָכֶם (Num 29:35a)

וַיִּקְרָא בְּסֵפֶר תּוֹרַת הָאֱלֹהִים יוֹם בְּיוֹם מִן־הַיּוֹם הָרִאשׁוֹן עַד הַיּוֹם
הָאַחֲרוֹן וַיַּעֲשׂוּ־חָג שִׁבְעַת יָמִים וּבַיּוֹם הַשְּׁמִינִי עֲצֶרֶת
כַּמִּשְׁפָּט (Neh 8:18)

There are a few considerations that appear to limit the referent of כַּמִּשְׁפָּט to בַּיּוֹם הַשְּׁמִינִי עֲצֶרֶת. First, the citation base and referent are distinguished from the preceding series of *waw*-conversive forms (italics) by taking the form of a disjunctive clause[18]. Secondly, the direct correlation between the terms בַּיּוֹם הַשְּׁמִינִי עֲצֶרֶת in both this disjunctive clause and Num 29:35a appears to make the qualification of other forms in Neh 8:18 unlikely.

Neh 8:18 is another example where the identification of the referent of a citation base is disputed. As he typically does elsewhere, Fishbane reads this *Vergleichspräpositionale* with a relatively broad qualification. As a result he identifies the reading of the law recounted at the beginning of v. 18 ("he read from the book of the law of God daily, from the first day to the last day") as a "festival lection" based on Deut 31:10-13. He maintains that the command to read the Torah in v. 10 was interpreted by Ezra "in a distributive sense; i.e., to read it 'during the festival' and not just 'on' its opening day"[19]. However, we hope that by this point in our analysis we have at least shown the propensity for citation bases in the form of a *Vergleichspräpositionale* to be read with a relatively smaller scope of qualification (most commonly Types III, II, and I) than comparative clauses introduced with כַּאֲשֶׁר (Types I, A, B, etc.) especially when it concerns a legal referent in the non-synoptic post-exilic historiography. Additionally, the understanding of Hebrew syntax reflected in Fishbane's reading of כַּמִּשְׁפָּט requires a qualification that we have not seen to be customary even of comparative clauses introduced with כַּאֲשֶׁר (Type A). That is, such a comparative clause typically qualifies a single main clause (Type I). In light of our analysis, we maintain that the burden of proof rests on anyone who would advocate the view of Fishbane. We would suggest that a more limited range of qualification is to be generally understood for citation bases in the form of a *Vergleichspräpositionale* in the non-synoptic post-exilic historiography. The few cases when one of these *Vergleichspräpositionalen* qualified an uncharacteristically large referent happened when it was also construed with one of the broadening terms (e.g., Esth 4:17). In Neh 8:8, no such broadening term is employed.

---

18 √עשׂה does not govern בַּיּוֹם הַשְּׁמִינִי עֲצֶרֶת.
19 Fishbane, 113.

b. The Pro-Form √עשׂה

The pro-form √עשׂה occurs once in this category of citation bases.

וְלֹא שָׁמֵעוּ כִּי אִם־כְּמִשְׁפָּטָם הָרִאשׁוֹן הֵם עֹשִׂים (2 Kgs 17:40)

The pro-form √עשׂה refers to the meaningful referent in v. 34 ("they neither fear the LORD nor adhere to the decrees and ordinances"; Type I).

c. Compound Citation Bases

Another relevant construction entails the legal term חֻקָּה which is linked together with כְּמִשְׁפָּט to form a compound citation base (enlarged) in Num 9:14.

...וְעָשָׂה פֶסַח לַיהוָה כְּחֻקַּת הַפֶּסַח וּכְמִשְׁפָּטוֹ... (Num 9:14)

The referent is √עשׂה ("to observe") which does not function as a pro-form here (Type I).

In Num 9:3b, the compound citation base is construed with various terms that generally widen the qualification of such comparative formulations.

בְּאַרְבָּעָה עָשָׂר־יוֹם בַּחֹרֶשׁ הַזֶּה בֵּין הָעַרְבַּיִם תַּעֲשׂוּ אֹתוֹ בְּמוֹעֲדוֹ
כְּכָל־חֻקֹּתָיו וּכְכָל־מִשְׁפָּטָיו תַּעֲשׂוּ אֹתוֹ (Num 9:3)

The immediate referent entails the pro-form √עשׂה (Type I). The meaningful referent is located in v. 2 ("observe the Passover"). There are features associated with the compound citation base in Num 9:3 that have typically occurred outside of the non-synoptic post-exilic historiography. These elements concern: the pro-form √עשׂה; a compound citation construction כֹל (twice); and the repetition of √עשׂה.

In 1 Chr 24:19, the Chr used a compound citation base that we addressed in the previous chapter. We observed there that the form of a compound construction is not part of the Chr's standard use of citation bases. It appears all the more significant that the function of this compound citation base, which included a כַּאֲשֶׁר clause, has a Type II qualification. Such a function is not typical of comparative clauses introduced with כַּאֲשֶׁר, but agrees with the Chr's use of *Vergleichspräpositionalen* as exegetical devices.

III. Conclusions

Unlike citation bases with כָּתוּב, כְּמִשְׁפָּט with non-legal referents does not recur in a consistent pattern. However, the distribution of the characteristics of the citation bases in this chapter nevertheless appears to relate them to the development of constructions we have observed before. Only outside of the post-exilic historiography is כְּמִשְׁפָּט used: with a Type A qualification (Lev 9:16; Josh 6:15; 1 Kgs 18:28; Psa 119:132); with a pro-form element (2 Kgs 17:34, 40; Ezek 5:7; 11:12); as a scaffolding device (Num 29); or in a compound citation base in both form and function (Num 9:3, 14). The only use of a citation base in a tautological expression, an undeveloped feature, occurred in the DtrH (1 Kgs 3:28).

Conversely, we have observed the careful distinction of a referent from its context only in the non-synoptic post-exilic historiography. This marking of the referent could be accomplished by a disjunctive clause (2 Chr 35:13; Ezra 3:4; Neh 8:18) or an inseparable suffix (2 Chr 4:7; an intermediate referent). In 2 Chr 8:14, a citation base was used in the type of complex sentence (one finite form, one or more infinitives, and a comparative citation base) that typically results in a lack of consensus regarding the identification of the referent. In this passage, the Chr positioned כְּמִשְׁפָּט in order to mark the qualification of the entire complex sentence: the citation base is adjacent to the finite form of the sentence. Elsewhere in the non-synoptic post-exilic historiography, the citation base in this type of complex sentence occurs at the end in order to qualify only the infinitival portion of the sentence (e.g., Neh 10:35 [34]). A similar careful use of an exegetical device is represented by the Chr's rewriting of his *Vorlage* in 2 Chr 4:20. Here the Chr represents conformity to the legal traditions to the greatest degree possible. The distinctive use of בְּמִסְפָּר כְּמִשְׁפָּט in 1 Chr 23:31 stems from the Succoth legislation cited in Num 29. This citation base restricts its qualification to one of three infinitive phrases. In the post-exilic historiography, the use of כמשפט with non-legal referents drops-off dramatically. Despite the form of the citation base in 1 Chr 24:19, it nevertheless functioned as several of the Chr's *Vergleichspräpositionale* citation bases.

In light of our analysis, there appears to be nothing inconsistent with concluding that כמשפט reflects the development of certain citation bases with legal referents in the non-synoptic post-exilic historiography. So far this group of citation bases includes כמשפט as well as the relative and comparative forms of כָּתוּב, √צוה, and מִצְוָה we have examined above. In a concluding chapter we will summarise the various features of all of these developed citation bases.

Chapter 5: Other Citation Bases

I. Introduction

The citation formulæ in this chapter are, for the most part, based on the following terms: תּוֹרָה; דָּת; חֻקָּה; עֵצָה; בְּרִית; טָהֲרַת הַקֹּדֶשׁ ("[in accordance with] the sanctuary's rules of cleanness", 2 Chr 30:19, NRSV); פֶּה (e.g, "according to the word of the LORD"); and רִשְׁיוֹן (e.g., "according to the authorisation of Cyrus"). In comparison to those forms we have previously addressed, these citation bases have a relatively small number of occurrences. These terms are generally used as citation bases with legal referents. This point is important when considering another group of constructions formed with √דבר and √אמר, or their nominal cognates[1]. The semantic variability of √דבר, √אמר and their nominal cognates is so diverse that, unlike many of the forms in our analysis, it appears that they were not the focus of the same development that we have seen in earlier chapters. We will present an overview of these terms below since an exhaustive analysis would take our inquiry too far afield. The *verba dicendi* √אמר and √דבר have understandably merited their own detailed examination[2].

II. Citation Bases with תּוֹרָה

Consideration of תּוֹרָה in citation bases does not require much space. In addition to the relative scarcity of its use in a citation base, we

---

1 E.g., the *Vergleichspräpositionale* כדבר can mean "as he said", or it can be used in an unrelated manner (e.g., "far be it from you to do such a thing [כַּדָּבָר הַזֶּה]" [Gen 18:25a, NRSV]). For the various semantic meanings of כדבר, see Jenni, 184.

2 For a recent exhaustive analysis of these *verba dicendi,* see Meier, *Speaking of Speaking.*

have already treated some of these passages among the compound constructions in the chapters above. תּוֹרָה is never used in a relative citation base. Since there are no verbal cognates for תּוֹרָה in citation bases we will not need to address clauses introduced by כַּאֲשֶׁר.

A. The Independent Citation Base

כְּתוֹרָה functions as an independent citation base only once[3].

וַיַּעַמְדוּ עַל־עָמְדָם כְּמִשְׁפָּטָם כְּתוֹרַת מֹשֶׁה אִישׁ־הָאֱלֹהִים
וְהַכֹּהֲנִים זֹרְקִים אֶת־הַדָּם מִיַּד הַלְוִיִּם (2 Chr 30:16) [4]

They took their accustomed posts according to the law of Moses the man of God; the priests dashed the blood that they received from the hands of the Levites (2 Chr 30:16; NRSV).

The referent of כְּתוֹרָה is the statement "they took their accustomed posts" (Type I).

Japhet is an example of a scholar who reads כתורת משה in v. 16 with a relatively broad scope of qualification. She considers the identification of the referent of this citation base to entail all of the details of v. 16[5]. In order to explain the tension that results from this view of the referent, she opts for the position that "the Chronicler did not refer to the written word as it stands, but rather to the way it was understood and interpreted, either by him or at his time"[6]. However, according to

---

3   The *Vergleichspräpositionale* in Psa 119:85 is used descriptively.

4   A few MSS of ⅙ and 𝕯 attest to a ו introducing the participial clause in v. 16b. In a chain language such as BH, we would expect this *waw* to occur.

5   Japhet, 950.

6   *Ibid.* Japhet prefers this route over against the assumption that the Chr was working with "a version of the Pentateuch which was different from the MT" (*Ibid*).

Japhet, "the remark that the priests 'receive the blood' from the
Levites…is an innovation when compared with the sacrificial laws of
Leviticus 1ff."[7] This is a conclusion which she admits is not followed
by the Mishnah. Japhet's identification of the referent, however, is not
supported by our analysis.

In light of our analysis, the following considerations appear to cast
doubt upon Japhet's treatment. First, it is noteworthy that the
Vergleichspräpositionale כְּמִשְׁפָּטָם qualifies וַיַּעַמְדוּ עַל־עָמְדָם in the
same manner that the *Vergleichspräpositionale* כְּתוֹרַת מֹשֶׁה modifies
וַיַּעַמְדוּ עַל־עָמְדָם כְּמִשְׁפָּטָם. The positioning of both of these
comparative expressions limits the scope of qualification to the first
clause.

Secondly, the subsequent appositive statement ("a man of God") is
followed by a disjunctive clause which we have seen the Chr use
elsewhere to facilitate the identification of the referent. Another
advantage to the Type I reading of כתורה is that it removes the need to
refer to the interpretative process as a departure from the law. Rather,
this passage has the two levels of exegesis that consist of a reference to
the law (v. 16a) and the facilitating measures taken to fulfil that law (v.
16b). The reestablishment of the priests and Levites in their posts in v.
16a was according to the law. Williamson explains that the citation base
here "is a purely general reference to the priestly sections of the
Pentateuchal law which assume the prominence of the cultic officials on
all such occasions"[8]. During Hezekiah's Passover, the Chr represents
these priests and Levites as having slightly different roles which cannot
be attributed to the legal traditions ("the priests dashed the blood that
they received from the hands of the Levites", v. 16b, NRSV). Vv. 17-
18 appears to state the basis for the interpretation in v. 16b.

B. Broadening Terms with the Independent Form

The citation base כְּתוֹרָה may be construed with כל or the pro-form
עשׂה√.

---

7   *Ibid.*
8   Williamson, *1 and 2 Chronicles*, 369-70.

1. כֹּל *with* כְּתוֹרָה

The citation base in 2 Kgs 23:25 occurs with כֹּל (enlarged).

וְכָמֹהוּ לֹא־הָיָה לְפָנָיו מֶלֶךְ אֲשֶׁר־שָׁב אֶל־יְהוָה בְּכָל־לְבָבוֹ
וּבְכָל־נַפְשׁוֹ וּבְכָל־מְאֹדוֹ כְּכֹל תּוֹרַת מֹשֶׁה וְאַחֲרָיו
לֹא־קָם כָּמֹהוּ (2 Kgs 23:25)

The referent consists of one clause (Type I). Despite the form used in
Deut 4:8, כְּכֹל הַתּוֹרָה הַזֹּאת does not function as a citation base[9]. This
phrase in Deut 4:8 is similar to כְּכָל־הַכָּתוּב in Josh 8:34 which also
does not function as a citation base. In the non-synoptic post-exilic
historiography, such forms always function as citation bases.

2. כְּתוֹרָה *with Pro-Form* עשׂה√

The citation base in Ezra 10:3 uses the pro-form עשׂה√.

וְעַתָּה נִכְרָת־בְּרִית לֵאלֹהֵינוּ לְהוֹצִיא כָל־נָשִׁים וְהַנּוֹלָד מֵהֶם בַּעֲצַת
אֲדֹנָי וְהַחֲרֵדִים בְּמִצְוַת אֱלֹהֵינוּ וְכַתּוֹרָה יֵעָשֶׂה (Ezra 10:3)

The referent is in v. 3a ("let us make a covenant with our God to put
away all the wives and their children"). It is significant that the use of
this formulation with the pro-form עשׂה√, an undeveloped feature of
citation bases that are concentrated in the law and deuteronomistic
material, is stated by Shecaniah. In Ezra 10, Shecaniah is the spokeman
for those who were guilty of intermarriage but who were also
responding to Ezra's prayer of confession. We probably should not

---

9   Jenni classifies the use of כ in Deut 4:8 as "Vergleiche bei Qualifizierungen"
     (66f.).

expect Shecaniah, who has just confessed the sin of intermarriage, to be represented as using a citation base in a developed manner; he includes himself among those who had "broken faith" (v. 2). As we have noted elsewhere, the use of a pro-form is an uncharacteristic feature of developed citation bases.

While we should not generally expect the use of such an undeveloped feature with a non-synoptic post-exilic citation base, a plausible purpose for such a formulation in Ezra 10:3 can be deduced. By putting a citation base with the pro-form עשׂה√ in the mouth of a recent transgressor, it would appear that the writer is suggesting that faithfulness to the traditions is inextricably connected with the use of careful exegetical practices. That is, the author may have wanted to represent Shecaniah with an undeveloped exegetical device in order to suggest that such a reference to the legal traditions could lead to unfaithfulness. According to this view, Ezra 10:3 would serve as an antitype in the overall use of citation bases in the non-synoptic post-exilic historiography. In Ezra 10, the writer appears to present Shecaniah as a warning to the reader that shoddy exegetical methods are a threat to the preservation of the traditions of the fathers (see further below).

A similar use of exegetical devices may be found in the Chr's use of citation bases in connection with Passover. Two negative citation bases were employed in the Chr's account of Hezekiah's Passover (2 Chr 30:5 [בְּלֹא כַכָּתוּב], 18 [לֹא כָלְרֹב עָשׂוּ כַּכָּתוּב]; cf. v. 19). The two negative formulations in Hezekiah's account were subsequently countered by several citation bases in the account of Josiah's Passover (2 Chr 35:10, 12, 13, 15, 26).

C. Compound Citation Bases

תּוֹרָה occurs three times in a compound citation base. One of these passages was already encountered in the most complex compound citation base in the Old Testament (2 Kgs 17:34). The use of כְּתוֹרָה in compound citation bases occurs only in the DtrH.

Josh 1:7 uses a compound citation base with both כֹל and a pro-form עשׂה√ .

רַק חֲזַק וֶאֱמַץ מְאֹד לִשְׁמֹר לַעֲשׂוֹת כְּכָל־הַתּוֹרָה אֲשֶׁר צִוְּךָ
מֹשֶׁה עַבְדִּי אַל־תָּסוּר מִמֶּנּוּ יָמִין וּשְׂמֹאול לְמַעַן תַּשְׂכִּיל
בְּכֹל אֲשֶׁר תֵּלֵךְ (Josh 1:7)

The referent consists of a hendiadys phrase (italics) in the form of two
infinitives (Type II).

2 Kgs 17:13 has nearly the same form of citation base.

וַיָּעַד יְהוָה בְּיִשְׂרָאֵל וּבִיהוּדָה בְּיַד כָּל־נְבִיאוֹ כָל־חֹזֶה לֵאמֹר
שֻׁבוּ מִדַּרְכֵיכֶם הָרָעִים וְשִׁמְרוּ מִצְוֹתַי חֻקּוֹתַי כְּכָל־הַתּוֹרָה
אֲשֶׁר צִוִּיתִי אֶת־אֲבֹתֵיכֶם (2 Kgs 17:13)

The referent consists of the contiguous clause (Type I). The most
noteworthy aspect of these two constructions (enlarged) is that they
reflect the fact that compound citation bases, pro-form עשׂה√, and כל
are characteristic of such formulations in the DtrH.

D. Conclusions

The use of תּוֹרָה in citation bases complements our analysis of the
use of certain *Vergleichspräpositionalen* as developed exegetical devices
in the non-synoptic post-exilic historiography. The independent citation
base reflect the same careful presentation of the referent and exegetical
process. In 2 Chr 30:16, a reference to the law is distinguished from its
interpretation by a disjunctive clause. The historiographer in Ezra 10:3
has carefully placed an undeveloped citation base in the mouth of a
leader of the community who had "broken faith" with the God of Israel
(v. 2) and just confessed the transgression of intermarriage. In light of
the use of citation bases throughout Chronicles, Ezra, and Nehemiah as
well as the development of certain exegetical devices in this literature, it
appears that the historiographer in Ezra 10:1ff. is issuing a warning
concerning the dangers of shoddy exegetical practice to the future of the
post-exilic community. The distribution of the other aspects of the use
of כַּתּוֹרָה was consistent with our broader examination of citation bases
in the Old Testament. First, the form כְּכֹל הַתּוֹרָה הַזֹּאת in Deut 4:8

does not function as a citation base. Secondly, the compound citation bases were restricted to the DtrH (Josh 1:7; 2 Kgs 17:13, 34).

III. Citation Bases with דָּת

A. Independent Citation Bases with דָּת

The independent citation bases with דָּת occur only in prepositional phrases introduced with כְּ.

1. Citation Bases that Qualify One Clause

The citation base in Dan 6:13 (12) qualifies the contiguous non-verbal clause (italics; Type I).

$$עֲנֵה מַלְכָּא וְאָמַר יַצִּיבָא מִלְּתָא כְּדָת־מָדַי וּפָרַס$$
$$דִּי־לָא תֶעְדֵּא \text{ (Dan 6:13c [12c])}$$

In Esth 1:15, כְּדָת introduces an interrogative clause introduced with מָה ("what is to be done to Queen Vashti"; Type I).

$$כְּדָת מַה־לַּעֲשׂוֹת בַּמַּלְכָּה וַשְׁתִּי עַל אֲשֶׁר לֹא־עָשְׂתָה$$
$$אֶת־מַאֲמַר הַמֶּלֶךְ אֲחַשְׁוֵרוֹשׁ בְּיַד הַסָּרִיסִים \text{ (Esth 1:15)}$$

A referent that consists of an interrogative statement has not been characteristic of any portion of the Old Testament.

2. A Citation Base that Qualifies an Infinitive

The referent of the citation base in Dan 6:9 (8) is a negated infinitive (Type II).

כְּעַן מַלְכָּא תְּקִים אֱסָרָא וְתִרְשֻׁם כְּתָבָא דִּי לָא לְהַשְׁנָיָה
כְּדָת־מָדַי וּפָרַס דִּי־לָא תֶעְדֵּא (Dan 6:9 [8])

The referent is "it [the document] will not be altered".

3. A Citation Base that Qualifies a Noun or Nominal Phrase

As the predicate of a non-verbal sentence, כְּדָת (enlarged) qualifies
a noun (Type III) in Esth 1:8a ("the drinking was done according to the
law/edict").

וְהַשְּׁתִיָּה כַדָּת אֵין אֹנֵס כִּי־כֵן יִסַּד הַמֶּלֶךְ עַל כָּל־רַב בֵּיתוֹ
לַעֲשׂוֹת כִּרְצוֹן אִישׁ־וָאִישׁ (Esth 1:8)

What immediately follows is probably a short paraphrase of the edict
("let there be no restraint"[10]).

4. A Citation Base that Qualifies a Particle

In Esth 4:16b, כַּדָּת is the predicate in an ellipted verbal clause
(Type IV, cf. בְּלֹא כַכָּתוּב in 2 Chr 30:16).

וּבְכֵן אָבוֹא אֶל־הַמֶּלֶךְ אֲשֶׁר לֹא־כַדָּת וְכַאֲשֶׁר אָבַדְתִּי אָבָדְתִּי
(Esth 4:16b)

B. Conclusions

For the few occurrences of דָּת in a comparative citation base, it is
used in a number of ways. Its use as a citation base does not appear to
be related to the development that we have observed among the
exegetical devices treated in previous chapters. כְּדָת occurs with
broadening terms in Esth 2:12 and 9:13. The evidence of the

---

10   Bush, 341.

independent forms appears to be sufficient to show that these citation bases are not developed formulæ.

IV. Citation Bases with חֻקָּה

There are only four citation bases in this category. Other than the most compound formulation in the Old Testament in 2 Kgs 17:34, חֻקָּה functions as a citation base only in Num 9. The citation bases in Num 9 are used in various ways with regard to the Passover celebration. Num 9:14 has the independent form כְּחֻקַּת הַפֶּסַח, and v. 12 adds the broadening term כֹּל. Both of these citation bases qualify a clause with √עשׂה which is not employed as a pro-form.

The form in Num 9:3 is part of a compound citation base which includes two occurrences of כֹּל.

$$\text{...כְּכָל־חֻקֹּתָיו וּכְכָל־מִשְׁפָּטָיו תַּעֲשׂוּ אֹתוֹ (Num 9:3)}$$

In each case in Num 9, these *Vergleichspräpositionalen* mark a Type I qualification.

By the use of כֹּל and compound formulations in the majority of these passages, the use of חֻקָּה in citation bases generally agrees with the undeveloped formulæ that have characterised the law and the deuteronomistic literature throughout our study. The association of this citation base with the Passover celebration (כְּחֻקַּת הַפֶּסַח) does not lead the Chr to use it in his representation of the Passovers of Hezekiah and Josiah. In 2 Chr 30 and 35, the Chr prefers ככתוב which occurs a total of four times with legal referents. This may further dissociate כחקה from the citation bases that are developed in the post-exilic historiography.

V. Additional Citation Bases

The citation bases in this section are not widely attested but they repay attention. Some directly support previous observations. Other forms should be addressed because they are close in meaning to the main forms we have addressed[11].

Hezekiah's prayer in 2 Chr 30:18b-19, a non-synoptic passage, employs the citation base כְּטָהֳרַת הַקֹּדֶשׁ ("in accordance with the sanctuary's rules of cleanness", NRSV).

כִּי הִתְפַּלֵּל יְחִזְקִיָּהוּ עֲלֵיהֶם לֵאמֹר יְהוָה הַטּוֹב יְכַפֵּר בְּעַד
כָּל־לְבָבוֹ הֵכִין לִדְרוֹשׁ הָאֱלֹהִים יְהוָה אֱלֹהֵי אֲבוֹתָיו וְלֹא
כְּטָהֳרַת הַקֹּדֶשׁ (2 Chr 30:18b-19)

This citation base qualifies the negative particle לֹא (Type IV). This is another negative citation base that the Chr has used in Hezekiah's Passover in 2 Chr 30 which is countered in chapter 35.

We previously observed how the use of כַּתּוֹרָה as an undeveloped citation base in Ezra 10:3 warned against shoddy exegesis. Another undeveloped citation base is used for the leaders of the community at the beginning of this chapter. In Ezra 10:8, כַּעֲצַת is used to qualify three clauses (Type B; italics).

וְכֹל אֲשֶׁר לֹא־יָבוֹא לִשְׁלֹשֶׁת הַיָּמִים כַּעֲצַת הַשָּׂרִים וְהַזְּקֵנִים
יָחֳרַם כָּל־רְכוּשׁוֹ וְהוּא יִבָּדֵל מִקְּהַל הַגּוֹלָה (Ezra 10:8)

The referent surrounds the citation base ("whoever would not come within three days, *according to the counsel of the leaders and the elders*, all his possessions should be forfeited and he himself excluded from the assembly of the exiles"). It appears that the historiographer has deliberately depicted the exegetical practices of the leaders of the community in an undeveloped manner (cf. our treatment of Ezra 10:3 above). One might also suggest that the choice of כַּעֲצַת for the

---

11 Generally, Jenni's semantic categories "Befolgung (Rubrik 7)" (130ff.) and "Bewahrheitung (Rubrik 6)" (125ff.) have served as reliable guides for determining terms that are relevant for the study of citation bases.

authority of these leaders is more appropriate than a form that was built on a legal term, i.e., כמצות or כמשפט. In Ezra 10:8, the undeveloped features entail the Type B qualification and the unique citation base כָּעֵצָה.

Our examination has detected the development of certain citation bases with legal referents. The use of these citation bases in Ezra 10:3 and 8 complement the manner in which developed forms are used elsewhere in Chronicles, Ezra, and Nehemiah. By using undeveloped citation bases to represent the advice of those caught in intermarriage, the importance of careful exegetical methods is enhanced.

כִּבְרִית is used as a citation base only once.

וַיַּעֲמֵד אֶת כָּל־הַנִּמְצָא בִירוּשָׁלַם וּבִנְיָמִן וַיַּעֲשׂוּ יֹשְׁבֵי יְרוּשָׁלַם
כִּבְרִית אֱלֹהִים אֱלֹהֵי אֲבוֹתֵיהֶם (2 Chr 34:32)

This citation base qualifies the contiguous main clause which has the pro-form √עשה. The meaningful referent consists of v. 32a ("then he made all who were present in Jerusalem and in Benjamin pledge themselves to it", NRSV).

Another uncommon citation base concerns the use of פֶּה in a *Vergleichspräpositionale*.

וְאֵלֶּה מִסְפְּרֵי רָאשֵׁי הֶחָלוּץ לַצָּבָא בָּאוּ עַל־דָּוִיד חֶבְרוֹנָה
לְהָסֵב מַלְכוּת שָׁאוּל אֵלָיו כְּפִי יְהוָה (1 Chr 12:24 [23])

The deed that was accomplished "according to the word of the LORD" was the establishment of David as king (cf. 1 Chr 11:10; 1 Sam 16:1, 3, 12, 13; etc.). The referent is the infinitive phrase (Type II; italics).

The second occurrence of this form occurs in the law and uses the pro-form כֵּן.

כְּפִי נִדְרוֹ אֲשֶׁר יִדֹּר כֵּן יַעֲשֶׂה עַל תּוֹרַת נִזְרוֹ (Num 6:21b)

It is difficult to attach much significance to these two uses of פֶּה in a comparative citation base even though their use generally corresponds to our findings in previous chapters.

The form כְּרִשְׁיוֹן כּוֹרֶשׁ מֶלֶךְ־פָּרַס ("according to the authorisation of Cyrus the king of Persia") is used once in the Old Testament. This passage consists of the same sentence structure that has resulted in the least consensus among scholars concerning the identification of the referent. That sentence structure consists of a finite verb, one or more infinitive phrases, and a *Vergleichspräpositionale*.

וַיִּתְּנוּ־כֶסֶף לַחֹצְבִים וְלֶחָרָשִׁים וּמַאֲכָל וּמִשְׁתֶּה וָשֶׁמֶן לַצֹּדְנִים
וְלַצֹּרִים לְהָבִיא עֲצֵי אֲרָזִים מִן־הַלְּבָנוֹן אֶל־יָם יָפוֹא כְּרִשְׁיוֹן
כּוֹרֶשׁ מֶלֶךְ־פָּרַס עֲלֵיהֶם (Ezra 3:7)

When it is positioned last in such a sentence, this type of developed citation base has consistently marked a Type II qualification in the post-exilic historiography. In contrast to this pattern, the citation of Cyrus' authority here qualifies the entire complex sentence (Type I). Cyrus' decree in Ezra 6:8b makes provisions for the payment of the expenses ("the cost is to be paid to these people, in full and without delay, from the royal revenue, the tribute of the province Beyond the River"). The importance of this passage in our study will be observed when we compare the placement of citation bases in this type of complex sentence.

VI. √אמר and √דבר and Their Nominal Cognates

Throughout our analysis, we have observed several passages where certain forms we have treated do not in fact function as citation bases. This situation is exacerbated by such semantically variable terms as the two main *verba dicendi* and their nominal cognates[12]. It will not assist our analysis to treat these terms in the same way as those above. It appears that the greater semantic variablility of these terms may be the reason why they were not the focus of the development that we observed in certain forms in previous chapters. Our main concern then

---

12   These terms clearly occur in many more semantic fields than the legal terms and כָּתוּב which have dominated our analysis heretofore.

will be to indicate some noteworthy passages and to demonstrate the
lack of development in those forms.

A. √אמר and its Nominal Cognate

1. Relative Constructions

The basic contiguous relation between an independent form and its
referent is attested among the passages in the post-exilic historiography
(Esth 4:7; Neh 2:18; 6:8 [participle]; 9:23; 2 Chr 2:14 [15]). A few
substantivised forms also occur (Esth 2:13, 15; 2 Chr 18:13). In Neh
5, the phrase וְיֵשׁ אֲשֶׁר אֹמְרִים is attested in vv. 2, 3 and 4. The
referent always follows √אמר in these latter verses.

2. Comparative Citation Bases

a. Citation Bases in a Comparative Clause

Type I qualifications occur among citation bases in the law (e.g.,
Gen 34:12), the DtrH (e.g, 1 Kgs 5:20), and the minor prophets. The
formulation in Joel 3:5 (2:32) demonstrates that it is not related to the
uses of citation bases we have been treating.

וְהָיָה כֹּל אֲשֶׁר־יִקְרָא בְּשֵׁם יְהוָה יִמָּלֵט כִּי בְּהַר־צִיּוֹן
וּבִירוּשָׁלַם תִּהְיֶה פְלֵיטָה כַּאֲשֶׁר אָמַר יְהוָה וּבַשְּׂרִידִים
אֲשֶׁר יְהוָה קֹרֵא (Joel 3:5 [2:32])

Scholars have debated the significance of the interrelation between Joel
and other prophets. Crenshaw begins his analysis by asking the
question: "to what does this allusion refer?"[13] In the end, he speculates
that the source referred to could be either "an independent tradition"
known to the writer of Obad and Joel (cf. Obad 17), or the promise in

---

13   James L. Crenshaw, *Joel,* AB (London: Doubleday, 1995) 169.

Joel 2:27[14]. The possible relation to Joel 2:27 ("you shall know that I am in the midst of Israel, and that I, the LORD, am your God and there is no other. And my people shall never again be put to shame") is difficult to establish. Bewer considers this citation base to be a quotation of Obad 17[15]. At any rate, none of these readings of כאשר √אמר in 3:5 (2:32) clearly relate to the use of citation bases we have studied in the Old Testament. Perhaps the significance of this construction should be seen elsewhere. Coggins has recently suggested that this citation base and the reversal of Isa 2:4 (= Mic 4:3) in Joel 4:10 [3:10] are perhaps the best indications that Joel is dependent on the prophetic tradition rather than the view that he was the source for several prophets[16].

The form of the citation base in this category does not occur in the post-exilic historiography. The two closest examples do not appear to be related to what we have observed in earlier chapters. These two examples consist of either the participial form in Neh 5:12 (כַּאֲשֶׁר אַתָּה אוֹמֵר) and the statement in 2 Chr 21:7 (וְכַאֲשֶׁר אָמַר ["and since he said"]).

b. *Vergleichspräpositionale* Citation Bases

In Psa 119, אִמְרָה occurs in a *Vergleichspräpositionale* five times (vv. 41, 58, 76, 116, 170). The exclusive use of this phrase in Psa 119[17] appears to distinguish it from those we have been analysing in the law, deuteronomistic material, and the post-exilic historiography.

---

14 *Ibid.,* 170.
15 J. A. Bewer, *A Critical Commentary on Obadiah and Joel,* 124-25, in J. M. P. Smith *et al., A Critical Commentary on Micah, Zephaniah, Nahum, Habakkuk, Obadiah and Joel,* ICC (Edinburgh: T. & T. Clark, 1912).
16 R. Coggins, "Interbiblical [*sic*] Quotations in Joel", in J. Barton and D. J. Reimer (eds), *After the Exile: Essays in Honour of Rex Mason* (Macon, Georgia: Mercer University Press, 1996) 77-80. For a similar treatment of Joel 3:5 (2:32), see H. G. M. Williamson, "Joel", in G. W. Bromiley, *et al.* (eds), *The International Standard Bible Encyclopedia,* Vol. 2 (Grand Rapids, Michigan: William B. Eerdmans Publishing Co., 1982) 1078.
17 Jenni, 182.

In BA, there is one occurrence of כְּמֵאמַר כָּהֲנַיָּא ("according to the request of the priests").

וּמָה חַשְׁחָן וּבְנֵי תוֹרִין וְדִכְרִין וְאִמְּרִין לַעֲלָוָן לֶאֱלָהּ שְׁמַיָּא חִנְטִין
מְלַח חֲמַר וּמְשַׁח כְּמֵאמַר כָּהֲנַיָּא דִי־בִירוּשְׁלֶם לֶהֱוֵא מִתְיְהֵב
לְהֹם יוֹם בְּיוֹם דִּי־לָא שָׁלוּ (Ezra 6:9)

The referent of this citation base consists of the noun phrase "young bulls, rams, or sheep for burnt offerings to the God of heaven, wheat, salt, wine, or oil". This nominal phrase is a parenthetical list of forms describing "what is needed [מָה חַשְׁחָן]" (Type III). The significance of the citation base is not clear beyond what we have stated above for all the forms in this category.

B. √דבר and its Nominal Cognate

There does not appear to be any substantial development in the form and function of the citation bases in this category.

Among developed citation bases, referents comprised of hendiadys constructions were not attested in the post-exilic historiography. However, כַּאֲשֶׁר דִּבַּרְתָ (enlarged) qualifies a hendiadys construction in Esth 6:10.

וַיֹּאמֶר הַמֶּלֶךְ לְהָמָן מַהֵר קַח אֶת־הַלְּבוּשׁ וְאֶת־הַסּוּס
כַּאֲשֶׁר דִּבַּרְתָ (Esth 6:10a)

The referent in Esth 6:10 includes both √לקח and √מחר (italics). The citation base in Deut 1:21 also qualifies a referent comprised of a hendiadys statement. The command "to possess the land" is expressed with the two imperatives of √עלה and √ירשׁ.

The *Vergleichspräpositionalen* in this category differ from the developed citation bases. For example, כרבר הזה may function as a virtual pronominal expression. In Neh 6:4-5, כרבר הזה is used in this manner three times.

They sent to me four times in this way [כַּדָּבָר הַזֶּה], and I answered them in the same manner [כַּדָּבָר הַזֶּה]. In the same way [כַּדָּבָר הַזֶּה] Sanballat for the fifth time sent his servant to me with an open letter in his hand (Neh 6:4-5).

The same phrase qualifies a pro-form √עשׂה in the post-exilic historiography (Ezra 10:5; Neh 5:12, 13; see also Ezra 10:12).

The citation base in 1 Kgs 22:38 contributes significantly to our analysis. At first, one observes certain undeveloped features in this passage. For instance, the compound citation base (enlarged) and its tautological nature is characteristic of undeveloped constructions.

וַיִּשְׁטֹף אֶת־הָרֶכֶב עַל בְּרֵכַת שֹׁמְרוֹן וַיָּלֹקּוּ הַכְּלָבִים אֶת־דָּמוֹ
וְהַזֹּנוֹת רָחָצוּ כִּדְבַר יְהוָה אֲשֶׁר דִּבֵּר (1 Kgs 22:38)

More importantly, the clause immediately preceding the citation base ("now the harlots bathed themselves there") is not the referent of this formulation. The prophetic judgment in 1 Kgs 21:19b ("thus says the LORD, 'in the place where the dogs licked up the blood of Naboth the dogs shall lick up your blood, even yours'") was made to Ahab for permitting the murder of Naboth and then possessing his vineyard. According to the writer, this statement in v. 19b was fulfilled by the dogs lapping up the water in the pool in Samaria where Ahab's blood-filled chariot had been washed. The referent in v. 38 ("the dogs licked up his blood") is not placed beside the citation base. A disjunctive clause which provides parenthetic information results in a non-contiguous relation between the citation base (enlarged) and the referent (italics).

Among developed citation bases in the post-exilic historiography, we have seen disjunctive clauses used to distinguish the referent from its context. However, in 1 Kgs 22:38, the disjunctive clause in fact impedes the identification of the referent. That is, if one was to read this passage apart from its extended context one would reasonably conclude that the act being ascribed to "the word of the LORD" was the contiguous clause ("the prostitutes washed themselves [in the pool of Samaria]"). The evidence of 1 Kgs 22:38 appears further to support the view that the use of a disjunctive clause to ease the identification of a referent is part of the development of citation bases.

Our last issue in this section concerns the compound citation base in
1 Kgs 15:29 which is rewritten by the Chr. Both S. R. Driver and
Kropat draw attention to the Chr's rewriting of the relative clause in 1
Chr 11:3.

...כִּדְבַר יְהוָה אֲשֶׁר דִּבֶּר בְּיַד־עַבְדּוֹ... (1 Kgs 15:29)

...כִּדְבַר יְהוָה בְּיַד־שְׁמוּאֵל (1 Chr 11:3)

Describing this type of rewriting in the Chr's history, Kropat states,
"dem Chroniker genügt attributive präpositionelle Näherbestimmung,
wo in älterer Sprache ein Relativsatz nötig war"[18]. Driver includes the
expression in 1 Chr 11:3 in "the heavy combined sentences such as
would be avoided in the earlier language by the use of the clauses
connected by אֲשֶׁר"[19]. Driver is correct to note several places where the
Chr omits אֲשֶׁר[20]. This observation of Driver, however, is not a central
concern of our study since this is the only form among the passages in
his list that entails the Chr rewriting one of these compound citation
bases into an independent form. This supports the view that we have
observed throughout this analysis that the differences between SBH and
LBH do not account for the bulk of the features that distinguish
undeveloped citation bases from the more sophisticated forms in the non-
synoptic post-exilic historiography. The only exception pertains to
Rooker's observation that the repetition of terms is not characteristic of
LBH. This pertains to the propensity for several legal terms to be used
with citation bases in the law and the deuteronomistic literature.

VII. Conclusions

In this chapter, we have addressed a range of forms and terms. Our
analysis suggests that כתורה is related to the development of citation
bases in the post-exilic historiography. Even the use of this form with

---

18   Kropat, §20.
19   S. R. Driver, *Introduction,* 539.
20   See Driver, *Ibid.*

an undeveloped feature in Ezra 10:3, along with כעצה in v. 8, appeared to share a related concern to that reflected in developed citation bases, i.e., to warn against shoddy exegesis. The two main *verba dicendi* and their nominal cognates were clearly distinguishable from the development of certain citation bases in the post-exilic historiography. Consideration of these *verba dicendi* and their nominal cognates revealed evidence that supports our previous conclusions regarding disjunctive clauses and the differences between SBH and LBH. The evidence of the remaining forms does not clearly identify them as developed citation bases. However, this evidence will prove helpful in our conclusions.

Chapter 6: Conclusions

In order to address the lack of consensus regarding the use of citation formulæ in the OT, we have attempted to advance the discussion by an examination grounded predominantly in syntax. At times, this analysis has required an extended treatment of the rival referents that scholars have deemed possible for a given citation base. Such an approach has enabled us to illuminate several debates regarding the use of citation bases. Some of these debates have existed throughout the modern era of biblical criticism, and when a legal referent is in view, it invariably has ramifications for the examination of inner-biblical exegesis. Additionally, this examination has offered insights into the syntax of comparative statements in BH. Once we have summarised the results of our syntactic analysis, we will present an overview of the use and development of citation bases. Throughout this summary we will also highlight the significance of these citation bases for the study of inner-biblical exegesis.

I. The Syntax of Comparative Statements

Our analysis of comparative citation bases has reflected on Jenni's view that the clauses introduced with כַּאֲשֶׁר and the prepositional phrases introduced with כְּ have equivalent functions. That is, Jenni classifies every example of כַּכָּתוּב, כְּמִצְוָה, and כְּמִשְׁפָּט that functions as a citation base as an abbreviation of a comparative clause (i.e., כַּאֲשֶׁר כָּתוּב, √צוה כַּאֲשֶׁר, and כַּאֲשֶׁר שׁפט√ respectively) in his section "Vergleichssätze und deren Verkürzungen"[1]. Jenni's study, which is the most up-to-date summary of the syntax of Hebrew comparative

---

1   Jenni, 30-31, cf. 130ff., 187, 189.

expressions, considers these two sentence constituents to have equivalent functions[2]. Our examination, however, does not support this conclusion without qualification. In short, the use of these two forms of comparative statements is more nuanced than Jenni's treatment suggests.

We will first summarise the range of qualifications that we have observed for clauses introduced with כַּאֲשֶׁר. As one might expect, such a comparative clause customarily qualifies a single main clause. We have observed several uses of a כַּאֲשֶׁר clause, however, that have another type of qualification. Not a few of these comparative clauses have qualified two, three, four, or five clauses (Types A-D). Furthermore, in Exod 39-Lev 8, twenty comparative clauses introduced with כַּאֲשֶׁר were employed as a "scaffolding device" (Type α). This distinctive function of a כַּאֲשֶׁר clause demonstrates one of the ways in which these citation bases may govern relatively large referents. For instance, in Lev 8:29, as many as seventeen clauses were governed by a single כַּאֲשֶׁר clause once the "scaffolding" of the seven constructions in Lev 8 was appreciated. Conversely, a comparative clause introduced with כַּאֲשֶׁר only rarely qualified an infinitive phrase.

In contrast to the characteristics above, only one *Vergleichspräpositionale* governed a referent larger than a single clause. This single exception occurred in Deut 26:13 where the form also included the term כֹּל and a compound citation base. These features used in this exceptional formulation are an important consideration since both of them frequently broadened the qualification of a comparative citation base[3]. Hence, Jenni's theory of the equivalent function of the clauses introduced with כַּאֲשֶׁר and the prepositional phrases introduced with כְּ finds most of its support in the qualification of a single clause (Type I). However, *Vergleichspräpositionalen* frequently qualify one of the following sentence constituents: an infinitive or an infinitive phrase(s) (Type II); a noun or nominal phrase (Type III); or even a single particle (Type IV).

---

2   See pp. 79ff. in Chapter 2.

3   For the Janus use of כְּכָתוּב, see our treatment of Josh 8:31.

In short, our study suggests that *Vergleichspräpositionalen* tend to qualify Type I and smaller sentence constituents while comparative clauses tend to qualify Type I and larger antecedents. In general, these propensities are even more stark when the comparative clause is used with a broadening term like כל.

The syntactic characteristics of these comparative statements can inform several of the debates that have resulted from the intuitive reading of comparative citation bases in the OT. We have treated the syntax of comparative expressions separately because of the intricacies inherent to this subject. In light of the nature of the syntax of comparative expressions in BH, it is not surprising that the most contested debates we have addressed in this thesis concern the use of such citation bases.

II. The Use, Development, and Significance of Citation Bases

As we have observed in our introductory chapter, the critical study of citation bases in the OT is inextricably connected to the discussion of Hebrew syntax. While we have already summarised some of the findings regarding comparative constructions, other syntactical issues are best treated by referring to specific citation bases. It is to be hoped that by this point in our study we have demonstrated the advantages and need for this approach. We will present the citation bases with non-legal referents as the background for considering those with legal referents.

A. Citation Bases with Non-Legal Referents

One of the most interesting syntactic features in this study concerns the four-part citation pattern used exclusively for non-legal referents:

1. an extraposed nominal phrase;
2. a *particle* plus a resumptive pronoun;
3. כְּתוּבִים; and
4. a literary source.

הִנֵּה and the negative interrogative הֲלֹא occurred interchangeably as the particle in the second position of this citation pattern (italics above). This sentence structure marks the highest degree of emphasis for a non-verbal sentence. Such a sentence structure may be employed to indicate off-line or tangential material. As we might expect, the resumptive pronoun customarily marks an adnominal relation to an extraposed nominal phrase. The analysis of the form and function of this four-part citation pattern, which was used exclusively for various non-legal topics, helps us to elucidate its various reformulations.

This four-part pattern could be adapted to cite other types of referents. First, this pattern could be adjusted to cite a non-extraposed referent. In this case, an anaphoric relation extending over three clauses was marked by using two resumptive pronouns (2 Chr 35:25). Secondly, the references to "the Book of the Just" in the OT all alter the standard form above. A *neutrum* could be employed instead of a resumptive pronoun in order to attribute a poetic fragment, rather than a nominal phrase, to "the Book of the Just". This is a discourse relation and occurs in two passages (Josh 10:12-13; 1 Kgs 8:12-13 [reconstructed[4]]). The participle of the four-part citation pattern above is altered to agree with the *neutrum* which marks a broad relation to the poetic fragment in the context:

1. a poetic fragment;
2. a negative interrogative הֲלֹא plus a feminine *neutrum*;
3. כְּתוּבָה; and
4. "the Book of the Just".

---

4   3 Reigns 8:53a preserves a more original text than the MT.

A larger poetic excerpt is attributed to the same corpus in 2 Sam 1:18. Due to the size of the referent (vv. 19-27), this poetic passage is given a title (קֶשֶׁת) in the formulation in v. 18[5]:

1. קֶשֶׁת;
2. הִנֵּה and a resumptive pronoun (repointed);
3. כְּתוּבָה; and
4. "the Book of the Just".

Even among these three citations of "the Book of the Just", הִנֵּה and the negative interrogative הֲלֹא occur interchangeably in the second position of this formula. The interchangeability of these two particles in regnal source formulæ and for ascriptions to "the Book of the Just" may indicate that this structure was a literary convention (see further below).

The last type of alteration of this four-part citation pattern occurred in the Chr's history. In order to bolster his distinctive histories of Abijah, Joash, and Manasseh, the Chr rewrote three of the regnal source formulæ and thereby transformed their off-line function.

This four-part citation pattern and its alterations are attested in the DtrH and Chronicles as well as in Esth 10:2. These forms are also employed for a diverse range of non-legal referents: "the rest of the deeds of a king", "laments", "genealogies", and poetic excerpts from "the Book of the Just". The distinctive provenance of the book of Esther[6], the interchangeability of הִנֵּה and the negative interrogative הֲלֹא, and the use of this structure among the range of non-legal topics above may further suggest that the four-part citation pattern reflects a literary convention for marking tangential information in narratives. In

---

5   For a discussion of the history of the text criticism of 2 Sam 1:18, as well as how the analysis of citation bases in the OT illuminates the much-discussed term קֶשֶׁת, see pp. 57-62.

6   The evidence is slim, but we cannot ignore certain facts. First, the use of such a trivial feature in a book which is so distinctive in relation to the rest of the Old Testament appears to be a weighty consideration. Based on the citation base and referent in 10:2, Gordis concludes that the book of Esther is a unique literary genre in the Hebrew Scriptures (375). Secondly, this citation base refers to a Persian corpus ("the annals of the kings of Media and Persia") which suggests a non-Palestinian setting.

the end, the evidence is inconclusive. The distribution of the three-part version of this pattern may indicate that the writer of Neh 12:23 was also aware of this putative literary convention, but this is uncertain.

כָּתוּב מִצְאָ√ and מִשְׁפָּט are used in other citation bases with non-legal referents. Unlike those above, the citation bases that use these terms manage both non-legal and legal referents. Furthermore, both of these latter citation bases may be associated with some of the development that is more observable in other post-exilic exegetical devices. The use of the citation base כְּמִשְׁפָּט with non-legal referents did not continue into the post-exilic period (see further below). The citation base מִצְאָ√ כָּתוּב is an innovation of this same era; among the exegetical devices in this study it uniquely recounts the citation process ("it was found written").

The use of these latter two citation bases further highlights the resilience of the four-part citation pattern above. This may further suggest that the four-part construction reflects an ancient literary convention. The use outlined above for מִצְאָ√ כָּתוּב and כְּמִשְׁפָּט appears to be associated with the development of citation bases with legal referents to which we turn next.

B. Citation Bases with Legal Referents

Certain post-exilic citation bases with legal referents appear to have been developed from their use in the law and the deuteronomistic literature. In order to demonstrate this, we will list the general features associated with the citation bases in the law and deuteronomistic literature over against those in the non-synoptic post-exilic material we have examined. This development appears to be the result of greater concern for the responsible use of the legal traditions in light of their vindication in the exile. The result is that citation bases with legal referents have undeveloped features before the post-exilic era. From 520 B.C. (cf. Zech 1:6), the developed use of citation bases with legal referents can be observed. The distribution of developed features specifically in the non-synoptic post-exilic historiography is striking. Along with these lists, we will provide some key examples which represent the development of these formulations.

The characteristic features of citation bases in the law and deuteronomistic literature provide the background for appreciating the manner in which certain forms in the post-exilic literature are developed. The features associated with citation bases that are concentrated in the law and the deuteronomistic literature consist of various pro-forms (especially עשׂה√ and כֵּן), rubrics, non-contiguous relations between the citation base and referent, tautological expressions, dissonance between the legal tradition ostensibly being cited and its observance, relatively large referents, substantivised citation bases, correlative constructions, and, less consistently, the broadening lexeme כֹּל. It is not uncommon to have several of these features converge in one passage or citation base which is vastly different for the forms in the non-synoptic post-exilic material[7].

The propensity for compound citation bases to occur in the law and deuteronomistic literature can perhaps best be represented by the following examples. The most complex compound citation base in the OT includes five independent constructions (enlarged) and the pro-form עשׂה√ (italics).

וְאֵינָם עֹשִׂים   כְּחֻקֹּתָם וּכְמִשְׁפָּטָם וְכַתּוֹרָה וְכַמִּצְוָה אֲשֶׁר צִוָּה
יְהוָה אֶת־בְּנֵי יַעֲקֹב אֲשֶׁר־שָׂם שְׁמוֹ יִשְׂרָאֵל (2 Kgs 17:34b)

Citation bases also occur in close proximity to each other in Ezra 3:4. However, unlike the overwhelmingly characteristic use of the forms in the law and the deuteronomistic literature, the close proximity of two constructions in Ezra 3:4 (enlarged) does not result in a compound citation base, i.e., each exegetical device has its own referent. It will be recalled that במספר כמשפט is the distinctive formulation for the Succoth stipulations of Num 29.

---

7   In the course of our examination we also noted that the common *verba dicendi* דבר√ and אמר√, together with their nominal cognates, are so semantically variable that they do not become developed citation bases in the post-exilic historiography.

וַיַּעֲשׂוּ אֶת־חַג הַסֻּכּוֹת כַּכָּתוּב וְעֹלַת יוֹם בְּיוֹם בְּמִסְפָּר
כְּמִשְׁפַּט דְּבַר־יוֹם בְּיוֹמוֹ (Ezra 3:4)

In 1 Kgs 22:38, there is a convergence of several undeveloped citation features: a compound citation base; a tautological expression (דָּבָר and רבר√); and a non-contiguous relation between the citation base and referent. Perhaps the most noteworthy feature is the disjunctive clause (enlarged) which *impedes* the identification of the act that is represented as having been accomplished "according to the word of the LORD...": "the dogs lapped up his [Ahab's] blood" (cf. 1 Kgs 21:19).

וַיָּלֹקּוּ הַכְּלָבִים אֶת־דָּמוֹ וְהַזֹּנוֹת רָחָצוּ *כִּדְבַר יְהוָה אֲשֶׁר
דִּבֵּר* (1 Kgs 22:38b)

The disjunctive clause merely states parenthetic information ("now the prostitutes bathed themselves [in the pool of Samaria]"). It is not to be attributed to דְּבַר יְהוָה despite it being placed in a contiguous relation to the compound citation base (italics). In contrast to the use of this disjunctive clause in 1 Kgs 22:38, we will see below how such clauses are used in the non-synoptic post-exilic historiography to ease the identification of the referent.

Other representative examples of undeveloped citation bases include Gen 6:22 and Deut 31:5b below. Both of these passages further demonstrate some of the ways that several undeveloped features may converge on one device in this literature.

וַיַּעַשׂ נֹחַ כְּכֹל אֲשֶׁר צִוָּה אֹתוֹ אֱלֹהִים כֵּן עָשָׂה (Gen 6:22)

The undeveloped features associated with the citation base in Gen 6:22 include: the correlative construction; כֹּל; the pro-forms עשׂה√ and כֵּן; a non-contiguous relation between the citation base and the referent; a large referent (vv. 14-21); and the general cumbersomeness of this form. Such features are concentrated in the law and the deuteronomistic literature. The convergence of all of these features on one citation base, as in Gen 6:22, is unattested in the post-exilic historiography.

וַעֲשִׂיתֶם לָהֶם כְּכָל־הַמִּצְוָה אֲשֶׁר צִוִּיתִי אֶתְכֶם (Deut 31:5b)

In Deut 31:5b, the referent of the citation base is: marked by the pro-form עשׂה√; located more than twenty chapters away from the citation base (7:1-6), and when compared with post-exilic legal referents, is large (six verses). Additional undeveloped features include the use of a compound citation base as well as the broadening lexeme כֹּל.

In contrast to the features that characterise the citation bases in the law and the deuteronomistic literature, the forms used as exegetical devices in the non-synoptic post-exilic historiography do not use rubrics or non-contiguous relations between the citation base and referent. Disjunctive clauses and *waw-explicativa* ease the identification of the referent by distinguishing it from the context, i.e., rival referents. *Vergleichspräpositionalen* are used as citation bases more frequently. Related to this comparative exegetical device is the increased use of Type II, III, and IV qualifications. There is no evidence for the unwieldy relations between the citation base and the referent that were observed recurringly in the law and the deuteronomistic literature. Large legal referents are only found with the מצא√ כָּתוּב formulations which, as we have previously observed, uniquely recount the citation process. Additionally, כַּכָּתוּב without a subsequent reference to its source (e.g., בְּתוֹרַת מֹשֶׁה) occurs only in this material (Ezra 3:4; Neh 8:15; 2 Chr 30:5, 18). Presumably, the source of these citation bases was obvious by the time these histories were written. כֹּ in CD 19:1 may indeed indicate a further post-biblical development of this abbreviated כַּכָּתוּב.

In 2 Chr 35:26, the Chr distinguished the referent חֲסָדָיו of the citation base כַּכָּתוּב by both extraposition and a *waw-explicativum*. The Chr's rewrite of 1 Kgs 9:4 in 2 Chr 7:17 adds a *waw-explicativum* which eases the identification of the referent.

In the non-synoptic post-exilic literature, the citation base כְּמִשְׁפָּט is used only with legal referents. In the DtrH and Ezekiel, כְּמִשְׁפָּט had also referred to the "custom of Sidionians", "the traditions of the nations", and even to a non-legal custom in Israel (i.e., "the king standing by the pillar"). All such non-legal uses of the citation base כְּמִשְׁפָּט are discontinued after the exile.

The use of כְּמִשְׁפָּט as a citation base with a legal referent provides us with another perspective on the attention given to the interpretation of the law in the reconstruction era. In Ezra 3:4b (see above), the author has introduced the referent with a disjunctive clause in order to facilitate the identification of the referent of במספר כמשפט. In 2 Chr 35:13, another disjunctive clause (italics) introduces the contemporary interpretation of the law and thus distinguishes it from the legal reference previously cited by כְּמִשְׁפָּט (enlarged) in this sentence.

וַיְבַשְּׁלוּ הַפֶּסַח בָּאֵשׁ כַּמִּשְׁפָּט וְהַקֳּדָשִׁים בִּשְּׁלוּ בַּסִּירוֹת
וּבַדְּוָדִים וּבַצֵּלָחוֹת וַיָּרִיצוּ לְכָל־בְּנֵי הָעָם (2 Chr 35:13)

In both Ezra 3:4b and 2 Chr 35:13, the use of a disjunctive clause which distinguishes the referent from its context is vastly different from the use of the same type of clause in 1 Kgs 22:38 (above).

We can observe more examples where the Chr uses a citation base as a developed exegetical tool. In 2 Chr 4:7, the Chr uses the form כְּמִשְׁפָּטָם with an inseparable suffix. By affixing this suffix to the citation base ("according to their [the מְנֹרוֹת] ordinance"), he carefully avoids attributing the presence of ten מְנֹרוֹת in the sanctuary to a legal tradition. In this way, the Chr represents the conformity to the law to the greatest extent possible.

The evidence for the relative formulations also corresponds to the development of citation bases above. The only relative participle with כָּתוּב was an example of the way the Chr used every available means to make the relation between the citation base and the referent clear. In 2 Chr 34:24, this included: the distinctive use of the participle הַכְּתוּבוֹת; the contiguous relation between a relative citation base and its referent (cf. Dyk); and the Chr's referent הָאָלוֹת which is more detailed than his *Vorlage*.

Some of the relative forms with אֲשֶׁר צוה√ in the post-exilic literature have been developed into sophisticated exegetical and, at times, homiletic devices (Zech 1:6; Ezra 9:11; Neh 1:7-8; Mal 3:22).

Based on the common characteristics among these passages, there may be a basis to extend Mason's concept of "preaching the tradition" to include certain prayers[8]. Some of these אֲשֶׁר צוה √ citation bases were integrated in post-exilic addresses at key places to elicit a response from an audience[9]. This was accomplished by putting the relative citation base in the form of an imperative or a rhetorical question. Such use of and reflection upon the traditions in the early reconstruction period was identified as a plausible context for the development of exegetical devices that has been observed.

The comparative citation bases with מִצְוָה have a distinctive distribution of functions within the non-synoptic post-exilic historiography. The כְּמִצְוָה citation bases that referred to הַמֶּלֶךְ were consistent with the use of exegetical devices in the law and the deuteronomistic literature while such *Vergleichspräpositionalen* with legal referents were employed with developed features.

The vindication of the legal traditions in light of the events of the sixth century B.C. would be an obvious reason for referring to these sources in a distinctive manner. This use of כְּמִצְוָה in the OT, together with other forms in this study, suggests that the characteristic forms and functions of citation bases in the law and deuteronomistic literature, i.e., undeveloped exegetical devices, may have been avoided by these post-exilic authors because such tools of interpretation were too unwieldy for referring to traditions whose authority had been vindicated by the fall of Jerusalem and the exile. Such development among citation bases with legal referents is best understood as a result of the new care given to the use of the legal traditions rather than a deliberate move to develop exegetical devices.

We have seen that the most controversial syntactic environment has been a sentence comprised of a finite verb, one or more infinitives, and a comparative citation base. Our examination demonstrates that the most scrupulously placed comparative citation bases are *Vergleichspräpositionalen* with legal referents in the non-synoptic post-exilic historiography. In Neh 10:35 (34), כַּכָּתוּב was placed in a

---

8   See pp. 128-47.
9   It will be recalled that Ezra's prayer to the LORD in Ezra 9:6-15, had a homiletic effect on those in earshot of his words (see 10:1).

contiguous relation to the second infinitive phrase, not the finite verb or the adverbial qualifiers of the first infinitive phrase, to indicate that only the latter portion of the sentence was being ascribed to the law. In 2 Chr 8:14, כְּמִשְׁפַּט is placed beside the finite verb in order to indicate that the entire complex sentence is being attributed to the law. In contrast to these examples, the citation base כְּמִצְוַת הַמֶּלֶךְ in 2 Chr 35:16, which governs a referent that is attributed to the king himself, is less carefully positioned than the developed citation bases which take the form כְּמִצְוָה.

וַתִּכּוֹן כָּל־עֲבוֹדַת יְהוָה בַּיּוֹם הַהוּא לַעֲשׂוֹת הַפֶּסַח וְהַעֲלוֹת עֹלוֹת
עַל מִזְבַּח יְהוָה כְּמִצְוַת הַמֶּלֶךְ יֹאשִׁיָּהוּ (2 Chr 35:16)

Like 2 Chr 8:14, the citation base above qualifies the entire sentence (cf. vv. 3-6), but it has not been placed beside the finite verb. By placing the citation base in a contiguous relation to the finite verb of the sentence, the qualification of the entire sentence is more explicitly represented than when it is placed at the end of the passage. Cyrus' authority is cited in a similar manner in Ezra 3:7.

וַיִּתְּנוּ־כֶסֶף לַחֹצְבִים וְלֶחָרָשִׁים וּמַאֲכָל וּמִשְׁתֶּה וָשֶׁמֶן
לַצִּדֹנִים וְלַצֹּרִים לְהָבִיא עֲצֵי אֲרָזִים מִן־הַלְּבָנוֹן
אֶל־יָם יָפוֹא כְּרִשְׁיוֹן כּוֹרֶשׁ מֶלֶךְ־פָּרַס עֲלֵיהֶם (Ezra 3:7)

In this type of syntactic environment, a citation base with a referent that concerned *Israel's* law was more precise. In such a case, the qualification of the entire complex sentence was more clearly marked by the contiguous placement of the citation base beside the finite verb of the sentence.

In 2 Chr 34:21, semantic features clearly differentiate the referent from the prevailing context. In this verse, the Chr once again rewrites his *Vorlage* by introducing a citation base into his history, i.e., the similar form in 2 Kgs 22:13 does not ascribe a referent to a source. The

semantic features in 2 Chr 34:21 concern a positive proposition
followed by a negative one[10].

לֹא־שָׁמְרוּ אֲבוֹתֵינוּ אֶת־דְּבַר יְהוָה לַעֲשׂוֹת כְּכָל־הַכָּתוּב
עַל־הַסֵּפֶר הַזֶּה (2 Chr 34:21)

This phrase כְּכָל־הַכָּתוּב, which occurs only four times in the Hebrew
Scriptures (Josh 1:8; 8:34; 2 Kgs 22:13; 2 Chr 34:21), shows another
way that citation bases are developed in the OT. In the DtrH, the form
כְּכָל־הַכָּתוּב functions as a citation base only once (Josh 1:8). This
form does not attribute a referent to a source in Josh 8:34 or 2 Kgs
22:13. In 2 Chr 34:21, the Chr rewrites 2 Kgs 22:13 so that
כְּכָל־הַכָּתוּב functions as a citation base, i.e., it attributes a referent to a
source. In the post-exilic historiography, the use of the form
כְּכָל־הַכָּתוּב, a variant of כַּכָּתוּב, is restricted to citation bases. The
use of כֹּל is less characteristic of chronistic citation bases and, as a
broadening term, customarily indicates a Type I or larger qualification.
In 2 Chr 34:21, כְּכָל־הַכָּתוּב, however, has a Type II qualification
which is more customary in these post-exilic citation bases. Despite its
form, כְּכָל־הַכָּתוּב nevertheless has a function characteristic of the
Vergleichspräpositionale exegetical devices in the post-exilic period.

The Chr has used a comparative clause introduced by כַּאֲשֶׁר in 1
Chr 6:34 (49).

וְאַהֲרֹן וּבָנָיו מַקְטִירִים עַל־מִזְבַּח הָעוֹלָה וְעַל־מִזְבַּח הַקְּטֹרֶת
לְכֹל מְלֶאכֶת קֹדֶשׁ הַקֳּדָשִׁים וּלְכַפֵּר עַל־יִשְׂרָאֵל כְּכֹל אֲשֶׁר
צִוָּה מֹשֶׁה עֶבֶד הָאֱלֹהִים (1 Chr 6:34)

The comparative clause is not the preferred form of citation base in the
non-synoptic post-exilic literature for two apparent reasons. First, as
we have seen, they tend to have a larger range of qualification than
Vergleichspräpositionalen. Accordingly, the comparative clause
qualifies the entire sentence even though it is contiguous to the infinitive

---

10 The citation base in 2 Kgs 17:33 has an antithetical relation between clauses
    which facilitates the identification of the referent, but this is a non-legal referent.

phrase. Secondly, they are less mobile than *Vergleichspräpositionalen,* i.e., the more cumbersome comparative clause is less capable of being strategically positioned. The evidence appears to highlight the use of *Vergleichspräpositionalen* as exegetical devices that are at once precise and unobtrusive.

Lastly, the development of citation bases in Esther primarily concerns their use in connection with the literary artistry of ironic reversal in this book. As a result, these bases should be distinguished from the non-synoptic post-exilic exegetical devices above.

The evidence appears to support the conclusion that the *Vergleichspräpositionalen* that use the terms מִשְׁפָּט, מִצְוָה, כָּתוּב, and תּוֹרָה, as well as the relative forms of כָּתוּב and √צוה, reflect development in their use as exegetical devices by the time of the writing of the post-exilic literature. A plausible reason for this development is the vindication of the legal traditions in light of the events of the sixth century B.C. There is some evidence also for the relative citation base with √צוה being used at times as a homiletic device. כָּתוּב √מצא appears to be related to the development of citation bases above.

The only way to come to an appreciation of the development of these forms is to undertake an extended analysis of the citation bases with legal and non-legal referents throughout the OT.

The analysis of citation bases with legal referents demonstrates that the post-exilic authors promote the responsible use of the legal traditions in different ways. First, as we have seen, this is done by carefully marking legal observances. Secondly, citation bases were used to support this concern in less direct manners. For example, by using an undeveloped form for people caught in intermarriage, the author of Ezra 10 appears to be depicting the outcome of shoddy exegesis and interpretation (vv. 3, 8; see also כֵּן כִּדְבָרֶיךָ עָלֵינוּ לַעֲשׂות in v. 12). In his history, the Chr similarly marks aspects of Hezekiah's Passover celebration which fell short of the law with negative citation bases (2 Chr 30:5, 18; see also v. 19). In his narrative on the Passover celebration in Josiah's days, the Chr uses eight citation bases to mark its conformity to the past traditions. Among the latter chapters of the Chr's history, in which there is a concentration of citation bases, כַּכָּתוּב is the preferred formulation (30:5, 18; 31:3; 34:21; 35:12, 26). In Ezra and

Nehemiah, it is used several more times (Ezra 3:2, 4; 6:18 [כְּכָתֵב, BA]; Neh 8:15; 10:35 [34], 37 [36]).

The evidence suggests that the post-exilic historiography reflects the careful citation of legal referents in order to refine the exegesis and interpretation of the legal traditions in the post-exilic community. In Chronicles, this distribution of exegetical devices has a distinct effect. The further the events of the Golden Age of the Davidic-Solomonic era recede into the past, and the nearer Israel's history approaches the debacle of the sixth century B.C., the greater care the Chr takes to use these exegetical devices to indicate the relationship between Israel and their legal traditions. The Chr was careful to indicate both positive and negative relationships between Israel's history and their law.

It is appropriate to summarise briefly the dynamics of the interpretation reflected in the use of the citation bases. The referents in the post-exilic historiography were frequently observed to relate to various stipulations in the law. Both direct citations were observed (e.g, Neh 8:18; cf. Num 29:35) as well as the general statement "to observe the law". In 2 Chr 35:26, Josiah's lifetime of faithfulness to the legal traditions is summarised in the single word חֲסָדָיו. It is important to note that a referent may consist of an obvious implication from a stipulation in the law. In Ezra 6:18, to state that the service of God in Jerusalem was כִּכְתָב סֵפֶר מֹשֶׁה implied the observance of the requirement for a central sanctuary in Deut 12:14-15. Similarly, the need to construct *succoth* כַּכָּתוּב in Neh 8:15 is implied by the requirement to live in such structures during the festival (Lev 23:40-43).

As we have discussed in the syntax section above, citation bases may also be employed to differentiate a reference to the law from the facilitating measures taken to observe it. In 2 Chr 30:16a, כְּתוֹרַת מֹשֶׁה refers to the requirement that the recently restored cultic officials should assume their duties ("they took their accustomed posts"). In v. 16b, the separate roles for the priests and Levites in the cult are stated ("the priests dashed the blood that they received from the hands of the Levites", NRSV). These measures in v. 16b are not attributed to the law, but merely designate the manner in which the required duties stated in v. 16a were accomplished in the time of Hezekiah. In 2 Chr 35:13a, כְּמִשְׁפָּט refers to the requirement that the Passover sacrifice be cooked.

V. 13b relates the specific measures undertaken in Josiah's time to see
that this stipulation was fulfilled ("they boiled the holy offerings in pots,
in caldrons, and in pans, and carried them quickly to all the people",
NRSV). In Neh 10:35 (34), the delivery or offering of wood was
devised in order to keep the fire continually burning on the altar.

Two hermeneutical horizons were also detected in the law in Num
27 where the ancient laws of inheritance were reinterpreted for the
daughters of Zelophehad. As we have come to expect from our
analysis, however, such exegetical activity is done with undeveloped
devices in Num 27. Notice that the meaningful referent (vv. 3-4) of
כַּאֲשֶׁר צִוָּה יְהוָה אֶת־מֹשֶׁה and the statement of reinterpretation (vv. 8-
11a) are comparatively much larger than those in the non-synoptic post-
exilic historiography[11]. Furthermore, the citation base used in Num 27
is a comparative clause and not the preferred *Vergleichspräpositionale*
for legal referents in post-exilic times. In short, the exegetical process
that is marked with a citation base in Num 27 is more unwieldy than
what can be observed in the non-synoptic post-exilic historiography.
Succinctness may indeed be the reason why כַּכָּתוּב without a
subsequent source statement (e.g., בַּתּוֹרָה) is attested only in this
literature. The desire for concise exegetical devices in the post-exilic era
would also explain why *Vergleichspräpositionale* citation bases are
preferred over כַּאֲשֶׁר clauses. The use of כְּ in CD 19:1 may be a
further development in post-biblical Hebrew.

The only disadvantage with the use of *Vergleichspräpositionalen* for
citation bases is that such constructions cannot be inflected to agree with
their antecedents as the relative citation bases may (see 2 Chr 34:24
above for the Chr's distinctive rewriting of אֵלוֹת הַכְּתוּבוֹת).
However, to overcome this limitation, the *Vergleichspräpositionale*
citation bases with legal referents in the non-synoptic post-exilic
historiography are placed in a contiguous relation to their referents.
This, together with the observation that *Vergleichspräpositionalen* tend
to have a smaller scope of qualification than comparative clauses
introduced with כַּאֲשֶׁר, is an important conclusion. It appears that such

---

11 See the treatment of Num 27 in chapter 3 for a full discussion of the
    undeveloped features that are present in this passage.

forms make succinct and mobile exegetical devices for marking conformity to the law. This also agrees with those instances in the post-exilic historiography where the referent consisted of only a portion of a series or list of nominals (2 Chr 4:20; 35:26; Neh 10:37 [36]). In the law and DtrH, the referent, at times, consisted of an entire list of forms (e.g., Num 29:6).

III. Previous Scholarship

We have interacted with the scholarly treatment of citation bases throughout our study. It will be useful to compare our conclusions with some of the arguments that have been put forward based on only a portion of this evidence. The syntactic principles discussed above appear to challenge those scholars who attribute a faulty memory or carelessness to the post-exilic authors. Based on the use of citation bases (i.e., explicitly marked examples of legal interpretation), such conclusions no longer appear to be plausible. The view that citation bases are ambiguous in their meaning cannot be supported by this analysis either. Recent scholars who have attributed the law of the post-exilic historiography to a tradition that is no longer extant have typically read the *Vergleichspräpositionalen* with a broader scope of reference than appears justifiable.

Previous studies of LBH have not accounted for the distinctive features we have noted in non-synoptic exegetical and homiletic devices above. Only Rooker's observation that repetition is avoided at the time of the Chr applies to the citation bases in our study.

The conclusions of this study have largely vindicated the treatment of those who have observed a responsible handling of Israel's traditions in the post-exilic citation bases. We have indicated throughout this analysis where the work of several scholars has been confirmed by our approach to the lack of unanimity on this issue. However, in order to address the lack of consensus in scholarship a new and exhaustive approach has seemed necessary.

We must relate our conclusions specifically to two recent examinations which have attached a great deal of significance to some of these citation bases. First, DeVries has categorised some citation bases in Chronicles as either an "Authorization Formula" (AF) or a "Regulation Formula" (RF)[12]. DeVries claims that these two types of formulæ cite the authoritative traditions in Israel in different ways and for separate purposes. This informs DeVries' assessment of the purpose of the Chr's history which, according to his view, is to strengthen David's role as cult founder and to legitimize the Levites in the cult of Israel. While we do not find DeVries' evaluation of the Chr's purpose problematic, our main concern is the value of his AF and RF categories.

An examination of DeVries' article and book demonstrates that his analysis of the AF and the RF is fundamentally flawed. In short, DeVries' description of the features of the AF and RF cannot all be maintained at once. First, at various points in his treatment, his AF appeals to different sources of authority. For example, in his article, DeVries argues that the AF is comprised of expressions that base "cultic practice on the authority of Moses and his law"[13]. In his book, however, he states that the AF cites a much broader range of authority. According to his book, the AF "is found frequently in 1-2 Chronicles and, appealing to the authority of Moses, David, or the prophets, aims to legitimize a specific cultic event or procedure"[14].

Second, DeVries maintains that כַּכָּתוּב, with its variants, is "the stereotyped expression" in the AF[15]. DeVries' list of the variants of כַּכָּתוּב is elastic enough to permit the form בִּכְתָב in 1 Chr 28:19 to be an AF. DeVries admits that this "formulation is somewhat distinctive"[16]. At the same time, however, he lists the form בִּכְתָב in 2 Chr 35:4, the same preposition and construct noun, as one of the three

---

12 Simon J. DeVries' treatment of these citation bases is contained in his two publications "Moses and David as Cult Founders in Chronicles", *JBL* 107 (1988) 619-39; and, *1 and 2 Chronicles*, FOTL (Grand Rapids, Michigan: Eerdmans, 1989).

13 *Ibid.*, "Moses and David", 620.

14 *Ibid.*, *1 and 2 Chronicles*, 68, see also 437.

15 "Moses and David", 621, see also 623.

16 *Ibid.*, 626.

main synonyms comprising his RF[17]. It is unclear how the identical term can at once be part of the stereotypical language of the AF and be listed as a RF.

Thirdly, in "Moses and David", DeVries argues, "what is surely the core element in the Authorization Formula is a prepositional phrase introduced by [כְּ], mentioning some specific mode or repository of revelation"[18]. It is unclear why this same statement cannot be made about the majority of the passages of his RF. For instance, the main expression comprising DeVries' RF, כְּמִשְׁפָּט, typically refers to such repositories. DeVries complicates his statement by proceeding to list the כְּמִצְוָה expression in 2 Chr 8:13 as an AF. He includes 2 Chr 8:13 as one of six "striking exceptions" of an AF occurring without "the stereotyped expression" כַּכָּתוּב, and its variants[19]. Later in his article, DeVries further compounds his treatment of 2 Chr 8:13 by stating that, "we recognize that 2 Chr 8:12-15, with both Authorization Formula [v. 13] and Regulation Formula [v. 14], is highly programmatic material for the Chr"[20]. How DeVries can maintain that the AF in v. 13, which is irregular by his own analysis, can be part of highly programmatic material is unclear. His analysis in the book finds an additional AF in v. 14b of 2 Chr 8:12-15 and results in a total of two AFs (vv. 13, 14b) and one RF (v. 14)[21].

Most troubling of all, DeVries lists some of the constructions in his analysis as both AF and RF: כַּכָּתוּב in 2 Chr 30:5[22]; בְּלֹא כַכָּתוּב in 2 Chr 30:18[23]; and כְּמִשְׁפָּטָם in 2 Chr 30:16[24]. On consecutive pages in

---

17 *Ibid.*, 627.
18 *Ibid.*, 621.
19 *Ibid.*, 621.
20 *Ibid.*, 634.
21 *1 and 2 Chronicles*, 268-69.
22 AF in "Moses and David", 622, 623, 625, 631 n. 37; RF in *1 and 2 Chronicles*, 385, 438.
23 AF in "Moses and David", 622, 625; RF in *1 and 2 Chronicles*, 385, 438.
24 AF in *1 and 2 Chronicles*, 377, 385, 437; RF in "Moses and David", 627, 628 n. 28.

his book, the expression הַכֹּל בִּכְתָב in 1 Chr 28:19 is listed under both formulations[25].

A related issue concerns DeVries' inconsistency with regard to the term כָּתוּב, and its variants, which he deems is "the stereotyped expression" of the AF[26]. DeVries excludes at least two passages containing כָּתוּב, and its variants, from his AF and RF typology (2 Chr 34:21; 35:26). While we have used his analysis at several points in our examination, DeVries' typology of AF and RF has been ignored.

Shaver has recently attached considerable weight to some of the citation bases in our study. He concludes that there are seven passages which the author of Chronicles and Ezra-Nehemiah ascribes to the legal tradition that are not found in the present version of the Pentateuch. From this he deduces that the Pentateuch had not reached its canonical form at the time of the Chr[27]. Shaver's thesis depends on whether he has correctly identified the word, phrase, clause, etc. in seven passages which the author attributes to his law book (Ezra 6:18, 20; 10:3; Neh. 8:15; 10:35 [34]; 2 Chr 30:16-17; 35:10-11). This is the point at which Shaver's analysis is flawed. Of these seven passages, six employ citation bases. First, the citation base in 2 Chr 35:10-11 ascribed the referent to the monarch and not a legal tradition. Hence, what this indicates about the law or legal tradition is unclear.

Secondly, Shaver has not addressed the debates that surround the use of citation formulæ. Our analysis has shown that Shaver's identification of the referent of each of these citation bases is not supported by syntax. The fact that Shaver has not broached the debates that surround these citations seriously undermines his conclusions. The use of the pro-form √עשׂה in Ezra 10:3 does not clearly establish the element in the prevailing context that is being ascribed to the law. Even if this form is to be understood in Shaver's way, we have identified this use as a citation base that warns against shoddy exegesis. One would not want to attribute too much significance to the use of this כַּתּוֹרָה since it is ascribed to Shecaniah who had just conceded that he had

---

25 AF in *1 and 2 Chronicles,* 437; RF in *Ibid.,* 438.
26 "Moses and David", 621.
27 Shaver, 127-28.

"broken faith". Finally, it is unclear how Shaver can use Ezra 6:20 to support his thesis since it does not ascribe anything to another source. A syntactic treatment of citation bases in the OT does not appear to support the view that the law book of the Chr contained laws that are not attested in the Pentateuch.

The conclusions reached by these two partial examinations of citation formulæ have been unsatisfactory. Hence, they further justify the need for a comprehensive study of citation formulæ and bases in the OT.

IV. Future Research

As we have already indicated, this study stands as the logical precursor of an examination of citation bases in post-biblical Hebrew[28]. However, there is another vista of inquiry that this study suggests would be worthy of future research. Insofar as this study has demonstrated that the proper reading of comparative expressions must rely on sound syntactic principles, a thorough study of such sentences would seem to be merited. In 1994, Jenni's semantic taxonomy of the preposition כ stated that there was a need for such an examination[29].

V. Summary

We conclude that the *Vergleichspräpositionalen* that use the terms כָּתוּב, מִצְוָה, מִשְׁפָּט, and תּוֹרָה, as well as the relative forms of כָּתוּב

---

28 For an overview of the fundamental issues that would have to be addressed in such a study, see p. 123, n. 259.

29 In the course of this study of citation bases, we have stumbled upon some tangential findings that appear worth summarising at this point. First, we identified a *Wiederaufnahme* in Josh 10:15 and 43 which indicated that the chapter should be read around the theme of the conquest of the southern kings. This view has several advantages to a chronological reading that has always proven to be problematic. Secondly, the analysis of the four-part citation pattern revealed a basis for retaining קֶשֶׁת in 2 Sam 1:18 (cf. Gordon, 211).

and √צוה, reflect development in their use as exegetical and, at times, homiletic devices by the time of the writing of the post-exilic literature. In the post-exilic community, there may have been devices that were used in a formulaic manner, i.e., "citation formulæ". If this is correct, it appears that such a designation would chiefly concern the developed constructions above. In BA, כִּכְתָב סֵפֶר מֹשֶׁה in Ezra 6:18 was also consistent with the distinctive features of the non-synoptic post-exilic citation bases with legal referents. The forms used in Esther are developed in accordance with the literary artistry of that book. The development of citation formulæ is attested as early as about 520 B.C. in connection with the renewed work on the Temple.

The analysis of citation formulæ with non-legal referents, especially the four-part regnal formulæ and the reformulations of this citation pattern, highlights the development of the bases with legal referents. Even the Chr's citation of the authority of a monarch was distinguishable from his reference to the legal traditions.

The evidence for the use of the citation base מִצָּא √ כָּתוּב is late, but it may only be loosely associated with the development above. This formulation uniquely recounts the citation process ("it was found written") and thus attributes relatively large referents to a source which does not occur among the developed exegetical devices we have listed above.

The impetus for the development of exegetical and homiletic devices in the post-exilic literature appears to be the vindication of the legal traditions in light of the fall of Jerusalem, the destruction of the temple, the experience of exile, and perhaps, the limited success of the initial wave of returned exiles. The post-exilic authors use citation formulæ to cultivate the responsible handling of the law in the reconstruction era. In Ezra and Nehemiah, this is achieved, as we have seen, by both type and antitype. For the Chr, another concern emerges. By concentrating several citation formulæ in the final chapters of Chronicles, the Chr achieves a distinctive effect regarding the use of the legal traditions for his day. In his history, the further the events of the Golden Age of the Davidic-Solomonic era recede into the past, and the nearer Israel's history approaches the debacle of the sixth century B.C., the greater care the Chr takes to use these exegetical devices to indicate the relationship between Israel and their legal traditions. The Chr was careful to mark both negative and positive relationships between the law and Israel's history late in the divided monarchy. By portraying Israel's history in this manner, the Chr was attempting to improve the exegesis and observance of the law in the reconstruction period. The way forward for his community included the careful use of the recently vindicated traditions.

This analysis has sought to demonstrate that certain post-exilic citation bases were developed exegetical devices used to improve the interpretation and observance of the law after its vindication in the events of the sixth century B.C. The most developed of these citation formulæ is כַּכָּתוּב.

Bibliography

Ackroyd, P., *The Age of the Chronicler* (Auckland: Colloquium, 1970).

_____, *I & II Chronicles, Ezra, Nehemiah,* TBC (London: SCM Press, 1973).

_____, "The Chronicler as Exegete", *JSOT* 2 (1977) 2-32.

Alfrink, B. J., *Josue* (Roermond en Maaseik: J. J. Romen & Zonen, 1952).

Allen, L. C., *The Greek Chronicles. The Relation of the Septuagint of I and II Chroniclesto the Massoretic Text. Part 1: The Translator's Craft (VTS 25), Part 2: Textual Criticism (VTS 27)* (Leiden: E. J. Brill, 1974).

Andersen, F. I., *The Hebrew Verbless Clause in the Pentateuch,* JBLMS 14 (New York: Abingdon, 1970).

_____, *The Sentence in Biblical Hebrew,* Janua Linguarum, Series Practica 231 (The Hague: Mouton, 1974).

Anderson, A. A., *2 Samuel,* WBC (Dallas, Texas: Word Books, 1989).

Auld, A. G., "Joshua: the Hebrew and Greek Texts", *VTS* 30 (1979) 1-13.

_____, *Kings Without Privilege: David and Moses in the Story of the Bible's Kings* (Edinburgh: T. & T. Clark, 1994).

Bardke, H., *Das Buch Esther,* KAT (Gütersloh: G. Mohn, 1963).

Barr, J., *The Semantics of Biblical Language* (Oxford: Oxford University Press, 1961).

Barton, J., and D. J. Reimer (eds), *After the Exile: Essays in Honour of Rex Mason* (Macon, Georgia: Mercer University Press, 1996).

Batten, Loring W., *The Books of Ezra and Nehemiah,* ICC (Edinburgh: T. & T. Clark, 1913).

Bauer, H., and P. Leander, *Historische Grammatik der hebräischen Sprache des Alten Testamentes* (Halle: Niemeyer, 1922).

Baumgartner, W., *et al., Hebräisches und aramäisches Lexikon zum Alten Testament* (Leiden: E. J. Brill, 1967-).

Bergen, R. D. (ed.), *Biblical Hebrew and Discourse Linguistics* (Winona Lake, Indiana: Summer Institute of Linguistics, and Eisenbrauns, Inc., 1994).

Bertholet, A., *Die Bücher Esra und Nehemia,* KAT (Tübingen: Mohr, 1902).

Blau, J., "Gibt es ein emphatisches *'et* im Bibelhebräisch?", *VT* 4 (1954) 7-19.

_____, תוארי־פועל כנושאים הגיונים ורקדוקים בעברית, *Leshonenu* 20 (1955/56) 30-40.

_____, "Adverbia als Psychologische und Grammatische Subjekte/Praedikate im Bibel hebräische", *VT* 9 (1959) 130-37.

_____, *An Adverbial Construction in Hebrew and Arabic: Sentence Adverbials in Frontal Position Separated from the Rest of the Sentence,* The Israel Academy of Sciences and Humanities Proceedings VI (Jerusalem: Central Press, 1977).

Blenkinsopp, J., *Ezra-Nehemiah: A Commentary,* OTL (London: SCM Press Ltd., 1988).

Blokland, A. F. den E., *In Search of Text Syntax: Towards a Syntactic Segmentation Model for Biblical Hebrew* (Amsterdam: VU Uitgeverij, 1995).

Boda, M., *Praying the Tradition: The Origin and Use of Tradition in Nehemiah 9,* BZAW 277 (Berlin: DeGruyter, 1999).

Bodine, W. R., *Linguistics and Biblical Hebrew* (Winona Lake, Indiana: Eisenbrauns, 1992).

Boling, R. G., and G. E. Wright, *Joshua: A New Translation with Introduction and Commentary,* AB (Garden City, New York: Doubleday, 1982).

Botterweck, G. J., and H. Ringgren (eds.), *Theologisches Wörterbuch zum Alten Testament* (Stuttgart: Kohlhammer, 1970-).

_____, *Theological Dictionary of the Old Testament,* trans. by J. T. Willis *et al.* (Grand Rapids, MI: Eerdmans, 1974-).

Bowman, R. A., "Introduction and Exegesis to the Book of Ezra and the Book of Nehemiah" in *IB,* Vol. 3 (New York: Abingdon, 1954) 551-819.

Braun, R., *1 Chronicles,* WBC (Waco, Texas: Word Books, 1986).

Bright, J., *A History of Israel,* 3rd edn (London: SCM Press, 1981).

Brin, G., "The Firstling of Unclean Animals", *JQR* 68 (1978) 1-15.

Brockelmann, C., *Grundriss der vergleichenden Grammatik der semitischen Sprachen* (Berlin: Reuter und Reichard, 1908-13).

_____, *Hebräische Syntax* (Neukirchen: Neukirchener Verlag, 1956).

Brockington, L. H., *Ezra, Nehemiah and Esther,* NCB (London: Nelson, 1969).

Bromiley, G. W., *et al.* (eds), *The International Standard Bible Encyclopedia,* 4 Vols (Grand Rapids, Michigan: William B. Eerdmans Publishing Co., 1979-88).

Brongers, H. A., "Some Remarks on the Biblical Particle $h^a lo$ '", *OTS* 21 (1981) 177-89.

Brooke, A. E., N. McLean and H. St. J. Thackeray, *The Old Testament in Greek According to the Text of Codex Vaticanus, Supplemented from Other Uncial Manuscripts, With a Critical Apparatus Containing the Variants of the Chief Ancient Authorities for the Text of the Septuagint* (Cambridge: The University Press, 1906-1940).

Brown, F., S. R. Driver and C. A. Briggs, *A Hebrew and English Lexicon of the Old Testament* (Oxford: Clarendon, 1907).

Browne, L. E., *Early Judaism* (Cambridge: Cambridge University Press, 1920).

Budd, Philip J., *Numbers,* WBC (Waco, Texas: Word Books, 1984).

Bush, F. W., *Ruth, Esther,* WBC (Dallas, Texas: Word Books, 1996).

Bussman, H., *Routledge Dictionary of Language and Linguistics,* trans. and ed. by G. Trauth and K. Kazzazi (London: Routledge, 1996).

Butler, T. C., *Joshua,* WBC (Waco, Texas: Word Books, 1983).

Carson, D. A., and H. G. M. Williamson (eds.), *It is Written: Scripture Citing Scripture. Essays in Honour of Barnabas Lindars* (Cambridge: Cambridge University Press, 1988).

Chester, A., "Citing the Old Testament", in D. A. Carson and H. G. M. Williamson, (eds.), *It is Written: Scripture Citing Scripture. Essays in Honour of Barnabas Lindars* (Cambridge: Cambridge University Press, 1988) 141-69.

Cheyne, T. K., *The Origin and Religious Contents of the Psalter* (London: Kegan Paul, Trench, Trübner, & Co. Ltd., 1891).

Childs, B. S., *Introduction to the Old Testament as Scripture* (London: SCM Press, 1979).

Clines, D. J. A., "Nehemiah 10 as an Example of Early Jewish Biblical Exegesis", *JSOT* 21 (1981) 111-17.

_____, *Ezra, Nehemiah, Esther,* NCB (London: Marshall, Morgan & Scott, 1984).

_____, "In Quest of the Historical Mordecai", *VT* 41 (1991) 126-39.

Coggins, R. G., *The First and Second Books of Chronicles* (Cambridge: Cambridge University Press, 1976).

_____, "Interbiblical Quotations in Joel", in J. Barton and D. J. Reimer (eds), *After the Exile: Essays in Honour of Rex Mason* (Macon, Georgia: Mercer University Press, 1996) 75-84.

Cottrell, P., and M. Turner, *Linguistics and Biblical Interpretation* (Downers Grove, IL: InterVarsity, 1989).

Crenshaw, J. L., *Joel: A New Translation with Introduction and Commentary,* AB (London: Doubleday, 1995).

Cross, F. M., "A Reconstruction of the Judean Restoration", *JBL* 94 (1975) 4-18.

Crystal, D., *A Dictionary of Linguistics and Phonetics,* 4th edn (Oxford: Blackwell Publishers, 1997).

Curtis, E. L., and A. A. Madsen, *A Critical and Exegetical Commentary on the Books of Chronicles,* ICC (Edinburgh: T. & T. Clark, 1910).

Dalley, S., "The Mesopotamian Background to the Hebrew Book of Esther", Oxford Old Testament Seminar, 3 ii 1997.

Davies, T. W., *Ezra, Nehemiah and Esther,* CB (London: Caxton, 1909).

Dawson, D. A., *Text-Linguistics and Biblical Hebrew,* JSOTS 177 (Sheffield: Sheffield Academic Press, 1994).

Day, J., "Baal (Deity)", in D. N. Freedman *et al.* (eds.), *ABD*, Vol. 1, 545-49.

Deboys, D. G., "The Chronicler's Portrait of Abijah", *Biblica* 71 (1990) 48-62.

De Vaux, R., *Ancient Israel: Its Life and Institutions,* 2nd edn, trans. by J. McHugh (London: Darton, Longman and Todd Ltd., 1965).

DeVries, S. J., *1 Kings,* WBC (Waco, Texas: Word Books, 1985).

_____, "Moses and David as Cult Founders in Chronicles", *JBL* 107 (1988) 619-39.

_____, *1 and 2 Chronicles,* FOTL (Grand Rapids, Michigan: Eerdmans, 1989).

Dillard, R. B., *2 Chronicles* (Waco, Texas: Word Books, 1987).

Donner, H., ",Wie geschrieben steht'. Herkunft und Sinn einer Formel", in his *Aufsätze zum Alten Testament aus vier Jahrzehnten* (Berlin: Walter de Gruyter, 1994) 224-38.

Dorothy, C. V., *The Books of Esther: Structure, Genre and Textual Integrity,* JSOTS 187 (Sheffield: Sheffield Academic Press, 1997).

Dörrfuß, E. M., *Mose in den Chronikbüchern Garant theokratischer Zukunftserwartung,* BZAW 219 (Berlin: Walter de Gruyter, 1994).

Driver, S. R., *A Treatise on The Use of the Tenses in Hebrew,* 3rd edn (Oxford: Clarendon Press, 1892).

_____, *A Critical and Exegetical Commentary on Deuteronomy*, 3rd edn, ICC (Edinburgh: T. & T. Clark, 1902).

_____, *Notes on the Hebrew Text and the Topography of the Books of Samuel,* 2nd edn (Oxford: Clarendon Press, 1913).

_____, *An Introduction to the Literature of the Old Testament,* 9th edn (Edinburgh: T. & T. Clark, 1913).

Dyk, J. W., *Participles in Context: A Computer-Assisted Study of Old Testament Hebrew* (Amsterdam: VU University Press, 1994).

Dyk, J. W., and E. Talstra, "Computer-Assisted Study of Syntactical Change, the Shift in the Use of the Participle in Biblical and Post-Biblical Hebrew Texts", in P. van Reenen and K. van Reenen-Steins (eds.), *Spatial and Temporal Distributions, Studies in language variation offered to Anthonij Dees on the occasion of his 60th birthday* (Amsterdam: John Benjamins, 1988), 49-62.

Eissfeldt, O., *The Old Testament: An Introduction,* trans. by P. R. Ackroyd (New York: Harper & Row, 1965).

Elliger, K., *Das Buch der zwölf kleinen Propheten. II. Die Propheten Nahum, Habakuk, Zephanja, Haggai, Sacharja, Maleachi,* ATD 25 (Göttingen: Vandenhoeck & Ruprecht, 1964).

Elliger, K., and W. Rudolph (eds.), *Biblia Hebraica Stuttgartensia* (Stuttgart: Deutsche Bibelgesellschaft, 1983).

Emerton, J., "The Priestly Writer in Genesis", *JTS* NS 39 (1988) 381-400.

Eskenazi, T. C., *In an Age of Prose: A Literary Approach to Ezra-Nehemiah,* SBLMS 36 (Atlanta, Georgia: Scholars Press, 1988).

Fensham, F. C., "Neh. 9 and Pss. 105, 106, 135, and 136, Post-Exilic
Historical Traditions in Poetic Form", *JNSL* 9 (1981) 35-51.
_____, *The Books of Ezra and Nehemiah,* NICOT (Grand Rapids,
Michigan: Eerdmans, 1982).
Fishbane, M., *Biblical Interpretation in Ancient Israel* (Oxford:
Clarendon Press, 1985).
_____, *The Garments of Torah: Essays in Biblical Hermeneutics*
(Bloomington, Indiana: Indiana University Press, 1989).
_____, "Inner-Biblical Exegesis", in M. Sæbø (ed.), *Hebrew Bible/Old
Testament, the History of its Interpretation. Vol. I: From the
Beginnings to the Middle Ages (Until 1300). Part 1: Antiquity*
(Göttingen: Vandenhoeck & Ruprecht, 1996) 33-48.
Fohrer, G., *Introduction to the Old Testament,* trans. by D. Green
(London: SPCK Publ., 1968).
Fox, M. V., *The Redaction of the Books of Esther: On Reading
Composite Texts,* SBLMS 40 (Atlanta, Georgia: Scholars Press,
1991).
Freedman, D. N., *et al.* (eds.), *The Anchor Bible Dictionary,* 6 vols
(London: Doubleday, 1992).
Fritz, V., *Das Buch Josua,* HAT (Tübingen: J.C.B. Mohr, 1994).

Galling, K., *Die Bücher der Chronik, Esra, Nehemia,* ATD (Göttingen:
Vandenhoeck & Ruprecht, 1954).
Geißler, J., *Die litterarischen Beziehungen der Esramemoiren,
insbesondere zur Chronik und den hexateuchischen Quellschriften*
(Chemnitz: J. C. F. Pickenhahn & Sohn, 1899).
*Gesenius' Hebrew Grammar as edited and enlarged by the late E.
Kautzsch,* trans. by A. E. Cowley, 2nd edn (Oxford: Clarendon
Press, 1910).
Gibson, J. C. L., *Canaanite Myths and Legends,* 2nd edn (Edinburgh:
T. & T. Clark, 1978).
_____, *Davidson's Introductory Hebrew Grammar - Syntax,* 4th edn
(Edinburgh: T. & T. Clark, 1994).
Goettsberger, *Die Bücher der Chr oder Paralipomenon,* Die Hl. Schrift
des AT (Bonn: Feldmann-Herkenne, 1939).
Gooding, D. W., "Problems of Text and Midrash in the Third Book of
Reigns", *Textus* 7 (1969) 1-29.

_____, *Relics of Ancient Exegesis: A Study of the Miscellanies in 3 Reigns 2* (Cambridge: Cambridge University Press, 1976).

Gordis, R., "Religion, Wisdom and History in the Book of Esther—A New Solution to an Ancient Crux", *JBL* 100 (1981) 359-88.

Gordon, A., "The Development of the Participle in Biblical, Mishnaic, and Modern Hebrew", *AL* 8 (1982) 1-59.

Gordon, R. P., *1 & 2 Samuel: A Commentary* (Exeter: Paternoster, 1986).

_____, book review, *VT* 44 (1994) 135-36.

Gray, J., *I & II Kings,* OTL (London: SCM Press LTD, 1964).

_____, *Joshua, Judges, Ruth,* NCB (Basingstoke: Marshall, Morgan & Scott Publ. Ltd., 1986).

Gross, W., "Satzfolge, Satzteilfolge und Satzart als Kriterien der Subkategorisierung hebräischer Konjunktionalsätze, am Beispiel der כֵּי-Sätze untersucht", in W. Gross *et al.* (eds.), *Text, Methode und Grammatik: Wolfgang Richter zum 65. Geburtstag* (Sankt Ottilien: EOS, 1991) 99-116.

Gunneweg, A. H. J., *Esra,* KAT (Gütersloh: Gütersloher Verlagshaus Gerd Mohn, 1985).

_____, *Nehemia,* KAT (Gütersloh: Gütersloher Verlagshaus Gerd Mohn, 1987).

Haag, "כָּתַב", *TWAT,* Vol. IV, cols 385-97.

Halliday, M. A. K., *An Introduction to Functional Grammar,* 2nd edn (London: Edward Arnold, 1994).

Hatch, E. and H. A. Redpath, *A Concordance to the Septuagint and the Other Greek Versions of the Old Testament,* 3rd edn, 2 vols (Oxford: Clarendon, 1892-97).

Herder, A., *Corpus des tablettes en cunéiformes alphabétiques découvertes à Ras Shamra — Ugarit de 1929 à 1939,* MRS 10 (Paris: Imprimerie nationale, 1963).

Hoftijzer, J., "Remarks Concerning the Use of the Particle *'t* in Classical Hebrew", *OTS* 14 (1965) 1-99.

Hoftijzer, J., and K. Jongeling (eds.), *Dictionary of the North-West Semitic Inscriptions,* 2 parts, Handbuch der Orientalistik. Erste Abteilung. Der Nahe und Mittlere Osten, (Leiden: E. J. Brill, 1995).

Hoglund, K. G., *Achaemenid Imperial Administration in Syria-Palestine and the Missions of Ezra and Nehemiah,* SBLDS 125 (Atlanta, Georgia: Scholars Press, 1992).

Holloway, S. W., "Kings, Book of 1-2", *ABD,* Vol. IV, 69-83.

Houtman, C., "Ezra and the Law", *OTS* 21 (1981) 91-115.

Jahn, G., *Die Bücher Esra (A und B) und Nehemja, Text-Kritisch und Historisch-Kritisch untersucht mit Erklärung der Einschlägigen Prophetenstellen und einem Anhang über hebräische Eigennamen* (Leiden: E. J. Brill, 1909).

Japhet, S., "The Supposed Common Authorship of Chronicles and Ezra-Nehemiah Investigated Anew", *VT* 18 (1968) 332-72.

_____, "Law and 'the Law' in Ezra-Nehemiah", in M. Goshen-Gottstein (ed.), *Proceedings of the Ninth World Congress of Jewish Studies, panel discussions* (Jerusalem: Perry Foundation for Biblical Research in the Hebrew University of Jerusalem, 1988) 99-115.

_____, *The Ideology of the Book of Chronicles and its Place in Biblical Thought,* Beiträge zur Erforschung des alten Testaments und des antiken Judentums 9, trans. by A. Barber (Frankfurt: Peter Lang, 1989).

_____, *I & II Chronicles: A Commentary,* OTL (Louisville, KY: Westminster/John Knox Press, 1993).

Jellicoe, S., *The Septuagint and Modern Study* (Oxford: The Clarendon Press, 1968).

Jenni, E., "Zur Semantik der hebräischen Vergleichssätze", *ZAH* 2 (1989) 14-44.

_____, "Zur Semantik der hebräischen Personen-, Tier-, und Dingvergleiche", *ZAH* 3 (1990) 133-166.

_____, *Die hebräischen Präpositionen Band 1: Die Präposition Beth* (Stuttgart: W. Kohlhammer, 1992).

_____, *Die hebräischen Präpositionen Band 2: Die Präposition Kaph* (Stuttgart: W. Kohlhammer, 1994).

_____, *Die hebräischen Präpositionen Band 3: Die Präposition Lamed* (Stuttgart: W. Kohlhammer, 2000).

Jenni, E., and C. Westermann, *Theologisches Handwörterbuch zum Alten Testament,* 2 vols (Munich: Chr. Kaiser, 1971-76).

Johns, A. F., *A Short Grammar of Biblical Aramaic,* Andrews
    University Monographs 1, revised edn (Berrien Springs, Michigan:
    Andrews University Press, 1972).
Jones, B. W., "Two Misconceptions about the Book of Esther", *CBQ*
    39 (1977) 171-81.
_____, "The So-Called Appendix of the Book of Esther", *Semitics* 6
    (1978) 36-43.
Jones, G. H., *1 and 2 Kings,* NCB (London: Marshall, Morgan &
    Scott Publ. Ltd., 1984).
Joüon, P., *A Grammar of Biblical Hebrew,* 2 vols, trans. and rev. by
    T. Muraoka, reprint of 1st edn (1991) with corrections, SB 14/I &
    II (Rome: Editrice Pontificio Istituto Biblico, 1993).

Kaufmann, Y., תולדות האמונה הישראלית מימי קדם עד סוף
    בית שני (Jerusalem: Ktav Publ., 1956).
_____, *History of the Religion of Israel. Volume IV: From the
    Babylonian Captivity to the End of Prophecy,* trans. by C. W.
    Efroymson (New York: Ktav Publ., 1977).
Keil, C. F., *Commentary on the Book of Joshua,* trans. by J. Martin
    (Edinburgh: T. & T. Clark, 1857).
_____, *Chronik, Esra, Nehemia und Esther* (Leipzig: Dörffling und
    Franke, 1870).
_____, *The Books of Ezra, Nehemiah, and Esther,* trans. by S. Taylor
    (Edinburgh: T. & T. Clark, 1873).
_____, *Josua, Richter und Ruth,* Biblischer Commentar über die
    Prophetischen Geschichtsbücher des Alten Testaments, zweite,
    verbesserte Auflage (Leipzig: Dörffling und Franke, 1874).
Khan, G., *Studies in Semitic Syntax,* LOS 38 (Oxford: Oxford
    University Press, 1988).
Kidner, D., *Ezra and Nehemiah,* TOTC (Leicester: Inter-Varsity Press,
    1979).
Knoppers, G. N., *Two Nations Under God: The Deuteronomistic
    History of Solomon and the Dual Monarchies. Volume 2: The
    Reign of Jeroboam, the Fall of Israel and the Reign of Josiah,*
    HSM 53 (Atlanta, Georgia: Scholars Press, 1994).
Koehler, L., and W. Baumgartner, *Lexicon in Veteris Testamenti
    Libros,* 2nd edn (Leiden: E. J. Brill, 1958).

_____, *The Hebrew and Aramaic Lexicon of the Old Testament,* trans. and ed. by M. E. J. Richardson *et al.,* 5 vols (Leiden: E. J. Brill, 1994-).

König, E., *Historisch-kritisches Lehrgebäude der hebräischen Sprache,* 2 vols. in 3 (Leipzig: J. C. Hinrichs'sche Buchhandlung, 1881-97).

Kosters, W. H., *Het herstel van Israël in het Perzische tijdvak* (Leiden: E. J. Brill, 1894).

Kropat, A., *Die Syntax des Autors der Chronik verglichen mit der seiner Quellen. Ein Beitrag zur historischen Syntax des Hebräischen,* BZAW 16 (Gießen: Alfred Töpelmann, 1909).

Kugel, J., *The Idea of Biblical Poetry* (New Haven: Yale University Press, 1981).

Kuhrt, A., *The Ancient Near East: c. 3000-300 B.C.,* 2 Vols, Routledge History of the Ancient World (London: Routledge, 1995).

Labuschagne, C. J., "The Particle הֵן and הִנֵּה", *OTS* 18 (1973) 1-14.

Lambdin, T. O., *Introduction to Biblical Hebrew* (New York: Charles Scribner's Sons, 1971).

Leech, G., *Principles of Pragmatics* (London: Longman, 1983).

Levenson, J. D., *Esther: A Commentary,* OTL (London: SCM Press, 1997).

Levine, "מִצְוָה", *TWAT,* Vol. IV, cols. 1085-95.

Levinson, S. C., *Pragmatics* (Cambridge: Cambridge University Press, 1983).

Liddell, H. G., and R. Scott, *A Greek-English Lexicon,* rev. by H. S. Jones and R. McKenzie, 9th edn (Oxford: Clarendon Press, 1940).

Lisowsky, G., *Konkordanz zum hebräischen Alten Testament* (Stuttgart: Württ. Bibelanstalt, 1958).

Long, B. O., "Framing Repetitions in Biblical Historiography", *JBL* 106 (1987) 385-99.

Loretz, O., "Der Torso eines kanaanäisch-israelitischen Tempelweihspruches in 1 Kg 8, 12-13", *UF* 6 (1974) 478-80.

Lyons, J., *Semantics,* 2 vols (Cambridge: Cambridge University Press, 1977).

Mandelkern, S., *Veteris Testamenti Concordantiæ Hebraicæ atque Chaldaicæ* (Berlin: Margolin, 1925).

Mason, R., "Some Echoes of the Preaching in the Second Temple? Tradition Elements in Zechariah 1 - 8", *ZAW* 96 (1984) 221-35.

_____, *Preaching the Tradition: Homily and Hermeneutics after the Exile* (Cambridge: Cambridge University Press, 1990).

Mathias, D., "'Levitische Predigt' und Deuteronomismus", *ZAW* 96 (1984) 23-49.

Mauchline, J., *1 and 2 Samuel,* NCB (London: Marshall, Morgan & Scott Publ. Ltd., 1971).

McCarter Jr., P. K., *II Samuel: A New Translation with Introduction, Notes and Commentary,* AB (Garden City, New York: Doubleday & Co., 1984).

McCarthy, D. J., "The Uses of W*e*hinneh in Biblical Hebrew", *Biblica* 61 (1980) 330-42

McConville, J. G., *Ezra, Nehemiah and Esther,* DSB (Edinburgh: The Saint Andrews Press, 1985).

_____, *Judgment and Promise: An Interpretation of the Book of Jeremiah* (Leicester: Apollos, 1993).

_____, *Grace In The End: A Study in Deuteronomic Theology,* SOTBT (Grand Rapids, MI: Zondervan, 1993).

McKane, W., *A Critical and Exegetical Commentary on Jeremiah,* 2 vols, ICC (Edinburgh: T. & T. Clark, 1986, 1996).

McKenzie, S. L., "1 Kings 8: A Sample Study into the Texts of Kings Used by the Chronicler and Translated by the Old Greek", *BIOSCS* 19 (1986) 15-34.

_____, *The Problem With Kings: The Composition of the Books of Kings in the Deuteronomistic History,* VTS 42 (Leiden: E. J. Brill, 1991).

McKenzie, S. L., and H. N. Wallace, "Covenant Themes in Malachi", *CBQ* 45 (1983) 549-63.

Meier, S., *Speaking of Speaking: Marking Direct Discourse in the Hebrew Bible,* VTS 46 (Leiden: E. J. Brill, 1992).

Meyer, E., *Die Entstehung des Judenthums: eine historische Untersuchung* (Halle a. S.: Max Niemeyer, 1896).

Michaeli, F., *Les livres des Chroniques, d'Esdras et de Néhémie,* CAT 16 (Neuchâtel: Delachaux & Niestlé, 1967).

Milgrom, J., *Leviticus 1-16: A New Translation with Introduction and Commentary*, AB (London: Doubleday, 1991).

_____, "Priestly ('D') Source", in D. N. Freedman *et al.* (eds.), *ABD*, Vol. V, 454-61.

Miller, J. M., and J. H. Hayes, *A History of Ancient Israel and Judah* (London: Marshall, Morgan & Scott Publ. Ltd., 1986).

Mitchell, H. G., J. M. P. Smith and J. A. Bewer, *A Critical and Exegetical Commentary on Haggai, Zechariah, Malachi and Jonah*, ICC (Edinburgh: T. & T. Clark, 1912).

Montgomery, J. A., *A Critical and Exegetical Commentary on the Books of Kings*, ICC (Edinburgh: T. & T. Clark, 1951).

Moore, C. A., *Studies in the Book of Esther* (New York: Ktav Publ. House, 1982).

Mosis, R., *Untersuchungen zur Theologie des chronistischen Geschichtswerkes*, FTS 92 (Freiburg: Herder, 1973).

Mulder, M. J., "Die Partikel כֵּן im Alten Testament", *OTS* 21 (1981) 201-27.

Muroaka, T., *Emphatic Words And Structures In Biblical Hebrew* (Jerusalem-Leiden: The Magnes Press/E. J. Brill, 1985).

Myers, C. L., and E. M. Myers, *Haggai, Zechariah 1-8: A New Translation with Introduction and Commentary*, AB (Garden City, NY: Doubleday & Co. Inc., 1987).

Myers, J. M., *Ezra-Nehemiah: Introduction, Translation, and Notes*, AB (Garden City, New York: Doubleday & Co. Inc., 1965).

_____, *I Chronicles: Introduction, Translation, and Notes*, AB (Garden City, NY: Doubleday & Co. Inc., 1965).

_____, *II Chronicles: Introduction, Translation, and Notes*, AB (Garden City, NY: Doubleday & Co. Inc., 1965).

New American Standard Bible (La Habra, CA: The Lockman Foundation, 1988).

Nicholson, E. W., *Preaching to the Exiles: A Study of the Prose Tradition in the Book of Jeremiah* (Oxford: Blackwell, 1970).

_____, *The Book of the Prophet Jeremiah Chapters 1-25* (Cambridge: Cambridge University Press, 1973).

_____, *The Pentateuch in the Twentieth Century: The Legacy of Julius Wellhausen* (Oxford: Clarendon Press, 1998).

North, R., "The Chronicler: 1-2 Chronicles, Ezra, Nehemiah", in R. E. Browne *et al.* (eds.), *The New Jerome Biblical Commentary,* 2nd edn (London: Geoffrey Chapman, 1990/1968) 402-38.

Noth, M., *Das Buch Josua*, 2nd edn, HAT (Tübingen: J. C. B. Mohr, 1953).

_____, *Könige,* BKAT (Neukirchen-Vluyn: Neukirchener Verlag des Erziehungsvereins, 1964-, issued in parts).

Patton, L. B., *A Critical and Exegetical Commentary on the Book of Esther,* ICC (Edinburgh: T. & T. Clark, 1908).

Peterca, V., "Ein midraschartiges Auslegungsbeispiel zugunsten Salomos 1 Kön 8,12-13 - 3 Reg 8, 53a", *BZ* N.F. 31 (1987) 270-75.

Petersen, D. L., *Haggai & Zechariah 1-8,* OTL (London: SCM Press, 1985).

Plett, H. F., *Textwissenschaft und Textanalyse* (Heidelberg: Quelle und Meyer, 1975).

Polzin, R., *Late Biblical Hebrew: Towards An Historical Typology of Biblical Hebrew Prose,* HSM 12 (Missoula, Montana: Scholars Press, 1976).

Qimron, E., *The Hebrew of the Dead Sea Scrolls* (Atlanta: Scholars Press, 1986).

Quirk, R., S. Greenbaum, G. Leech and J. Svartvik, *A Comprehensive Grammar of the English Language* (London: Longman, 1985).

Rad, G. von, "Die Levitische Predigt in den Büchern der Chronik", in *Festschrift für Otto Procksch* (Leipzig, 1934) 113-24.

_____, *Gesammelte Studien zum Alten Testament* (München: Kaiser, 1958) 248-61.

_____, "The Levitical Sermon in I and II Chronicles", in his *The Problem of the Hexateuch and Other Essays*, trans. by E. W. T. Dicken (London: Oliver & Boyd, 1966) 267-80.

Rahlfs, A. (ed.), *Septuaginta id est Vetus Testamentum graæce iuxta LXX interpretes* (Stuttgart: Württembergische Bibelanstalt, 1935).

Rehm, M., *Das erste Buch der Könige: Ein Kommentar* (Wurzburg: Echter Verlag, 1979).

Richter, W., *Grundlagen einer althebräischen Grammatik*, ATSAT, Bd. 8: I. *Das Wort (Morphologie)*, Bd. 10: II. *Die Wortfügung (Morphosyntax)*, Bd. 13: III. *Der Satz (Satztheorie)* (Sankt Ottilien: EOS Verlag, 1978-80).

_____, *Untersuchungen zur Valenz althebräischer Verben 1: 'RK*, ATSAT 23 (Sankt Ottilien: EOS Verlag, 1985).

Röllig, W., "Baal-Shamem," in Karel van der Toorn *et al.* (eds), *Dictionary of Dieties and Demons in the Bible*, 2nd edn (Leiden: Brill, 1999) 149-51.

Rooker, M. F., *Biblical Hebrew In Transition: The Language of the Book of Ezekiel*, JSOTS 90 (Sheffield: Sheffield Academic Press, 1990).

Rosenbaum, M., *Word-Order Variation in Isaiah 40-55: A Functional Perspective*, Studia Semitica Neerlandica 35 (The Netherlands: Van Gorcum Publ., 1997).

Rosenthal, F., *A Grammar of Biblical Aramaic*, Porta Linguarum Orientalium ns 5 (Wiesbaden: Harrassowitz, 1961).

Rudolph,W., *Esra und Nehemia*, HAT (Tübingen: J. C. B. Mohr, 1949).

_____, *Chronikbücher*, HAT (Tübingen: J. C. B. Mohr, 1955).

_____, *Jeremia*, 3rd Aufl., HAT (Tübingen: J. C. B. Mohr, 1968).

Ryle, H. E., *The Books of Ezra and Nehemiah*, CBSC (Cambridge: Cambridge University Press, 1897).

Sæbø, M. (ed.), *Hebrew Bible/Old Testament, the History of its Interpretation. Vol. I: From the Beginnings to the Middle Ages (Until 1300). Part 1: Antiquity* (Göttingen: Vandenhoeck & Ruprecht, 1996).

Savran, G. W., *Telling and Retelling: Quotation in Biblical Narrative* (Bloomington & Indianapolis: Indiana University Press, 1988).

Schneider, H., *Die Bücher Esra und Nehemia*, HSAT (Bonn: Peter Hanstein, 1959).

Schneider, W., *Grammatik des biblischen Hebräisch* (Munich: Cladius, 1974).

Schniedewind,W. M., "The Source Citations of Manasseh: King Manasseh in History and Homily", *VT* 41 (1991) 450-61.

_____, *The Word of God in Transition: From Prophet to Exegete in the Second Temple Period,* JSOTS 197 (Sheffield: Sheffield Academic Press, 1995).

Segal, M. H., *A Grammar of Mishnaic Hebrew* (Oxford: Clarendon, 1927).

Septuagint: Vetus Testamentum Graecum Auctoritate Societatis Litterarum Gottingensis Editum (Göttingen: Vandenhoeck & Ruprecht, 1931-).

Seybold, K., "כִּ", *TWAT,* Vol IV, cols. 1-7.

Shaver, J. R., *Torah and the Chronicler's History Work: An Inquiry into the Chronicler's References to Laws, Festivals, and Cultic Institutions in Relationship to Pentateuchal Legislation,* BJS 196 (Atlanta, Georgia: Scholars Press, 1989).

Smith, R. L., *Micah - Malachi,* WBC (Waco, TX: Word Books, 1984).

Soggin, J. A., *Le livre de Josué,* CAT (Paris: Delachaux & Niestlé Neuchatel, 1970).

Soulen, R. N., *Handbook of Biblical Criticism,* 2nd edn (Atlanta: John Knox Press, 1981).

Stade, B., *The Books of Kings: Critical Edition of the Hebrew Text* (Leipzig: J. C. Hinrichs'sche Buchhandlung, 1904).

Steiner, R. C., "Ancient Hebrew", in R. Hertzon (ed.), *The Semitic Languages* (London: Routledge, 1997) 145-73.

Stoebe, H. J., *Das zweite Buch Samuelis,* KAT (Gütersloh: Gütersloher Verlagshaus, 1994).

Stuart, D. K., *Old Testament Exegesis: A Primer for Students and Pastors,* 2nd edn (Philadelphia, PA: Westminster, 1984).

Sweeney, M. A., book review, *JBL* 116 (1997) 336-38.

Tanakh תנ״ך *The Holy Scriptures. The New JPS Translation According to the Traditional Hebrew Text* (Jerusalem: Jewish Publicaltion Society, 1988).

Taylor, J. G., *Yahweh and the Sun: Biblical and Archaeological Evidence for Sun Worship in Ancient Israel,* JSOTS 111 (Sheffield: JSOT Press, 1993).

_____, "A Response to Steve A. Wiggins, 'Yahweh: The God of Sun?'", *JSOT* 71 (1996) 107-19.

The Holy Bible. New International Version (London: Hodder &
    Stoughton, 1973, 1978, 1984).
The Holy Bible. New Revised Standard Version (Cambridge:
    Cambridge University Press, 1989).
*The Holy Bible. Revised Standard Version. Containing the Old and
    New Testaments,* 2nd edn (Cambridge: Cambridge University
    Press, 1971).
Thiel, W., *Die deuteronomistische Redaktion von Jeremia 1-25,*
    WMANT 41 (Neukirchen-Vluyn: Neukirchener Verlag, 1973).
_____, *Die deuteronomistische Redaktion von Jeremia 26-45,*
    WMANT 52 (Neukirchen-Vluyn: Neukirchener Verlag, 1981).
Thiselton, A. C., *New Horizons in Hermeneutics* (London:
    HarperCollins, 1992).
Throntveit, M., "Linguistic Analysis and the Question of Authorship in
    Chronicles, Ezra and Nehemiah", *VT* 32 (1982) 201-16.
Toeg, A., "Numbers 15: 22-31 – a Halakhic Midrash
    [מדרש הלכה - לא - כב : טו במדבר]]", *Tarbiz* 40 (1960-61) 1-
    20.
Toorn, K. van der, B. Becking and P. W. van der Horst (eds.),
    Dictionary of Deities and Demons in the Bible (DDD) (Leiden: E. J.
    Brill, 1995).
Torrey, C. C., *Ezra Studies* (Chicago: Chicago University Press,
    1910).
Tov, E., *The Text-Critical Use of the Septuagint in Biblical Research,*
    JBS 3 (Jerusalem: Simor, 1981).
_____, "Some Sequence Differences Between the MT and LXX and
    Their Ramifications for the Literary Criticism of the Bible", *JNSL*
    13 (1987) 151-60.
_____, *Textual Criticism of the Hebrew Bible* (Minneapolis, MN:
    Fortress Press, 1992).

Waldman, N. M., *The Recent Study of Hebrew: A Survey of the
    Literature with Selected Bibliography* (Cincinnati: Hebrew Union
    College Press; and Winona Lake, IN: Eisenbrauns, 1989).
Walters, P., *The Text of the Septuagint: Its Corruptions and Their
    Emendations,* ed. by D. W. Gooding (Cambridge: Cambridge
    University Press, 1973).

Waltke, B. K., and M. O'Connor, *An Introduction to Biblical Hebrew Syntax* (Winona Lake, Indiana: Eisenbrauns, 1990).

Weinfeld, M., *Deuteronomy and the Deuteronomistic School* (Oxford: Clarendon Press, 1972).

Welch, A. C., *The Work of the Chronicler: Its Purpose and Its Date* (London: The British Academy, 1939).

Wellhausen, J., *Der Text der Bücher Samuelis* (Göttingen: Vandenhoeck und Ruprecht's Verlag, 1871).

_____, *Die Composition des Hexateuchs und der historischen Bücher des alten Testaments,* 2nd edn (Berlin: Georg Reiner, 1889).

_____, "Die Rückkehr der Juden aus dem babylonischen Exil", *Nachrichten von der königlichen Gesellschaft der Wissenschaften zu Göttingen. Philologisch-historische Klasse* (1895) 166-86.

Wenham, G. J., *The Book of Leviticus,* NICOT (Grand Rapids, MI: Eerdmans, 1979).

_____, *Numbers. An Introduction and Commentary,* TOTC (Leicester: Inter-Varsity, 1981).

Whybray, R. N., *The Making of the Pentateuch: A Methodological Study,* JSOTS 53 (Sheffield: JSOT Press, 1987).

Wiggins, S. A., "Yahweh: The God of Sun?", *JSOT* 71 (1996) 89-106

_____, "A Rejoinder to J. Glen Taylor", *JSOT* 73 (1997) 109-12.

Willi, T. *Die Chronik als Auslegung,* FRLANT 106 (Göttingen: Vandenhoeck & Ruprecht, 1972).

_____, *Chronik,* fasc. 1, BKAT (Neukirchen-Vluyn: Neukirchener Verlag des Erziehungsvereins, 1991-, issued in parts).

Williamson, H. G. M., *Israel in the Books of Chronicles* (Cambridge: Cambridge University Press, 1977).

_____, "The Origins of the Twenty-Four Priestly Courses: A Study of 1 Chronicles XXIII-XXVII", *VTS* 30 (1979) 251-68.

_____, *1 and 2 Chronicles,* NCB (London: Marshall, Morgan & Scott Publ. Ltd., 1982).

_____, "Joel", in G. W. Bromiley *et al.* (eds), *The International Standard Bible Encyclopedia,* Vol. 2 (Grand Rapids, Michigan: William B. Eerdmans Publishing Co., 1982) 1076-80.

_____, *Ezra, Nehemiah,* WBC (Waco, Texas: Word Books, 1985).

_____, "History", in D. A. Carson and H. G. M. Williamson (eds.), *It is Written: Scripture Citing Scripture* (Cambridge: Cambridge University Press, 1988) 25-38.

Woudstra, M., *Joshua,* NICOT (Grand Rapids, Michigan: Eerdmans, 1984).

Yamauchi, E., "The Archaeological Background of Esther", *BSac* 137 (1980) 99-117.

Indices

Subjects

four-part citation pattern 22ff.,
    188-89, 197, 203, 238-41
    the Chr's alterations of 40-
        48, 240-41
    a putative ancient literary
        convention 26-30, 39-40,
        46-47, 57, 70, 121, 240-
        41
    see "The Book of the Just"
footnote
    see four-part citation pattern

hermeneutical horizons, two
    failure to acknowledge 8
    see citation bases, exegetical
        devices
hermeneutical ramifications of the
    reading of citation formulæ
    6ff.

inner-biblical exegesis 1, 11, 14,
    20, 236, 241-251, *passim*
intermediate referents 49-50, 52,
    65, 67, 68, 77, 121, 210, 216

Jeremiah tradents 127

laments 49-51
law
    dissonance between the law
        ostensibly being cited and
        its observance 91ff., 156-
        57, 163, 184, 242
    implications drawn from the
        law 103-4, 111-12, 118-
        19, 120, 250
    observance of the law to the

greatest extent possible
    98-101, 208-9, 217, 245
use of the law 241-52
see citation base, exegetical
    devices distinguishing
    between two
    hermeneutical horizons
linguistics 18-19

method 14ff.
    lack of 2ff.

negative citation base 78, 140
neutrum 52-53, 55, 56, 65, 121,
    172, 239

PAR 31-32, 37-38
Passover in Chr's narrative of
    Hezekiah and Josiah 115-16
pragmatic issues 18-19, 91, 101,
    161ff., 212-14, *passim*
Präpositionale 80
"praying the tradition" 144, 147
"preaching the tradition" 128-47,
    152, 246
Pro-Forms 18, 68-69, 97, 107,
    142, 173-80, 208, 210, 215,
    216, 221, 222, 228, 242-43,
    244

referent 1, 19
    legal referents 17, 71-123,
        124-89, 192-97, 204-217,
        218-29, 234-35, 241-51,
        256-57
    non-legal referents 17-18, 22-

Authors

Biblical Texts

Septuagint

New Testament

Ancient Texts